THE SCOTTISH
MOUNTAINEERING
CLUB JOURNAL

| Vol. XXXV | 1995 | No. 186 |

SALAMANDER

By John Mackenzie

LIKE GHOSTS from the past, our memories constantly remind us of previous aspirations, those waking dreams that haunt us so mercilessly and so effectively. Driven by past endeavour and future challenge, the inner demon gnaws at the soul to restlessly explore and turn over each sod as if our version of truth could only be realised by that next journey into the unknown. Some of us are content with our previous lot, past challenges met and overcome, resting on those dreams of success and failure that provide the buffer, the bulwark, against age and failing powers. But why, one asks, are some not content to share this accepted norm; what is it about us as a breed that defies easy categorisation as simply mad, bad or sad? Do we turn our collective and individual thoughts upwards to escape intolerable low ground pressures or inadequacies or have we, individually, found the true discipline and the only worthwhile path to salvation as we see it? We have enough trouble explaining all this to ourselves, let alone to those of more sceptical bent; rather than bend the metaphysical into the merely plausible, by conjuring with abstract words, to arrive at a satisfactory solution that temporarily rests until displaced by better, let's take a journey to see if any of this can be explained while it is actually happening and note what is done.

For a start let's get over this ridiculous notion of 'we' in the article, which puts you in the role of a passive spectator, and instead include you as a fellow traveller, because in the real world 'we' are concerned about 'us' as individuals. Rather than generalise and try to take in all aspects of our game and spread the load over-thinly, I will concentrate on a single adventure; replaying the concept and resolution as it actually happened with the sole purpose of seeing if it helps resolve or explain any of our motives. You, as reader, will have to tag along as the invisible third-party, judging and approving or disapproving of our actions as the story unfolds.

I will choose a remote, lonely crag in a remote, lonely spot; no audience, no critical crowds, no applause, no jeers. Perhaps you prefer the limelight, the spotlight of critical opinion that looks for the slightest waver that robs the chance of success. Bear with me, I have had my fill of that down south, and living in the far north I have a chance to explore. I could have chosen innumerable roadside crags, each with their own strong characters and routes to match, some bold some not, but somehow at the end of the day do you not agree that when pressed, it is the major line, the big route which has to more closely explain our motives. A person is judged, after all, by their best work, not by their doodles.

Perhaps the most important single element is the dream. My friend Bob says he has seen this amazing line left of The Lizard; so has Martin. Robbie has even tried the first 100ft or so, but no farther. A great grey ghost of a slab, pale and probably hostile – would we have it any other way, would we be interested in it if it was broken and manifestly easy? – It is smooth, there are no give-away secrets of weakness; the element of doubt and even trepidation creep in just talking about it. And it is the talking about the unknown which is, of course, so fatally attractive. The known has been mapped, the imagination is left with dry statistics. We can either do it or not, the outcome is only in doubt if we push the limit of skill or conditions.

The best dreams of the unknown plague with angles, and in those dreams the slabs rear up impossibly steep and smooth; holds, cracks and protection are noticeable by their absence. In my imaginings I am pushed to my limit, miles up, a pimple on the proverbial elephant's backside and looking at ripples that give no hint as to their helpfulness. How far do you want to push it? Are you so young and bold that the thought of death or disablement lies easily in the equation? On this I draw back, a frightened slug withdrawing its horns in a blue funk. Pragmatic dreaming suggests that to boldly go where no man has gone before might be fine for the 'Starship Enterprise' but not for me. Sorry. I see perhaps you are bolder than me and more talented, but there we are, imperfections do tend to raise their heads in times of stress. On sight in winter is fine as, often, what you see is what you get, but on long hostile looking summer lines then at least an abseil inspection to clean off the scruffiest bits of moss and to see if any protection is possible is surely allowable. Deep down I want to both enjoy the success and live to tell the tale; obviously I take my hat off to those who can whoop it up doing impossible looking lines at first glance but I am not one of them. So, mentally, the adventure is already made less so by the admission that a 'ground-up' approach is not on. Fear is a great leveller. I am long in tooth, Bob even longer, and at the least I wish to equal his longevity.

The next consideration is the competition – already in our minds there are hordes of climbers at that very moment thinking of our very route. Names rapidly come to mind. Perhaps they are on it at this very hour, gleefully reappearing in the pub later to crow of their success at the expense of ours. I'm sure you recognise the paranoid tendencies in yourself; no punishment is keen enough for the new-route stealer on what you consider is 'your' crag. We console ourselves that since cleaning is important and remoteness a fact, the competition, if any, can probably, but not entirely, be discounted. New routes are therefore seen as select trophies, prizes whose worth is directly proportional to the amount of effort needed to attain them. Sometimes I wonder if there is any material object on this earth as satisfying as a classic new route; it is an art object, a natural sculpture, an acquisition which both personally identifies you and yet is seen as an aspiration by others, though at no time can it ever belong to you in any real sense except the spiritual. How can man's baubles and trinkets compare with a great line on a great cliff? This unworldly possession is one of the keystones of why we climb.

Now that the germ of desire is sown, a plan for action is needed. We will need all the cleaning ropes, wire brushes, the cut-down redundant ice-axes to clean cracks, climbing gear and ropes. All this weighs! There is 1000ft of extra-steep heathery and be-cragged hillside before we even reach the base of the cliff and then tortuous and probably precarious scrambling up its flanks to get to its crest, something like 1500ft in all. At least we can drive along the lonely glen near its base. We have been talking and dreaming of this route for long enough, putting off the evil day, for despite all those dreams, the effort needed in cleaning heathery cracks is well known to us and softer options have been appearing throughout the year, leaving us in late summer with nowhere else to go but here.

I love the long, dead-end glen, itself the off-shoot of an even longer and lovelier dead-end glen. The track is rough and stony, and dirt is spitting up from the wheels of this ridiculous vehicle I find myself in, a fully grown Campervan, complete with toilet and kitchen, bumping along this narrow road fit only for extraction vehicles. However, the trees hide the view and what with the swirl of dust the crags are reserved only for those who are sitting in the front. I always find approaches psychologically interesting, as I'm sure you must do as well. Sometimes it's light hearted, sometimes it's a grim silent business, thoughts kept well to oneself; often you hope to see the chosen line looking easier than your imagination has built it up to be. The whole balancing act between simply dreaming about it and then actually setting out to do it can be difficult, a slightly uncomfortable act of faith.

Bob and I have grown to become Bob, Colin and I. Three is bad for speed but good for cleaning. It is a fine day, cold but clear with the crag above visibly dry. Going up a steep hillside overladen with gear is a trial by any definition. This is not the first time, neither will it be the last I expect. Isn't it curious what goes through one's head when placing one foot in front of another on an arduous slope? Initially there is little rhythm, the mind wanders fairly loosely about, cannoning off aspects either underfoot or ahead, but when the first hard breathing sets in and the easiest line chosen is topmost in thought then the mind sets itself little jingles or incantations to ease the physical labour, higher mental processes having been subsumed in order to create a wholeness with the body. It is the first stage in trance, a narrowing of objectives and, most importantly, the mental sloughing off of the everyday world.

While Bob wilfully chooses a line independent of ours, we take a more direct line up a horrible scree-filled gully with short outcrops. This was not a good idea, laden as we are. Handfuls of heather and clutches of loose blocks occupy us for awhile until we clear this barrier. There is something very trying about stepping over little terraces of rank heather; no step ever seems high enough to properly clear it. At the foot of the crag the steepness of the slabs is now apparent, great plaques of a light grey schist with corner lines filled with heather. Tenuous possibilities rise up from the base, often to fade into obscurity and a frightening blankness. Like the sea, there is little to hide behind, few areas of visible comfort ease the eye. There are a few thin heather ledges perched here and there but the connection between them is problematic.

The central rib where the original line, The Lizard, wends its way up a groove, borders a fantastic slab that stretches up for 500ft with every chance of improbability on its journey to the top. A big dog-legged crack covers the initial 140ft, human progress having been stopped where the crack thins and angles left. Above, a smooth slab appears to form a wall, very unlikely looking from where I'm standing and above that another slab sports a great crescent-shaped shield before running into a hidden corner. Finally, a near vertical wall ends the route where an off-width crack cuts it directly in half. All in all it is some line and potentially very good indeed. Will my ambition be realised, and how much would I really give for something which I, – you, – really wish for? A fingernail? A finger? An arm and a leg? Your life? Don't dismiss this as trite; many climbers have died for such prizes like the Eiger North Wall. Some tread the thin line between reason and unreason better than others. Some are doomed to die, they have it marked on their faces, others have the bearing of survivors, sadder, wiser, but still here. Mostly we err on the safe side but always in the background there is the choice for that great leap into the unknown, the game of chance between the devil within and the poised statistics of real risk.

After much havering about and ferreting here, there and everywhere, we reach the crest. The top wall is set back from a terrace and it makes sense to set up an abseil from this and clean the top wall later. I play around for a few minutes on the wall, an off-width chimney that soon narrows to a soaring crack, stuffed with heather and perched blocks. It looks amazing but needs those blocks cleared first. Once embarked on action it is extraordinary – as I'm sure you'll agree – how you slip into a mechanical

Bob Brown climbing 'Salamander' on the West Buttress of Creag Ghlas, Sgurr A' Mhuillin. Photo: John Mackenzie.

Sgurr Alasdair, Skye. Photo: Alastair Mathewson.

mode. Abstract philosophy, so important in defining our motivation now has no place once the actual climbing starts. All such thoughts outwith the actual event therefore belong to the realm of retrospection and a dimming memory.

We have absolutely no idea at all what lies below. The ropes spin in the air for a moment and are gone. Each of us has set up a course of action mutually independent of the other. Colin is to clean the corner below. Bob to set up his ropes from any available anchor below that and I to set up a flotilla of ropes to reach the ground after having descended down the other two. We have a fair amount of gear but no pitons as they seem unnecessary. At least Colin's rope is well secured as I slide down after Bob. A brilliant corner is going past my nose, pink rock with few holds and a heather stuffed corner crack. Colin will be spending his time cleaning this!

Bob has now shuffled alarmingly off to the left and is busy digging out what looks like a pathetic little ear of rock to abseil off. There is something stomach-churningly gripping about shuffling about on one's bottom on a narrow ledge between the end of one abseil rope and the beginning of another. The evaluation of genuine risk has to come in here. Is there justification in these heart stopping manoeuvres, unroped and hundreds of feet off the ground? Easy enough ground perhaps but only justifiable up here due to the past accumulation of experience.

Climbing, in essence, is a series of alternating states between fear and relief, doubt and hope, each individual using his or her own very special mental faculties to deal with these in a way unique to them. We all know one man's terror is merely another's marginal niggle.

Bob's little ear has grown somewhat between the start and finish of my shuffle and a chance to see him test his creative anchor is sufficient enticement for me to follow down the next stretch. This is the great shield of rock perched like a scab atop a slowly steepening convexity. Thin, V-shaped cracks split the rock like shallow wounds, a feature of this crag. It did not look, taken objectively, too difficult but then abseils always lie. I like floating down this great inclined plane, a grey ocean of rock set on its lonely hillside amidst the cold clear air of the North. I reach a ledge worthy of the name and a really solid set of blocks where a less worrying anchor can be arranged.

Initially, my ropes go over the ominous bulging slab above the great dog-legged crack. A couple of bulges and sparse but good gear offer hope. I have an intuitive sense based on past routes that the top bulge is going to provide the crux. The ropes have ended two-thirds of the way down the lower slab, but since I will only have to clean the section above the dog-leg, then I should be able to swing across on to rising ground to escape, leaving the lower crack as it is.

Gardening as we euphemistically call grouting out of cracks and scrubbing clean lichen is probably frowned upon by our greener brethren. However,

The Yard-arm on Cioch Direct, Sron na Ciche, Skye. Photo: Jas Hepburn.

in defence may I quickly add there is simply so much rank heather here that the occasional cleaned crack makes no difference, visually or botanically, to the overall health of the crag, so I will simply draw a veil over the matter. My case rests on the over-proliferation of common vegetation and the relatively marginal impact sensitive cleaning does. The repetitive and muscle-crunching nature of hanging off a rope and cleaning a deep crack is immensely satisfying. Here is real sculpture, releasing the rock from its bondage of roots and seeing fresh crystals shine in the light of day. No person has ever touched this rock before; its sinuosity and simplicity of form – a single crack amid blank slabs – is stunningly attractive.

It is also desperately tiring. We have all been cleaning for seven hours by the time we reach the base of the crag and late August days are not so long as those in May. I do a precarious swing to one side, just managing to reach bottom at the very end of the ropes. It is imperative to get some fluid intake to lessen the cramps in my arms. A late lunch follows over on the boulders well to the right of the crag, our usual gearing up and eating spot. We brush the dry earth off ourselves, poke out lichen from our eyes, don rock boots and gear and head in an optimistic threesome towards the base of the crack. The moment of truth to test all those dreams – is it going to be a desperate fight or a piece of cake or somewhere in between? No moves have been practised on the rope so nothing is sure. Funny how we have to invent artificial rules in order to make life just that little bit harder for us, to subtly weight the balance so that something is probably, but not definitely, possible.

Bob shoots up the lower straight bit of the crack and takes a belay just before it jinks out left. I follow on delightful wafers of rock, crinkly crisps and little horns and nubbins that fingers can pinch and pull on carefully. A feature of the climbing here is that the holds often appear as rather superficial crusts, wind and chemically eroded into less than substantial objects. Often all the holds, especially in cracks, lie to the right, giving a very awkward and sometimes blind form of movement as they are hidden. Rarely is it as difficult as it looks but equally rarely is it easy and a commitment to what lies above, the 'faith' part of climbing, is necessary.

Bob has unearthed an ancient stub of a piton. Someone had retreated here a long time ago; indeed the crack to this point was quite clean. Now while Colin lounges around below, escaping from the quite chill wind, I set off up the newly cleaned dog-leg part of the crack. Gone are the encrustations that decorated the rock below, indeed gone is anything visibly helpful on the steep slabs above me. The crack is curious. It is more a shallow scoop that undulates, narrows and dilates again like a stone snake. By placing feet within the undulations and laying off the right edge, a surprisingly easy balance is reached. Fine as long as I keep my nerve and trust this frictional trickery. The whole feel is uncertain, the relative ease of progress is offset by an aura of difficulty. Apprehension remains that the ever steepening angle will force a retreat just short of the ledge above and I am deeply suspicious of a snarling setback.

Every route on this crag has this apparent atmosphere of slickness, of the need for panther-like stealth, the lonely leader out on the edge of the world battling with the ever present threat of flesh ripping falls. But in fact it was simply not true, merely mind games, imagination borrowing from the stuff of nightmares. Optical illusion said that the last move was going to be 'something else'. I doubt it was more than a very sustained 4c, unbelievable but true, HVS but not high in the grade. One of the great and unexpected joys is to undertake what seems a difficult task only to find that fate laughs at your own fears as it reflects the mirror of doubt back at you.

We are now all reassembled on our stance, a perch in the wind and with glorious views over to the Torridon mountains. The smell of autumn is in the air, heavy scents cut across us and the purple of the heather and grey of the rock create that unique feeling that at this moment, unlike any other, we would rather be here than anywhere else on earth. These are wonderful, transient moments that reinforce the bonding between the earth and us. They never last long enough and the intensity is only dimly remembered afterwards. For a few seconds insight and intuition go hand in hand, a true freedom preciously gained, the very stuff of the visionary.

I am now elected to lead the next pitch, the unprotected one, on the principle hastily proposed by Bob that since I cleaned it I deserve it. Thank you, dear friend, I can always rely on you in a tight spot. Weak but dry humour is part of our game, like understatement; it serves to reduce the seriousness of a given situation, a mental armour that works best (only!) for those who propose it.

The slab is steep and looks distinctly unfriendly above a half-height overlap. A chance line of flakes runs across the lower section, exposed and unprotected, to the overlap above. This takes some good gear, which is as well as I end up doing a scruffy mantel on to a very thin heather ledge. My nose is pressed against holdless rock, so another gearless shuffle left leads to the only weakness in the top slab, an unhelpful looking affair that seemed distinctly easier from the abseil rope. Fooled again! In fact it is, like all else so far, easier than it appears to be with the occasional hold and a single good piece of gear. There is definitely a crux though, and with a considerable fall penalty – only by climbing can the truth be known. As people we are easily pleased, a bit of gear, the odd good hold and our world sparkles with sunshine again.

The afternoon is well advanced; the light getting low and the temperature distinctly chilly. The far West has louring dark clouds gathering gloom around the skirts of the hills; night is in the air and we are little more than halfway on our voyage. The suppressed panic of darkness begins to grow as a dark flower in my guts, the little tendrils growing like a cancer and instilling fear. An epic is brewing as Colin is climbing painfully slowly.

Impatience with one's fellow man in such circumstances is understandable but pointless.

Bob has a choice on the long shield-topped slab above. Broken cracks on the left have been left uncleaned and an obviously better but sterner central crack gardened instead. It is evidently more technical than his dismissive comments from the abseil indicated. Nasty, off-balance and shallowly flared to start, we are willing him to succeed on this precarious section and audible is our relief when he does. Above it is easier and off his restraining leash of technical difficulty, Bob flies up to the great curved overlap of the shield, a half-moon that blocks access to what lies above.

While he is engaged in finding his own solutions, I let the cool of the evening air relax me. Colin is an interesting man, full of the great days of the past and as we talk, I watch the sun find a brief glory as it dips below the indigo clouds, flooding the low ground with an orange light. The orb grows bigger as it lowers, a cold fire races across the hills tingeing everything it touches with that peculiar sadness of colour that is so hauntingly beautiful.

The ropes now ran up out of sight, Bob having turned the shield on the right. Our turn to climb comes soon after and I note that the initial moves are of a sustained, rather negative type of climbing leaving you wondering if it was difficult, awkward or what. You will no doubt recognise the feelings well enough. Above though, delightful moves on flakes lead swiftly to the overlap, much bigger now that it is at hand. An awkward step right then easier ground separates me from Bob, now athwart a rock like some Biblical patriarch, his sharp profile cutting the last of the evening wind.

Colin, climbing in the gloaming does well, perhaps I was too harsh in my thoughts earlier on. We might, with just one pitch left to the terrace, get down before true night begins. Bob's belay is inadequate, a pathetic hollow flake. The acceptance of the old adage that 'The Leader Never Falls' is of necessity now. The ropes are beginning to get twisted and to save time Bob will lead through while I unravel a vast amount of what is rapidly becoming the climbing equivalent of the Gordian Knot. A tricky slab undercuts a hanging corner, the depths of which are hidden to our left. Colin and I watch the initially tenuous moves across the slab lead unprotected to the overlap that guards the corner. Whatever you do Bob, don't fall here please! The cracks under the overlap are very wet and after an anxious moment he arranges some solid looking gear. Thank God for modern equipment. Hidden now by the corner we are startled by great guffaws and chortles as the sheer quality of the experience is relayed down to us. If it can be that good in near darkness, just imagine what it must be like in daylight.

It is good. Solidly sustained every inch of the way, a perfect end to a perfect route, bridging on dimples, constantly provoking. Colin emerges beaming, he cannot believe his luck, telling us that down south people would kill for a route like this. We will have to come back for that top wall though, as the route should properly finish up it, but tonight is not the night. Our groping way off the terrace is probably the most dangerous part of the day, traversing over little walls that are effectively bottomless. The descent gully, a mirage of safety amid vertiginous heather and broken rock is scuttled down with that urgency which only those racing the night will ever know. We reach the boulders where the gear is stowed and then, hobbled by inadequately packed sacs, and festooned with ropes, descend the grim slopes back to the welcome lights of the Campervan, many, many hours after first setting out.

A short while later, so impressed are we by the quality, that Bob and I cleaned the soaring crack above the terrace and the left-hand cracks of the shield-topped slab. We climbed the route on a faultless sunny day, warm and windless with the scent of heather wafting up on thermals. The cracked slab was a grade easier than the original way and the top chimney cracks gave superb steep climbing at merely VS despite every appearance to the contrary. We still feel that the crag has given us its best route; certainly not its hardest, simply its best.

So, our dream had been fulfilled, were we then satiated, ready to look back upon those two days as some kind of highlight? Did the experience, realised without hint of disappointment, explain any more clearly the deeper questions? For a few days we were content, basking in the reflected glory of our own satisfaction. But then the ache returned. Why can we not be content with merely passive appreciation as in an art gallery? We have to crawl all over our 'art' to get to some deeper and fundamental understanding of the meaning of life itself. Perhaps we are driven souls, haunted by the promise and occasional realisation of great peace – and beauty – both within ourselves and within our surroundings. Despite jobs and restrictions of all shapes and sizes, despite great fears and self doubts, 'up there' represents a true life force, an essence of what is good and worthwhile; despite even our flawed personalities, we strive to attain a moral freedom based on self-integrity.

At times this integrity is circumscribed by our actions; we make the end justify the means even at the expense of our fellow man. Ambition can be naked, ugly and truly selfish. Perhaps it is simply not possible to pursue great goals without sacrifice. Indeed, if pressed sorely then that little inner voice might claim we are an elite, a Praetorian Guard, looking down on a lesser humanity who are struggling through a mire of mediocrity and dullness while we juggle with the forces of Eros and Thanetos like protogods. Dark though these thoughts are, there is much that is light. On balance, though, as a group we are no saints, we have evidently found a method of passing through life which is deeply fulfilling for mind and body. It may not be much of a conclusion, but at least we are willing to explore the possibilities, understanding ourselves better in the process, and by so doing, beginning to comprehend our fellow men.

THE TRAP

By P.J. Biggar

SQUAT AND black and inimical to progress the fabled Mantrap barred the way. As I climbed the arete towards it, Dave Meldrum gave a shrug of aversion and backed off down to the Tough-Brown variation. His partner, Phil Gribbon, waved me towards the ample belays in the Mantrap's crack. That piece of rock was a physical obstacle we could not overcome, but we had another more pressing though intangible enemy – time. The moon was shining brightly on Carn Mor Dearg as I brought Mike Jacob up. We had been climbing for more than 11 hours. Jacob arrived only to hurry off in Meldrum's footsteps. Gribbon and I were left to contemplate nature which was extremely beautiful, and our feet, which were becoming cold.

To the right of our ledge, painfully hacked out of the most recalcitrant snow-ice, lay the steep and narrow way to the Forty-Foot Corner and possible salvation. Hideous depths plummeted in shadow below it. To the left, the foreshortened glassy walls of Little Brenva swept into the gentle basin of Coire Leis.

Normally, when Gribbon and I share a stance the atmosphere is genial, the talk humorous and bantering. This time we were like two old men who have met at the same bus-stop for 30 years and have nothing to say. Each wisp of warm vapour from dry lips was grudged. One short exchange contained a confession: 'We might need torches.'

'Mine's in the hut.'

'That wouldn't be intentional?'

'No.'

And the bus wouldn't come. The delicate curve on the frosted ropes remained unaltered. Minds flinched away from the subversive cold, seeking release in thought.

Why had we been so long? The weather was perfect. The condition of the snow almost too perfect – excessively hard, a stubborn unyielding material, points and picks had to be placed with abnormal exertion which was especially bad for the ancient Terrordactyls of the Gribbon-Meldrum rope; stances took many blows to cut and even then were cramped and full of aches . . . Excuses, excuses! We'd got off route. Gribbon swore he'd been that way before with Smart, but all that followed from that, I muttered to myself as I clawed my way along the chosen icy ledge, was that they'd been off route then as well! This had been confirmed by the two lads finishing Minus Two; we'd had to follow them up the exit chimneys of that route. And some time before that, of course, Gribbon's crampon had worked loose from its ancient strapping system, and that had entailed a minor retreat; Meldrum's dazzling smile had become slightly strained.

It hadn't been a great night either. We'd been in a position to get to the hut early, and were in our bunks as the first little light was seen ascending from the Fort. Sleep? Scraps of the conversation we had been forced to overhear came back to me as I stood in the cold, punctuated by the rhythmic percussion of the hut door: 'She was a most peculiar woman seemingly!'

'Oh really?'

Crash!

'. . . maybe I will have another, just a wee one, it helps you to sleep.'

Crash!

'Aye, Craig-y-Barns last week . . . good route . . . desperate . . .'

'Oh! He is is He? We'd better clean this pan tonight then!'

Raucous guffaws.

'Aye, most peculiar . . . she made him perform in a harness!'

Sleep after hours of this becomes impossible, and getting up a great relief.

'I think they're shouting.' At intervals we had heard words being exchanged by our partners; now their deliberations had issue. The instruction was for Phil to untie one of his ropes; the end vanished upwards, leaving us still cold and perplexed. Some grim struggle was being fought out up there, on which depended our chances of avoiding benightment, and we could only wait; we weren't even onlookers. Ice chips hissed down the slope to rattle, it seemed for ever, into the gulch below the Minus Face.

Gribbon occupied himself in putting his balaclava over thinning locks. I contemplated getting my jacket out of my sack, but the thought of fiddling with frozen ropes, removing outer layers and securing vital equipment on the glazed surface deterred me. Inertia threatened. My companion muttered darkly each time the wind blew.

Thoughts burrowed again. Where had the daylight gone?

Above the Second Platform there had been a definite mistake. I had gone left when I should have gone right, leaving my partner to lead the last pitch of Frostbite, putting still more pressure on the leg he had injured playing squash: a dangerous game that . . . My penance had been to stand on a lower shelf for more than an hour as the sun set, watching and hearing, so still was the air, the footsteps of little black figures crunching down Coire Leis to warmth and supper and bed.

The witch-burners in the Hut would be alight now; wine bottles warming by the stove; the Ogre enthralling the company with Fell Tales: running over the mountains and gobbling up intruders into his ancient Sanctuary . . . No little figures now. Even the belated travellers on Tower Ridge had followed their torch beams along the extension to the Eastern Traverse, to disappear in Tower Gully. We were alone in a cooling world whose softened shapes and blunted forms concealed its extreme steepness and menace. I imagined looking up at N.E. Buttress from below and saw it as a monstrous Helter-Skelter. I saw us all on little fairground mats flying round and round the stripey tower to land like breathless children at the very door of the Hut. Oh how the mind yearned towards the odorous warmth of the drying room! . . . Why so long?

At times a little cloud would cross the moon's surface. I could only hope it would be clear if our bus ever came: big and maroon and white, rumbling down Gorgie Road, full of warmth and beery breath and old men discussing the Hearts. Another little puff of wind found chinks in our armour and made us cry out against our imprisonment.

One coil detached itself from the pile at Gribbon's feet, to slip ever so leisurely down the slope; then nothing, then another. This was tortuously repeated until his one remaining rope was almost gone. He shouted. There was no reply. The rope never came taut. There were no urgent, comforting tugs, it just lay like a tired dog's tail with only an occasional twitch. No message from the beyond, only this ambivalent motion of the messenger:

'Look with what courteous action
It wafts you to a more removed ground:
But do not go with it.'

My face was too numb to smile, but I recalled that this was the rope which Gribbon had purchased from Meldrum for a jar of peanut butter, and I felt secretly glad that my ropes were still attached to Jacob.

Gribbon acted at last, not because there was sufficient warrant for doing so, but because further passivity was unbearable. With an economy of motion proclaiming the experience of a long life, he moved backwards and downwards from our desolate shelter, paused once on a cut step, then, with a 'See you later,' to me, and a hopeful cry to those above which lost itself in the great spaces, he moved up and out of my sight.

I looked down at my feet, encased in honest, frozen leather and tattered canvas gaiters. The boots were old friends, the feet older still, and numbness was setting in. Fifty steps, I thought, then count to 25, and then another 50. The tramping began. My sentence now included the treadmill as well as being tied to a legendary rock.

The stars were bright now: the light of each denoting a body of huge mass, of whose origin, motions and destiny I was profoundly ignorant. My life seemed miniscule and measured out in trivialities; a few climbs, a few drinks, a few books read, a few words written: sitting in armchairs thinking vaporous thoughts. The whole was like a match struck in a blind alley; it revealed nothing for a moment and then went out; one puff of wind and its smoke would be gone too. My world was contracted to what shivered below my vest and hunched its shoulders against the draughts. It was linked to other similar worlds by two strands of frozen rope. And the ropes never moved. Only my feet resumed their dreary tramping.

Speculations flitted through my tired mind like bats through a clearing. I was alone in this dreadful place . . . my companions had been phantasms . . . there was no-one on the end of the ropes . . . no-one else in this cold universe. Perhaps I had died and become immortal? This tramping on one spot was a penance for crimes on earth. But surely I was not dead? For one thing I was too uncomfortable, and for another I was too afraid.

What was I afraid of? Of Death of course! Yet, if one examined it coolly, was that the real object of fear? Not really. Not the state itself, but the process: the loss of control, the sickening slither, the cartwheel into space, the bone crushing impacts; these perhaps, and the loneliness of it. The blackness or light beyond them was not fearful.

'God is very merciful,' I muttered. It was a Mantra. I was chanting my Mantra below the Mantrap. A horrid gurgling sound, like water leaving a basin, told me I was laughing.

I jiggled it this way, I rattled it that way, I turned it upside down but it would not budge. My mitts were chopped to shreds and my hands belonged to somebody else. The unknown powers smiled on the folly of my actions. This particle of warmth feebly struggling to get free from the rock to which, an instant before, it had clipped itself. But the struggles continued until krab and sling were in my hands. And then I dropped them, and they slid, ever so gently, out of sight.

The universe, after all, contained some other agency. The ropes were tightening inexorably. A moment ago I'd had too much time, now I had too little. The unseen agent might have forgotten that, before he could encourage me by pulling on the rope, I had to climb at first downwards; a pull at this stage was not what I wanted. It became a race backwards down the polished curvature; legs shaking, wooden hands prodding picks for balance, shuddering inwardly, I just made it.

We had climbed all day on abundant thick ice. The paradox of the Corner was that its covering was vanishingly thin. Steep rock smeared with glass. As I came to it in the moonlight I found signs of the great struggle. A deadman at the bottom grinned like a skull in the desert; it was half embedded and had been left as a runner. A few feet up the corner some shallow scrapes had been hacked in the smears, and an ice-screw protruded, rather too much, from its placement. I could only pick up the pieces and wonder.

Blue sparks shot out as my picks repeatedly struck rock. I bridged and heaved, pulled on shaky axes, scraped, scratched and gritted my way upwards. As my body came back to life, a fierce exhilaration swept through me. Just as every means of continued upward progress ran out, and it seemed as if my feet must lose contact with the rock, a long flailing reach with the hammer brought the security of perfect névé and a moment of knowledge and peace. My hand tightened round the shaft and one last convulsive heave took me over the top.

As I crouched, spent, on the slope above the Corner, a boulder-like shape stirred and a familiar Irish accent offered comfort:

'Well done, now! That deserves a biscuit! Just let me get my headlamp out of this bag . . . But wait now, this isn't a headlamp . . . it's ... . a piece of cake!'

A little farther up the ridge I encountered the good shepherd, Jacob, looking as drawn as I've ever seen him. Despite his injured leg he had led his little flock to salvation. At his wise insistence we followed him to the Summit Shelter. The wind was rising and our faces were stung by drift. Meldrum produced an orange and unselfishly quartered it; I can taste the juice yet.

Down in the hut all was snoring tranquillity. The Ogre, betraying a heart of gold, had put a pan of soup on the stove for us, and Sandy Reid got up to make us tea. One remembers these things.

Time was still out of joint next morning. Dave produced a bottle of wine and we had dinner for breakfast. Outside, the gentle elements of last night had fled, and even the young bloods of the SMC came back, snow-bespattered, from the entrance to Coire na Ciste. Someone asked why we had taken so long. The Ogre himself pronounced a kindly absolution.

'You see,' he said, 'they were using old-fashioned equipment.' But we knew that the tumbling grains had qualified our proceedings in more than one way. Yesterday, it seemed, had occurred at just the right time.

CHANCE ENCOUNTERS OF A FLEETING KIND

By Bill Shipway

A CENTURY ago a member of the SMC wrote that members of the club might be divided into two classes: the Ultramontanes (deeds of derring-do) and the Salvationists (safety first). Subsequently, this distinction[1] has been suggested to be false – many early members exhibited both tendencies. Nevertheless, the labels survive in story and verse100 years later.

Talking about it not long ago, a friend asked me what groups I would put hillgoers into nowadays. That will not be difficult, I thought, and began to make some notes of stravaigers I had encountered over the years. But the task was more awkward than I had imagined. The strong, silent men, yes, they were self-reliant and knowledgeable, even if having rather much of the loner in their make-up. But the blethers were by no means a bunch of softies. Some were beyond doubt princes of the hills, brightening the day with warm friendship. In between, a collection of gangrels interested in the experiences of others, ready to help with the route, or tell you of a better B & B down the road. There is only one thing to do, dear reader – turn the question over to you, and give you my notes to add to your own. Send entries to the Editor to reach him by December 31. A mystery prize for the first correct solution opened.

A year or two back on a breezy July morning, I set off for Beinn Dearg of Atholl from Old Blair. The route is served by good estate roads and it was not long before I reached Allt Sheicheachan bothy, all spick and span with table, forms and chairs in place but no-one about. After leaving the burn the path follows a long shoulder to the cairn, rather a cold tramp now against a bleak wind blowing strongly, making the dyke at the trig point a welcome shelter. To the north, waves of featureless brown crests led one's eyes to the Cairngorms. Towards the Gaick deer forest in the west the empty landscape was much the same. The wind at the cairn never let up and I was glad to think I would have it behind me on the return journey. As I left the summit rocks my eye caught a solitary figure crossing the peat moss from the west on what I guessed was the route in from Calvine and Bruar Lodge. Here was a chance to exchange greetings with a fellow walker and add to one's information about the hill. I altered direction to intercept him. But the focus of my attention only called: 'Blowy, in't it?' and passed on without slackening his stride. Clearly, a man saving his breath for better things. Or was he one of those 'head down get to the top as fast as possible and on to the next Munro' types that one meets occasionally these days?

In June 1992 I spent a week on Skye. Sandy had only six Munros left to climb to compleat the round, five on the Cuillin Ridge, plus Blaven. The weather was good and on our first day we climbed Sgurr nan Eag and Sgurr

---

[1] See R.N. Campbell in SMCJ, XXXIV, p. 219.

Dubh Mor; on our second day the Inn Pin followed by Sgurr Mhic Choinnich. We then took a day off and paid our respects at the last resting place of John Mackenzie and Norman Collie at Struan. The weather held and next day we returned to the Ridge for Am Basteir.

That left Friday for Blaven, and again it was a fine morning. I had been up this hill before, knew it would not present any difficulty, and donned my kilt as glad rags for the big occasion. Sandy was not quite as exuberant. Now retired, he had climbed his first Munro as a schoolboy, and was finding it hard to believe he was about to be translated from a common Munro-bagger to the aristocracy of the Compleat Munroists.

Loch Slapin sparkled in the sun, Blaven looked magnificent and we set off up the Allt na Dunaiche with lightsome step, passing some faithful members of the John Muir Trust at work on the path. It was sun hat and shirt sleeves down here, but some three hours later we were glad of anorak and woollies as we crossed the final slope to the cairn and trig point. Bravo for Sandy, he had finished the round, and as befits a couple of pensioners we celebrated with a sip of Drambuie. Other walkers came across from the South Top and helped with the obligatory photographs. It was sunny and clear in the keen wind and the views of the Cuillin Ridge and the Red Hills were superb.

We had just left the cairn to begin the descent when we met three climbers coming up. They had made the climb via Clach Glas and had left their sacs where the gully comes in at the Great Prow. Perhaps the Drambuie had loosened my tongue. I had to tell them of Sandy compleating. 'Wow!' their leader exclaimed: 'I finished myself last year and you are the first man I've met who has done the same.' He congratulated Sandy with enthusiasm and sounded as thrilled as we were ourselves. We learned that his name was Matthew and that Clach Glas was a warm up for a visit to the Cioch next day.

Gladdened by this encounter we left our three friends to finish their climb and continued downwards ourselves. The coire was warm in the afternoon sun and we paused for a breather by the side of the track above the little meadow on the coire floor. Suddenly, there was a clatter of stones behind us. It was Matthew and his two friends again. He pulled a bottle of Johnnie Walker from his sac. 'We can't let this pass without a toast, have a dram!' Then the three stalwarts hastened on down, but Matthew told the tale ahead of us to others on the path, so that Sandy's progress was marked by even more handshakes. A man of good cheer, charismatic, friendly – meeting Matthew made a great day even more memorable.

Mountain guides are not a corps I've had much to do with, and I suppose like other professionals they have to be economical with information in order to safeguard their livelihood. Not long ago I was in a party making its way along the Cuillin Ridge from Sgurr Mhic Choinnich to Sgurr Thearlaich. After leaving the airy crest of Mhic Choinnich we trod gingerly over the slabby roofs and then crept across the face of the hill toward the bealach below the tumbled rocks leading to the upper ramparts of Thearlaich. Here we paused and I asked our leader: 'When do we reach Collie's Ledge?' He turned round and, in a voice that told me all too clearly that some mothers do have 'em, replied: 'Collie's Ledge? You've just come down it!'

Another meeting I am less happy about recounting occurred back in August 1977 when a few of us decided to attempt Ben Nevis, Carn Mor Dearg and the Aonachs Mor and Beag in one day. We left the Glen Nevis camp-site at 7.30a.m. and made our way up the pony track on a glorious summer morning to reach the summit plateau of the Ben at 11a.m. The view was almost too much to take in, a wonderful panorama of peaks and ridges, with gleams of light from lochs and sea. Then it was on across the plateau to find the descent to the curving Arete, with its bouldery spine leading towards the pink screes of Carn Mor Dearg. After threading the ragged switchback above Coire Leis and a halt for lunch, we reached the cairn on Carn Mor Dearg at 2p.m. This time it was not the distant hills which held the eye, but the towering cliffs of Nevis across the glen. When mantled in mist and snow they present a fearsome aspect, but today they were smiling and peaceful in the sun, with only a few scattered patches of snow to remind one of their mighty winter couloirs.

It was time now to turn round and descend from Carn Mor Dearg by its east ridge to a grassy bealach where we filled our water bottles from the first trickle of a burn. A steep grassy wall split by crags faced us, demanding many a grunt and gasp ere the angle relented and we found ourselves on the broad back of the Aonachs. Dumping our sacs we walked up the wide expanse and reached the cairn on Aonach Mor at 5p.m., there to have an argument as to whether we were looking across the Mamores to the Aonach Eagach or to Bidean nam Bian.

Then back to retrieve the sacs and head for the short craggy path leading up to the summit dome of Aonach Beag. Oddly, the ground underfoot was mossy and tundra-like, differing from the grassy sweeps of its neighbours close by. We sprawled around the cairn discussing the distances still to cover. It would seem three miles down Glen Nevis from Steall to road end, and thereafter perhaps four on the road to the camp-site . . . but first we must reach Steall.

Leaving the cairn at 6.30p.m. we began the downward journey, picking our way among the outcrops, down and still down. Suddenly Ronnie fetches us up, pointing to a lone figure descending the Allt Coire Guisachan towards Steall, a long way below us. 'If he had a car at the road-end and were going down Glen Nevis . . .'

Hastening down we reach a pool on the burn and await the approach of the walker. No elaborately accoutred climber this man, just baggy flannel trousers, a cotton shirt and an ancient canvas rucksack. We hail him as though we have no other motive but the honest friendship of the hills, fall in beside him with chat about this and that, trying to conceal the high stakes for which we are playing. Ah, the deceit in the heart of man. At last Alex takes the bull by the horns. 'Are you staying in Fort William?' Five pairs of ears strain for his reply. 'No, I'm camping at Steall . . .' Ouch, no car, no lift. Immediately, all interest in our erstwhile friend departs, and we are as keen to extricate ourselves as we were to ingratiate ourselves minutes before. We slip away with as much grace as we can muster and hasten on down the burn towards Steall, the Nevis gorge and the road-end. Happily, there were still folk about when we reached the road-end in the gloaming, and we were lifted in more than one car before we had walked as far as Polldubh. So ended a great mountain day.

Let's pass now to the Fannichs. Stewart and I thought we would have a try for Beinn Liath Mhor and drove to the parking place on the A835 at the west end of Loch Glascarnoch. Another two walkers, man and woman, were kitting up by their car and said they were going for Am Faochagach, on the north side of the road. I said we were hoping to go there ourselves on the following day, and asked them where they intended to cross the Abhainn a' Gharbhrain, a river said to involve wet feet even in normal conditions. They joked about it, the man saying we would see the tide marks on his breeches when they got back. With that they were across the road and away.

It was a surly kind of late summer morning, blowy and overcast, difficult to say how the day would turn out. The route for Beinn Liath Mhor was simple and about two hours later we reached the col below the long curving ridge leading to the summit. We started up, the mist blowing round us, the ground stony and shattered. The Deargs were clear – it is strange how weather patterns can be different over relatively short distances. We reached the double cairn and sat down for some lunch.

Stewart thought he would like to return. I was keen to reach Sgurr Mor, so we agreed to separate. It was fairly rough walking over the wet scree, easy to slip, and I had not given it more than a few minutes before I began thinking I had done a very foolish thing in not staying together in the mist. I turned and set a bearing to contour the hill and rejoin our route of the morning. Some minutes later I was surprised to see a figure loom out of the mist, compass in hand. 'Have you passed a man going down?' I asked. 'No, I haven't seen anybody.' I was filled with alarm, but mercifully when clear of the mist I saw Stewart below me. Such episodes teach lessons.

Lower down there was a blink of sun, though behind us the ridge remained cloud-capped, dense and gloomy. As we approached the parking place, I was sorry to see that the other car was no longer there. Unlocking the car, I noticed a sheet of paper with a message on it tucked under the wiper blade. I have kept the paper with my log of the day. Here is what it said: 'Re ascent of Am Faochagach: For your information, it is possible to cross the Abhainn a' Gharbhrain without getting your feet wet! The location is GR282753 where the river splits into two. The SW branch is easy to cross and the NE branch can be crossed where it is split by a small grassy island. There is a small cairn on the far bank. Good walking! Hope you had a good day. From the couple you met this morning.'

Who says you do not meet some wonderful folk in the hills?

My last story concerns a visit to Ben Alder. Marcus had arranged with the estate that we might have the use of the bothy at Black Burn of Pattack for two nights. Permission to take our car up had been refused and we were faced with a six-mile walk from Gallovie. None of us had any experience of back-packing: we found the heavy packs very different from our usual day sacs, and were mighty glad to throw them down at the wooden bothy, light the fire and have some supper. The messages on the walls went back to 1913 and some were quite funny e.g. 'This would be a nice place to die in'. But as we sat round the fire we would not have exchanged our bothy for Buckingham Palace.

We had only just rolled out our sleeping bags when there was the sound of a car outside and a solitary man came in. He sounded friendly and quickly made himself at home.

We awoke to a perfect June morning: even at 7a.m. the sun was warm. We left in high spirits for the round of Ben Alder and Bheoil – the early sun in a clear sky, a skylark singing, a good path underfoot and our mountain ahead, its massive flanks still streaked with snows of winter. Bill from Aberdeen, the stranger of the night before, had departed ahead of us, but as we made our approach by the Long Leachas he appeared in silhouette on the Short Leachas, stepping up the ridge with the easy stride of a hillman. Taking a breather near the cairn, we saw him coming towards us: 'I've run out of film, would you have a spare?' 'Haven't a spare', said Alex, 'but if it's slides you need maybe I could take some shots for you!' That seemed to solve the problem and he joined us for the remainder of the day.

Our new friend was a grand companion. He had a marvellous knowledge of the mountains, and of those who climbed them, and of the books written about them, all recounted in an unselfconscious fashion which assumed we knew as much as he did. He pointed out that the retreating snowfields delineated the coires and ridges in a way which made the hills particularly lovely at that time of year. 'See this boulder', he would say 'It's granite, while the rocks of this hill are schistose. It's been carried from the Moor of Rannoch in the Ice Age and deposited here.' He took a lizard from a rock by the burn and showed us its beautiful markings, did the same with wild flowers and mosses.

Back at the bothy he pulled a bottle from his sac. 'Have a drink on me, this is home-brewed red wine.' We had a wonderful evening of talk and laughter round the fire. Our shadows danced on the walls as the logs crackled and flared, and he talked of ice climbs on Lochnagar, and the hazards of the Aonach Eagach, and mountain rescue, and training young people, and the friendship of climbing companions whose names we knew, and half a hundred other things. Even the deer came to listen, for later we found a hind at the bothy window, and others grazing nearby. The warmth of friendship matched the warmth of the hearth and when it was time to get into our sleeping bags again we could not think of when we had spent a happier evening.

Next day we decided to visit the Laggan hills before returning. Our new friend offered to take our packs down to Gallovie in his car – that was a real bonus. He was not coming out with us, so we took some last photos and said our goodbyes. 'I'm B– B–', he said: 'Look me up if you are ever in Aberdeen.'

These are a sample of the chance meetings which have come to me over years given to hillwalking. For me such encounters enrich an outing, and their recollection sings in the memory for many a year. Perhaps not everyone is of the same opinion: perhaps you prefer your own company. And as for classifying hillgoers into groups, I'll have to admit they are as different as individuals as the folks walking in Princes Street or George Square.

REFLECTIONS

For W.H. Murray

His writings brought the mountains alive for me
his exploits in ice-choked gullies on Buachaille and Ben
inspired generations to dare and to know
the steep and challenging places.

This morning our eyes met through an hotel window
as I strode to the mountains and I saw reflections,
reflections on comrades lost in war, reflections on past glories
and above all reflections on the physical limitations of age.

Charlie Orr
Alexandra Hotel, Fort William.
4th December, 1994.

THE CONNOISSEURS' ROUTE

By Peter Warburton

I HAVE never been on friendly terms with an ice axe. Even corks carefully affixed to the spike fall off – unobserved. This can make for unpopularity on buses and aeroplanes. Some people do so over-react. What principally undid me were those illustrations of climbers toppling backwards, forwards or sideways down steep slopes but saving themselves by deft manipulation of an axe on which adversity has not loosened their grip. There could be no more vivid reminder of my own lack of prowess in similar dire circumstances. I dismissed out of hand, as imprudent in the extreme, the advice that beginners gain practical experience of 'self arrest' by voluntarily hurling themselves down suitable slopes. So, where the high hills are concerned, I became a May to October excursionist. Snow and ice are best admired in other peoples' photographs.

One of the benefits this heresy confers is the increased time made available for one of winter's safer pleasures – the study, purposeful or otherwise, of maps. The awkward squad find perverse delight in devising approach routes that, usually for excellent reasons, have escaped the notice of the corps of mountain guide writers. When I feel able to keep a straight face, I am apt to refer airily to such discoveries as connoisseurs' routes.

There are also connoisseurs' addresses to be found on the Highland sheets – remote habitations that fascinate by their isolation or because of the evocative quality of a name. Visiting them can become as much a mission as collecting Munros. The reality often falls short of expectations. Marble Lodge, although built of the specified material, is still rather a let-down if the picture in the mind's eye has featured one or more stately pleasure domes. Iron Lodge – another estate workers' dwelling in character – is definitely fraudulent in its present incarnation. I fear that Abyssinia, held in reserve as a suitable outing for my declining years, will also disappoint. Wag and Glut are others that hint at more than they are likely to deliver.

Some sites stir the imagination whatever the weather – Bachnagairn is a good example – but judgments are inevitably coloured by conditions on the day. Altanour Lodge (ruin) on the late afternoon of a very wet October day with darkness falling, five sodden miles ahead to Inverey and soaked breeches chafing inside thighs at every step: the verdict was unfavourable. In contrast, I have always been lucky with Slugain Lodge (ruin). The approach up a lightly-wooded, nicely watered ravine, with a resident population of woodland birds, twittering incongruously in a high moorland setting is rather special. There is even a Slugain bypass from which you can look down on the ruins and speculate on the logistics of supply in the days when it was in use. In fact, many of the remoter sporting lodges had a brief and limited active life. McConnochie, writing a hundred years ago, notes that Altanour and Loch Builg Lodges were only in occasional seasonal occupation.

One place that long eluded me is Patt, or rather Patt Lodge, since the keeper's house at Patt went under when Loch Monar was enlarged. There are few references in the literature. Brenda Macrow writes of Iron Lodge and she and Tom Weir of Benula Lodge (a casualty of the Mullardoch dam), Hamish Brown and Iain Thomson are informative about Maol Buidhe, but Patt Lodge seems quite off the literary beat. Thomson who lived (1956-60) at Strathmore, now submerged, on the northern shore of the loch writes of his friends and neighbours, the keeper and family at Patt, but the Lodge hardly enters the narrative, although he includes an undated photograph. On my maps it remained safely above the new water line, still sheltered by several acres of woodland. This was not conclusive evidence. Corndavon Lodge has lost its plantation and Cabuie is no more, despite having survived the raising of Loch Fannich. Eventually, I shall become reconciled to metric maps, but not yet. There is something to be said for the possibility of imperial surprise.

A day devoted solely to the Patt experience would have been extravagant of holiday time, especially as it might well end in contemplation of a few stones in a clearing among tree stumps. You need not be of the romantic 'rickle ae stanes' school to feel melancholy on such occasions. The map suggested a solution: a return visit to Lurg Mhor by way of Meall Mor, starting from the east end of Loch Monar would take in Patt en-route, providing a second objective for the day as well as promising a potential connoisseurs' route. My only previous outing to Lurg Mhor had been by the conventional approach from Strathcarron over Beinn Tharsuinn and Bidein a'Choire Sheasgach, but I had so run out of steam and time that Meall Mor had proved a top too far. Instead, I had cut down to the head of Loch Monar and up to the Bealach Bhearnais (a genuine connoisseurs' short cut, this). Later, I had been slightly affronted to read that the Gilbertian tough guys do not consider that these hills offer a notably Big, Classic, Wild or even Challenging walk.

At one time access by car to Glen Strathfarrar involved considerable ceremony. The applicant presented himself, not at the Big House, but at a substantial subsidiary establishment where a lady of military manner, seated at an imposing desk, inquired his motives and completed the paperwork. Those intending a round of the Strathfarrar Munros would be handed a Struy Estate day pass giving permission to visit Glen Strathfarrar 'for the purpose of sightseeing'. Such preliminaries were time consuming, but the pass allowed 13 hours (8.30a.m. to 9.30p.m.) in the glen. In 1989 time was saved by collecting a pass from the gatekeeper, but it only gave a 10-hour licence, which must have caused unease to many another late breakfaster. A more welcome change was the omission of the Estate pass footnote which had read: 'The Private Road to Monar Lodge and across the top of the Hydro Electric Board Dam are out of bounds to Visitors.'

A wink being as good as a nod, I drove across the dam, hoping that no frolicsome keeper would padlock the gate during the day. In Gleann Innis an Loichel two parked cars offered qualified reassurance on that point. The first stage of the walking route was a 500ft climb to a bealach at 1250ft between Meallan Odhar and Beinn Dubh. A promising path left the glen but quickly faded, leaving me high-stepping through primeval heather mixture. The col was wide and wet, inadequately drained by slow moving, meandering streams broad out of all proportion to their flow. The going looked better on the far bank, but never was. After some long time I was granted a possible distant sighting of the Patt plantation, only to be denied confirmation by a combination of drifting mist and minor undulations not recorded on the map. This process was several times repeated, raising in the explorer's mind the subject of mirages. I encouraged my steps with the notion that perhaps I was trampling heather that not even stout Butterfield had trod before: only wild surmise of course. One who certainly came this way was the Rev. A. E. Robertson. He notes that the path fades away at the bealach but that it was 'fair going' down to Aultfearn, which stood by the loch shore about 1½ miles east of the keeper's house and the jetty at Patt. His photographs suggest that muir burning was practised at that time (1905).

Having cautiously negotiated the Riabhachan burn, which was carrying a lot of snow water, I made directly for Meall Mor, by then in full view, intending to hold Patt in reserve for the return journey. A mistake, since the next burn was unfordable and I was obliged to follow it downstream to a bridge close by the Lodge. Behind protective fencing a cultivated plot was visible and, looking up, I could see the windows of a habitable, probably an inhabited house.

Over the bridge the going gradually improved and, after what had gone before, the 2400ft climb of the Meall Mor ridge was a pleasant change. At the top however there was one of those irritating winds that seems to come from all directions and calls for so many precautionary measures that it is impossible to relax with the flask and sandwiches. The convenient rock seat is in the full blast. Nicely established in the second best situation, you find that your arrival has coincided with the briefest lull in the gale. The final resting place, 50ft below the summit, proves very wet, a fact not initially apparent. In these distressing circumstances, I reminded myself of a typically rueful aside of Stevie Smith that seemed obliquely relevant: 'I will say this about Shrimpton-on-Strand, you can always get out of the wind one side of the breakwater or the other, or under the bathing machine.' Then, as there was no one about, I declaimed the even more appropriate lines of Victor Hugo:

> *'Le vent qui vient a travers les montagnes*
> *Me rendra fou'.*

Meall Mor, intermittently visible during the meal, presented a striking picture. It had attracted a wreath of bluish black cloud of the sort that usually crosses the sky slowly and in bulk, but these were mere fragments and they were circling the summit rocks at a smart pace against a fiery background of filtered sunlight. It had all the look of a stage set. I should not have been in the least surprised to find fat Brunnhilde up there awaiting the arrival of thick-witted Siegfried.

Only about half-a-mile of ridge with an intervening drop of 200ft separates Meall Mor (3190ft) from Lurg Mhor (3234ft). I reckoned, first, that Naismith, a more energetic man, would have allowed no more than 40 minutes for the return trip and, second, that I was already that much behind a schedule that would get me out of the glen by the prescribed deadline. These calculations took time. Another consideration was that the oasis of Patt might prove to be one of those places where the householder, esteeming his rarity value, presses a cup of tea and conversation on the passing traveller. Time should be allowed to accommodate that possibility. It would have been a different matter if Mozart or Verdi were involved, but Wagner is not a favourite: in the circumstances I decided not to intrude. Incidentally, the preoccupation with timekeeping was occasioned by reports, perhaps ill-founded, that the glen authorities were inclined to be difficult with late arrivals.

The only feasible route from the bridge at Patt lay through the policies, along a drive between gardens and loch. There was no visible sign of life in or about the Lodge, but everything looked solid and serene. Every prospect pleased, even the raising of the water level from 663ft to 740ft appeared to have enhanced the outlook, at least when the loch is full. Patt Lodge evidently belonged with the minority that had lived up to every hope.

This glowing citation was interrupted by the loud, excited barking of a pack of dogs. A bend in the drive revealed kennels on a knoll to the left and on the right a modern bungalow. A man, alerted by the noise, had come out in anticipation of developments and was standing, back to the track, ostensibly studying the pile of logs stacked against the bungalow wall. I

called a greeting. He turned, stared fully long enough to leave no doubt that
the snub was deliberate, then, without change of expression, resumed his
contemplation of the wood stack. He had no words for his dogs either and
they, keenly regretting their confinement, voiced their frustration with
redoubled fervour. They were not the bald, athletic type – all teeth and chest
and genitalia – these were hairy brutes, but big and their bark had a serious
baritone quality. Perhaps they were only well-intentioned, friendly doggies,
but I was rather glad that Pattman had not thrown them a key.

I re-entered the 'here be dragons' country without enthusiasm. In fact
there was little wildlife: just the occasional covey of vultures and the odd
yeti. I suppose the well organised travel between Patt and Gleann Innis an
Loichel by boat, if at all. By land there does not seem to be any right or
wrong way and consequently little advantage to be gained from limited
previous experience. I did avoid some of the minor misjudgments of the
morning, but without striking a significantly better line. A planned detour
to Carn na Cosaig to see whether anything remained of the deer watcher's
cottage mentioned by Robertson and Thomson was abandoned without
remorse. This desirable residence was put up by Winans, the celebrated
high-spending and notoriously litigious shooting tenant of the 1880s. Hot
and fractious, I negotiated the wetlands of the bealach to see below a small
party variously loping and trotting along the track from the direction of
Sgurr na Lapaich towards the parked cars. They conveyed an infectious air
of urgency. I caught the mood, but was unable to emulate the action.
Lurching as briskly as possible down the slope, I had a grandstand view of
the admirable speed with which they divested themselves of rucksacks,
boots and outer clothing and made a dashing getaway, leaving twin dust
trails.

Installed in my own driving seat with every window open, clothes
gradually came unstuck from body and spirits rose. An unexpected lorry
progressing ponderously down the glen allowed me to catch up and join the
convoy. At the checkpoint a leader of men emerged from the middle car to
make a joint presentation of three passes with all our apologies for having
slightly overstayed our welcome. He was evidently well received. As we
drove through the gate, the lady with the keys acknowledged our further
thanks with a friendly smile.

Not a bad day at all really, although I reserve the right, if anyone should
ever talk to me about the heathery horror of Lochan Fada (north), to take
up quarter-of-an-hour of their time with a full account of the hell of Loch
Monar (south).

FLIGHT OF THE CONDOR

By John Ashbridge

An account of the first ascent of the Flight of the Condor, Grade VI, 5, Indicator Wall, Ben Nevis.

THE ROUTE was going well until Robin Clothier popped his head over the arete I had just negotiated with some difficulty.

He inquired: 'You doing the traverse?' 'Yeah,' I replied, concentrating on traversing away across the ice banked ramp. 'You with Simon?' he persisted.

I couldn't deny it. Simon Richardson was belayed some distance away over a series of aretes and bulges. He had guessed that Robin had been below us on Riders of the Storm and had suspected he might catch us up.

'Hello Simon,' hollered Robin

From that moment, things started going wrong.

After a long winter season, that last route is always difficult to predict in advance. So often, end-of-season days can be wasted by poor conditions brought on by prevailing warm westerly winds. April routes, high on Ben Nevis can however often prove an exception, for that extra 1000ft can hold good ice and névé when the surrounding hills are touched by the first taste of spring.

We had reports of good ice from the previous weekend and it had remained cold all week. Simon had called me at work on the Thursday, tentatively suggesting a visit to the Ben. He was writing the new SMC guidebook to the mountain and had his eye on an unclimbed line. I had half arranged a cragging trip to the Lakes, but the northern England weather had been pretty wet all week and the weekend forecast was for much of the same. It didn't take much to cancel the trip to England.

We arranged to meet at 4a.m. in Inverurie, a small Aberdeenshire town, for the drive across to Fort William. Since moving to Scotland, early rises and long drives along windy Highland roads have become an almost ritualistic feature of my winter climbing experiences. Two-and-a-half hour's later we arrived at the golf course car park. A few other climbers were stirring into life as we sorted our gear.

'Do you want to see the line?' Simon produced a glossy A4 print of Indicator Wall, captured on one of those rare sunny Ben days. A rising traverse-line was obvious from the angle of the photograph, the ground above barred by a steep, overhanging headwall, and below by a vertical wall of corners and aretes.

'Looks a good line, a natural weakness,' I said. But would it go? What grade would it be?

I have only ever really enjoyed the walk up the Allt a' Mhuilinn on the very rare occasions when the peat bog is frozen and the footpath can be negotiated with ease. Normally, as on this occasion, the path is at its boot-sucking worst. At least it wasn't raining. We chatted idly and made steady progress, even pulling ahead of a party, and the CIC hut arrived sooner than I had anticipated. Perhaps the previous five months of carting heavy sacs around numerous Scottish glens and mountains had paid off and I was getting fit.

The ground was still not frozen when we reached the first snow at the base of Observatory Gully. Avalanche debris had piled up as contorted mounds of ice blocks in a huge fan. At least the cornices wouldn't be that unfriendly, they were lying in front of us. While gearing up, a party from the CIC Hut caught up. They were friends of Simon and we talked for a while and arranged to meet at the hut that evening, before leaving them to their preparations for Point Five.

The climb up to Indicator Wall is a long slog. It is 2000ft up Observatory Gully beneath the imposing Observatory Buttress, to the highest cliff in Britain. With its base at 4000ft, the Wall took its name from the viewpoint indicator erected by the SMC on the plateau above the wall in 1927 (and destroyed by vandals in 1942).

The Observatory Gully snow was mercifully hard-packed, with wide swathes having been compressed by the tracks of numerous avalanches. We entered the mists and remained immersed throughout the day. Beneath Gardyloo Gully, the snow steepened considerably, and a careful traverse was required above a steep rocky buttress beneath the Wall.

In the swirling cloud, Simon found the start of the line and was digging out a belay as I arrived. It took some time to get ourselves sorted out as decent belays always seem to be a problem with Ben Nevis andesite. This one had to be good as we were climbing into unknown ground.

'I'll take this first pitch, it's crucial we find the ramp line.'

'Fine, you've got the photo,' I replied.

He led off, up and rightwards across a series of ice falls towards more mixed ground and was fixing the first runner as another team arrived. They were surprised by our line, until I explained who I was with. Scottish winter climbing is a small world.

Simon reached the mixed ground, disappeared out of sight and was soon belayed. I moved off to join him. Traversing across steep icy ground has always unnerved me and it took a while to feel comfortable. I felt rusty and uneasy for the first 50ft, and tried to relax at the first runner. Moving onto rockier ground I felt more at ease, and was happier by the time I pulled over the small spike that required an 'à cheval' approach.

'How are you feeling?' Simon inquired, perhaps sensing my unease at the start of the icy traverse. 'Yeah, OK, fine now,' I replied.

The second pitch involved a short corner with rotten ice at its base but good névé over the top. I planted the axes deep and heaved up and away from the belay onto easier ground and traversed up and right to a belay below the third pitch of Albatross.

The route was going well. I could see the third pitch clearly now and the ramp line we had seen on the photograph was to my right.

'I reckon that's Clothier beneath us on Riders of the Storm,' Simon remarked as he arrived at the belay. An old climbing partnership and now joint guidebook writers, Simon and Robin revel in friendly rivalry about new routes and their subsequent grades, especially on the Ben. This route was no exception.

'Give him a hard time if he tries to overtake,' joked Simon as he moved quickly off on the ramp-line proper. It looked straightforward, and was. He quickly covered the 130ft to a hidden belay beneath the imposing headwall. I moved off to join him. The snow was in excellent condition and allowed for rapid progress. I was enjoying the climbing immensely and my initial trepidation about traversing had dissipated.

It was difficult to ignore Robin's forceful questioning, especially as I was concentrating on staying upright on the traverse. When it became clear who I was climbing with, Robin did as Simon had predicted by abandoning Riders of the Storm, and following us across the ramp-line. I subconsciously speeded up my movements to keep ahead of him. Who ever said climbing isn't competitive.

Quickly, I joined Simon, who had managed to find an excellent three-point belay, much to my relief, as the ground ahead of us looked more difficult. A delicate technical axe-torquing move across a thinly-iced buttress got me onto easier ground. I left Simon and Robin to their jovial banter and continued traversing across and upwards over thinly-iced ramps and walls until the traverse ended beneath an overhang, with the ramp tumbling away in a series of corners and aretes. I belayed to a rather loose looking block to the left of Stormy Petrel and brought Simon across. The gear and belay were poor, and as Simon moved off, I could still hear the nattering as I started bringing in the rope. Suddenly, a gasp of alarm and the rope twanged tight. The jovial banter stopped. On the delicate icy buttress one of Simon's axes had pulled, depositing him back at the belay. He tried again, and soon arrived at the stance.

'My axe pulled.'

'I noticed, that move needed a bit of concentration, you should have stopped chatting to Clothier,' I jested.

The atmosphere had become more relaxed since Robin had appeared but the route had become more challenging and required more concentration. Simon's ebullient mood continued as he considered the next pitch.

'Do you reckon it'll go?' I asked. 'Yeah, no problem,' was the confident reply. Gear exchanged he moved off, directly upwards over two thinly-iced bulges to a steep, icicle-draped chimney.

There ensued a waiting game. I suspected the chimney would be desperate and as I got colder and more battered by falling ice, my suspicions were confirmed. Simon couldn't find any gear and in the process had removed most of the ice.

'I can't do this, so I'm traversing right,' he yelled from above. I was relieved, mainly because of the reduction in the pounding I had been getting on the very exposed belay. The rope moved out faster now. Thankfully, the verbal barrage between Simon and Robin had also ceased as they concentrated on the climbing. Meanwhile, Robin had led a very steep icy corner cutting through the overhanging headwall to our left.

'I'll call this the Mickey Mouse finish,' he whooped as he pulled over the final bulge.

I joined Simon at a drive-in and peg belay beneath a steep, rotten icefall, 40ft beneath the easy summit snow slopes. I collected the gear and led off. The rotten ice was soon passed and I planted the axes into good névé. Something felt wrong, my right boot just didn't seem to be holding firm. I looked down and saw the crampon hanging off the boot. Time just stopped; 10ft above a poor belay, 300ft up Indicator Wall, and 4000ft up Ben Nevis my crampon had come off.

'How're your axes?' asked an alarmed Simon.

'Good, good,' I panted. I tried desperately to firm up the left boot placement as I hung off the tools. I had to get back to the belay quickly, before my arms gave up. I took my weight on my left side and threaded a tape through the unweighted hammer wrist loop. Groaning, left arm pumping, I struggled to get the tape through the frozen loop. Mind racing, arms failing, I clipped a cow's tail to the axe and took the weight off my arms. Through! I clipped the ropes. Relieved, panic subsiding, I lowered down to the belay, the hammer wiggling ominously as the frozen ropes jerked through the crab. I was down.

'Jesus, that's the second time I've lost a step-in leading a pitch this winter,' I said, panic receding from my voice. The front bail had sprung off its mount, on the current set, a different pair from the earlier incident in which the same failure occurred at the top of the ice fall on West Gully, Lochnagar. I suppose practice makes perfect. Simon led the pitch without further incident. My hammer, to which we had trusted our lives, alarmingly, just lifted out of its placement. With my crampon temporarily repaired, I gingerly cleared the icefall. I negotiated the snow slope and awkward cornice. Robin and his partner, Jim McGimpsi, were chatting to Simon.

'What took you so long?' Robin yelled, grinning.

Lost for words, I muttered something about step-in crampons and joined in the rope coiling. My elation at climbing a hard new route on the Ben was tempered by the experience of life-threatening gear failure. I tried to push the thoughts of the consequences of falling from the icefall out of my mind as we descended to the CIC Hut. A cup of coffee in the steamy warmth of the hut soon cleared my depressive thoughts, a process helped by the genial atmosphere among the climbers recounting their exploits at the end of a memorable day.

Later, in the darkness of the Allt a' Mhuilinn, I promised myself a new pair of crampons, with straps!

THE DREADFUL BUSINESS OF THE ABERNETTY BROTHERS

Edited by Robin N. Campbell

from the case notes of John H. Watson, M.D.[1]

I WAS summoned out of my reverie by a tap on the knee. I stared down at Holmes's long bony finger, then into his cool grey eyes.

'Watson,' he said, 'I will come with you to Skye.'

'But how could you imagine that I wish to go there?' I exclaimed.

Holmes lounged back into his old chair, propped his feet on the coal scuttle and released a thick coil of smoke. He grinned through the fog like the Cheshire Cat.

'Really, Watson. This secrecy regarding your summer holidays in Scotland is wholly preposterous. Do you presume to try to deceive me? You have spent an hour this evening delving in *Thomas's handbook of the Bowel*[2]. I have noted that you consult this work each Spring, when you plan your holiday. Of course it is not Thomas's tedious monograph which you have been reading. It is a copy of *Munro's Tables of Scottish Mountains,* which you have glued into the case of a surplus Thomas in the hope of concealing your vice from me. A feeble stratagem, indeed! You then proceeded to massage your old war-wound and to peer anxiously at that picture.' He waved his calabash at the picture of the rocky Reichenbach Falls above the mantel. 'Next, after much head-scratching, you gazed at me speculatively and began the agitated ruminations that accompany the flaming of an awkward request'.

'Plainly you had decided that you must *bag* the difficult Skye peaks before your bad leg entirely refuses to bend. You doubted whether the dull Glasgow physician who normally accompanies you would be of much use in this venture. You thought of recruiting me. What could be more elementary?'

'Holmes, this is mind-reading!' I sputtered.

'Nonsense, it is merely the product of close observation, together with analysis of a trivial sort – child's play when it is the actions of an old acquaintance which must be deciphered. There were other clues. You have absent-mindedly knotted the rope of your gown with a bowline, for example! But it is wearisome and futile to explain – let us rather make our plans. I shall be glad to accompany you. London is deadly in summer, without musical or criminal diversion. The Coolins are hardly the Alps, but they will serve well enough for amusement. I know them passably well,

---

[1] These case notes were discovered some years ago in the bottom of a box of old lantern slides, thought to have been donated to the Club by Norman Collie. The first set of notes formed the basis of *The Adventure of the Misplaced Eyeglasses* (SMCJ [1979] xxxi, p360); the second set resulted in *The Case of the Great Grey Man* (SMCJ [1986] xxxiii, p241). The sorry tale recounted here is based on the third and last set of case notes. I am greatly indebted to Robert Aitken for assistance in interpreting Watson's notes.

[2] Holmes is probably referring to H.O. Thomas's *The Past and Present Treatment of Intestinal Obstructions,* first published in 1877 – a standard work of the period.

from a previous excursion with my cousin, who is a great enthusiast. Indeed, I believe I have a mountain named after me – Sgurr Tearlach, Gaelic for Sherlock's Peak?[3]'

-----o-----

It was late in the evening when we arrived at the Sligachan Inn, having left London early on the previous day. Despite the long and weary hours of travel I felt my spirits lift as the coach rounded the last bends beyond Sconser and the Coolins came into view, the jagged peaks of Sgurr nan Gillean glowing brightly in the evening sunshine. After dinner Holmes went off to his room, pleading fatigue. I passed some time with the other guests, who instructed me in the use of the local spirit – a fiery potion named Talisker, reeking of peatsmoke and the sea. With a few of these inside me, and my head filled with their talk of climbing, I went off to bed looking forward to the exertions of the coming fortnight.

I will not weary you with an account of our campaign. Holmes performed with his customary agility and I followed him over and around the convoluted razor-backed ridges. Each evening we sipped Talisker at the smoking-room window and on most of them I was pleased to put another mark in the Holy Tables of Munro. We were often joined by a droll Scotchman from Hamilton, by name Naismith, who shared an interest in pugilism with Holmes and common acquaintance with his cousin Norman[4]. One evening Holmes was entertaining him with a tale of some battle between Cockney bruisers, when another guest, overhearing this colourful narrative, joined in with some observations of his own. He introduced himself as John Abernetty. He and his brother, Henry, had recently arrived from Weymouth in Dorset for a climbing holiday. I felt obliged to make some remonstrance over this dreary talk of boxing.

'How should civilised gentlemen, in middle years, interest themselves in this brutal sport?' I complained. 'It serves no useful purpose except to provide the science of medicine with unusual sorts of brain injury!'

'Well said!' cried Henry Abernetty. 'But you forgot the benefit it brings to bookmakers and the unusual injuries to the pockets of the followers!'

This sally brought a black look from brother, John, and some amusing

---

[3] According to Colin Phillip – the principal authority on Cuillin names – (see SMCJ [1916] xiv, p11) this peak was named by Collie and Naismith. Phillip reports that it was named after Charles Pilkington but adds: 'I cannot recall who suggested this.' Certainly, Tearlach is the usual Gaelic equivalent of Charles, but its pronunciation (roughly, 'tcherluch') bears such a close resemblance to Holmes's name that it seems likely that Holmes's given name is an anglicisation of the Gaelic name. As for his claim that it is named after him, this is an obvious jest. It is interesting that Holmes's spelling of the peak agrees with Phillip's and with the spelling on Professor Harker's SMC map of Skye published as an endpaper to Volume IX of the Journal in 1907 – a wonderful map, far superior to the ugly Priestman map which replaced it in 1923.

[4] The reference is to Norman Collie, identified as Holmes's cousin in the stories mentioned in Footnote 1. Watson's description of the habits and character of our Founder, here and below, are confirmed in Gilbert Thomson's illuminating obituary of Naismith in SMCJ [1936] xxi, p40.

arguments from Holmes and Naismith, but I was pleased to have found an ally. However, Henry Abernetty's enthusiasms turned out to be scarcely less repellent than his brother's. He proclaimed himself as a student of 'comparative religion' and soon began to prate about the teachings of the Bible and the Cabbala on the subject of fighting. Worse still, he found a willing partner in Naismith. Before long they were deep in a stultifying debate regarding the authorship of Old Testament histories. I left the company in disgust and retired to bed with a copy of Whymper's Scrambles.

-----o-----

The following day, which was a Sunday, had been deemed an 'off' day by Holmes. When I descended to breakfast shortly before 10 o'clock, I found the room empty apart from Holmes.

'Where is everybody?' I inquired.

'Well, I have not seen the Abernettys, but their plan last night was to traverse Sgurr nan Gillean. As you know, this is their usual place,' he waved a hand towards a neighbouring table littered with the debris of a meal, 'and as you can see they have eaten and gone. Have you no eyes, my dear Watson, or is it that you see but do not observe?'

'Come now, Holmes. I saw it well enough, but merely wished to make conversation.'

'Ah, just so. So where is Naismith?'

'Indeed I have no idea. Perhaps he is still abed.'

'What deuced poor conversation you make, Watson. Look, he sat at our table, to keep me company, for here in the ashtray is the dottie from his pipe – an unmistakably pungent leaf, but not so strong as to mask the odours of his cologne and the mothballs in the pockets of his best black suit. He has gone off to Portree in search of an English Service. If you are to assist me as we both would wish, you must master these simple deductions! Let us persevere. When did the Abernettys leave?'

'Good gracious, Holmes, I have no idea. Shall we ask Mrs Sharp[5]? She will surely know.'

'But you do not even try, Watson! Observe their table. The butter served with their haddock bore a sprig of parsley which has now sunk a half-inch into the dish. At room temperature, according to the prescriptions of my monograph *Clues Useful for Estimation of the Passage of Time,* this gives us an approximate time of service of one hour twenty minutes ago. Allow them twenty minutes to finish their meal and put on their boots. They left at nine o'clock[6].'

'It is much too early for such bravura, Holmes!' I pleaded. 'Let us

---

[5] The Sharps were proprietors at Sligachan until 1900 (see G.D. Valentine's excellent paper: *At Sligachan – The Classic Age.* SMCJ [1945] xxiii, p224).

[6] Sherlockians will recognize the present case as that mentioned in *The Six Napoleons* in the following terms: 'You will remember, Watson, how the dreadful business of the Abernetty family was first brought to my notice by the depth to which the parsley had sunk into the butter on a hot day.' Holmes's description of the case is, as will be seen, a somewhat colourful exaggeration.

abandon conversation. I am sorry that I spoke. Pray leave me in peace to eat my haddock.'

'I am happy to do so, even though it is plainly a kippered herring. I shall be in the smoking lounge, dealing with my correspondence, should you require further conversation.'

I have made it a fast principle during my walking holidays to exercise every day, since otherwise my game leg is prone to stiffen disagreeably. I therefore consigned only the morning to leisure. After a light luncheon of cold salmon and lamb, I followed a recommendation of Naismith's and took a turn up the Red Burn to look at the Bhasteir Gorge, an impressive and sinister declivity bounding the path to Sgurr nan Gillean on the west, apparently passable only by swimming – which I could well believe[7]. I made my way back out of the gorge and onto the track shortly before three o'clock. I had not descended far when I was astonished to see John Abernetty hurrying across the moor from the Tourist Route, and in obvious distress.

'Watson,' he gasped, 'Henry has fallen from the ridge. I think he must be dead!' The poor fellow blurted out his story to me. They had crossed the mountain and were about to tackle the 'Policeman', an obstacle on the difficult lower portion of the western ridge. John had been on the point of suggesting that it was time to tie on their Alpine line, which he was carrying, when Henry had slipped and fallen down into the Bhasteir Corrie. Believing him to be killed by the fall, and lacking the confidence to negotiate the awkward Policeman section alone, John had traversed back over the mountain. My long experience of such affairs prompted me to ask him if he had noted the time of the accident. He guessed that it had been about 12.25: a few minutes beforehand they had discussed the idea of carrying on to the next peak and had determined the time as 12.20.

It seemed to me that Abernetty was in no condition to climb back up to the site of the accident. I knew the place well enough – Holmes and I had made the same expedition some days before – so I sent him down to the hotel to recruit a stretcher party and turned back up the mountain to see what I could find. It was a stiff pull of an hour and more up to the cliffs below the Policeman. As I turned east to approach them I could make out a motionless figure draped over the screes. I judged that Henry had fallen about 100ft and must have died almost immediately. I made a brief examination: lower limbs, pelvis and spine were fractured. Evidently, he had landed on his feet, but of course after such a fall there are always massive internal injuries. I laid out the body ready for the bearers and thought to pass the time in waiting for them by examining the rocks above. He had fallen from a point on the ridge some distance to the east of the

---

[7] This tremendous gorge is well described in B.H. Humble's *The Cuillin of Skye*. Humble's description is taken from Clinton Dent's account of the first ascent (by Hastings, Slingsby and Hopkinson) in his *Alpine Journal* paper *The Rocky Mountains of Skye*. (Vol. XV, No. 112, p422). For some unaccountable reason, its ascent is nowadays unfashionable.

Policeman. Though the rocks hereabouts were impracticable, I found that some way to the left an easy-looking gully angled up to meet the ridge[8]. It struck me as odd that Abernetty had not let himself down here to assist his brother. He had rope enough, surely, to secure it to some flake of rock and thereby provide a safe means of descent. Perhaps he was so shaken by the incident that he did not think of it.

As I returned to poor Henry's body I could see a party making its way over the slabby rocks at the entrance to the corrie. Soon three local men arrived carrying a stretcher. They were not disposed to linger, nor equipped for English conversation, so we quickly loaded up and began the descent. It was a long and exhausting business and I was very happy to see Naismith and Holmes join us to share the burden over the last interminable mile or so across the bogs to the hotel. Meanwhile, one of the men went ahead to warn Mr Sharp of our arrival and to make arrangements for accommodation of the body. Sharp and John Abernetty stood waiting in the hotel yard as we walked in. Abernetty shuffled up to the stretcher and put a hand on his dead brother's cold face.

'Poor Henry!', he muttered,'I hope he did not suffer much. Did he . . . Was he dead when you got up to him, Watson?'

'He had been dead a while,' I replied shortly. 'His injuries were very severe. There was nothing you could have done for him, I'm afraid.'

Sharp then guided us to an outhouse beyond the stables. We laid the body on a table within and prepared to take our leave.

'Mr Abernetty would like a few moments with his brother,' said Sharp. 'I will wait with him and lock up. I will have to send word for Dr McLeod and the Portree Sergeant to come tomorrow. They'll want to examine the body and prepare a report. There should be two doctors present. Would you be so good as to assist the local man, Dr Watson?' I nodded agreement and walked over to the hotel with Holmes and Naismith. Mrs Sharp had left out sandwiches and refreshment, which we took into the porch. I recounted the day's events, including my conclusion that Abernetty might have made more of an effort to go to the aid of his brother.

'True enough,' put in Naismith, 'that gully is an easy enough place to come down[9]. Or he might have gone down into Lota Corrie – that is not difficult – and come around by the Bealach a' Bhasteir. The route is plainly marked on Harker's map. That would be a long road, but a deal shorter than the road he took.'

'I have to say, too,' I added, 'that I was surprised that he did not at least come up the path to meet us. Should he not have been anxious to know as

---

[8] Evidently Nicolson's Chimney (1873).

[9] The rocks around Nicolson's Chimney were nevertheless the scene of another fatal accident in August 1901, when Mr Whincup – climbing in the (unroped) company of another Aberdeen solicitor Mr Fraser – fell to the screes and then bounced over the lower cliffs to the corrie below. Fraser descended immediately, found Whincup all but dead and raced to Sligachan in one hour. Fraser returned with help in two hours, but to no avail (see SMCJ [1902] vii, p41).

soon as possible whether his brother had survived the fall? I wonder if perhaps there is more to this incident than a simple fall. He acts like a man with something on his conscience.'

'Indeed,' said Holmes, 'so you presume to speculate regarding a death in the mountains. You have been discreet, I trust, since proof of mischief in such places is almost impossible to secure. In general, the matter is quite hopeless. Guilty conduct means little in such a case. Think of it: you are alive and the other is dead. Who is there to blame but yourself? Certainly, mountains are the ideal place in which to dispose of an enemy. Means and opportunity lie everywhere at hand. All that is needed is a slight push, and gravity will complete the job! Moreover, where a fatal accident is always a distinct possibility, those who would inquire must do so under enormous disadvantages. Since the ground itself is murderous, establishing means and opportunity are of no value. Putting aside the remote chance of a direct witness, we are left with motive. But motive alone is never enough for conviction. If a good motive were sufficient to commit murder, you would have done for me years ago, and I you!' 'And between brothers,' said Naismith, 'a good motive is seldom hard to discover.'

'I am chastened, but I am also sure that you exaggerate the difficulties. Look, here is Abernetty coming now. At least ask him a question or two, Holmes.' Abernetty approached the porch doors with downcast eyes, but turned towards us as he entered.

'Thank you, Watson, for what you tried to do for Henry. I still can't believe that this has happened.' He dropped into a chair and put his head in his hands.

'Unexpected death is always shocking,' said Holmes after some moments, 'especially so when one is a witness to it. Were you close beside him when he fell?'

Abernetty jerked upright. 'Good gracious, no!' he cried, and plunged his head in his hands again.

'Where were you, then?' asked Holmes gently.

'I was ahead,' he mumbled, 'I had just turned a corner of the ridge. Henry was perhaps 15ft or so behind me. I heard him cry out, just once and not very loud . . . I did not even see him fall! Oh! I cannot bear to talk about it.' Abernetty turned a stricken face to us, lurched to his feet and staggered through the hotel doors.

A few moments later Sharp entered. He asked me to hold the outhouse key until Dr McLeod arrived tomorrow and passed it to me. Then Naismith made his apologies and disappeared into the hotel with Sharp.

'Well, Watson, you may have something,' said Holmes after a moment. 'Let us enjoy the evening air. If we are to talk about this further we would do well to do so privately.'

We walked over the bridge and followed the Sligachan river down towards the shore. Eventually, we stopped to sit on a convenient boulder. Holmes produced a flask and two silver cups. I poured while he stoked his pipe.

'The principles of interrogation are simple,' said Holmes. 'It is necessary to interrogate as soon as possible, before the suspect has had time to manufacture convincing lies. And it is necessary to ask questions which a guilty man is disposed to answer with lies. You heard his answers. What do you think? If he did push his brother to his doom, then of course he was beside him. "Good gracious, no!", he answered, and vehemently. And then he was in front when it happened. That is the safest place for a guilty man to pretend to be. Naturally, he would have been behind, so that he could choose the spot and so that he could look around for possible witnesses before closing on his victim. And "he cried out", but "not very loud". When there is a violent accident of any kind, it is usually the onlookers who cry out rather than the victim, who is desperately trying to save his life. Since that is so, in this case probably there would be no cry. But of course the common expectation is that the victim would scream as he fell. So it is safest to say "he cried out", but "not very loud" for someone else may have been nearby, approaching the ridge from the other direction perhaps, and would be able to say "No, I heard nothing". Yes, my friend, perhaps you have something after all.'

'But how can we proceed? Surely it is impossible to tell whether he fell or was pushed?'

'Well, as I said earlier, in general terms it is indeed impossible. But in particular cases there may be indications. We have already discovered some, have we not? Now let us suppose that we are in such a place and that I slip and plunge to my doom. What will you do?'

'Do? I should be devastated, of course. I would observe your fall, so far as I was able, and mark the place where you came to rest. I should look for any sign of movement. I should also take care not to fall myself!'

'Indeed, Watson, I am sure you would do that. And then . . . ?'

'I would seek out the shortest safe route to where you lay and go there as speedily as possible.'

'Why?'

'Well, you might perhaps still be alive. If so, I would treat your injuries, wrap you in my clothes, leave you my flask and descend rapidly to the hotel to fetch help, taking careful note of the route, of course.'

'Very good, Watson. An excellent plan. Would anyone act differently in these circumstances?'

'No. I do not think so. I would take no credit for these actions. They are obvious duties which anyone would fulfil.'

Holmes paused to refill our cups.

'Now, Watson, attend. Suppose, *per contra*, you have pushed me: my habit of butchering Paganini's Caprices at 3a.m. has finally fractured your

patient soul. I plunge below, combining the conventional cry of horror with a reproachful stare. What now?'

I meditated my way through a half-inch of Talisker. 'Goodness, Holmes, I should do exactly the same. After all you might not be absolutely killed. Supposing that you were not, I could not leave you alive to accuse me. I would find a convenient boulder and crush your skull. A bloody and cruel business no doubt, but it would have to be done.' We paused to contemplate this unlikely nemesis of Holmes.

'Quite so. That is why it is in general impossible to tell. Victims of a push or a fall excite the same response in their companions, although for different reasons. But let us suppose that your disposition is somewhat squeamish. You have courage and malice enough to cast me down a mountain, but to administer the *coup de grace* is beyond you. That is surely plausible, even if the fatal push was coldly planned and premeditated. If it was, on the other hand, impulsive – perhaps caused by some offensive remark of mine about your want of skill with pen or stethoscope – then it is even less likely that you would compound your felony by doing me to death with a hand-axe. So what may we conclude?'

'I see what you mean, Holmes. A companion who does not make his best efforts to get to the body of the fallen man must be viewed with some suspicion.'

'Absolutely, Watson, and not entirely elementary. Such conduct indicates foul play and squeamishness at once, and it indicates them quite strongly.'

'Of course!' I exclaimed, 'so that is why I felt so much concern in the present case. Now I understand it! A rogue and a coward to boot! Let us fetch him out of his room and confront him.' I rose to my feet in anger.

'Calm down, old fellow!' said Holmes, pouring the remains of the flask into my cup. 'We are barely halfway to our quarry. Now consider further, you have impulsively thrust me off the ledge to my probable death. So far so good. You peer downwards to observe my corpse strewn on the hillside. Does it move a little? Perhaps it does. You are not sure. But nothing will persuade you to descend to the remains. You fear that life still lingers in that shattered bloody ruin, that I will twitch an accusing finger, groaning "Why, friend, why?". You know that you could not stomach the measures necessary to still that accusing finger for ever. So you go down for help, since you are bound by every human duty and by ordinary prudence to do at least that. As you go, you fabricate a plausible story: you could not find your way down to me alone, you were confused and distraught, etc. Do you go down quickly by the shortest route?'

'No indeed. I linger, since every passing minute makes your demise more certain.'

'Just so. You will take your time. Indeed you might take rather a lot of time and may consider lying about the time of the unhappy event, postponing it to such a time as will make your descent appear prompt, although this ruse is plainly hazardous.'

'And can we glean any clue from the times in the present case?'

'I do not believe so. Naismith is expert in the estimation of times. We know, thanks to my calculation at breakfast, which you so brutally derided, that the Abernettys left at 9 o'clock. According to Naismith they should have been on the peak at around midday, so 12.25 is a perfectly plausible time for the accident to happen. You met Abernetty on the path just before three. His descent was a little slow, perhaps, but not unreasonably so.'

'So what shall we do now? Do we have enough evidence to denounce Abernetty?' 'No, we have nothing approximating proof, only an accumulation of indications. We must bide our time and keep our counsel. In any case, I am on holiday and have no client. Perhaps Henry Abernetty was a black-hearted villain who deserved his fate! However, when you carry out the examination tomorrow, please attend to the curious condition of the dead man's fingers.'

'His fingers? But I have already attended to them. There was nothing whatever curious about them. They were clean and well-groomed.'

'That, Watson, is the curious condition[10]. Except under very odd circumstances a slip will result in a fall to the ground followed by an accelerating sliding descent which becomes in due course a free fall. What would you do in these first moments of the catastrophe? You would dig your fingers into the rock in a desperate search for a hold, would you not?'

'Indeed I surely would. And I am also sure that you are about to tell me that this is yet another circumstance or indication which does not amount to proof.'

I rose up in disgust, drained the last of the whisky and set off to return to the hotel somewhat unsteadily, I confess – as the last light drained from the peaks of Sgurr nan Gillean and Bhasteir. It had been a long and exasperating day and I was more than ready for the benison of sleep.

-----o-----

In the morning I conducted Dr McLeod and Sergeant McLean to the outhouse. McLeod cut off the clothing and we began to inventory the injuries while McLean examined the personal effects.

Suddenly he spoke up. 'Here's a very curious thing, gentlemen! Look at his watch, will you?' He flipped the watch open and passed it over.

It was an odd watch, certainly, having two small dials set one above the other in the face. The upper dial gave the time in the usual way, and the lower dial gave the date. It was stopped, of course, and the glass was gone.

'The time, man, the time!', said McLean impatiently.

'Of course!', I said, 'Eight minutes past four o'clock! It is hopelessly wrong, since he fell at 12.25! Perhaps it ran on for a while. But the date is

---

[10] Watson is a slow learner. Holmes used exactly this type of deduction, in relation to 'a dog which did not bark in the night-time' in an earlier case – *Silver Blaze*.

wrong also. The hand points to the 1st, but this is the 15th!'

'Aye, so it is. And besides, how does broken glass fall out of a closed watch? Tell me that, sir!'

I hurried through the examination, impatient to consult Holmes about this bewildering matter of the watch, signed the certificate and rushed over to the hotel to wash. I found Holmes and Naismith deep in conversation in the smoking lounge. The combined effect of their pipes had reduced the lounge to a condition recalling the thickest of London fogs.

'Good heavens, Holmes, what an appalling fug!' I cried. 'Be so good as to open a window!'

Holmes rose and threw the windows open. 'Watson, Naismith has interesting news. He was up with the lark, and off to Portree in the dogcart. We now have a motive. Tell him, Naismith!'

'My father owns a newspaper, Watson, – *The Hamilton Advertiser,*' he said, 'so I sent a telegram to our office, who forwarded it to *The Weymouth Telegram*. They then replied directly to me in Portree.' He produced a telegram. 'It seems that John Abernetty has heavy gambling debts and that he will inherit a considerable sum on Henry's death. So there is motive enough, although – as we allowed last night – it is a question whether this would count for much in Court.'

'Let us review the case,' said Holmes, 'and then you may give us the new evidence which you are bursting to deliver, Watson!'

Holmes paced back and forth before the window, enumerating the several indications of foul play so far discovered in what seemed to me to be an unnecessarily pedantic fashion, while I fretted to have the mystery of the watch explained. Eventually, I was allowed to speak.

'His watch! There was no glass in it when Sergeant McLean opened it! It was stopped - broken - and gave the date as the 1st and the time as eight minutes past four! He must have consulted his broken watch after he fell! Why would anyone do that?'

'Come, Watson,' said Holmes, 'your question is surely rhetorical. The answer is that no-one would do such a thing. You know my methods. Since the glass is gone, he must have opened his watch, but not to consult it. Rather he moved the dead hands of the watch to 4.8 on the 1st. Why? To pass a message, of course! In the context the message is clear enough – I was pushed! – but can we perhaps make it clearer?'

While they pulled at their pipes I struggled to think of what the dead man's message might be. One – four – eight? Could it be the number of some kind of locomotive, perhaps?

'Of course!' cried Naismith. 'I have it! Abernetty was a Rosicrucian and an adept of Scripture. Such folk even take decisions by using date and time as a code to divine a guiding text, or so I have heard[11]. One is the Book, four is the Chapter and eight is the Verse. Genesis 4:8.'

SCOTTISH MOUNTAINEERING CLUB JOURNAL

As I rose to fetch a Bible he stilled me with a wave of his pipe. 'I have no need of the Book. I learned it in my cradle.' Naismith stood up, turned to face Sgurr nan Gillean and intoned: 'And Cain talked with Abel his brother: and it came to pass, when they were in the field, that Cain rose up against Abel his brother, and slew him!'

As these awful words rang in our ears we saw a figure jump to the ground from above the open window. It was Abernetty. He rose to his feet, turned to stare at us briefly and despairingly, then ran off in the direction of the Sgurr. I reached for my stick and moved to pursue him.

'No, Watson, let him run,' said Holmes, 'He will not get far. I had forgotten that his room lay directly above. I fear that he must have heard everything.'

-----o-----

Holmes was right: Abernetty got only as far as the Bhasteir Gorge, with Sergeant McLean in futile pursuit, and promptly cast himself into it. Accordingly, when we made our melancholy departure from Sligachan on the following day, we had for company two coffins consigned to Weymouth and lashed to the roof of the coach.

Several days later, we were once more before the hearth in Baker Street. I finished the last of my notes describing this appalling case, tied up the file and laid aside my pen.

'Holmes,' I said, 'I have spent the day talking to a lawyer friend and studying medical reports of men who have suffered falls. I have come to three conclusions and would value your opinion about them.'

'Certainly, Watson, what is it you have discovered?'

'I have discovered that there was no case against Abernetty. He could have stuck to his story and gone free. The business of the watch meant nothing. It might have been broken days before. I have also discovered that it is next to impossible for a man recently fallen from a height, severely shocked and bruised, at best semi-conscious, to remove a watch, adjust it in the manner required and return it to his waistcoat pocket. My third conclusion is that you contrived the whole dreadful business. You made sure that I drank too much Talisker that night, so that you could remove my

---

[11] This method of divination is a variant of the *sortes Biblicae* – in which a page of scripture was selected at random, and a verse obtained by random pointing. This method was widely used in mediaeval monastic traditions but, following proscription, it was used only by secret religious and occult groups such as Rosicrucians and Freemasons. Rosicrucianism enjoyed a considerable vogue in late Victorian England: among our own members Aleister Crowley was associated with the London Order of the Golden Dawn until he abandoned white magic for the more interesting sort. Naismith's knowledge of these arcane methods may well have been due to acquaintance with Crowley. Contemporary applications of the *sortes* may be found in Tennyson's *Enoch Arden* (1862) and Conrad F. Meyer's *Der Heilige* (1879). More recently, Ellis Peter's novel of mediaeval detection *The Holy Thief* provides a dramatic example.

key as I slept and tamper with Abernetty's watch. You did not *forget* that Abernetty's room lay above us, but rather chose to reveal our suspicions in his hearing, speaking loudly before an open window. You wished to spare yourself the tedium of attending an inquiry in Inverness and the ignominy of giving evidence in an unsuccessful murder trial, so you persuaded Abernetty to his death!'

'Tut, Watson, these are hard words to come from a friend. And where is there any proof? Did I force the Talisker down your throat? No. Was it I who wished the windows opened? No. Was it I who saw the hands of the watch pointing to Genesis 4:8? Again, no. A scholar like Naismith would have found a suitable text from almost any setting of the watch.'

Holmes reached down a Bible from his shelf and began to thumb through it. 'Let me see, the deed was done at 12.25 on the 14th. The 14th Book is Second Chronicles . . . Ah, yes . . . In the code used by some Rosicrucians it is the minute hand which gives the chapter, and the hour which gives the verse . . .   So Chapter 25, Verse 12 . . . I have it: "And other ten thousand left alive did the children of Judah carry away captive, and brought them unto the top of the rock, and cast them down from the top of the rock, that they were all broken in pieces." Surely a better text! As you say, the broken watch meant nothing. John Abernetty took the time from his own watch, read his pocket Bible and took the text as excuse to kill his brother!'

'But I see that you are quite incredulous, Watson. How then shall we resolve this matter? Let the Good Book decide.'

He glanced at the clock.

'It is now eight minutes past ten on the 21st . . . That would be Ecclesiastes 10:8: "He that diggeth a pit shall fall into it; and whoso breaketh an hedge, a serpent shall bite him". Justice was done, Watson, let that be an end of it.'

'So be it, Holmes,' I said, placing the file on the highest shelf, 'although I am sure that any verse from the misanthropic author of Ecclesiastes would have served as well. At least you will agree that this story cannot on any account be published?'

'Absolutely, Watson. On mountains we must remain Idealists: no *real* crimes are to be found there, alas; for none may be detected.

DALWHINNIE

By I.H.M. Smart

*Dalwhinnie even now can be a dour place to wait for something to happen.
Two of the following stories tell of waiting there for lifts in the days of long
ago, while the third is an update . . .*

The days of innocence.

IN APRIL 1945 we put up our cotton tent in the wood at the Loch Ericht
turnoff. The time passes slowly when you are 15 and we lay for interminable hours wrapped in our blankets waiting for some vehicle to pass. The
roof with its camouflage pattern flapped monotonously in the grey wind.
It was painted thus because of wartime regulations. A white tent would
have attracted enemy bombers.

We were on our way back from an expedition into the fastnesses of
Rothiemurchus, boldly going beyond the remote village of Coylum Bridge,
along the pot-holed cart track to uninhabited Loch Morlich and then by the
narrow footpath through the primeval forest to the Clach Bharraig bothy.
We spent the night in this half-legendary, now-vanished howff whose
presence we had known about through the oral tradition. The next day we
climbed Cairngorm and felt we had accomplished a great feat. We really
were that naive. Then we camped in the woods over by the mouth of the
Lairig and had a little fire under the stars, intimidated by the old trees that
loured darkly around us. On our second day by the bleak snow-dusted
roadside we heard an engine, not a bomber but a military vehicle of some
kind. Usually, army lorries did not stop as it was against regulations to pick
up civilians. We had been hoping for a commercial traveller, the only
civilians who made long journeys by road in these years. We hurriedly
packed up just in case. A long flat-bedded lorry lumbered up with a ruined
aircraft on board. We thumbed it despondently. It stopped! The driver, a
genial soul, told us to hop on the back but to lie down out of sight if he blew
the horn as this would mean the approach of other military traffic. We
climbed aboard and found half-a-dozen people already there. There was a
dignified, fine-featured woman with two windswept children; they were
from Glen Fruin and spoke Gaelic. We gathered her husband had been
killed in the Western Desert. The Highlands were still largely inhabited by
Highlanders at that time. It would be strange today but then it was quite
normal. They were, however, already unprofitable anachronisms, the
Scottish equivalent of Red Indians. We did not understand that after the war
they would be surplus to requirements and would have to go. We in our
innocence treated them with deference; we felt we were visitors to their
inalienable native heath. The other passengers were three dishevelled

civilian men who looked down on their luck. They were very old, maybe even in their 40s. We all crouched together under the wreckage in what little shelter we could get from the slipstream.

The Highland family got off at Calvine, the rest of us at Dunkeld. Nearer to Perth the road got busy, maybe a car an hour and our driver didn't want to chance his luck any further. We thanked him and, chilled to the gizzard started to walk south into a hard blue gloaming. We reached Birnam where there was a Youth Hostel in the old school, now levelled to the ground. There was no resident warden and it was a cold draughty place with a high ceiling. We had a whole tin of beans left, also some dog biscuits. (Food was rationed at the time and we were quite rightly never allowed to take our ration books away from home: besides, financial constraints were such that the less you ate, the longer you could stay away). After supper round a smoky coal-burning grate that shed heat grudgingly we retired to the bunks and lay under a heap of blankets, converting our beans and dog-biscuits into heat by shivering. We were, I repeat, so naive we thought that this was the normal way of doing things. I can remember being aware of the luxury of finally feeling warm and the blessing of shelter from the night wind that was making the rafters creek. There were no lights in the darkness outside; the war had another month to go.

Ship of the road.

Later in the same year we were once again becalmed on the north-south traffic watershed at Dalwhinnie, this time on the return from our first trip beyond the Great Glen, until then a closed area requiring a military pass to enter. We had seen the fabled country to the north, reached the remote Cuillins and climbed the Window Buttress and the easy side of the Inaccessable Pinnacle with an ancient, inadequate hemp rope. I think we thought we had really made it into the first rank as rock climbers; we were obviously still very naive, but then we had only read books on the craft, had no friends who were rock climbers and youth leaders had yet to be invented.

As petrol was rationed traffic was sparse, but then so were hitch-hikers, and most vehicles would pick you up; there was still a sort of camaraderie in the air. After a few hours something approached from the north. It emitted black smoke and rode the undulations of the old road like a well-found vessel, for this is what it was, a steam-driven ship of the road, probably one of the last of the puffing billies. It clanked to a halt smoking and hissing. Three black faces with bright shining smiles beamed down us: 'If youse come wi us, ye'll hae tae pass us coal fae the back,' said Para Handy, indicating room beside the coal on the back platform. MacPhail and Sunny Jim beamed down in confirmation. We gratefully accepted. Steam lorries even then were archaic vehicles; this might be the last possibility of riding a live and working dinosaur and a paradoxically early carboniferous one at that. *Vitalsparkosaurus Rex* weighed anchor and set course for its home port of Inverkeithing. I can't remember much about the journey but we must have steamed our way all day along a rambling archaic version of the A9. I can remember climbing the narrow winding road up Glen Farg, because we had to stop at the Bien Inn to do something mysterious to the engine. The crew made a brew over the fire in blackened syrup tins with wire handles. They generously decanted some of the creosote into our mugs. At Inverkeithing the ship of the road berthed and the crew disbanded. 'Ye'll be in Embro the nicht,' they said waving farewell. We too were now the colour of the crew and undeniably proletarian. Thus promoted, we got friendly greetings from passers-by in the street and were addressed as equals by the lassie in the chip shop as she wrapped up our suppers. Like ship-wrecked mariners we trudged to the Queen's Ferry, signed up for the passage and managed to reach home in douce, perjink, bourgeois old Embro that evening. I remember my mother saying: 'Thank goodness you arrived after dark.'

Selling the Pass.
Recently, I spent an August day exploring the mysterious territory around Gaick and was returning in the late afternoon to my car near the old Dalwhinnie road end. From the heights of Carn na Caim I could see the great new road crowded with traffic streaming north out of Atholl and skailing bumper to bumper into Badenoch and Strath Spey (or the Spey Valley as the new owners call it). It was some sort of holiday in the dark south and a major population shift was taking place. Cars and caravans trying to make the best time they could mingled with lorries and vans bent on maximising their speed. None of these vehicles were dangerously ramshackle, rusty and bald-tired like so many cars of the frugal Fifties: they all had heaters and radios and cassette players and did not need to rely on hand signals. I had sufficient recall of the elder days to realise the magnitude of the new wealth blessing the land and the inordinate increase in happiness that must surely have accompanied it. However, the memory suddenly came of a postcard I once bought in Tombstone City, Arizona. It was a photograph of the great Apache chief, Cochise. It depicted a man with a noble demeanour. His visage was intelligent and dignified but, nevertheless, wore a deeply-puzzled expression, probably the same look he wore when he sat on his horse watching yet another covered wagon train appearing over the eastern horizon. No matter how many palefaces his Apaches killed, replacements arrived in increasing numbers. On such an occasion he was heard to remark with weary incomprehension: 'Is there no end to these people?' The norms of his world had collapsed. An alien population explosion could no longer be controlled by the tomahawk. Yet, had he but realised it, these people coming over the horizon were mobile profit, potential customers rather than potential scalps. With a good lawyer

he might have negotiated the Arizona Big Mac franchise for himself and scholarships to West Point and the Harvard Business School for his sons. He could have become a real Big Mac, that is, a Highland instead of a Red Indian Chief.

And so I stood with my arms across my chest, tried to look noble, watched the covered wagons rolling endlessly over the southern horizon, muttered: 'Is there no end to these people?' And then tried to realise that these were not really people but customers, profit on the hoof, a source of wealth. Dignified surrender may be all very well for making tragic postcards but has no real biological future. After all, even we in the SMC, toffee-nosed elitists though we are, depend on increasing the numbers of customers who stay in our huts and buy our guide books and so increase the cash flow of the Trust. I could feel my belay taking the strain as my expression started to become streetwise and speculative.

TABLE MOUNTAIN

It's done. Sign on.
Carry your stone to the cairn.
Initial the mist.
Then go down
Add your own
name to the list.

A long climb.
For a long time.
Hundreds of thousands of feet.
And after each top
another one yet to go up.
But now you can stop.

Compleat.
And the sun has come through, what a sight.
Every mountain in Scotland laid out
neat underfoot, your friends will delight
hearing each night your account of this great
incomparable view.

Mostly of you.

G.J.F. Dutton.

REMEMBERING A CUILLIN PIONEER

By H.M. Brown

1993 WAS the centenary of the death of Sheriff Alexander Nicolson, whose name is remembered in the name of Skye's highest summit. He was the first to climb Sgurr Alasdair and that was only one of several outstanding discoveries and climbs by this largely-forgotten pioneer, whom Ben Humble in his history of Skye climbing called 'the great explorer'. *(B.H. Humble: The Cuillin of Skye* – Hale 1952, is a collector's item but is available in a modern reprint from the Ernest Press.)

The first real explorer of the Cuillin was another remarkable figure, Professor James Forbes, 'the wonder child of his generation' who gained his chair at the age of 23 and was to pioneer the science of glaciology. For two decades after his appointment he went to mountains regularly, whether Alps, Pyrenees, or Skye. He and a local man first ascended Sgurr nan Gillean (1836) by what is now called the Tourist Route. Nine years later he made the first ascent of Bruach na Frithe and drew the first accurate map of the range. Most other early travellers had been romantics, in the wake of Scott, Turner, Horatio MacCulloch, etc., heading for Loch Coruisk with its wildly inaccurate description of being sunless and surrounded by unscalable precipices. It needed a Skye man to explore and extol the rich reality – Alexander Nicolson.

Nicolson was born in Husabost, Skye, in 1827, where his father was a tacksman under Macleod of Macleod. He made himself an able student but abandoned his original vocation of the church to try and earn a living as a writer. Journalism was then left for law and he became an advocate in 1860.

Nicolson was unlucky in life. Success, fame, wealth always eluded him and while many men could have been made bitter in these circumstances, his nature kept him content enough. Perhaps he lacked the killer-instinct, the greedy self-seeking, to soar as many of his peers did. He was known as a charmer, a singer, a wit, a rhymester, a big man of open features and warm heart, 'perhaps the most popular man of his time in Edinburgh'. Fun, rather than ambition, lay behind his Skye ploys, and the love of the place, for itself, rather than as a scientific objective (as with Forbes) kept him returning whenever possible. His long Sligachan romance was to be repeated a generation later by the climbing academician, Norman Collie. Even when Nicolson's active days were over just being there was enough. He was one of the first to climb, and say so, purely for fun.

Sligachan greeted him (as it has done a few folk since) with a thunderstorm but he evidently revelled in this. ' . . . among the towering black mass of the Cuillin rolled and seethed a lurid array of lead-coloured clouds, grim and threatening'. His name cropped up continually in the Bible-thick Visitors' Book at Sligachan, a treasure I browsed through by the hour as a youngster and in which we so diffidently added our record of the now commonplace Ridge Traverse. The book has been stolen and, being irreplaceable and unique, it can never be sold or passed on. (If the selfish culprit should read this, can I plead for the book to re-appear mysteriously somewhere, to take its rightful place again.)

Many of Nicolson's doings were described in *Good Words*, a magazine edited by Dr Norman Macleod – Queen Victoria's chaplain, a famous preacher and influential churchman. Good Words was an immensely popular publication (with a circulation which would be the envy of most outdoor magazines today), its rather unfortunate title hiding plenty of stories of outdoor activities. It is a pity Nicolson never produced a Skye book for he wrote good clean prose. Perhaps that innate talent for missing the boat applied again. He was no Skye ostrich though. He foresaw the vast tourist potential of the island and lived long enough to see it happen. As early as 1872 he was suggesting a bridge at Kyle might not be a bad idea. Camasunary he envisaged would have its Grand Hotel de Blaveinn. Today's bothy was a Victorian 'establishment for reforming drunkards'.

Thinking of books, the first, the SMC guidebook, was to come in 1907 and, in 1908, A.P. Abraham's *Rock-Climbing in Skye* had an even bigger influence. The Abraham brothers climbed all the known routes and made several notable first ascents to produce this classic. The superb photos were all taken with whole-plate cameras. They were early motorists. Such were the changes. Nicolson had none of these aids. Not even Munro's Tables. Scotland, never mind Skye, was *terra incognito*.

Few briefs came Nicolson's way and some law reporting, lecturing and general writing barely kept him going till he was appointed Sheriff-substitute of Kircudbright (1872) and, later, of Greenock (1885). Before going to Kircudbright he had been offered, and turned down, the chair of Celtic Studies at Edinburgh University, which would have appeared the perfect place for his talents. He was a notable Gaelic scholar, with a delight in Gaelic poetry and song. Plenty of the Sligachan Visitors' Book entries are in Gaelic. He retired to Edinburgh and died in January 1893, aged 66.

His first real mountain visit to the Cuillin was in 1865 (he was then 38) and if the weather was wild, well, he could wait, warning the impatient: 'If they are in a hurry, Skye and its clouds (and its inhabitants) are in none, and the Cuillin will unveil their majestic heads, in due time and no sooner.'

'To see them is worth a week's waiting – to see the black peaks start out like living creatures, high above the clouds which career up the cleft ridges, now hiding and now revealing their awful faces . . .' For Nicolson it was all 'life and music'.

Skye saw 'few strangers except yachtsmen, bagmen and a stray geologist', yet locals (shepherds and keepers) obviously had a peripheral knowledge and were occasionally enrolled to guide visitors. When Nicolson climbed Sgurr nan Gillean in 1865 MacIntyre, the Sligachan keeper, went with him (just as MacIntyre *pere* had gone with Forbes in 1836) and they went up by the Tourist Route. But the character of the man then appears. Instead of descending the same way he persuaded his companion to try a new traverse of the mountain.

So they made the first descent of the West Ridge until they came up against the late, lamented gendarme and, perforce, made a 'vermicular descent' down a chimney to the screes of Coir' a' Bhasteir, a route now known as Nicolson's Chimney and still regularly used as a way up the peak. Nicolson returned to climb up the West Ridge shortly after. He was the first to comment on the super-adhesive qualities of gabbro.

After descending Nicolson's Chimney our explorer traversed under the Tooth and up Bruach na Frithe, a day which obviously well-satisfied and led to many similar ventures. When Knight climbed his eponymous peak on Gillean's Pinnacle Ridge he wrote to tell Nicolson of his climb. Some years later Nicolson and Gibson were to find Knight's card in a bottle on its summit. Nicolson was a Vice-President of the Scottish Mountaineering Club and a lifelong friend of some of its members. Nicolson didn't hesitate to wander alone if shepherd or friend was unavailable nor did he hesitate to bivvy on the Cuillin, lying wrapped in his plaid (none of our soft gear and equipment) and eating cold fare and water. He wrote lyrical descriptions of his nights out and how 'the rich gloaming still lingers tenderly in the north west till bars of yellow light are seen in the east heralding the dawn'.

A trip, as unconventional, and tough as any today, was largely done at night and is worth recalling; almost incidentally, it included the first ascent of that elusive and tricky Munro, Sgurr Dubh Mor.

This was in September 1874. He and a friend had been visiting an artist at Loch Coruisk so it was 4p.m. when they set off for this unknown hill, which was bold, rather than rash, given Nicolson's unique experience of the Cuillin, a steady barometer and the promise of a full moon.

They went up An Garbh Coire, between Sgurr Dubh and Gars-bheinn, a coire choked with a mass of huge boulders and giving difficult passage. Once, coming down the coire, I was glad to shelter, quite dry, in its subterranean depths during a thunderstorm – as did Nicolson on this ascent for a less worrying shower of rain. Then, as now, route-finding was intricate and the summit was reached at sunset (7p.m.) and the descent was started in the gloaming, again, choosing deliberately to head into unknown country down into Coir 'an Lochain, still rarely visited and from where an ascent of Sgurr Dubh is specifically not recommended by guidebooks.

They soon ran into trouble. Halfway down a steep wall barred progress and Nicolson brought into play his secret weapon – his plaid. He was lowered down and backed against the wall so his (lighter) companion could hang down to stand on his shoulders. They fought down in shadowed blackness for two-and-a-half hours, finishing with a water-spraying gully, their finger tips shredded and mighty relieved to be down safe and sound into the moonlit valley bottom. The plaid could be put away.

Nicolson described this item of clothing and its usefulness: with a belt it could be made into a dress for a man, serve as bedclothes, as a bag, as a sail for a boat, a rope for rock climbing, a curtain, an awning, a carpet, a hammock . . . and it had one superiority in that 'there's room in it for twa'.

Their adventures were not yet over. Nicolson tried to take a new short cut over Druim nam Ramh to Harta Coire and Glen Sligachan. It didn't 'go' (the moon disappeared again) so they had to descend and go along to the other end of the loch for the usual crossing of Druim Hain. Blaven, which Nicolson considered the finest hill in Skye, loomed in the east. They reached the Sligachan Hotel at 3a.m.

A year earlier (1873) Nicolson had made the ascent of the peak which would be named after him. At that time everything thereabouts was lumped together as Sgurr Sgumain, the name now used for the lower, seaward subsidiary crest. He had wandered up from Glen Brittle on a wild, wet day and had reached Lochan Coire Lagan when the driving cloud cleared briefly to reveal a monster peak overhead 'one of the wildest objects I had ever seen'. He was back next day with Macrae, a local shepherd and able hillman.

The fine day began with an ascent of Sgurr na Banachdich (he'd recently made its first recorded ascent) from which they traversed the by no means straight-forward ridge to Sgurr Dearg on what may have been a first ascent. Bypassing the Inaccessible Pinnacle he wrote: 'it might be possible with ropes and grappling irons . . . but hardly seems worth the trouble.' What a pity he did not take the trouble, but his priority was exploration, movement, the 'leaping from rock to rock' and not any seige of a single problem. The Pilkington brothers in 1880 proved his opinion as to its feasibility to be correct. His was the first close encounter of the Inn Pin by a real climber. Everything that day was new.

Nicolson looked across the coire to his objective and at once spotted the single line of weakness, the Great Stone Shoot as we now know it (even though, today, it has largely shot its boulders). Right of the huge gully two other great exploratory routes were to go up: Collie's climb in 1896 (Collie, Howell, Naismith) and Abrahams' Climb in 1907. But Nicolson was before them all – and recording the success with an understatement worthy of Tom Patey: 'I have seen worse places.'

The early Seventies saw a rapid rise in ascents being made from Sligachan. Faster and faster times were recorded in the Visitors' Book and our gentle giant tartly made the following entry in 1872. 'Spent four nights here with great satisfaction. Climbed Sgurr nan Gillean with ditto in what precise space of time it matters not to anyone else, especially to Brown, Jones and Robinson. Supposing I should say '1 hour and 49½minutes', they might stare, but they might also say, not inaccurately, Walker! The view from the top was not so fine as I have seen there before, being limited by atmospheric conditions to a radius of about a dozen yards.'

Nicolson had his hard core too. He could come out with comments like: 'The loss of life is a small thing compared with the full and free exercise of our powers and the cultivation of a bold adventurous spirit; and any nation which has ceased to think so is on the fair road to decay . . .'

Nicolson travelled extensively. He once listed some of the other islands he knew and compared them with Skye: Arran – more delightful; Islay – fairest of all; Mull – beauty and grandeur, more green and woody; Jura – queenly but lacking variety; Tiree – too flat yet many charms; Staffa and Iona – a sense of wonder; Barra – rough and rocky; Lewis – boggy; Harris – almost like Skye in mountain grandeur; Skye – *Queen of them all.* And who would argue with such a regal judgment, given by the man who could rightly be regarded as the Cuillins' Prince of the Peaks?

Sgurr nan Gillean, from a photograph taken by Howard Priestman. Readers may wish to refer back three years to p.122 of the 1992 Journal, where R.N. Campbell presented two puzzles about the peak. The third puzzle, obviously, is why this illustration was missed out in 1992.

THE SMC HUT ROUTE

By Alec Keith

FOR ALL its varied landscapes, and despite the efforts of Grieve et al (SMCJ, 1978, p227) Scotland has no definitive summer or winter outing to compare with the Alpine Haute Route. Such was the topic chewed over by Hamish Irvine and myself one Christmas Eve as we retreated from the Coire Cas car park, our attempts at climbing repulsed in a spray of gravel and small shrubs. Skiing, we decided, should be ignored, the snow too fickle, the province, after all, of the worms; and clearly it is no bad thing that the vibram-shod hordes do not have too many classic summer routes to churn up and bury under gas canisters and toilet paper. We gave up and wondered instead if the present shape of the Club (angular and stooped, with a discernible bulge at the midriff) had anything to add to its fine history of long days on the hills, and so it was that Hamish conceived the SMC Hut route.

It was a basic idea, the simple linking of the four SMC huts on foot by any reasonably aesthetic line. Obviously the huts were to be used, and the journey should take as little time as possible, each day leading to a new hut, though for reasons of human frailty the 73-mile stage from the CIC to the Ling could be split with a night at the Cluanie Inn, in keeping with the finest traditions. While countless variations are possible, the distances involved (the route described is 140 miles) mean that the shortest lines are to be preferred. Like any grand plan we agreed it should be done and then many months passed and the Hut route was spoken of only in moments of idle pub banter.

I made a tentative foray from the Ling in the gloom of the following November, but got no further than Achnashellach before a tendon in one of my knees complained. I hitched home with a clear conscience but was secretly relieved. A sharp exchange with Hamish revealed his unhappiness with my disloyalty, and it was agreed that this was to be a joint project. But I reckoned this pledge could be overlooked for a bit in the light of Hamish's next conception, a conception with a shorter and more predictable period of gestation.

In this window of opportunity I slunk guiltily into the Raeburn one Sunday early last May for a second try. The weather was forecast to be fairly settled but cold, and much snow still lay on the hills. Good conditions, but I was nervous, unsure if my body was capable of four days' sustained effort without a good rest in between.

I'd not stayed in the Raeburn before; it's a typical committee hut, and its location doesn't inspire. The hut was empty, which was a problem for someone who sees flushing a toilet as a technical challenge, the frighteningly large gas cylinders meant that the cooker was out of the question; the water pump made a lot of noise but would only produce air; and the electricity tripped out at breakfast in the dark.

I was away shortly after five, trotting along the road towards Dalwhinnie, chilled by the morning air but happy to have started at last. The plan was to run a fair amount of the way, but my sack turned out heavier than expected, crammed as it was with a clutter of shoes, maps, bananas, cakes, pit and so on, and my jogging would fade into a painful thrashing motion after a few hours each day. Also there were a lot of bags of a horrible white powder which would no doubt have interested the Constabulary, but it was only an energy drink of uncertain flavour, slightly better swallowed than inhaled. I followed the track along the side of Loch Ericht and made good time jogging in the sun to Culra.

On Ben Alder it was still more winter than summer, and I was lured off the Bealach Dubh path on to the Long Leachas ridge, kicking the odd step in hard old snow, topping out on the plateau just as a band of cloud blew over the sun and sat on the summit. As I dropped down to the Uisge Labhair and ran down to Loch Ossian my legs began to seize up and my movements became more sluggish. I stopped for lunch at the hostel with Tom Rigg, receiving an enthusiastic welcome from a puppy called Beinn Eibhinn and a more circumspect one from a stag called Windswept.

After cutting over a boggy shoulder on Leum Uilleum I came down to Loch Chiarain and managed a half-hearted trot down to the Blackwater Reservoir, kept going by the sight of the Buachaille and the Blackmount hills peering round Beinn a'Chrulaiste at me. The final treat was the low pass between the Blackwater dam and Altnafeadh, a real Slough of Despond in which I wallowed haplessly.

It was half past five when I reached Lagangarbh, finding the builders busy with Phase Three of the renovations. There were plenty of signs of their efforts as well as a large hole where the toilet block used to be. After a ritual meal of tuna and pasta I just managed to crawl upstairs to the bunks before falling asleep.

Tuesday was cold, windy, misty and unfriendly. But it was the easy day, the goal being the CIC, so there was time for a lie-in. I plodded stiffly over the Devil's Staircase in drizzle, to indulge the previous day's food fetish (half a chicken) in Kinlochleven, creating an unnecessarily heavy pack for the rest of the day with other, additional goodies. The route was due to cross the Mamores to Steall then go over the Ben to the CIC, but the snow on the higher slopes was going to be pretty icy and my running shoes were a bit

inadequate for that and yes it was still very windy . . . Looking back it was
the right decision, although an unsatisfactory one. I sneaked round the
Mamores on the West Highland Motorway which took me to an unavoidable
tea-stop at one of the Glen Nevis cafes. The youth hostel track up to the
Halfway Lochan was as tedious as ever, and great blasts of wind tore down
the Allt a'Mhuillinn on the traverse round into Coire Leis. Hadrian's Wall
appeared briefly through the murk, icy and complete.

The midweek section of one of our kindred clubs (which can remain
anonymous for the usual fee) was in residence in the CIC, including in their
number the Hut Guest from Hell, whose activities dominated the hours
ahead. His climbing companion freshly choppered off the Ben, the Guest
rapidly reduced himself to a state fit for admission to the Belford on a
mixture of (other people's) drinks and it was midnight before his rantings
turned to garglings and his lights went out. The night was made complete
when my mantelshelf on to the top bunk went horribly wrong and I
plummeted shins-first on to the wooden frame of the bunk beneath.

After these excitements I slept in on Wednesday, woke, panicked, and
shot out of the hut shortly after eight for the next leg, a 33-mile flog to the
Cluanie Inn via Banavie and the Caledonian Canal towpath to Gairlochy.
I eluded a pack of baying dogs while passing through some private-looking
grounds in Achnacarry on the way to Loch Arkaig, then followed a vague
path up the Allt Dubh, passing a Geal Carn on its east, then going down to
another path by the Allt Ailein. My body ground to a halt up here, afternoon
nausea caused by a powdered drinks' overdose on top of weariness and a
general lack of inspiration. I sat down and thought about being sick. In
retrospect any true entrepreneur would have dug in and waited for the
arrival of the rescue teams and some cheque-book-waving journalists.
Meandering on, mind elsewhere, I fell off the path and tumbled into a bog;
thus refreshed I cantered down through forestry to the bridge over the
Garry at Aultnaslat.

The weather's foggy ambivalence began to clear now, hazy sunshine
peering through, and my mood improved too. After a mile on the road, a
path by the Allt a'Ghobhainn took me out of Glen Garry and over into Glen
Loyne where there was a big and still and deep river to cross. A pull up steep
grass led to the old road and I jogged down at about six o'clock to the
Cluanie, which sat in pleasant evening sun, surrounded by a patchwork of
green and white hills.

Staying in the hotel was an unaccustomed luxury, and it is easy to see
why this lifestyle appeals to Club members both past and present; we
younger ones of course would quickly become outsized and indolent if
such pleasures were afforded to us on too regular a basis. My aching body
enjoyed the comforts of a bar meal, a hot bath, and a soft bed. Sadly it was
all over by six as Friday was to be a long day, 40 miles over fairly rough
country. From the moment my feet touched the ground it was all pain; it
was clear that there was no bounce left and that a day of attrition lay ahead.

I passed by Alltbeithe then headed west to Gleann Gaorsaic and down into Glen Elchaig. It was a clear and cool spring day and I watched wisps of mist being teased off the tops of Beinn Fhada and A'Ghlas-bheinn by a strong north-easterly wind. From Carnach a good path took me over between Faochaig and Aonach Buidhe to Maol-bhuidhe bothy for a lunch of the last of the Dundee cake.

The generally mindless content of the entries in the bothy book indicated that, with the increase in the number of people enjoying the freedom to roam these days, there is a correspondingly greater number of extremely sad people in the hills; by the time I had circumnavigated Beinn Dronaig there was one more. I squatted on a tussock in the middle of a bog near Bearnais, gripped by an energy burnout, strength sapped by the wind, listlessly recalling the tale of a small group of soldiers from colonial days who were surrounded and vastly outnumbered by a ferocious and extremely agitated Enemy. Prospects were grim. A frightened private (let him be called 'Perkins') asked his commanding officer (let him be called 'Sir') 'Why us, Sir, why us?' To which he received the answer, 'Because we are here, Perkins, because we are here.' Mallory wasn't so far off the mark, really. Thus comforted I walked slowly on past Bearnais bothy, up the hillside behind it, and down the other side to splash through the Carron at Achnashellach.

My mood swung back now; it was in the bag. I almost revelled in the grind up from the station to Coire Lair, watching as the evening sun picked out every detail on the hills around me, ignoring my poor battered feet. The bealach between Sgurr Ruadh and Beinn Liath Mhor appeared at last and Torridon spread out ahead, colour fading in the calm of advancing darkness. I stumbled down the last miles to the Ling at about nine, shattered but satisfied. The quality of my celebratory meal of soup and rice left something to be desired, but it no longer mattered. The night was restless, my muscles taking their revenge with some acute cramp attacks. Next day was hot and joyous in Torridon and I made my way back to my car at the Raeburn by bus, train, hitching and bicycle, ready for the weekend's trip to Skye.

The future of the Hut Route is uncertain now, as the Huts sub-committee ponders how to extend its empire. The Hon. Secretary appears to have ignored my suggestion to make a bid for the Cluanie, so the Hut Route may shortly require an extension.

And Hamish? After some cursings he duly abandoned wife and wean a few months later (only temporarily, of course) to complete his own Hut Route, a New, Improved and undoubtedly Better Hut Route; but that's another story.

HOW MANY HILLS IN SCOTLAND?

By Peter Drummond

THE READER might care to guess at the answer now, and pencil an estimate in the margin. (No peeking at the last paragraph, please.)

Look at Iona on the 1:50000 OS map. It shows four hills – two druims, a cnoc and the highest point Dun I at 100m (332ft). The 1:25000 OS map, with space for more detail, has 10 heights named. Compare these with a map folding out from the book *Iona Past and Present* published in 1934, in which local authors A. and E. Ritchie revealed the depth of the iceberg effect. For they list not 10 but 106 hills on the island, reflecting the islanders' Gaelic culture and their tradition of linking hill-names with history or geography – 62 of them are cnocs, but there are 16 different elements of hill-names. The OS mapmakers show us only the tip of the iceberg, by comparison.

To the question of how many hills there are in Scotland altogether, some people have provided partial answers, in the form of Tables. Munro identified 283, Corbett 219 and Donald 86, totalling 588, plus 302 other tops in the first and last of these Tables, a grand total of 890 – since revised and re-revised to the current total of 876. Of course, Munro and Corbett called their hills 'mountains', with significant contours of 3000ft and 2500ft respectively, separating the mountains from mere hills. But most people who call themselves Munro-baggers or Corbetteers would define their activity as hill-walking, and speak of going on to 'the hill' for the day.

It has long been accepted that using 3000ft or 2500ft contours as cut-offs is quite irrational, since a hill a few feet less is just as grand, possibly harder of access, and subject to promotion or demotion in the Tables as the OS sophisticate their measurement techniques. In the present age of metrication the cut-off heights of 914m and 762m look particularly silly, and defenders must wrap themselves in the mantle of tradition.

Not only is the absolute height a problem, but so too is the degree of differentiation from other hills: Corbett demanded an ascent on all sides of 500ft, a clear if arbitrary rule; Donald had a complex formula in which tops needed an ascent of 100ft on all sides (although only 50ft was allowable if there was 'topographical merit' present), while separate 'hills' needed a 17-unit separation from other tops, a unit being one-twelfth of a mile distance or a 50ft contour drop. Munro had no such rules, clear or arcane, basing his distinction between mountains and tops on subjective judgment as to what made a separate mountain, thus laying the basis for much subsequent controversy about which summits should be Munros.

Similar problems are found in greater mountain areas: speaking about the Alpine 4000m peaks, McLewin says: '. . . there is no list of the 4000m peaks that is definitive. All (lists) are unsatisfactory in some way, reflecting the ill-defined nature of the basic concept . . .' (*Monte Viso's Horizon'*, p13). While Reinhold Messner, first to climb all 14 Himalayan 8000m peaks, wrote: 'I am not completely sure that there are 14 eight-thousanders, yet this is what the geographers assert . . . But this only takes free-standing mountains into account, not the innumerable subsidiary summits. But, (for example) Lhotse is the south summit of Everest, and perhaps it should never have been counted as an independent 8000er at all.' (*All the Eight-Thousanders*, p13.)

Returning to Scotland, everyone knows there are many good hills not in any of the Scottish Tables, revised or unrevised, many famous like Stac Pollaidh or Bennachie. More recently, in 1989, E.J. Yeaman published his highly informative *Handbook of the Scottish Hills* which lists circa 2500 hills (including 66 added since publication – personal communication): his definition of a hill is an eminence with an ascent of 100m on all sides or 5km distance from the nearest height. While this is subject to the same problems of arbitrariness as the other tables – what about ascents of 95m? – it does have the merit of including most of the hills missed out by the famous tables. Perhaps 'doing the Yeamans' along Munro-bagger lines hasn't caught on because of the four-figure total involved.

Now 98% of Yeaman's listed hills have names, marked on maps. To each of the 50 or so eminences without map names he has given a locating name – though probably many of these will have a local spoken name. So we can accept that virtually every hill of consequence in Scotland has a name. Past generations of Gaels, lowland Scots and Borderers did not need precise contours or measured re-ascents as cut-off points, in order to decide which eminences had significance as recognisable hills. Therefore one way we can assess the number of hills in Scotland, free of the classification problems of the Tables above, is to count up the number of hill-names. Easier said than done.

Let us start with Yeaman's listed total of 2450 hills with names (this excludes the 50 nameless on maps, and discounts the double names, such as Ben Arthur's doppelganger The Cobbler). There are certain to be more hill-names than this, because of his 100m cut-off criterion – but how many more? One could of course spend a few weeks with OS maps, counting them; the 80 or so Landranger sheets covering Scotland might seem quite a mountain to climb, but it becomes Himalayan when you accept that you will have to use the 1:25000 scale maps (there are about 600 of them!) because they contain names that 1:50000 maps don't.

Or you could spend much time with the OS Gazetteer which lists every place-name appearing on all of Britain's 1:50000 maps, alphabetically. This latter course is not too hard for the Gaelic hill-names, since the generic element (beinn, meall, carn, etc.) is often – but not always – at the start of the name, and conveniently appears in alphabetical blocks to be counted: but to pick up all the hill-names ending with a generic element, whether Gaelic or English or Scots (e.g. – Glas Bheinn, Carnethy Hill, or Traprain Law), would require a search through all the 250,000 entries. Even then you would have to go back constantly to maps to check whether a Creag or a Sron, for example, is simply a crag or nose, or is actually a hilltop (as Creag Meagaidh and Sron a'Choire Ghairbh are): in upper Deeside, for instance, just more than half of the Creags listed in Adam Watson's book are rocky hilltops, the others being crags or outcrops.

So how can we arrive at a reasonable estimate of the number of Scottish hill-names? With the emphasis on estimate, here is one possibility. Starting with Yeaman's list, I extracted and counted only those beginning with some of the commoner generic Gaelic elements (and a few English elements like Hill of . . .) so that I could make a comparison with the numbers listed in the OS Gazetteer. Some Gaelic elements, like dun, I ignored because of the ambiguity in the Gazetteer – they could be forts as well as hills. The elements I chose are listed in the table at the end of this article.

I found that there were 1494 hill-names beginning with these chosen elements in Yeaman, and 7125 beginning with the same elements in the OS Gazetteer. On the assumption that other name-elements, Gaelic or English, in Yeaman's Handbook (altogether 2450) are in the same ratio of 1:4.77, then the OS Gazetteer probably contains approximately 11,686 Scottish hill-names, from the 1:50000 maps.

We will return to this figure in a moment – while noting that the assumption of the 1:4.77 ratio includes a variation ranging from 1:2.2 for the more mountainous categories of beinns and sgurrs, through 1:4.75 for the mid-height mealls, to 1:16 for the lower cnocs and torrs. (The fact that the mean ratio virtually coincides with that for meall, which is also the median and the probable mode in height terms, strengthens the case for the 1:4.77 ratio applying.)

Adam Watson and Elizabeth Allan's book *The Place Names of Upper Deeside* (1984) is a very comprehensive guide to the 7000 names in their chosen area, names coming from OS maps, local informants, and other sources. Almost exactly 10% of these – 698 in my count – are names of hilltops. Of this 700 or so, only 180 appear on 1:50000 maps, a further 95 on 1:25000 maps, and 425 came from local informants (or old estate plans, books, etc.), not being on published maps. Now upper Deeside has not been a Gaelic-speaking area for many decades, and it is highly probable that the number of local names for hills here is less per square mile than in western areas where the Gaelic language still is, or was recently, the main tongue. The example of Iona given at the start of this article, with four 1:50000 mapped hills compared to 106 known on the ground, would support this. If we make the reasonable assumption that the ratios on upper Deeside hold good for Scotland as a whole, then we can advance our cautious calculations further.

Returning to the 11,686 figure of 1:50000 mapped hill-names, and applying the ratio of 1:1.54 from upper Deeside (of 1:50000 to 1:25000 names), we can conclude that current OS maps of all scales show in total probably 17,996 Scottish hill-names. And further, taking upper Deeside's ratio of mapped to unmapped names, which is also, intriguingly, 1:1.54, we can expect 27,715 hill-names not on current OS maps. Adding OS-mapped and unmapped names together we can estimate that Scotland has around 45,711 named hills. Let us say 45,000 for a round figure. Since Scotland is just under 79,000 square kilometres in area, this suggests just more than two mapped hill-names and three unmapped in every block of nine square kilometres, which does not seem unrealistic in a country as unsmooth as ours.

As it happens, Watson and Allan's study of upper Deeside turned up 700 hill-names in an area which is circa 1.5% of the Scottish landmass: if this area is typical, Scotland would indeed have just more than 46,000 hill-names. It may be objected that upper Deeside is not typical of Scotland's topography. True. But it contains grand sweeping mountains that may yield fewer names per square area than in lower undulating country – a glance at a map of, say, the Buchan lowlands will show this – and further, it is an area where the Gaelic tongue fell silent much earlier than in the huge areas west of the Great Glen, losing many hill-names in the process. In effect upper Deeside is probably a good average for the country, erring possibly even on the low side.

As the Iona experience demonstrates, we have probably lost thousands of names with the decline of the Gaelic language as the repository of local knowledge, both during the enforced Clearances from the glens last century, and from the ongoing decline of the culture. Further proof comes from a survey of the Back area of Lewis, still today at the heart of a Gaelic-speaking area: in a single square kilometre there, there were 27 hill-names – 20 cnocs, 6 creag(an)s and a sithean. (School of Scottish Studies – personal communication, Dr Ian Fraser.)

So 45,000 may well represent the minimum number of hills (of known name) in Scotland, from the highest mountain to the smallest rocky cnocan, but nevertheless recognisable hills to local people. And to think that Munro compleaters rest on their laurels after a mere 277! How does the figure square with the reader's guesstimate?

ELEMENT	A YEAMAN	B OS GAZETTEER	A as % of B
An	49	c.123	40%
Aonach	9	26	34%
Barr	6	c.45	13%
Beannan	1	8	12%
Beinn	361	789	45%
Ben	118	174	68%
Bin/n	2	6	33%
Bidean/ein	7	11	64%
Binnean/ein	8	18	44%
Biod	5	13	38%
Braigh	5	45	11%
Cairn	29	c.300	10%
Caisteal	2	24	8%
Carn	124	740	16%
Cnap/knap	3	42	7%
Cnoc/an	66	1035	6%
Creag (50% of OS-listed creags used)	101	c.510	19%
Cruach/an	45	279	16%
Druim	21	300	7%
Fell -	4	18	22%
Hill of -	52	c.400	12%
Knock	20	280	7%
Maol	7	125	6%
Meall	217	1030	21%
Monadh	6	38	31%
Mullach	21	66	31%
Sgiadh	3	14	21%
Sgor/r	26	52	50%
Sgurr	97	213	45%
Sidh/ean	6	83	7%
Spidean	4	5	80%
Stob	37	c.100	37%
Stuc/hd	4	15	26%
Torr/an	9	160	6%
Vord, Ward	19	38	50%
TOTAL	1494	7125	21%

NEW CLIMBS SECTION

SCOTTISH WINTER CLIMBS
Keynote Grades compiled by Simon Richardson

Grade	Snowed-up Rock	Mixed	Ice Gullies	Thin Face	Ice
	Techniques mainly include torquing and use of frozen turf. Great care must be taken not to damage the rock with peg placements, axe and crampon scratches etc.	Mainly turf, iced cracks or sections of thin ice. Normally less well protected than snowed-up rock routes.	Classic Scottish gullies - mainly ice.	Typical of many Ben Nevis routes - thin ice or neve over steep open slabs. Often very bold with limited protection	Icefalls or ice smears. Harder routes may involve thin brittle ice or free hanging sections.
IV,3	-	Tough Brown Traverse	Green Gully	Brimstone Groove	Fahrenheit 451
IV,4	Fingers Ridge	Observatory Ridge	Emerald Gully	Platform's Rib	The Screen
IV,5	Aladdin's Buttress Original	Route Major (Etchachan)	-	-	-
IV,6	The Message	-	-	-	-
V,4	-	1959 Face Route	Zero Gully	Indicator Wall	The Pumpkin
V,5	Mitre Ridge	Scorpion	Point Five Gully	Orion Direct	Poacher's Fall
V,6	Savage Slit	Sticil Face	-	-	-
V,7	Hooker's Corner	-	-	-	-
VI,5	-	Die Riesenwand	North Post Direct	Slav Route	Astral Highway
VI,6	Parallel Buttress	Tower Face of the Comb	Minus One Gully	Galactic Hitchhiker	Mega Route X
VI,7	Fallout Corner	Crypt	-	-	-
VI,8	Savage	-	-	-	-
VII,6	-	The White Elephant	The Fly Direct	Pointless	The Shroud
VII,7	Central Grooves	The Shield Direct	West Central Gully	The Ayatollah	Tubular Bells
VII,8	Citadel	Trail of Tears	-	-	-
VII,9	Ventricle	-	-	-	-

OUTER ISLES

HARRIS, SOUTH UIST: Leac Shleamhuinn (NF 775147) – see SMCJ 1993.
The routes described in SMCJ 1993 were all repeated by B. Davison. Slippery Slab
was considered overgraded and the routes over length by about 8m.
A new crag about 300m around (east) the hillside from the existing routes offers
a 30m slab of around the same steepness. There are three or four lines of about Diff.
or V. Diff. 20m right of the slabs (which are clearly seen from the road) is a short
steep wall about 40m long. It is approx. 10m high with a crack up the left nose/arete
and an overlap near the right end. The top of the slabs slope back giving rounded
and often difficult finishes.

Arete Crack – 10m VS 4b. B. Davison. 22nd May, 1994.
Climb the crack at the left end of the crag.

Flakey – 10m HVS 5a. B. Davison. 22nd May, 1994.
Climb the line of flakes right of the last route.

Flakey 2 – 10m E3 6a. B. Davison. 26th May, 1994.
The line of flakes right again which end before the top of the crag. A long reach for
small holds at the top.

Crack Route – 10m E2 5c. B. Davison. 26th May, 1994.
Right of the last route is a crack with heather in it. The crack branches at the top.
Follow the left branch.

Wall and Crack – 10m E3 6a. B. Davison. 26th May, 1994.
Climb the wall right of the crack and cross the right branch of the crack to finish
up flakes at the top.

Wall and Crack 2 – 10m E2 5c. B. Davison. 22nd May, 1994.
Climbs the wall to finish up the extreme right-hand crack line of the right branch.
A long reach in the middle.

Variations connecting the previous three routes have been done.

Crack and Roof – 10m VS 4c. B. Davison. 22nd May, 1994.
Right of the cracks and at the left end of the overlap is a vertical crack running
through the left end of the overlap.

Roof and Crack – 10m E1 5b. B. Davison. 26th May, 1994.
Right of the last route, in the middle of the overlap, is a vertical line of flakes/crack.
Climb to the overlap and through it and follow the crack. Avoid stepping left at the
top.

Ledge Route – 10m E2 5c. B. Davison. 22nd May, 1994.
Climb the wall to the right end of the overlap, then pass this and step left on to a ledge
above the overlap. From here finish directly (rounded).

Ledge and Crack – 10m HVS 5a. B. Davison. 22nd May, 1994.
Follow Ledge Route to the ledge, then move right along a diagonal crack.

The central of the three largest hills of South Uist (NF 819329), 1723ft contains the
following route.
Chimney Buttress – 50m H. Severe. B. Davison. 19th May, 1994.
The west face of the peak contains a chimney. The route climbs the pink buttress
immediately left of the chimney. Climb up cracks for about 20m until the angle
eases, then continue to the top, finishing up a steep off-width crack if desired. About
a 90-minute approach walk in dry conditions.

IONA: Several descriptions have been received. Since there are many recent routes
– and they will appear in the Skye and Hebrides Guide due out this year – they have
not been duplicated here.
RHUM, Trollaval, Harris Buttress:
Left of Central Rib, the crag's most obvious feature is a small grey buttress low
down, seamed by right-slanting cracks and bounded on its right by a big corner
which fades in its upper reaches.
Peer Gynt – 110m VS. A. Hume, A. Matthewson. 23rd July, 1994.
Start at the toe of the grey buttress.
1. 50m 4c. Climb a crack to a slot, step left, then go up to an easing at 15m. Continue
on slabs, heading slightly rightwards to a blocky ledge.
2. 25m 4a. Take the inset corner on the right for 3m until a move left gains a bigger
ledge with a huge block. Work up to a right-facing corner which leads left to a ledge
below a Y-groove – well seen from below.
3. 25m 5a. Climb the groove, smear into the right-hand branch, and continue more
or less directly up the nose above.
4. 10m. Scramble to the terrace.

The Dwarfie – 35m HVS. A. Matthewson, A. Hume. 23rd July, 1994.
Above the terrace, directly above the finish of Peer Gynt, is a small two-tiered
buttress of impeccable rock which offers this excellent small route.
1. 20m 5a. Climb the wall between a roof and a thin crack on the left, then a steep
flaky crack on the right.
2. 15m 4b. Continue up the middle of the cracked slab behind the ledge.

EIGG: The following two routes lie on the upper tier in the centre of Ocean Wall
on the south side of An Sgurr. They both start near the left end of Le Jardin where
the wall, although low, is composed of immaculate pitchstone assuming a smooth
convex character.
Sense of Porpoise – 30m E4 6b. K. Howett, G.E. Little. 21st August, 1994.
Start right of centre of the smooth convex wall (just right of a shallow pocket),
below an arching overlap. Pull over the bulge with great difficulty, then move up
to the right end of the arching overlap. Gain a good flat hold above, then make a very
thin move to gain the base of a left-trending ramp. Climb the ramp, then move up
and right on good pockets and then to the top.

Frolicking with Freddie – 25m E3 6a. G.E. Little, K. Howett. 21st August, 1994.
Start in from the left end of the smooth convex wall, below a short knobbly groove,

where the skirting roof starts to relent. Move up and pull strenuously over the bulge (Friend 0 over the lip) into a short groove. Climb this with a difficult exit, then go straight up the face above on generous holds.

SKYE

SGURR MHIC COINNICH, Coireachan Ruadha:
Exiguous Gully – 145m V. M. Fowler, A. Cave (alt). 4th March, 1995.
Fine climbing up the obvious gully immediately left of King Cobra. It must be exiguous because it says so in the Skye Guide. Start at the foot of the gully just left of King Cobra.
1. 40m. Take the left-hand corner of the gully until about 10m below a marked steepening. Transfer on to the right-hand corner and belay 5m below an obvious groove-line forming the right-hand corner of the steep section ahead.
2. 25m. Steep strenuous climbing in the groove/corner leads to a good belay at a slight easing of the angle.
3. 45m. Continue up the groove/corner line. More fine climbing eventually easing on to a broad, snowy ramp.
4. 35m. Follow the ramp up to the left and break out right to join the ridge at the first opportunity.

West Face:
This is the short, clean face at the back of Coire Lagan just below the ridge. The routes start from a narrow ledge. The face was approached from Jeffrey's Dyke. At the right side of the face are three right-slanting corners, the right one is the descent.

Routes described right to left, climbed by C. Moody, A. Petrie, 7th August, 1994.
Vanishing Beads – 50m VS 4b.*
Right of the descent is a rib. On the right side of the rib is a short, wide bulging crack. Climb the crack, then the slab to reach twin cracks; follow these to a large ledge and climb the cracked buttress above.

Raven's Rib – 30m E1 5b.*
Start at the left side of the rib. Move up right and climb the rib to the large ledge.

Mud Wrestler – 30m V. Diff.*
The corner left of the descent is climbed after climbing past the chokestone.

Huffy Messiah – 30m Severe.*
The next corner on the left. Avoid the large overhang by stepping left and climbing the corner crack.

Up the Down Stoneshoot – 30m Severe.*
Start below a jutting overhang and climb the corner crack leftwards past hollow flakes; trend left and climb flake cracks.

Starless Bay – 40m VS 4c.
Climb the bay by a series of corners. To get from the base of this route to the next is V. Diff.

Flap Cracker – 60m HVS 5a.**

Start up a dyke, then climb the obvious corner crack leftwards; step left and finish up a corner. It should be possible to extend the route by adding a pitch below the start.

SGURR SGUMAIN:

Raynaud's – 110m HVS. M. McLeod, C. Moody. 2nd July, 1994.

Start close to Frostbite.

1. 45m 4c. Climb up to the left-hand corner and follow it moving left at the top to belay on the slanting fault.

2. 40m 5a. The bay above on the right is taken by Direct Route. Gain and climb the corner left of it (directly above the belay) which is guarded by a bulge. After mounting a shelf at the top of the corner, move out left and continue to a belay.

3. 25m. Climb easily up right. Traverse off rightwards.

SRON NA CICHE:

Helen – E3 6a. S. Hill, C. Moody. 31st July, 1994.

Climbs the arete between Trojan Groove and Spartan Groove. Climb the initial bulge of Spartan Groove, then move up left to a slanting crack which starts from a horizontal crack. Climb the slanting crack, then the wall just right of the arete to finish up the arete.

BLAVEN, Lower East Face:

Serious Picnic – 240m III. A. Cave, M. Fowler, C. Jones, D. Rcerz. 5th March, 1995.

The route takes the prominent left-to-right rising ramp-line low down on the north wall of the east ridge of Blaven. It almost certainly takes the other two arms of the Crucifix formation (SMCJ 1994). The route is obvious from the point where the approach track leaves the Elgol road and is above a lower ramp.

Approach: Ascend the snow slope leading up to the Prow area to the point where an easy gully leads up left to a notch on the east ridge and an obvious pitch gives access to the lower end of the ramp line. Easy soloing leads to the foot of the pitch.

Climb up left and then back right on tufts to gain the ramp line (40m). Climb up the ramp line for several pitches over a col and on up past a short difficult step to the top (200m).

A1 Gully – 300m II. D. Bunker, K. Law, M.E. Moran, A. Nolan. 9th March, 1995.

From the tourist path at 400m altitude, as it climbs steeply leftwards towards the upper coire, a deep gully line runs up rightwards into the broad cliffs at the base of the East Face. This cleft cuts through the cliffs and from a col drops down into the Crucifix gullies on the true east face. The cleft was well filled with snow and allowed a simple passage through its deep narrows and up to the col. Above the col on the left, a short fierce wall bars access to easier mixed ground and the top of the buttress. This was climbed with a nut for aid. It seems almost certain that this is the same col as Serious Picnic, but approached from the other side. It therefore can be climbed free at a higher standard.

CLACH GLAS, South East Face:
The Big Ramp – 400m II. M.E. Moran, J. Singh. 26th January, 1995.
Follows the big snaking ramp on the right-hand side of the face. Needs a good plating of snow. Finishes 30m right of B Gully. From the top a steep, but simple, snow line was followed left across the top of B Gully and up ramps to finish at the summit cairn of Clach Glas. This avoids The Imposter, but needs a good banking of snow.

NEIST:
Warmer, Cleaner, Better – E3 6a. I. Taylor, C. Moody. 24th May, 1994.
Left of Patricia is a crack starting at a niche. Climb the crack.

Between Bays 2 and3:
Agfa – 30m HVS 5b. C. Moody, A. Petrie. 6th August, 1994.
Start left of Trilobite Groove below the left-facing corner crack. Climb the corner crack, then step left and climb the right-slanting crack to the top.

Bay 3:
Tourist Attraction – 25m HVS 5a. C. Moody, A. Petrie. 6th August, 1994.
Start just right of Solar Furnace. Climb the crack on the left side of the clean pillar which trends right to finish at the top of the pillar.

Cameras Clicking – 25m Severe. C. Moody, A. Petrie. 6th August, 1994.
The shallow chimney on the right side of the clean pillar.

KILT ROCK, Elishader Wall:
Easter Island – 30m HVS 5a. M. McLeod, C. Moody. 30th July, 1994.
Climb the corner crack left of Bandasky to the top of the statue, then climb the corner crack above.

NORTHERN HIGHLANDS

SOUTH AND WEST (VOLUME ONE)

LURG MHOR:
The Far Side – 60m M. Severe. R. Blackburn, A. Keith. 13th June, 1993.
The route lies on a clean area of slabs some 200m east of, and slightly lower than, the start of Munroist's Reward. Starting at the lowest point of the slabs, climb directly up aiming for a notch to the left of the steep upper wall at the top. Belay below this wall (45m). Climb the wall by any of a choice of unappetising lines to the top (15m).
Note: Munroist's Reward was repeated, a route of high quality, grade about right.

GLEN SHIEL, Druim Shionnach, West Face:
Bow Peep – 100m V, 6. J. Lyall, A. Nisbet. 11th January, 1995.
On the face right of the obvious central gully (Cave Gully) is a left slanting, slightly bow-shaped fault finishing up a wide chimney. The fault was climbed throughout, the first pitch being the hardest.

Cross-Bow – 110m IV, 5. S. Dring, K. Grindrod, J. Lyall, Z. Webster. 8th February, 1995.
A left-to-right slanting line crossing Bow Peep. Start at the foot of Cave Gully.
1. 50m. Climb straight up on vegetated ledges until an easy traverse right crosses Bow Peep to belay.
2. 30m. Continue right and up a chimney to a ledge below a steep corner.
3. 30m. Avoid the corner to the right and regain the fault which is followed to the top.

Boxer's Buttress – 90m III. A. Nisbet. 25th March, 1995.
The central buttress on the crag, between Cave and Capped Gullies. Climb it direct by a central turfy line. Steep but helpful. Perhaps IV, 4, since an ascent of Cave Gully by M. Welch thought it IV, 4.

Silver Slab – 100m V, 5. B. Davison, A. Nisbet. 24th January, 1995.
The relation to the summer route is unknown but it is the buttress left of Capped Gully. A serious first pitch, then a steep but well-protected second. Start up the right hand of two short chimneys at the base of the buttress. Trend slightly right to belay on flakes below a big right-facing corner (40m). Climb the corner (20m), and continue more easily to the top.

Deceptive Chimney – 70m III. S. McKenna, A. Nisbet, I. Stewart. 26th March, 1995.
A left-slanting line of weakness close on the left of Silver Slab buttress. It contains a section of narrow chimney hidden on the approach from below.

Creag Coire an t-Slugain (SMCJ, 1994):
Left Ridge – 130m II. J. Hart, A. Nisbet. 16th February, 1995.
The blunt ridge bounding the left edge of the crag. Start at the lowest rocks, which are about 15m right of the base of the crest. Climb up right to a barrier wall (which could be climbed direct in better conditions, but hard?). Traverse left to the crest (25m). Climb the crest into a shallow gully on the left. Go up this to regain the crest, followed to the top.

Tipperary – 140m III. J. Ashby, M. Dennis, R. Jarvis, A. Nisbet. 1st February, 1995.
Start about 30m right of the left bounding ridge of the buttress (Left Ridge) where a ramp leads up left towards the ridge. Climb the ramp to a depression ahead of slabby ground before the ridge (35m). Go up the depression until forced by steep ground to traverse right (crux) and slightly up to a flake on a small ridge (35m). Climb the fault on the right (40m) and continue up to finish by the crest of the ridge.

The Triangle – 120m IV, 4. P. Clayton, A. Nisbet, A. Partington. 8th February, 1995.
Climbs through a big triangular niche/snow patch at half-height and right of centre on the cliff. Take a left slanting line into the triangle, out its top (crux) and straight up to the cornice.

Speckles – 120m II. A. Nisbet. 25th March, 1995.
A right-slanting line of weakness left of Pioneer Gully, which shows up as speckled

snow patches. Start just left of The Triangle, cross it rightwards and continue up the line to the top.

Flakey Ridge – 110m III. A. Nisbet. 25th March, 1995.
The unusual arete of stacked flakes between Pioneer Gully and the Grade I at the right end of the crag (which was descended). Start up a groove in its base, then follow the crest as directly as possible. Take many slings (and not much else).

AONACH AIR CHRITH, North West Face:
Mother Knows Best – 150m II. I. Foskett, G. Moore, M.E. Moran, I. Reid. 8th February, 1995.
Climbs the narrower gully just left of My Mother Says No. Identifiable by a large finishing capstone. The gully gave a short awkward chokestone on its third pitch. The final chimney and fierce capstone were avoided by climbing the sheaf-like ribs on its right-hand side.

THE SADDLE, Forcan Ridge:
My Learned Friend – 100m III. J. Gillman, A. McGuffie, A. Nisbet, K. Wigley. 22nd February, 1995.
Climbs the shallow continuous groove in the centre of the first and lowest buttress on the south east side of the Forcan Ridge (left of a shorter wider roofed groove). A good build up of ice meant low in the grade.

The winter ascent of Easter Buttress recorded in SMCJ 1994 was probably an ascent of a buttress noted as Diff. in the Northern Highlands Guide. Cioch Buttress seems a suitable name. Easter Buttress is probably a cleaner, sharp ridge up and left. Close on the left of this sharp ridge is a more broken buttress with two toes forming a bay and providing the following route.

Biped Buttress – 120m II. A. Nisbet, G. Nisbet. 30th December, 1994.
Climb to the top of the bay and up the groove above. Below a steepening, move out on to the left leg. Up this and the main crest to the Forcan Ridge.

BEINN FHADA:
P. Grant and D. Morrison note that they climbed Instructor's Gully (SMCJ 1994, p. 451) in 1991.

FUAR THOLL, South East Cliff:
Fuar Folly Direct – 190m VI, 8. J. Lyall, A. Nisbet. 12th January, 1995.
This was the original intention of Fuar Folly, climbing direct up 'the great rock bastion' right of Fuhrer. It criss-crosses the summer route Fuar Feast to take the natural winter line. Start up Fuar Folly (which is harder than IV) for two pitches but belay on the crest just before the ledge curves round into Fuhrer (70m). Climb a left-slanting ramp (groove) to a short overhanging corner. Climb this and pull left on to a smooth rock terrace with a big block at its right end (20m). Fuar Feast crosses here and goes up a short overhanging groove on the left. Instead, pull up right on spikes to the base of a shallow right-facing corner with a perfect crack. Climb this (excellent protection) to a precarious finish on to the ledge above (10m). A long pitch straight up leads to the right-slanting break of Fuhrer (45m). Finish by this (45m).

Via Wellington – 100m HVS. A. Nisbet, G. Nisbet. 18th July, 1994.
Climbs the slabby wall right of Pipped at the Post. Start just above the step in the Cold Hole introductory gully.
1. 45m 5a. Climb the wall just right of Pipped at the Post (avoiding wet streaks) to the big spike belay.
2. 35m 5a. Move 3m right and climb a thin crack to a ledge, then another wall to a ledge.
3. 20m. Finish straight up, keeping to rock.

East Cliffs:
Solicitor's Rib – 200m III. J. Gillman, A. McGuffie, M.E. Moran, K. Wigley. 19th February, 1995.
Climbs the buttress between the central and right hand of the three parallel gullies in the right-hand section of the face just before it turns to the north and bends back into Mainreachan coire. One interesting mixed pitch up the broad, lower tier, then pleasant scrambling up the rib above.

SGORR RUADH:
Academy Ridge, True Finish – 25m IV, 5. A. Keith, D. Bearhop. 2nd January, 1994.
The present winter description of Academy Ridge is brief, but implies that the summer line is followed throughout. At II/III, however, this seems this cannot incorporate the summer crux, 'the steep upper section'. At the grade described, the original winter line seems likely to have involved a short descent into the upper section of Post Box Gully, regaining the ridge above the steep section. Climbed direct, this upper section gave a sustained pitch. Gain grooves just to the right of the arete by a 3m traverse, then follow the grooves to a loose spike. Gain the arete by awkward steps, and follow the arete more easily to the top. Repeated by C. Dale and party in March, 1995; 'an excellent pitch'.

Raeburn's Buttress, North Wall:
Tophet Gully – 200m IV, 5. S. Duncan, A. Nisbet. 20th March, 1995.
The obvious left-slanting fault towards the right side of the face and mentioned in the description of Fox's Face. Access to the fault appears to be blocked by a big overhang but a thinly-iced slab tucked in on the right was used. A second barrier wall was climbed on ice at its left side leading to an easier upper gully. The upper crest of Raeburn's Buttress led to the top (not included in length).

The Key – 170m II. A. Nisbet. 18th March, 1995.
Start about 50m up the right-bounding gully (the name North Gully is suggested for this obvious Grade I), where an easy ramp leads out left. Follow the ramp to the first crest after which it continues as a traverse line. Traverse initially, then make a difficult move on to a higher ramp leading to the main crest. Follow this easily to the top.

Highland Scottische – 150m IV, 4. A. Nisbet. 18th March, 1995.
Start about 15m above the previous route and 5m below Tango in the Night. Climb the vague scoop in the buttress diverging slightly from Tango in the Night, to finish up the easy crest, joining The Key. Steep, but helpful.

Upper Buttress:
Riotous Ridge – 140m II. D. Bradshaw, J. Colverd, A. Nisbet. 1st March, 1995.
The right-bounding ridge of the Upper Buttress, started by a depression on the left.

BEINN BHAN, Coire na Feola:
Note: On an ascent of Suspense Buttress, A. Keith and M. Shaw note that after the
initial traverse above the steep lower wall, a further traverse of about 40m was
required to climb the upper section at Grade III. Grade III, not II/III, has been
confirmed by others.

Coire nan Fhamhair:
The Magician's Boy – 150m IV, 5. R.G. Webb, N. Wilson. 4th March, 1995.
Immediately right of Der Rise and Shine, between it and another icefall just right
of the crest of the buttress, is a steep turfy groove.
1. 30m. Climb the groove to a stance below a steepening.
2. 30m. Continue to reach a steep terrace and thread belay top right.
3. 30m. Climb a corner crack 2m left of the belay to a terrace.
4. 60m. More easily to the top.

Note: M. Welch and R. Clark note an ascent of the icefall just right of the above
route. 50m, IV, 5. Two pitches of steep ice followed by an abseil off. Apparently
this was climbed by B. Jardine and partner in 1986.

Coire Toll a' Bhein:
Right of the Main Buttress (with pinnacle) is a broad gully, Grade I and used for
descent to the following route. This gully has a left branch, steep but looks Grade
I, and between these branches is a buttress which provides the following climb.
Solitary Confinement – 130m III, 4. A. Nisbet. 10th February, 1995.
Start just inside the left branch and gain a shelf leading out right to the crest. Climb
the crest or just right of it until blocked by a steep wall. Move right and up steep
blocks (crux) to the crest again. On the right is a short, icy corner leading to the
upper snow slopes.

Missing Persons – 250m II. A. Nisbet, G. Nisbet. 10th February, 1995.
The big buttress right of the Main Buttress. Start left of the crest up a short gully,
then slant up right to a horizontal section of crest overlooking Toll a' Bhein Gully.
Continue generally up the line of the crest to an easy finishing section.

Toll a' Bhein Gully – 250m I. A. Nisbet, G. Nisbet (in descent). 10th February,
1995.
The big deep gully right of Missing Persons. Has a rounded exit not prone to
cornicing. The four big Grade I gullies in the coire have now been climbed or
descended in recent years, and perhaps previously.

Criminal Trespass – 200m II. P. Clayton, A. Nisbet, A. Partington. 8th February,
1995.
The rightmost buttress in the coire (next right of Missing Persons, although there
is a more broken one farther right) has a deep hidden gully cutting into its right side.
One chokestone pitch (and cave belay below) and a smaller pitch higher up. The

start was reached by descending a Grade I gully from the col at GR 795 472 and traversing a terrace right (south).

SGURR A' CHAORACHAIN, A' Chioch:
North Gully – 160m III. B. Davison, A. Nisbet. 23rd January, 1995.
North Gully is complex but only one line avoids big overhangs. Start by the right hand of three gullies (ice), as for Voyager. Climb this, curving left to merge with the central gully. Follow this to the Cioch col.

A' Chioch Ridge, South Face:
Yodel – 200m IV, 5. M. Welch, R. Shillaker. 3rd January, 1995.
Most of this face is broken, with easy gullies leading down from cols on the ridge, most of which have been descended. At the top end, next to the descent slope from near the radio mast, is a well-defined steep straight gully. Pitches 3 and 4 involve steep ice.

Summit Buttress: P. Potter notes that his route Synergy starts approx. 20m right of Big Daddy – between the two gullies (icefalls) and not where described in the guide.

The following description is agreed by several correspondents to be the same as Excitable Boy, although with a different finish:
Triple Echo – 70m V, 5. M. Fowler, S. Sustad. 24th February, 1994.
Takes the central of three icefalls. Sometimes it seems that only two icefalls form. Triple Echo takes the main drainage line in the centre of the face and the shallow gully which continues down the slope below is the most prominent one hereabouts.
1. 40m Climb up to a very large ice umbrella at 25m. Pass this on the right and continue to take a stance on the right.
2. 35m Take the ice streak on the right wall (steep at first) to the cornice. The ice streak could be avoided by snow on the left.

Far North Buttresses:
North of the North Buttresses are two large, more broken buttresses separated by a descent depression marked on the map as a break in the cliffs at GR 788 430 (just south east of a small lochan).
The Gully in 3D – 400m II. A. Nisbet, D. Parr, D. Walsh, D. Williams. 26th February, 1995.
The left buttress has a well-defined gully and shallower left branch on its right side (next to the descent, directions looking up). Climb the gully, with one awkward pitch, past the fork to a big chokestone (which might ice in good conditions, steep) –170m. Traverse left on to the far side of the buttress between the branches, regain the crest and follow many short grooves and terraces to the top.

MEALL GORM:
Global Warming – 300m III. D. Bunker, K. Law, A. Nisbet, A. Nolan. 7th March, 1995.
Climbs the right hand of three big gullies at the bottom end of the cliff, just left of the buttress with the Spiral Terrace. The right branch was taken, the left being easy. The three chokestone section was avoided by a groove on the right.

The Vegetable Sheep – 270m III. A. Nisbet, G. Nisbet. 25th February, 1995.
The obvious gully right of the Trident Gullies and before the 'broad buttress', strangely not mentioned in the Northern Highlands Guide. A chimney pitch at half-height and subsequent boulder choke were passed on the buttress on the left. Climbed semi-frozen; IV, 4 on the day.

Gormless Grooves – 130m III. P. Bass, A. Lockley, M. Welch. January, 1995.
The buttress to the left of Gorm Gully. Keep slightly left of centre up a series of stepped tiers following the natural grooves. The first tier is the crux. A. Fyffe notes that he and party climbed Gorm Gully in 1970. (This should be noted as first ascent –Ed).

BEINN DAMH:
All the correspondents below have found the Northern Highlands Guide difficult to interpret; the grid references in the guide do not refer to the cliffs. M. Moran has used the 1:25000 map, which names Beinn Damh's second summit Spidean Toll nam Biast and the cliff below it Creagan Dubh Toll nam Biast; in which case Creag na h-Iolaire is the wrong name. P. Biggar considers the top to be named Creag na h-Iolaire, and therefore also the cliff below the top. The routes in the guide, however, are on a steeper section of cliff farther left, just before (north west of) a huge snow bowl below the col between the two highest summits. If the snow bowl is Toll nam Biast, then only this section of cliff would be referred to as Creagan Dubh Toll nam Biast. The two sections of cliff are separated by Boundary Gully (see below).

The Professor's Lum (GR 883 521) – 135m II. P.J. Biggar, R.A. Biggar. 3rd January, 1991.
To the left (east) of the path leading to the first col on Beinn Damh there is a small compact buttress split by an obvious gully (near the name Creag na h-Iolaire on the maps). The gully is steep and interesting in places and contains a passage under a jammed boulder. Seldom in condition.

Stalker's Gully (GR 888 513) – 400m III. D. Bradshaw, J. Colverd, M.E. Moran. 28th February, 1995.
The big gully bounding the buttress of Traveller's Trail on the right. Two lower steps and a big cave at mid-height were avoided by mixed climbing on the left wall. Above, a short awkward chockstone led to the narrow upper gully and finishing snowfield. In exceptional conditions all the steps might form ice and a direct ascent would be a fine climb.

Traveller's Trail – 200m III, 4 (GR 888 512). J. Ashby, R. Jarvis, M. Moran. January, 1995.
Climbs the broad buttress to the right of Stag Gully. Start at its right-hand side at the foot of Stalker's Gully and climb a left-slanting line of weakness through the steep tiers of the lower buttress, gaining the easier upper crest in five pitches. This is followed for 200m finishing by a variable line through bands of crags to emerge just a few metres north of the summit of Spidean Toll nam Biast (MM name).

Stag Gully (Left Fork) – 75m II. P.J. Biggar, R.A. Biggar. 13th February, 1994.
Stag Gully is the next main gully left. Below the main pitch of Stag Gully, make a leftward rising traverse on snow to beneath a chockstone; climb this and easy snow above.

Boundary Gully (GR 889 508) – 275m II. P. Moffat, P.J. Biggar. 3rd February, 1991.
Between the face containing Stag Gully and the steeper rockier buttress containing Aquila Gully, there is a long gully ending at a minor col to the left of the summit of Creag na Iolaire (PM name). The large ice pitch at its foot would make the standard Grade III but is seldom in condition. Avoid by turf on the right. Above there are icy steps and one good short ice pitch.

Note: Above the buttress containing The Professor's Lum, cradled between the north west ridge of Creag na Iolaire and the west ridge which runs down to the obvious col, there is a small coire containing a row of buttresses split by easy gullies and chimneys. Five of these (120m, Grade I/II) have been climbed by P. Biggar and R. Biggar between 1987 and 1994. GR 881 516.

LIATHACH, Coire na Caime:

Forking Gully – 160m IV,4. A. Fyffe, J. Hepburn. 25th March, 1995.
This is the left-slanting gully which starts from the snow bay of Jerbil.
1. 45m. Climb the left-slanting gully to the first terrace.
2. 30m. Move left and climb the deep fault on the left side of the main depression.
3. 45m. Above the gully forks. Climb the left fork on steep ice to reach easy ground and the next terrace. Move right to above the main fault. (With a good build-up it should be possible to climb the right fork which starts with a short step. This would probably make the climb Grade III.)
4. 40m. Climb the very open, turfy corner to a left-slanting fault leading to the ridge.

Red Herring – 140m IV, 4. E. Herring, A. Nisbet, R. Perriss. 19th January, 1995.
The buttress right of Gully 5. Start just right of the toe of the buttress (which is next to Gully 5). Climb a steep, turfy groove until a narrow ledge leads left to the crest (30m). Climb a groove on the left leading to a pinnacle, its top gained by a narrow chimney. Belay just above (20m). Continue near the crest past a level section (45m). A shallow chimney on the right and the crest leads to the top (45m).

Bannock Gully – 150m II. I. Dillon, A. Nisbet. 15th March, 1995.
The well-defined but easy gully right of Bannockburn. One ice pitch.

Eagle Gully – 220m III, 4. K. Grindrod, J. Lyall. 9th February, 1995.
Start 30m left of Titanium Gully at an icy depression. Climb this (50m, crux), then go straight up and climb the left-slanting gully to the top.

The Faultfinders – 250m IV, 5. S. Blagbrough, J. Lyall. 13th April, 1994.
Follows a faultline between Fat Man's Folly and Valentine Buttress. Start below the chimney of Valentine Buttress. Slant up left on mixed ground and climb a bulging ice wall to gain the fault. Follow this to the top.

Bell's Buttress:

The Doctor's Ear – 230m IV, 6. K. Duncan, A. Nisbet, I. Stewart. 29th March, 1995.
Climbs the crest at the left edge of Bell's Buttress. Start about 10m left of Bell's Buttress Left Chimney below a narrow chimney. Climb the chimney to the terrace above the steep lower tier and move slightly right to a small bay round the corner from Left Chimney's block belay (30m). Climb a vague groove above to steep ground, then traverse right and go up another groove (40m). Turfy ground leads to a steep wall (25m). Climb a chimney formed by a distinct ear of rock (10m, crux). Finish easily up the crest to the top.

Cube's Chimney – 280m IV, 5. S. Blagbrough, J. Lyall. 13th April, 1994.
The central chimney on Bell's Buttress, which fails to reach the base of the cliff, despite the attempts of an icicle to bridge the 10m gap. Start up the right hand start to Vanadium Couloir and where it joins the left start, take a traverse line right on diminishing ledges. Cross above the start to Left Chimney (or start up this) and continue right to gain the central chimney just above the icicle. Starting steeply, then easing, the ice-choked chimney gives superb climbing to the buttress top.

Bell's Buttress – 150m IV, 4. I. Dillon, A. Nisbet. 15th March, 1995.
Climbs the buttress between Cube's Chimney and Last Orders – the buttress left of the following route. This seems the most likely buttress to have been climbed by the Bells. The very steep first tier was passed by starting easily up Last Orders and moving left. The crest was followed for two pitches before the route merged with Campanology for a final chimney pitch on the right of an isolated tower. As with Campanology, the length excludes easy ground at the start and finish.

Campanology – 150m IV, 6. J. Lyall, A. Nisbet. 10th January, 1995.
Climbs the buttress between Last Orders and Bell's Gully. Start above the first steep tier, passed by the easy start to Bell's Gully. Climb a fault just right of the crest, moving on to the crest higher up

The Final Gong – 200m III. J. Lyall, A. Nisbet. 10th January, 1995.
A good easier route up the terminal buttress right of Bell's Gully. Start up an easy chimney in the lower tier, then trend slightly right to avoid slabby ground on the left. Return left to the crest between two steep tiers, climb the second, then a right-facing corner and continuing line to easy ground.

Pyramid Buttress:

Busman's Holiday – 130m V, 5. A. Nisbet, G. Nisbet. 24th February, 1995.
The icefall in the depression between Pyramid Right Icefall and Pyramid Right Edge. Steep thick ice left of the depression corner (45m), the continuation in the corner on thinner ice (35m), then a thinly-iced corner and right traverse into the finishing gully of Pyramid Right Edge, entering it lower than the latter (50m).

Spidean's Sting – 90m III, 4. M. Welch, D. Green, I. Grimshaw. 21st March, 1995.
Above the hanging coire south east of the summit of Spidean and east of the descent gully (opposite side from Way Up) is this crag with a prominent chimney in its centre. The chimney was climbed to a capstone. The traverse out right below it to a shelf and subsequent short steep wall was the crux.

BEINN DEARG, Carn na Feola:
North Ridge – 500m II. D. Broadhead. 6th April, 1994.
Hard to believe that this fine ridge has never been climbed in winter, but there seems to be no record of any ascent. Approaching from Coire Dubh Mor, skirt below the evil-dripping crag at the foot of the ridge, traversing back up a series of short icy steps to gain the crest.

Note: A. and G. Nisbet climbed the ridge in June, 1994. A scramble with some short tricky walls, the drier the better.

BEINN EIGHE, Coire Mhic Fhearchair:
Eastern Ramparts:
Happy Ever After – 100m E1. A. Nisbet, G. Nisbet. 17th July, 1994.
Climbs a prominent groove in the rib right of Fairytale Groove. Start right of Gnome Wall and below the groove.
1. 40m 5a. A crack in a pillar was chosen as a start, but there are other options.
2. 25m 5b. Traverse right along the Upper Girdle underneath the undercut rib. Climb a groove just before the Gnome Wall recess and traverse left on to the rib as soon as possible. Climb the rib into the base of the groove.
3. 35m 5b. Climb the groove using a wide crack on the left wall, then moving on to the right arete before finishing up blocky ground.

Central Buttress:
The Generation Game – E1+ 5c. A. Cave, J. Brown. 15th September, 1994.
A direct version of Central Buttress, picking good pitches. Climbed when damp; grade a little unsure. Start to the left of the grassy start to Piggot's Route. Go left to a vague/shallow groove, then trend right to a small ledge (4c). Go up an obvious pod, then straight up a vertical wall to belay just left of Piggot's lower ramp line (5c, thin). Cross Piggot's and climb easily up and right to the terrace. On the quartzite, start below a corner halfway between Piggot's and Hamilton's (which has some dangerous blocks). Climb the wall to the right of the corner and over a couple of overlaps (50m, 5b/c). Now a direct line to the final tower. This was climbed by a chimney and flake line starting as for Hamilton's but cutting back left on to the tower itself on gigantic flakes to the top (4c).

BEINN ALLIGIN, Sgurr Mhor:
Black Opal – 200m IV, 4. A. Gorman, S. Chadwick. 25th January, 1995.
On the right-hand side of this large north face is a buttress with a steep line of weakness clefting its centre.
1, 2. 80m. Approach by steepening snow slopes till beneath the main pitch.
3. 50m. Two icy steps lead to the ice runnel. Climb this and the continuing corner-groove to gain the wall below an overlap. Pull over into the upper groove, rock belay 5m up and left.
4. 30m. Steep snow to the exit gully.
5. 40m. Climb the gully and move right over final snows to reach the NW ridge.

Ruadh-Stac Mor, Creag Mhor:
Sidestep – 110m IV, 6. B. Davison, A. Nisbet. 26th January, 1995.
By the summer route. Although a tower, it appears from below as a parallel ridge to Spog aig Giomach.

DIABAIG:

Grandad's Wall – 18m VS 5a. M. Moran, J. Copping, T. Rankin, B. Riley. 10th May, 1994.
Climbs the black, compact crag directly above the village, in the birch wood 120m above the Marine Harvest warehouse. Take a start just left of centre, up left past a black streak, then step right on to a cleaner shield of steeper rock, and go direct to the top.

Copping's Crack – 28m V. Diff. M. Moran, J. Copping, T. Rankin, B. Riley. 10th May, 1994.
On the left side of the crags overlooking the stream gorge up above Grandad's Wall. Takes a pleasant crack in a clean grey crag, with a steepish start.

Dental Trauma – 30m HVS 5a. M. Moran, J. Copping, T. Rankin. 10th May, 1994.
Takes the main central break in the crag above The Mynch at the left hand side of the main crags. Climb steeply through a bulge to the base of a heather-filled groove, then break out right and climb a clean wall to the top.

The Little Big Wall:

(Once upon a Time in) The Wild West – 25m E5 6a. S. Crowe (unsec). 1994.
Takes the left arete of the unclimbed right-slanting fault. Two No. 2 Friends useful. Start in the recess. A couple of layback moves lead to a comfortable ledge on the left. Move up rightwards to gain a bulge in the arete proper. From an undercut gain layaways over the bulge. Continue with decreasing difficulty up the groove in the arete to a comfortable position. It is possible to escape up left to the ledge with start of Diabaig Pillar etc. Move up slightly left, then step rightwards to gain the continuation groove. Up this to the top.

The Main Cliff:

Big Glossy Book Route – 50m Severe. C. Moody. 27th May, 1994.
The gully right of the main section of wall. Walk to the back of the gully, back and foot up and out to the edge of the chimney, then traverse back in. Step off a large chokestone and climb the gully wall; traverse in again and follow the easy gully.

C. Moody notes that Dire Straights was climbed by J. Brown and A.C. Cain in 1986. A. Nisbet notes that while writing the Diabaig section for the Northern Highlands Guide, he soloed around the slabs above the described climbs in search of easier routes but decided the lines were not distinct enough to be worthy of description. The following route is open to opinion, but persuasion will be required to accept any more.

The Gooseberry – 60m Severe. A. Tibbs, H. Tibbs, A. Matthewson. 28th May, 1994.
The route starts at a small bealach at the top of the gully which bounds the right wall of the Main Crag. Climb slabs directly to a large ledge (30m). Climb just left of a left-slanting diagonal crack on good holds, then up slabs to the top (30m). The diagonal crack can also be climbed at 5a.

SEANA MHEALLAN:

Sandwich – 30m E3 5c. I. Taylor, C. Moody. May, 1994.
Climb the arete left of Crack of Ages, pulling left out of the niche to finish up the
final crack of Sandpiper.

The following routes were climbed by C. Moody and R. Watson on 3rd July, 1994.
Walk west from the Main Crag, keeping at the same level, past several small crags
till the sill changes direction after a large rowan. Right of the rowan is an easy shelf
which slants up left and gives a useful descent.

Nasal Abuse – 20m E2 5b.* Start right of the descent, move up right to a ledge on
the left side of the arete. Climb up from the left side of the ledge and finish up an
easy corner.

Mechanical Sheep – 20m E1 5b.** Right of the arete is a clean-cut corner with an
overhang at one-third height and another near the top.

Skate – 20m VS 4b.* Right of the corner is a short rib. Climb the rib then a crack
past the left side of an overhang. Finish up a corner.

Polythene Bag – 20m V. Diff. Farther right is another overhang with a grassy corner
just right. Climb past the left side of the overhang.

Clingfilm – 20m V. Diff.* Farther right is another grassy corner. The pillar right of
it has a crack which is climbed.

Right of Clingfilm is a wide, grassy bay just beyond which is a clean, slabby
buttress.

Moaning Minnie – 20m H. Severe 4b. S. Kennedy, C. Grindley. 16th July, 1994.
Start left of the edge of the buttress and climb past an old peg (!) to a steepening.
Traverse delicately right to the edge which is followed via a short groove on the left
to the top.

A few feet right of Moaning Minnie is the most continuous and clean section of rock
known as the Pink Walls.
Fleeced – 20m VS 4c. S. Kennedy, C. Grindley. 16th July, 1994.
Climb a prominent rib close to the left end of the wall to a crack in a steepening.
Climb the crack and continue up the rightwards-slanting corner above.

Immediately right of Fleeced is a steep wall with a rightwards-slanting groove line
and an obvious corner just right again. Beyond the corner is an obvious leftward-
slanting corner.
Unmasked – 20m VS 4c. S. Kennedy, C. Grindley. 16th July, 1994.
Climb the slabby corner, starting up a wall on the right.

Flaky – 20m Severe. S. Kennedy, C. Grindley. 16th July, 1994.
Climbs the slabby wall a few feet right of Unmasked. Start just left of a dirty corner
and climb flakes to finish up a crack on the left.

To the right of Flakey is a fine, steep wall and, right again, a very obvious overhung corner. On the wall just right of the corner is a steep crackline.
The Brotherhood – 20m E1 5b. S. Kennedy, D. Ritchie, S. Thirgood. September, 1994.
Climb the crackline to a small roof. Pull over the roof and finish up a small corner.

Right of The Brotherhood are more steep cracklines until a narrow, clean buttress is reached.
Big Cigar – 18m V. Diff. S. Thirgood, S. Kennedy, D. Ritchie. September, 1994.
Climbs the narrow buttress, starting about 20m right of The Brotherhood. About 20m right of Big Cigar is a wall with a large prominent roof in the lower section.

Mr Bean – 15m VS 5a. D. Ritchie, S. Thirgood, S. Kennedy. September, 1994.
Climb directly up a crack to the left end of the biggest roof in the centre of the buttress. Pull steeply out left and finish up slabs.

About 90m right of Mr Bean, beyond some broken slabby rocks, is a small compact buttress with a prominent crack up the middle.
Archangel – 15m VS 4c. S. Kennedy, C. Grindley. 16th July, 1994.
Climb the prominent crack with an awkward steep start.

Bedrock – 15m VS 4c. S. Kennedy, C. Grindley. 16th July, 1994.
Takes the corner left of the arete to the left of Archangel.

BEN DAMPH FOREST:
A low-lying line of sandstone crags are well seen from the Ben Damph Bar about 250m above the A896 Torridon road (grid ref 888 535). Start up the hill from the road bridge about 100m west of the Bar car park. The climbs are situated on the upper buttresses which are partially obscured by trees. A lower band of smaller crags lie directly below. The crags are reached in 20 minutes from the road.
The upper crags are split into two distinct sections by a grassy gully/corner. The left-hand section is more slabby and the right section is characterised by two prominent groove lines on either side of a prow.

Crystal Horizon – 30m Severe. S. Kennedy, C. Grindley. 6th August, 1994.
Follows a flake line running left to right up the obvious slabby scoop on the left side of the left-hand section of crag. Start about 10m right of the fence line at the lowest point of the crag. Climb a short awkward corner. Pull out right and climb the flake line to the top of the scoop. Climb up and slightly rightwards to finish just right of a small roof.

Maculate Slab – 8m 4b. S. Kennedy. 6th August, 1994.
The short immaculate slab up and left of the previous route directly above the fence. Climb directly up the middle.

The following routes lie on the right hand section.
Tombstone – 25m VS 4c. S. Kennedy, C. Grindley. 6th August, 1994.
Climbs the prominent groove running up the left side of the prow. Start by climbing the left edge of a coffin-shaped rock directly below the groove (about 5m left of the

right edge of the crag). Step right into the groove and continue to a short overhanging wall. Step out right and climb around the wall into the upper groove. Climb the groove to below the prow. Swing out left to the left edge and climb directly to the top.

Fiery Cross – 25m E1 5a. S. Kennedy, C. Grindley. 6th August, 1994.
Climbs the short groove running up the right side of the prow. Climb Tombstone to below the prow. Traverse right past some loose blocks to the groove which is climbed directly.

Procession – 25m HVS 5a. S. Kennedy, C. Grindley. 6th August, 1994.
Takes the leftward-slanting groove line on the wall right of Fiery Cross. Climb slabby rocks at the rightmost edge of the crag to the foot of the groove. Climb a crack and follow the groove out leftwards. Pull over a block at the top of the groove. Finish up the wall above just right of Fiery Cross.

LIATHACH CRAGS, Creag nan Uaimh (894 570):
This south-facing cliff is on the hill 100m past the last house in Torridon village going west. It consists of several short ridges.
Reach the Road – 15m HVS 5a. C. Moody, I. Taylor. 23rd May, 1994.
Climbs the right hand of the left-hand buttress. Climb the corner crack, move up right on a large flake (left of the chimney with the holly trees) and finish up the wall.

Caterpillar Ridge – 20m E1 5b. C. Moody, I. Taylor. 23rd May, 1994.
Farther right is a prominent arete. Climb up just right of it, pull on to the arete and climb it.

En Route – 20m Severe. C. Moody. 23rd May, 1994.
Climb the wide crack left of Holly Tree Rib and the continuation corner to the ledge; climb the ridge on the left.

Holly Tree Rib – 20m Diff. C. Moody. 23rd May, 1994.
Climb the easy ridge, at the top move right and descend the easy gully.

Kanko the Bone – 20m E2 5b. I. Taylor, C. Moody. 23rd May, 1994.
Climbs the clean, east-facing wall. Start past the tree, pull left, climb to and follow a flake crack to the top.

Creag nan Leumnach (GR899569):
The crags can be seen directly above Torridon village shop at the top of an open gully; the approach is slightly faster than Seana Mheallan. There are two long crags; the lower is very steep, the crag directly above gives easier climbs. Both face south. As the village is directly below, trundling has to be avoided.

Lower Crag:
Descend by:
1. scrambling down a right slanting gully right of the water streak.
2. By scrambling down a chimney at the right end of the crag.
3. Walking right for a distance past all the rock.

Global Warming – 25m Severe.* C. Moody. 13th February, 1994.
There is an arete at the left end. Start left of it, step right and climb it.

Blind as a Frog – 25m E1/2 5b.** C. Moody, S. Kennedy. 14th May, 1994.
The slanting corner crack just right of Global Warming; start from a flake ledge.

Squeezin' Yir Hied – 30m E4 6a.** I. Taylor, C. Moody. 23rd May, 1994.
Climbs the wall just right of Blind as a Frog. A boulder problem start gains the flake ledge. Climb the middle of the wall (gear), trend rightwards to stand on a pinnacle (small flexible friends). Move up and left and continue to the top. It is possible to go straight to the top of the pinnacle but this would avoid some good climbing.

Torridown Man – 25m E2 5c.* C. Moody, I. Taylor. 25th May, 1994.
In the centre of the wall right of the access route is a steep crack. Climb the crack to a ledge, step left and climb another crack, move left and climb a third crack. Possibly E3.

The White Streak – 20m E1 5b.* N. Smith, C. Moody. 26th March, 1994.
Halfway up the wall left of Warmer Cleaner Drier is a white streak. Climb the crack left of it. A detour to the left was taken low down; a more direct route would probably be E2 5b.

Warmer Cleaner Drier – 20m E2 5b.* C. Moody, I. Taylor. 23rd May, 1994.
Climb the steep crack at the right end of the wall, trending right then back left.
Upper Crag: The right half of the crag is split by a terrace. At the right end of the terrace is a structure, possibly a burial cairn. Descent is on the right.

Block and Beak – 25m E1 5b.* S. Kennedy, C. Moody. 14th May, 1994.
At the left side is a block; the cliff above it starts with a small overhang. Start left of the overhang, move right above it and follow the line of weakness above. From a ledge step right (crux) and continue to the top, or move left which reduces the grade to HVS 5a.

The Great Brush Robbery – 25m E4 6a.** I. Taylor, C. Moody. 25th May, 1994.
High in the grade. Climb the chimney of the next route; from the top of the block, place runners on the right. Move left to flat holds and climb straight up to a ledge. Finish up the cracked wall. there is a crucial rock 3 placement halfway up on the left hand crack.

A Million Years BC – 30m E1 5b.** C. Moody, S. Kennedy. 14th May, 1994.
Right of Block and Beak is a bigger block. Climb the chimney formed by its left side; move right and climb the obvious crack in the left facing corner, passing a large perched block.

Don't Just Sit There – 25m VS 4b. C. Moody, S. Kennedy. 14th May, 1994.
This route climbs the clean buttress above the terrace. Climb a right-slanting crack below the buttress. Move left, then step right on to the buttress and follow the line of weakness up right.

Big Tree – 25m Severe. C. Moody. 14th May, 1994.
Start below the biggest tree on the terrace; climb a right-slanting crack to the terrace. Climb the right-slanting crack up the ramp just right of the tree.

Sky a Jy – 25m VS 4c. S. Kennedy, C. Moody. 14th May, 1994.
Start just right of the previous route. Move up to gain a flake, step right and climb cracks to the terrace. Follow the edge to the top.

SLIOCH, Coire an Tuill Bhain: *Reconciliation Gully* – 130m I. J. Groves, J. Fleetwood, S. Scott. 3rd April, 1994.
The obvious gully to the left of the summit buttress of Sgurr an Tuill Bhan and to the right of the large easy-angled snow bay at the left end of the main cliffs. Well defined for 70m, then opens out to a snow fan. Large cornice avoided on the left by a narrow snow arete at the head of the adjacent buttress.

Magellan's Gully – 120m II. R. Webb, N. Wilson. December, 1993.
The gully immediately left of Far Away Buttress.

GAIRLOCH, Raven's Crag:
Though admittedly curiosities, the crag was climbable when higher areas were stormbound.
Bright Star – 50m II/III. I. Davidson. 1st January, 1995.
Climb the slabs and grooves at the extreme east end of the crag. The entire end of the crag was under snow and ice and several variations were possible.

Constabulary Slab – 65m III. I. Davidson, J. Fraser. 2nd January, 1995.
Start as for Hydro Hek, then up and right to the large flake. Climb this on the left to easier slabs, then up the corners and grooves to the top (choice of corners to finish).

An Groban:
Alleyway – 80m H. Severe. D.F. Lang. 25th June, 1994.
This route takes a line parallel to the grassy grooves mentioned in the guide. Climb slabby rock immediately to the right of the grassy grooves, overcoming several steep steps, move rightwards and climb obvious corner at half-height. Exit left to emerge below a steep wall barring entry to a large recess. (Crack should be climbable in the dry). Move right and ascend via two jammed blocks, then move left into the recess (crux). Exit the recess by the left-hand wall and crack; proceed to the top.

GRUINARD CRAGS:
The numerous crags within the areas bounded by Gruinard Bay offer some excellent and easily accessible climbing. Though most of the outcrops are short, there are longer routes on more impressive crags as well. The rock is perfect gneiss, comparable to the main slab at Diabaig. Since the crags are isolated summits, there is little drainage and dry very quickly after rain. The crags will be described individually in order of increasing distance from the car park at Gruinard Bay (MR NG 953 899).

Very Difficult Slab (954 898):
This is the pink slab well seen on the hillside from the car park. It consists of a wall

of slab with a vegetated break left of the central rib. The routes are easier than they look and are described left to right.

Two Minute Slab – 20m V. Diff. J.R. Mackenzie. 8th May, 1994.
Climb the rib left of the vegetated break to blocks and continue straight up.

Small but Perfectly Formed – 25m V. Diff.* J.R. Mackenzie. 1st May, 1994.
To the right of the break is a steep, clean rib, giving the best route on the slab. Step off a boulder and climb the rib direct avoiding a heather patch. Step left and climb a steepening to the top.

Five Minute Crack – 25m V. Diff. G. Cullen, J.R. Mackenzie. 8th May, 1994.
This is the thin crackline just right of the rib.

Flakey Wall – 15m V. Diff. G. Cullen, J.R. Mackenzie. 8th May, 1994.
A line of flakes lies right of the crack.

Gneiss Groove – 12m V. Diff.* J.R. Mackenzie, G. Cullen. 8th May, 1994.
The fine groove which cuts up the slab near the right-hand end.

Triangular Slab (954898):
This is just beyond the crest of Very Difficult Slab in a hollow. Steeper than it looks and with a central crack. The routes are described left to right.
Gneiss – 20m VS 4c.* G. Cullen, J.R. Mackenzie. 8th May, 1994.
Left of the crack is a water-washed streak. Climb the streak towards some parallel cracks and exit (crux) to the right of them.

Gneisser – 20m VS 4c.* J.R. Mackenzie, G. Cullen. 8th May, 1994.
Takes the central crack, climbing past a downward-pointing flake and exiting awkwardly at a notch.

Gneissest – 20m VS 4c.** J.R. Mackenzie, G. Cullen. 8th May, 1994.
Start right of the crack and climb up to an overlap; break through this at a notch and up to the top.

Not Bad – 30m V. Diff. J.R. Mackenzie. 1st May, 1994.
Start as for Gneissest and climb up to where it steepens. Traverse right to a break and climb this to a smooth slab finish.

Gruinard Crag (957 900):
This is the rather retiring crag that can be seen from the road. It is both bigger and better than it looks. The rock is less coarse, especially on the lower half of the upper tier, but makes up for it by having excellent holds. The crag is in three tiers, the lower being short, the second being a smooth wall with a break on the left and a thin vertical crack with a small tree on the right, and the upper crag being the highest with a prominent C-shaped recess in the centre.

Second Tier:
The routes are described left to right.
Halcyon Days – 25m HVS 5a.** R. Brown, J.R. Mackenzie. 14th May, 1994.

The recessed break on the left has a prominent flake on its right edge. Layback the flake to a large jug. Step right on to the blank-looking wall which is covered in holds and either exit up right at a break or, better but bolder, go left and finish up the steep slab.

Utopia – 20m E1 5b.*** J.R. Mackenzie, R. Brown. 14th May, 1994.
This is the thin, vertical crack near the right edge. Climb the wall right of the lower crack and step left below the upper crack. Climb the crack to the top. Well protected and low in the grade.

Simple Perfections – 25m Diff.** J.R. Mackenzie, R. Brown. 14th May, 1994.
The right border of the wall is a slab, covered in jugs and the best line follows the left edge.

Upper Tier:
Lies above the middle tier and is much steeper than it looks. The climbing is generally well protected. Some of the lines have a certain amount of heather higher up but this in no way detracts. One of the characteristics of this crag is that some of the steeper lines are easier than they look, giving exhilerating climbing.
Baywatch – 45m E1. A. Nisbet, J.R. Mackenzie, R. Brown. 28th May, 1994.
A short, sharp crux. Left of the holly tree of Paradise Regained is a slabby rib. Start as for Paradise Regained.
1. 25m 4c. Climb straight up the groove to belay on the large block.
2. 20m 5c. Climb the blank, red wall slightly left of the block and trend back right higher up to finish left of Paradise. A good route of VS can be made by joining the first pitch of this route with the last pitch of Paradise Regained.

Paradise Regained – 50m E3 5c.*** The open chimney on the left side of the crag with a holly tree at its base. Varied, but bold climbing.
1. 30m 5c. Climb the rib just left of the holly and step right into the groove above. Climb the groove and short chimney to a hard move on to the mantelshelf above. Move to the right end of the exposed shelf (0 Friend) and climb the bold crozzly wall to an easing. To the right of the blunt rib is a steep slab with a flake handrail. Climb the handrail to the top and step over a bulge, step left and finish up the rib to a pair of jammed blocks.
2. 20m 4c. Climb the wall 2m right of the blocks moving left, or better, climb the blank wall above the topmost block to the same spot (5a) and follow rough rock to the nose which is taken on the right.

The Big C – 30m HVS 5a.** R. Brown, J.R. Mackenzie. 3rd May, 1994.
This is the central line taken by the C-shaped niche. Start directly below the niche and climb a shallow corner to step left into the niche. Swing right on to the airy wall and follow the right-trending line to below a holly. Climb up to the tree and step right. Climb up to a crack above and finish by a sporting mantle to its right.

Red John of the Battles – 25m E2 5b.*** J.R. Mackenzie, R. Brown, A. Nisbet. 28th May, 1994.
Right of The Big C is a straight crack running up an overhanging wall. Climb this on excellent holds to gain a ledge and holly. Continue straight up to finish by the 'sporting mantle' of Big C.

Dave Hainsworth climbing 'Osiris' on the South Peak of the Cobbler. Photo Andy Tibbs.

Overlord – 25m E1 5b.*** R. Brown, J.R. Mackenzie, A. Nisbet. 28th May, 1994.
To the right of Red John is an overhanging corner. Climb into the corner and up it
via crozzly holds to some blocks. The daunting wall above is climbed leftwards into
a hidden crack and the climb finishes up a right slanting ramp.

Dome Crag (960893):
This south-facing crag is situated on the north-east shore of Lochan Duibh. By far
the best of the outcrops in the area, it is composed of perfect rough gneiss with the
occasional loose block; clean and devoid of vegetation. The crag is dome-shaped
and up to 65m high, with an overhanging wall running almost the full height, split
by a slight crack, with more amenable ground to the right. With a great outlook to
both hills and sea, this is a very pleasant place to climb.
Edgebiter – 60m VS 4c. R. Brown, J.R. Mackenzie. 14th May, 1994.
This climbs the left edge of the crag, with a good first, but scrappy second pitch.
Start a few metres right of the edge at a prominent crack.
1. 35m 4c. Climb the overhanging rib just left of the crack (crux) and move into the
crack above. Climb straight up to a broken corner and rib on the left edge.
2. 25m. Climb the corner, then step left on to the rib and follow this to the top.

The Silk Road – 55m E3 6a.** J.R. Mackenzie, R. Brown. 14th April, 1994.
Left of the overhanging wall is a prominent leaning corner, which is taken by this
route's second pitch. Left of a left-slanting rake is an overhanging wall of which
the left side is taken by Edgebiter. Edgebiter's crack borders a recess; start on the
right rib of this.
1. 20m 5b. Climb up the overhanging wall slightly right to a prominent hold. Pull
over the bulge and continue up the break on rough rock to a smooth corner.
2. 15m 6a. The smooth corner is as difficult as it looks; sustained (0 Friend useful).
Mantel on to the airy slab on the right.
3. 20m. Pull over the bulge on the right and climb rough rock to the top.

Grand Recess – 65m E1 5c.** J.R. Mackenzie, G. Cullen. 8th May, 1994.
This excellent route follows the first line of weakness right of the overhanging wall.
To the right of the overhanging wall is an easy-angled corner topped by a large
block.
1. 20m 5c. Start up the corner, step right and climb a crack on the right of the block
to gain a small ledge. The overhanging wall above is split by a pair of thin cracks.
Climb the wall (crux) and gain the large recess.
2. 20m 4c. Move up to the ledge behind and step right on to a shelf. Follow the line
up to the left.
3. 25m. Climb easier but pleasant rock to the top.

Abrasion Cracks – 60m VS 4c.* G. Cullen, J.R. Mackenzie. 8th May, 1994.
Takes probably the best line right of Grand Recess. Start at a pointed block near a
tree growing from the loch shore.
1. 10m. Scramble up the open chimney on the left to reach an easy shelf which is
traversed to its far left end.
2. 25m VS 4c. Climb the hanging corner, which has a projecting block on the left,
to a slab. Left of the little tree is a pair of jam cracks. Climb these and step right over
a block and slab to a rib. Climb the fine rib direct to a stance.
3. 25m. Continue up easier ground to the top.

Breidablick and Mount Thor from Summit Lake, Cumberland Mountains, Baffin Island. Photo: Greg Strange.

Scrabble – 65m H. Severe 4b. J.R. Mackenzie, R. Brown. 14th May, 1994.
On the right of the crag is a well-defined corner. Start well right of the tree by the lochside at a recess right of an overhanging wall.
1. 25m. Climb the recess and continue up a slight bulge to belay above a slab at the base of the corner.
2. 20m 4b. The corner is steeper than it looks and gives a traditional tussle with small trees and an overhanging finish.
3. 20m. Straight up to finish.

Creag Carn an Lochain Duibh (961 888):
This is the smooth triangular face high up on the hillside overlooking the Inverianie River, easily reached by walking up the track on the east side of the burn. Like the other crags, composed of a rough sound gneiss. There is a lower tier of crag that blocks direct access to the main face, but the grassy shelf below it can be reached from the left by contouring or by a scramble up the gully walls from the right.
Pink Streak – 45m HVS 5a.*** G. Cullen, J.R. Mackenzie. May, 1994.
A prominent pink streak can be seen running centrally up the full height of the face. Start from the grass shelf and climb a little wall on to the glacis. A slight rib lies centrally on the face. Climb this in a very open position to some cracks where the face steepens. Step right, then back left, following a crack that runs up the steepest part of the headwall. Good holds and protection where it matters.

LETTEREWE and FISHERFIELD, Creag Beag:
Into the Valley – E5 6b. P. Thorburn, R. Campbell, C. Forrest. 29th May, 1994.
Right of Central Groove are two cracks; the left one is E2 5b (C. Forrest, S. Turner) and the right one is E2 5b (R. Campbell, P. Thorburn). This route climbs left of the left-hand crack. A scoop leads up into a short awkward wall and groove. Move left round an edge before following a fine crack in the headwall.

Creag na Gaorach:
The following routes lie on the small buttress mentioned in the guide just below the col just to the east of the large east (third) buttress (containing Zebra Slabs). All climbed by S. Kennedy and D. Ritchie on 24th July, 1994.
Ugly Duckling – 50m V. Diff. Climbs the rib at the right side of the buttress starting at a quartz-studded overhang. Trend up and leftwards from a small grassy bay at half-height.
Note: A Diff. done in 1967 climbed rock to the right of the above route.

The Little Mermaid – 45m VS 4b. Start up a small rib 5m left of Ugly Duckling, just right of a damp groove. Climb to a roof at 10m, then traverse hard left into a short corner containing a prominent flake. Up the corner, then trend up and slightly left to a corner crack. Up corner and easy slabs above.

Red Shoes – 45m VS 4c. Start up a black wall at the left end of the lower roof running across the middle section of the crag. Climb flakes to the next roof, then traverse 2m right to the foot of an obvious scoop in the centre. Pull into the scoop, then make a short traverse right to a prominent crack. Up cracks, pull out left at the top and finish up easy slabs.

BEINN A' CHASGEIN MOR, Torr na h-Iolaire:
Arabic – 100m Severe. C. Moody, M. Shaw. 23rd July, 1994.
Approx. 100m left of Hieroglyphics is a grassy gully leading to a cave. Start right of the gully and left of the black-streaked wall. Climb up to the ledge, follow a right-slanting crack past an overhang and continue to the top.

AN TEALLACH, Toll an Lochain:
Fiona Verticale – 250m III. D. Litherland, M.E. Moran. 13th April, 1994.
The face between Sgurr Fiona and right of Lord's Gully holds three obvious ice lines, all gained from a big ramp which cuts across the face from the foot of Lord's Gully. This takes the right-hand line, following the easiest line up the ice in two pitches and continuing by mixed climbing up a chimney line to finish by a narrow cleft at the north ridge of Sgurr Fiona 50m below the summit.

BEINN DEARG MOR:
An ascent is noted of the Grade I gully right of Flake Buttress (Grade II direct in lean conditions). It has been climbed several/many times before, certainly in March, 1992 by the New Routes Editor, and is usually known as Central Gully.

NORTHERN HIGHLANDS

NORTH AND EAST (VOLUME TWO)

STRATHFARRAR, Sgurr na Muice, Coire Toll a' Mhuic, North East Face:
Sty in the Eye – 190m III. G. Cullen, I.M.F. Smith. 11th March, 1995.
Mixed climbing, requiring only hard frost. Follow the 200m couloir (Grade I) right of the rib that separates the south east from north east faces to the rock band between the icefalls of Pearls before Swine on the left and Three Little Pigs on the right. Climb steep snow up a ramp left of the left-hand icefall (or, harder, climb the icefall) to rock belays above (40m). Step right and climb snow or ice to the snow apron above and belay to the right of a dead-end snow groove which is left of Pearls before Swine's deeper entrance gully (50m). Climb up the groove and step left round the rib and traverse left to the foot of a square-cut turfy groove which lies to the right of an easier snowy one with a prominent small pinnacle (25m). Climb the turfy groove up over chimneys and other narrowings (50m, a fine pitch). Continue up a narrow chimney and exit up a shallow one above which is right of easier snow (25m).

Three Little Pigs – 200m III/IV. G. Cullen, J.R. Mackenzie. 10th February, 1995.
Climb the couloir for 200m as for Pearls Before Swine and Sty in the Eye to the rock barrier. Climb the icefall on the right of the rock barrier, crux (50m). Continue straight up the snow apron to the obvious gully/groove ahead (30m). Climb the delightful groove by jinks and turns to a small alcove on the rib on the right (50m). Step left and continue in the same line to the top (70m). If the lower icefall, which will vary in grade according to the build up, is avoided on the right, the grade is a soft III.

The Wolf – 165m IV, 5. J.R. Mackenzie, R. Brown, G. Cullen. 10th February, 1995.
To the right of the left hand couloir is a more pronounced gully running up to the crags, which gives 250m of quite exposed grade I climbing. Continue to the base

of a deep V-groove on the right side of the face. To the right of this groove is another which provided a ribbon of ice running over an overhang via an icicle. Climb into the groove to an impasse. Traverse neatly left to below the overhang and surmount the strenuous icicle (crux) which is well protected. Continue up the unprotected and steep V-groove above, over the inevitable bulge, and up to an icefall. Step left to a snow patch (45m). Climb the icefall to snow and up a groove on the left (50m). Continue straight up to belay on the summit cairn. A useful but quite steep descent to the base of the face or to reach the snow apron below the main crags at Grade I is to descend just to the right (looking down) of Pigsty Gully and to curve right where that route forms a more prominent gully.

SGURR A' MHUILLIN, Creag Ghlas, West Buttress:

Salamander – 160m HVS. J.R. Mackenzie, R. Brown, C. Powell. 12th August, 1994 and 24th September, 1994.

The best and most enjoyable route on the cliff, taking a central line and giving sustained climbing which is quick to dry. To the left of The Lizard is a sweep of smooth slabs split by a prominent dog-leg crack.
1. 40m 5a. Climb the crack which is noticably harder after the dogleg to a narrow ledge; a superb pitch well protected by Friends.
2. 25m 5a. Trend up right on hidden edges to a narrow heather ledge and creep left along this to some holds. Climb the bold slabby wall above, exiting left along a diagonal crack, block belays on the left.
3a. 40m 5b. There are two methods of climbing this pitch. Either climb thinly up to hollow flakes and climb straight up to the curved overlap. Traverse left under this and pull over on the left to shelves. Climb straight up to a narrow rake and a hollow flake right of a hidden corner. Vital $^1/_2$ Friend belay up the edge at a horizontal crack.
3b. 45m 5b. Harder but better. Step right from the belay and climb the thin crack which is difficult for the first 6m, but eases with the lessening of angle. Take a line directly to the overlap above and turn this delicately by the right edge. Easy climbing up left leads to a belay beside the hollow flake.
4. 25m 4c. On the left is a hidden corner; climb up the edge, step left on to the slab and undercut into the corner. Belay on the rock glacis below the top wall.
5. 25m 4c. Left of a big block is a superb narrow chimney which narrows to a crack. Layback the edge boldly (easier than it looks) to finish up the short steep crack. To the left and below the main crag is a subsidiary slabby wall seamed by cracks and with a square-cut recess near its right-hand end.

Centipede Crack – 20m HVS 5b. J.R. Mackenzie, R. Brown. 24th September, 1994.

On the left side of the slab is a heathery wide crack and a small pedestal. Start below a thin crack to its right. Climb thinly up to the crack (crux) and more easily up the crack. Finish delicately.

Gloaming Wall – 20m Mild VS 4b. R. Brown, J.R. Mackenzie. 24th September, 1994.

Left of the recess at the right end is a heathery crack. Start to the right and pull through the overlap. Climb a thin crack to the top.

BAC AN EICH, Coire Toll Lochain:

This scalloped coire lies above Glenn Chorainn and presents a moderately graded slope of 150m in vertical height, the potential home of countless Grade I and II variations depending on conditions. The marginally-fiercer nose that forms the south east spur from the summit (GR 232 485) gives the following line.

Angel's Delight – 100m II. J.R. Mackenzie. 27th December, 1994.
The nose has a central rocky spur, shorter than it looks. Start centrally where initially awkward slabs weave through overlaps. This promising start is not sustained and easier ground leads to a steeper turfy rib just left of a pronounced gully. Climb this rib to the top.

STRATHCONON, Glenmarksie, Top Crag:

Jumping Jack Splat – 10m E2 5c. J.R. Mackenzie, R. Brown. 3rd September, 1994.
To the right of Gritstone Corner is a gently overhanging wall split by a very thin crack. A PR below the crux protects. Start in the corner below the crack and climb to the glacis. Gain the niche and jump for the jug! (unless very tall).

Left Unprintable – 10m E2 6b. J.R. Mackenzie, J.M.G. Finlay. 3rd May, 1994.
A harder companion to Right Unprintable, taking the blank corner just left. The crux is trying to gain and sustain the finger lock just out of reach (medium RP and Rock 4 protect).

Red Ant Crack – 10m VS 4b. R. Biggar. 25th May, 1994.
At the extreme right end of Top Crag lies an obvious flake. Climb this and finish by the most obvious crack above.

Scatwell River Slabs:

Piles of Smiles – 25m MVS 4b. J.M.G. Finlay, Miss D. Henderson. 15th April, 1994.
Belay as for Boundary Ridge and climb small ledges on the arete for 3m until a short traverse left leads to the base of an obvious crack 4m left of the arete. Climb this to a good ledge and move right to finish up short slabs and ledges.

Meig Crag:

The Touchstone Maze – 25m E3 6a. J.R. Mackenzie, R. Brown. 22nd August, 1994.
Between Nicked in Time and Gabbro Slab is a smooth slab. This gives the best delicate climbing on the crag. Start centrally and climb to a hole. Step right (side runners in Gabbro Slab) and pull up to a ripple. Step left and climb thinly to the break (crux) and then more easily straight up to finish rightwards by a ramp to exit as for Blueberry Hill. This avoids the heather cornice and is also the best finish for Gabbro Slab.

Milk and Alcohol – 20m E4 6a. N. Main, S. Raw. June, 1994.
The corner capped by a roof between Limited Liability and Yellow Streak. Very bold.

Hind Quarters – 20m E4 6b. N. Main, K. Grant. June, 1994. The overhanging cracked arete to the left of Meig Corner. Bold to start. Start at a spike to the right of the arete and go left into the crack.

THE FANNAICHS, Carn na Criche:
Boundary Rib – 360m IV, 4. J.M.G. Finlay, A. Huntington. 2nd January, 1995.
Climbs the rib bounding the left side of the central scoop.
1. 40m. Approx. 30m right of the start of The Boundary, climb turf and ice groove
trending right. Step left to a large ledge and belay.
2. 50m. Continue up the groove for 5m, then move right to a wide shallow gully.
3 etc. Trend right to bypass a band of slabs and roofs. Continue to the top, keeping
slightly to the right of the broad rib.

BEINN DEARG, Gleann na Squaib:
Edgeway – 220m IV, 4. M. Franklin, C.P. Schiller, M.R. Sinclair. March, 1994.
Start left of the start of Archway at an obvious icicle fringed cave.
1. 45m. Climb up to the right and over some short steep ice steps, heading for an
obvious icicle forming down the rock band halfway up the crag.
2. 45m. Climb up to and ascend the 5m icicle and continue up to belay on the left.
3. 40m. Climb up to and into the start of the fault of Archway.
4. Move up through the Arch and climb very steep ice on the left wall to easier
ground.
5. 50m. Bear slightly left and up across a steep ice wall to gain a runnel, leading past
a large cracked block on the left, to the cornice. Diagram supplied.

Note: G. Strange notes that the route named No Surrender (SMCJ 1994) was
climbed on 29th March, 1975 by Mike Freeman, Denis King, Greg Strange and the
late Bob Smith. The ascent was never recorded partly due to our sympathies with
the Rowe/Tiso moratorium and partly because the line did not seem particularly
significant at the time. Judging by the name given by the 1994 ascentionists, they
must have experienced similar snow and weather conditions to ourselves.

ULLAPOOL, Royal Hotel Buttress:
Crack and Corner – 12m E1 5b. A. Hardy, H.M. Yates.
At the far right end of the crag. Climb the flake-crack to a prominent horizontal
break, then the corner above and right.

ARDMAIR, Big Roof Buttress:
Boreal Flipper – E3 5c. A. Wren, G. Szuca. 1992.
The wall between Grumpy Groper and First Fruits.

Note: The first ascent of Ten Seconds (SMCJ 1994) was by A. Wren, D. Gregg.
Blanka: In the first ascent list in the Northern Highlands Guide, P. Hanus should
be added to G. Szuca and G. Lawrie.

Slabby Buttress:
The following routes were not in the guide because the location of the buttress was
not known. It is situated a few hundred metres beyond and slightly down from the
descent path from Big Roof Buttress (presumably the descent path direct to the
road. The crag is therefore to the north of the main section in the gully and facing
the road.).
Czech Mate – VS 5a. B. Reid, G. Szuca. 1990.
Follow the obvious crack on the small slabby buttress.

Pawn in the Game – H. Severe. G. Szuca.
The arete left of Czech Mate.

Evening Wall Access:
The crag is found about 2km west of Ardmair on the A835 and a large layby can be found below the crag on the left. A five-minute walk up the hillside reaches it.
Layout: A 20m-high wall of sound Torridonian sandstone, well equipped with holds and protection, very steep in the central and right-hand areas and giving excellent climbing. It receives much evening sun.
Descent: Walk off to the right. Routes described from left to right.
Gee Gee Rider – 25m HVS 4c. G.G. Cullen, J.R. Mackenzie. 1st October, 1994.
To the left of Natural Sculpture is a recessed groove with a small oak. Climb the edge of the wall left of Natural Sculpture for a few metres, then step left into the crack. Negotiate the oak and climb to a groove. A cheval the rib with determination and finish straight up. Given a clean, this will be good.

Natural Sculpture – 20m HVS 5a.*** J.R. Mackenzie, R. Brown. 14th April, 1994.
The most enjoyable route on the crag, low in the grade and well protected. A clean cut left-facing corner lies near the left edge of the crag. Start at the left edge and traverse delicately up to the base of the corner. Climb the corner direct to a ledge near the top where there is a 'sculptured' runner. Gain the ledge on the left and finish up the ramp.

Sandstone Messiah – 20m E2 6b.* J.R. Mackenzie, G.G. Cullen. 1st October, 1994.
To the right of Natural Sculpture is a triangular niche. Climb a short overhanging wall below it and enter by a thin mantel (crux). Climb the back wall and a diagonal crack to exit via the short corner above.

Feint Attack – 20m HVS 5a.** G.G. Cullen, J.R. Mackenzie. 1st October, 1994.
Just to the right of Sandstone Messiah are a line of flakes. Start below the right end of the overhang and climb up to and across it. Climb up the flake edge and finish as for Sandstone Messiah. Easier than it looks.

Stone Monkey – 20m E2 5c.** J.R. Mackenzie, J.M.G. Finlay. 24th April, 1994.
This is the big corner in the middle of the crag. Start a short way left of the impending grooves and climb the overhanging walls to gain the corner. Climb the top corner on the right wall. A sustained and strenuous lower half with good, but fiddly, protection.

REIFF: Notes from T. Redfern.
Pinnacle Walls (Guide, P178):
1. A direct line up the wall from the start of Pop Out, and to the left of Puckered Wall, finishing by an obvious circular handhold. G. McEwan, T. Redfern. 25th May, 1993.
2, A shallow recess (black) between Krill and Xyles. Done before? Severe. T. Redfern. 25th May, 1993.
3. Wall between Midreiff and Descent Route. Severe. T. Redfern. 27th May, 1993.
4. Hy Brasil. A direct start from undercut base of arete. Up recessed corner and exit left on to original route. 5a. R. Cooper, T. Redfern. 25th May, 1992.

Seal Song Area:
Atlantic Crossing (p197). Should be a right-slanting crack, not left. Guttersnipe (p198) is left of Reiffer, not right.

Howk – 15m HVS 5c. B. MacLaughlan, G. Szuca. 28th May, 1994.
After the initial starting moves on Every Which Way But Loose, move on to the short, left arete. Follow the thin crack in the wall above to a strange move through the bulge at the top.

Golden Wall Area:
Necrophilia – 20m E3 5c. W. Moir, P. Allen. 21st May, 1994.
The stepped crack line 5m right (south) of Necronomican (p212).

Stone Pig Cliff:
Headstrong – 20m E3 5c. W. Moir, P. Allen. 22nd May, 1994.
The arete left of Strongbow. Start up Strongbow and head out on to the prow.

Anchors Away – 8m E4 6a. W. Moir, P. Allen, M. Atkins. 22nd May, 1994.
Start up Hard Tack to the horizontal crack. Move in right and climb boldly up the line of flakes.

The Stoned Pig – 8m E4 6b. W. Moir, P. Allen. 22nd May,1994.
The prow right of the prowl. Layback up to underclings and reach up to a horizontal break (good RPs just above). Powerful moves gain the top.

STAC POLLAIDH, West (No. 1) Buttress:
Egoterrorist – 130m IV, 5/6. S. Campbell, J. Walker, N. Wilson. 19th March, 1995.
Start below and right of the obvious square-topped pinnacle at the right side of the west face.
1. 40m. Climb up to the pinnacle, and up the corner above, to belay above chokestones.
2. 120m. Traverse left a few metres, climb a short corner crack and hand traverse right over a steep slab.
3. 25m. Climb a short chimney and the open groove above. Belay at the top of the wide terrace above.
4. 25m. On the upper tier, take a line trending right, swinging round a detached pinnacle to belay on ledges on the south face.
5. 30m. Traverse right and then climb steep walls trending right to finish by through route in a chimney (same finish as Party on the Patio).
Note: Party on the Patio, Variation. The first pitch can be improved thus: Having gained and followed the rib, instead of traversing up and left, continue up steep, clean rock on the rib to belay in the hidden chimney at the top of the second pitch in the guide (35m). Some good rock on this variation, making it out of character with the rest of the climb! The aid nut was not used on pitch 4 – combined tactics instead.

No. 3 Buttress:
Since there is confusion over this route, J.R. Mackenzie provides a description.
Summer Isles Arete – 120m V. Diff. J.R. Mackenzie, H. Murray. July, 1974.

This is the third buttress going east and just right of Pinnacle Amphitheatre. Start at a crack right of the lowest rocks and up this to a ledge. Climb a short chimney to level ground and then traverse the arete avoiding a big gendarme. Step down right at its end and climb a deep chimney with a chockstone to a niche. Go right up a groove and quit it for the steep face on the left and climb to a ledge. Climb up a crack and flakes to a small ledge and climb to the base of the 'monolith'. Avoid this on the right easily and climb a steep crack to finish on a level arete.

Slovo – 120m IV, 5. G. McKnight, R. Webb, N. Wilson. February, 1995.
Takes the turfy chimney to the left of the bottom left corner of the buttress.
1. 30m. Climb the chimney line to belay behind a large pinnacle.
2. 30m. Continue up the chimney, over chockstones, to belay on a ledge system (escape right possible at this point).
3. 15m. Climb a crack system in the steep wall above and belay on the narrow arete above.
4. 10. Pass two gendarmes on the arete on the right.
5. 35m. Continue along the arete for a few metres, drop off the left-hand side and finish up easy snow on the left flank to a notch on the main ridge of the hill.

QUINAG, Spidean Coinich, Bucket Buttress:
This small quartzite cliff lies directly below the summit of Spidean Coinich, curving round from a short east face to a longer and colder north face. Access is down a broad, rocky gully 10m east of the summit cairn and the toe of the buttress is on the left (looking down). A clamber over boulders gives access to a terrace curving round into a sheltered bay.

Although short, the crag provides some excellent sustained pitches on very helpful quartzite and has a real winter cragging feel if you do a couple of routes in the day.

Access (apart from the drive) is easier than other quartzite cliffs, with a walk of 1hr. 15min. from the car park at GR 229 266. A beautiful backdrop and friendly atmosphere make it a worthy training ground for the longer and harder routes on Beinn Eighe.

Buckets of Snow – 50m IV, 5.* J. Lyall, M. Sclater. 26th January, 1995.
Starts just right of the toe of the buttress at a deep chimney, which cuts behind the toe forming a large block.
1. 25m. Climb the chimney to a big ledge and go up the wall above to belay below large blocks.
2. 25m. Go left across the top of the blocks to gain the edge and climb this to the top.

The Frontline – 45m V, 7.*** J. Lyall, M. Sclater. 25th January, 1995.
1. 30m. Climbs the steep crack up the front of the buttress 5m right of Buckets of Snow and the continuation flake crack.
2. 15m. Move right and up a rock crevasse, then pull left on to a higher ledge and climb the headwall centrally by a niche and overhang turned on the left. Next are some large boulders forming a step at the foot of the crag. The next route starts on top of the boulders.

Kane Mutiny – 45m IV, 6.** J. Lyall (unsec). 3rd January, 1995.
Climb cracks up the wall and step right to climb a right-facing corner. Follow the continuation crack up the next wall and the short headwall at a rock cornice.

Bounty Hunter – 40m III, 5.** E. Kane, J. Lyall. 3rd January, 1995.
Next right is a small bay with a deep groove above. Climb the initial wall (crux) to gain the deep groove and follow this steeply to the top. Right of Bounty Hunter are twin hanging aretes with an off-width crack in a corner between them. The next route climbs the left side of the left arete.

Pick 'n' Mix – 45m V, 6.** J. Lyall, M. Sclater. 26th January, 1995.
Climb up under the left arete, pull over a chokestone and up a chimney. Exit the chimney and follow cracks up the left side to the top.

The Touchline – 45m V, 6.** J. Lyall, A. Nisbet. 17th February, 1995.
Climbs the off-width crack between the aretes. Aptly named!

Pick Nicker – 45m V, 6.*** S. Aisthorpe, J. Lyall. 3rd April, 1992.
Right of the twin aretes is an open fault leading into a corner. Start on the right of the open fault and move left to gain a wide crack behind a flake. This leads to the superb upper corner and the top. The terrace now narrows at a step before turning into a sheltered bay.

Peak Viewing – 45m III, 4.* S. Aisthorpe, J. Lyall. 3rd April, 1992.
Climb straight up the rib above the narrow step, and follow the crest overlooking Pick Nicker.

The sheltered bay has a short deep chimney in the right corner, with a steep wall to the left with two obvious corner lines. The next route starts left of these below a horizontal block at 7m.
Picket Line – 40m III, 4.* E. Kane, J. Lyall. 3rd January, 1995.
Climb the block-covered wall to reach a big vegetated ramp which is followed leftward to the top.

Lightfoot – 40m VI, 6.* J. Lyall, A. Nisbet. 17th February, 1995.
Climbs the lefthand corner/groove on the back wall of the bay.

Sworn to Secrecy – 40m VI, 7.*** J. Lyall, M. Sclater. 25th January, 1995.
Climbs the hanging corner to the right. Gaining the foot of the corner was bold, but more technical climbing followed. Very icy conditions; may be easier under powder.

Headline – 40m IV, 4. J. Lyall. 3rd January, 1994.
Start in the deep chimney below the first chockstone and climb the crack on the left wall. Airy climbing up the edge leads to an easier finish.

Barrel Buttress:
Y Gully Buttress is undergraded – should be III.
Several different starts, all easy, have been used to reach the big corner in the

centre of the upper buttress, the focus of attention for the following two routes (several attempts on Badazjoz). These include starting up Cave Gully, the buttress on its left, or even via Y Gully right branch – 200m, not described but included in length. Each was followed by a traverse right to the base of the corner.

Raeburn, Mackay and Ling Original Route – 270m VI, 7. S. Richardson, R. Webb. 3rd January, 1995.
This compelling line follows the exact route taken on the original ascent of the buttress in 1906.
1. 35m. Follow mixed ground for 15m to the base of the chimney-corner. Traverse a break in the right wall, and follow cracks and grooves past a large upright perched block for 15m until it is possible to make an unlikely step left on to a grass ledge in the main corner line.
2. 15m. Climb the chimney to a good platform.
3. 20m. Pull strenuously around a roof guarding the upper chimney and follow it to a short exit gully and the top.

Badazjoz – 285m V, 6. S. Steer, R.G. Webb, March, 1994.
1. 20m. Climb the corner of Raeburn's original route until stopped by a smooth-walled off-width crack.
2. 45m. Break diagonally left along the obvious steep ramp to gain an isolated pedestal, then up the hanging groove and climb this to gain a large ledge.
3. 20m. Finish by the chimney at the right end of the ledge (common with Raeburn's route).

Western Cliffs:
Lenin – 95m IV, 5. N. Stevenson, N. Wilson. January, 1995.
The route lies on the square-topped tower.
1. 35m. Climb the gully lying to the right of the subsidary buttress abutting the bottom of the face, traversing left at the top to belay below a right-slanting corner.
2. 35m. Climb the corner, initially by the right wall, and continue on the same line to climb the steep wall above and belay on a terrace.
3. 25m. Traverse easily left along the terrace to the left edge of the front face, and finish up easy ground.

SHEIGRA, First Geo, South Wall:
Acid Jazz – E1 5b. S. Younie. 13th September, 1994.
Start 3m left of Rescue Alcove, at a grey flakey handhold. Follow the thin crackline to the top, passing a ledge at mid height.

North Wall:
Just down from the descent groove is an obvious black gully, to the left of which is an angular, tower-like buttress which Haddie crosses. The following two routes are on this buttress.
Red Lead – Severe. T. Redfern. 13th September, 1994.
Start at the foot of the black gully and climb up the centre of the reddish slab on the left.

Rampart – VS 4b. T. Redfern, S. Younie. 13th September, 1994.
A direct line up the centre of the tower-like buttress, finishing at the top of Haddie.

The next route starts a few metres to the right of In the Pink.
Credit Zone – Diff. T. Redfern. 13th September, 1994.
Climb directly up the broken slab to its apex.

R & R Direct Variation – H. Severe. T. Redfern, S. Younie. 13th September, 1994.
Turn the small roof on the left and continue direct to the top. It is noted that the blocks and flakes where the original route rejoins are now shattered and loose.

Treasure Island Wall:
Guillemot Wall – 45m HVS 5a. A. Nisbet, G. Nisbet. 1st May, 1994.
Climbs the wall left of Plum McNumb. Abseil approach from the first slight crest 20m north of the burn (which is more of an occasional trickle), down to a large boulder (covered at high tide, but one then belays on the initial flakey ramp of the route). Climb the left slanting line of flakes (the right of two similar). After 10m, break out right on to the steep wall (crux) and climb it. Go up a right-slanting corner, return left and finish up slabs.

FOINAVEN AREA, Creag Dubh:
Essential Travel only – 330m. IV. S. Pearson, I. Stevens. 2nd January, 1995.
Climbs a prominent left-to-right-slanting groove 20m left of the deep gully which bounds the main cliff on the right. It enters a snow basin at hlf-height. Belays awkward. Climb turf and ice to a narrowing (40m). Continue past a ledge to belay below easy ground trending left (30m). Go up left to finish on slabs below blocks (60m). Continue into a snow basin, then trend right to a continuation gully (40m). Climb the gully (30m). Trend left for 20m, then right round a corner to reach an arete (50m). Either continue up the arete or traverse 5m right into an easy gully which can be followed to the top (80m).

Seer's Corner – 200m V, 5. C. Cartwright, N. Wilson. February, 1995.
Climbs the summer route entirely on ice.
1. 45m. Climb a steep slab, runners under shattered overlap, step right and climb a groove to a belay on a spike on the right.
2. 45m. Climb the groove above. Continue halfway up the corner.
3. 50m. Exit from the corner and continue up broken ground.
4, 5. 60m. Finish up easier ground.

Columbian Couloir – 200m V, 5. J.L. Bermudez, N. Wilson. 31st December, 1993.
To the left of Overseer is an icefall. Climb this to a snow bay, then climb a hanging ramp on the rock tower bypassed to the right by Overseer. Finish by a narrow gully line, turning an impasse on the left.

The Third Way – 200m IV, 4. M. Harvey, P. Miller, N. Wilson. 3rd January, 1994.
On the slabs to the left of Columbian Couloir is an obvious icefall. Climb broken ground to belay to the right of it. Climb it in two pitches, and continue to the top via an icy cave and a square-cut chimney.

The Shining Light – 160m V. G. Cohen, D. Rubens. 20th February, 1994.
Follow The Third Way for about a pitch, then diverge leftwards up a steep ice choked groove. Very steep bulge to start, then sustained climbing.

Second Sight – 110m IV, 4. N. Stevenson, N. Wilson. February, 1994.
Hidden to the left of the clean, rounded pillar mentioned in the crag description in Vol. 2 is a gully. Climbed in two pitches to finish up mixed ground.

Achned's Gully – 100m IV, 4. A. Forsyth, N. Wilson. January, 1994.
To the left of Second Sight is a gully slanting from bottom left to top right. This is climbed in two ptches, the second being the crux.

Lower Coire Duail:
Icefall – 250m IV. G. Cohen, D. Rubens. 18th February, 1994.
The obvious fall to the right of Windfall (with which it forms a twin). Where the fall steepens and divides at one-third height, the narrower right-hand fork was followed, giving a delicate move right at one point. A fine icefall.

Lord Reay's Seat:
The North Face – 200m IV. G. Cohen, D. Rubens. 19th February, 1994.
Approached from the north, Lord Reay's Seat presents a mixed face. There is a pinnacle about 30m below the summit. The route starts at the right-hand end of the face, climbs a left-trending ramp and aims towards a rocky bowl to gain the gap behind the pinnacle. The crux is the two mixed pitches gaining the pinnacle.

Creag na Faoilinn:
The Reluctant Accomplice – 25m E3 5c. R. Campbell. 1st May, 1994.
Climb an orange pillar straight up to a crack through the triple overhang. Nut lower-off above.

Ceannabeinne Crag (GR 442 657):
The crag is directly above a sandy beach a few km east of Durness. Numerous short routes up to HVS were soloed. The best worthwhile climb lies on the obvious east-facing wall of clean gneiss.
Rock Lust – 10m HVS 5a/b. A. Tibbs, A. Milne. 7th July, 1988.
The highest section of clean rock. Start on a large block and climb curving cracks above the left side of the block.

MID CLYTH, The Stack Area:
The Annunciation – 20m E2 5b. S. Clark, G. Milne. 26th June, 1994.
The arete right of Sprockletop, moving from the right side to the left at half-height (Friend 0).

Blood Hunt – 15m HVS 5a. S. Clark. 25th August, 1994. The prominent crack and V-groove right of Frog Stroker.

Overhanging Wall:
Psychedelic Wall – 10m HVS 5a. S. Clark, G. Milne. 31st May, 1994. Centre of buttress left of Slow Boat.

Seal Bomber – 12m E2 5c. S. Clark, G. Milne. 31st May, 1994.
Wall right of Thanksgiving, right to arete, then crack above.

LATHERONWHEEL:
S. Clark agrees with E2 5b for The Serpent (SMCJ 1994).

ORKNEY, Castle of Yesnaby Area:
Sea Hawk – 30m Severe. A. Tibbs, D. Bearhop. 21st July, 1994.
This route provides an escape back up the main cliff without resorting to climbing the abseil ropes. Start at low tide at the left edge of the buttress about 10m left of the abseil descent. At higher tide the start can be reached by a traverse in from the right. Climb up by short corners and ledges leading rightwards to belay 5m left of the abseil stakes.

SHETLAND, Grind o' The Navir:
Navir Direct – 25m E5 6b. W. Moir, N. Ritchie. 9th August, 1994.
A direct on Navir-Navir Land. Start below and right of the niche. Climb up via tiny ramps and cracks to a short jam crack through the roof. Climb this and the thin crack leftwards to join the original route at the large bowl hold. Continue up the crack to the top. Superb protection, brilliant route.

The Peat Stack – 15m E3 5c. W. Moir, N. Ritchie. 9th August, 1994.
The vague crack up the pillar from the starting ledge of Sylvi.

Shetland Times – 20m Hvs 5a. N. Ritchie, W. Moir. 14th August, 1994.
From the belay ledges of The Udge move left and climb the left edge of the wall to gain and climb the obvious chimney cracks.

Tushkar – 20m E4 6b. W. Moir. 14th August, 1994.
Climb the fine corner which Satori starts up, all the way.

Crabbie, Crabbie Is Do In – 20m E3 5b. W. Moir, N. Ritchie. 14th August, 1994.
The bold arete right of Tushkar.

Nibon:
Shetland Silvercraft – 15m E2 5c. W. Moir, N. Ritchie. 12th August, 1994. The prominent line of grooves on the south face of the Grey Pillar, Starting at a wide crack.

The Dancin' Water – 15m E3 5c. W. Moir, N. Ritchie. 12th August, 1994.
The intermittent jam-crack just left of Silvercraft to gain a ledge on the left. Step back right to climb the edge of the pillar to the top (long slings desirable to extend runners at the top).

I See Foula – 20m E3 6a. W. Moir, N. Ritchie. 11th August, 1994.
A line up the frontal face of the pillar between Black Magic and Bootie. Climb twin cracks direct to the grey niche, exit the left side of this and climb cracks and flakes to finish up a deep crack in the slab above.

The Tango o' The Isles – 22m E4 6a. W. Moir, N. Ritchie. 11th August, 1994.
A line up the wall right of Bootie. Start up a distinct corner to gain a ledge. Continue up the vague crackline directly above to a horizontal break. Hand traverse left to climb a corner, then hand traverse right to gain the final corner.

The next two routes are on the big south east-facing wall opposite Puissance.
Yogi Braer – 30m VS 4c. N. Ritchie, W. Moir. 11th August, 1994.
Abseil down the landward side of the big slabby face to a good black ledge below a corner, 15m above the sea. Move left to gain a groove. Climb this and the continuation crack to gain the fine twin cracks up the slab, continuing directly to the top.

Boo Boo – 35m HVS 5a. N. Ritchie, W. Moir. 12th August, 1994.
Abseil down the seaward side of the face to a black ledge 8m above the sea. Climb a corner, then the continuation twin cracks over a bulge (crux). Continue up the crack system to the top.

Notes. Nibon: Slice of Life is not in the geo with the 'protruding buttress'. It is 200m south of the geo containing Cattle Rustler. The Cattle Rustler Geo would be better described as directly seaward from the obvious cairn. Route lengths here need sorting e.g. Cattle Rustler is longer than Hermless although it is given 40m as opposed to 60m in the guide.
Warie Gill: Vampire and Silly Arete are not on the same cliff as the other routes hereabouts but are on the other side of a small inlet (just north), facing south.

CAIRNGORMS

Since a new edition of the Cairngorms Guide is due out soon after this Journal, new routes have not been repeated here. The style is similar to the previous guide, in that not all routes have been fully described. It is, however, slightly expanded, particularly for crags which are currently popular. Most recent routes are therefore described, but for those which have been summarised, full descriptions, if useful, will be in next year's Journal.

NORTH EAST OUTCROPS

COVESEA:
Hacuna Matatta – 30m E3 5c. J.A. Hall, J.T. 3rd May, 1994.
From the coastguard lookout (as for Honeycomb Wall) walk west for approx. 300m until just before the second dry stream bed. Four old abseil stakes can be seen beyond the gorse on the north side of the path. The route ascends the obvious overhanging groove (invisible from above) in the seaward nose. Abseil down the east side of the nose of rock, small sloping grass ledge to ease take-off. Care with sharp edges. Clip *in situ* thread (after 10m) and a poor peg (after 20m) to allow the belay to be reached. Hanging belay just above the very soft lower tier of sandstone. Climb the first groove using the left wall and groove to the break. Poor peg only necessary on the abseil. Continue up to and past the thread (crux) into the top groove. Ascend the final groove and arete in a spectacular position. Well protected throughout.

BEN RINNES, Scurran of Well:

The hill forms a prominent landmark near Dufftown and the routes are located on the prominent granite tor located 1500m north west of Ben Rinnes summit.

The Curse of the Neep – 50m HVS 5a. I. Davidson, P. Heneghan, A. Ross, M. Sutherland. August, 1990.

Start at the toe of the buttress and follow a steep groove and flakes to a stance. Left over an overlap and up the long, easy slab to finish. Treat the flakes like your best bottle of malt.

Unnamed – 20m VS 4c. M. Sutherland, A. Ross. August, 1990.

Climb the open corner near the top of the gully wall, finishing to the right.

GLEN CLOVA, The Doonie:

Guinness – A. Fyffe notes that a tree is missing near the top of pitch 1. It is now much harder, unless this section is turned on the left.

HIGHLAND OUTCROPS

BINNEAN SHUAS:

Turning a Blind Eye – 50m E5 6b. R. Campbell, P. Thorburn. 11th June, 1994.

Climbs the arete right of Fortress Direct in one long pitch. Protection very hard to arrange for an on-sight ascent, so might be harder. Start at the toe of the buttress and meander up with no great difficulty to an overhang at the start of the vertical climbing. Climb first up and left to a jammed RP1; then up and back right to a flake on the right-hand wall. Finish straight up.

Native Stones – 115m VS. N. Kempe, D.F. Lang. 9th May, 1993.

About 50m right of Tip Top there is a prominent chimney. Start about 10m right of this, to the right of vegetated ledges and before the final arete of the crag, at the bottom of a leftward slanting corner.

1. 25m 5a. Follow the corner, pass over a projecting block and enter a groove for a couple of moves, then move on to the right wall and up to a ledge on the right with a prominent block.

2. 25m 4b. From the block, step right on to the face of the buttress, then up rightwards and back leftwards to a large belay ledge on the edge of the buttress.

3. 25m 4b. Follow the mossy crack above, then up, keeping a prominent corner-crack system to the left. Join this where it steepens to a vertical corner and follow up and left to belay. Easier ground then leads to the top.

Far Eastern Chimney – 115m HVS. N. Kempe, D.F. Lang. 22nd May, 1994. This is the prominent chimney about 50m right of Tip Top.

1. 35m 4b/c. Climb the mossy chimney.

2. 25m 5a/b. Gain a platform below the steep corner and crack above and climb these direct, exiting right at the top to belay by large blocks.

3. 30m 4c. Climb the chimney above directly (very airy) to a belay well back. Finish up easy rocks as for Native Stones.

CREAG DUBH:
A Lethal Affair – 150m IV, 5. S. Allan, M. Atkins. 3rd January, 1995.
Climbs the right-slanting fault which divides Great Wall and Lower Central Wall.
A variable amount of ice forms slowly and the initial icefall has been climbed
before. Start about 1m left of Rib Direct.
1. 10m. Climb ice for 6m, then left and up to a tree belay.
2. 35m. Climb the right slanting groove (ice) to a tree belay.
3. 45m. Climb directly left of the tree belay to reach round and into a corner, which
is followed.
4. 40m. Continue up the corner.
5. 40m. Icicles at the top of the corner were not complete so a finish was made on
the left.

STRATHYRE CRAG (OS Sheet 57, 555183):
Travelling northwards on the main road through Strathyre there is a garage on the
left, then a small newsagent's shop. Immediately beyond the shop turn left, go over
the narrow humpbacked bridge and follow the single track road up right to go
northwards through the woods for about 3km. There is a house on the right
(Bailefuill) and a straight. Just beyond the pines there is a small clearing on the left
where the small lower crag becomes visible. The main crag sits immediately above
this. Continue along the road for a few hundred metres, around a bend to where a
forestry track goes off up left.
  Park immediately opposite this on the right where there is space for two or three
cars. Walk back to the clearing, through the pines and find a small footpath leading
up to the left side of the crag.
  The hotel opposite the single track road is good for cheap tea and toast. 50m up
the road from this hotel there is an excellent little tea room with a fine selection of
tasty cakes.
  The routes are described from left to right.
Shock Horror – 7b+. R. Anderson. 1st May, 1994.
Wall left of arete.

Electrodynamic – 7a. R. Anderson. 24th October, 1993.
Prominent left arete.

Bridging the Gap – 6c+/7a. R. Anderson. May, 1994.
Prominent groove to lower-off of previous route.

Short Circuit – 6b. R. Anderson. 6th November, 1993.
Slim groove beside main groove (common start).

Clam Chowder – 6c+/7a. G. Ridge. 1st May, 1994.
Wall to right through ledge.

Unnamed – 7b+. P. Thorburn. 30th April, 1994.
Wall to finish up Static Discharge.

Static Discharge – 7b. R. Anderson. October, 1993.
Central line through diagonal crack.

Project –Line through crack (D. McCallum).

Project – Line straight up from base of crack (P. Thorburn).

Cracking the Lines – 7a+/7b. R. Anderson. 21st May, 1994.
The crack from its base.

Unnamed – 7a+/7b. R. Anderson. 21st May, 1994.
Short steep leaning wall and less steep wall.

Power Surge – 6c+. R. Anderson. October, 1993.
Leaning wall and scoop on right.

Spark Thug – 6b. R. Anderson. May, 1994.
Short corner and wall to lower-of of Power Surge.

GLEN NEVIS, Black's Buttress:
M. Garthwaite notes an ascent of Centrepiece without the peg. E6 6b.

TULLIEMET CRAG (NO 013 496):
The Sleeping Sickness – 20m E5 6a. P. Thorburn, R. Campbell. October, 1993.
The leaning wall above a slab in the middle of the crag. Gain a standing position
on the flake by swinging in from the left; crank up to the top.

GLEN LEDNOCK, Eagle Crag:
Cranium Wall Direct – 10m E2 5c. G. Lennox, C. Adam. July, 1994.
This route takes a line straight up the middle of the overhanging face left of the route
Cranium Wall. Follow the large edge to a PR and finish slightly rightwards.

CENTRAL HIGHLANDS

**MEALL NAN TARMACHAN, East Face of Meall Garbh (named Carn
Chreag on OS map):**
Lozenge Buttress – 120m III. M. Shaw, A. Keith. 23rd January, 1994.
This buttress is the central and highest part of the Carn Chreag, and lies about due
east of Meall Garbh (approx. GR 581384) and to the left (west) of the Meall Garbh-
Meall nan Tarmachan col. Its lozenge shape is readily identified by the two gullies
that start nearly at the same point and curve upwards to embrace the rock face.
    Start underneath the overhanging rock at the lowest point of the buttress. Skirt
the overhang on the left, traverse back right to above the belay and continue directly
to the top. Warthogs in frozen turf used for runners and belays.
    The buttress was first noted and named by W. Inglis Clark and J.W. Inglis in
December, 1898. They declined to climb it, instead tackling the right-hand-
bounding gully (article and photo in SMCJ Vol.5, Jan 1899, p153). A more recent
sketch of the Carn Chreag is in SMCJ 1988 in which the buttress is clearly shown.
Inglis Clark's gully is dismissed as I/II although the first ascentionists seem to have
had it tougher in early-season conditions.

BEN LAWERS, Coire nan Cat:
This wide coire holding Lochan nan Cat and a variety of crags and gullies belongs jointly to Ben Lawers, An Stuc and Meall Garbh. 1:50000 Sheet 51. The two main crags are the slabby Creag an Fhithich (GR 640 421), at the termination of a short spur jutting east from the north ridge of Ben Lawers, and the large but more broken Creag nan Cat (GR 640 427) on the south west flank of An Stuc. Both these crags lie at an altitude of over 800m and are turfy in nature. However, their easterly aspect tend to give best climbing conditions in early to mid winter.

Creag an Fhithich:
Felinity – 125m II/III. G.E. Little. 14th November, 1993.
Start well right of the centre of the crag where a low snow ledge runs out to the right. Follow the ledge for about 15m to below a shallow groove. Climb the turfy groove to reach an obvious small pinnacle on the right. Traverse right, then follow a ramp to reach an easy angled tapering snowfield. Ascend this to a pointed block, then climb a short section of mixed ground to the top of the crag.

Cool for Cats – 125m VI, 5. G.E. Little, C. Schaschke (alt). 27th November, 1993.
The general line of this route can be identified by an obvious thin chimney, just below mid height, near the centre of the crag. To the right of the lowest point of the crag are two well-defined corners with a big block roof between them at 15m. Start farther right at a vague open groove (collinear with the aforementioned chimney).
1. 45m. Climb the vague open groove which proves a lot harder than it looks (poor protection) to gain a better defined turfy groove. Follow this to belay about 5m below the thin chimney.
2. 25m. Move right and climb an icy slab to under the right end of an overhang where protection can be arranged. Step right around the edge to the base of a turf-filled crack (running roughly parallel to the thin chimney). Climb this to a tiny ledge below a band of small overhangs.
3. 25m. Step left and up to good protection under a roof (this provides an alternative belay for pitch 2). Move left into a turfy groove and follow it to a ledge on the left.
4. 30m. Easy-angled snow leads to the top of the crag.

Cataract – 85m IV, 4. C. Bonington, G.E. Little (alt). 19th March, 1994.
The obvious wide icefall, left of centre, just below a low band of roofs running out left.
1. 40m. Climb a short ice step, then up to below the main icefall. Ascend this to take a good, but exposed, rock belay on the left before the top of the steepest section.
2. 45m. Step right, then climb steep ice to a rock overlap. Move right into a groove. Ascend this, then up an easier-angled snow scoop to belay at a big block on the left.

BEN NEVIS, AONACHS, CREAG MEAGHAIDH

BEN NEVIS, North East Buttress:
C. Stead notes that the start of Newbigging's 80-minute Route is some 200m downhill from the ledge leading out to the First Platform of North East Buttress, not 45m (p64 of the new guide). On p67, route 8 on the diagram should be 8a, Newbigging's Far Right Variation.

Orion Face:
Orion Directissima – 375m VI, 5. S. Richardson, R. Webb (AL). 16th April, 1994.
A sustained climb to the right of Orion Direct, starting up Beta Route, and finishing up the prominent curving corner in the Orion headwall. Although many of the pitches have been climbed before, the complete route is a logical line and the most direct route up the face.
1, 2. 90m. Climb Beta Route to a stance just right of the Basin.
3. 50m. Step right, and follow wide icy grooves on the right side of a rocky rib to belay below the Second Slab Rib.
4, 5. 90m. Turn the Second Slab Rib on the right, then trend back right by icy grooves to a snowfield (as for Orion Direct).
6. 50m. Climb the snowfield and step right to belay below the steep bow-shaped corner on the right side of the headwall.
7. 45m. Climb the corner to its top. An excellent pitch.
8. 50m. Finish easily up snow to the top.

Indicator Wall:
Shot in the Foot – 50 V, 4. J.L. Bermudez, N. Wilson. 4th April, 1995.
A icefall starting on the left wall of Gardyloo Gully below the chockstone.

Gardyloo Buttress:
Murphy's Route – 130m VI, 6. R.G. Webb, A. Shand. March, 1983.
Between Kellet's Route and Smith's Route is a short, icy groove.
1. 50m. Climb the groove to its end, then up steep mixed ground to a shallow cave beneath the icicle fringe hanging down from Smith's Route Left Hand. Pull out through the overhang above to a precarious belay on Smith's Route.
2. 30m. Continue steeply trending left to the foot of Augean Alley.
3. 50m. Finish up Augean Alley.

Douglas Boulder:
Note: D.F. Lang and C. Stead repeated the North West Face of the Douglas Boulder, unaware of its earlier ascent, and considered the grade of IV, 5 to be a substantial undergrading. Certainly V. Two French parties also climbed the route and commented their agreement in the hut book.

West Face:
Jacknife – 90m Severe. D.M. Jenkins, C. Stead. 23rd July, 1994.
This climbs the V-groove with twin parallel cracks 30m right of the Cutlass corner.
1. 50m Climb slabs to the base of the groove.
2. 25m Climb the groove, finishing by the right-hand crack to a grass ledge.
3. 15m Climb a crack with a loose flake and move right to the South West Arete.

Walking Through Fire – 130m VS. D.M. Jenkins, C. Stead. 23rd July, 1994.
Climbs the groove system just right of Cutlass.
1. 40m 4b Climb slabs to the ledge below the Cutlass corner.
2. 25m 4b Traverse left along the ledge to its end. Climb the groove above, avoiding a loose block on the right and move left into a parallel groove which is climbed to a stance below an inverted V-overhang.
3. 25m 4b Step down right and climb the overhanging wall to easier ground and a belay some way up a long V-groove.

4. 40m 4b Continue up the groove, avoiding the final chimney on the left arete. Move right past dangerously -loose blocks to the SW Arete.

Note: It would be safer for the leader to belay at the top of the groove to avoid the risk of stonefall to the second, as happened on the first ascent.

Secondary Tower Ridge:

The Gutter – 110m IV, 4. R. Webb, S. Richardson (AL). 8th April, 1995.

The summer line regularly forms a prominent icefall on the right side of Glover's Chimney. Low in the grade. Start by climbing Glover's Chimney for 80m and belay at the foot of the icefall.

1, 2. 60m. Bear right to where the icefall steepens and climb it to its top (easiest on the left).

3. 50m. Continue up snow slopes to finish below the final steepening on Tower Ridge.

D.M. Jenkins and C. Rowland note that they made a winter ascent probably of this line in the early 1970s.

Number Two Gully Buttress:

The Blue Horizon – 100m IV, 4. S. Richardson, R. Webb (AL). 8th April, 1995.

A worthwhile ice climb taking the easiest line in the centre of the steep headwall above the traverse of Raeburn's Easy Route. Start 25m right of Le Panthere Rose below a short steep icefall.

1. 50m. Climb the icefall and continue up the gully on the right to an easing in angle.

2. 50m. Follow ice runnels up and right to the cornice. This was outflanked by a 70m traverse left to finish just right of Tower Ridge.

Creag Coire na Ciste:

Place Your Bets – 100m V, 6+. J. Blyth, J. Briel; G. Perroux, D. Colin. 12th April, 1994.

The obvious 40m overhanging icefall to the right of Wendigo. Seldom forms.

South Trident Buttress:

Rien Ne Va Plus – 50m V, 5. G. Perroux, J. Blyth. 10th April, 1994.

Prominent icefall on the right as you head up Number Four Gully. Seldom forms. Short vertical walls.

Jubilee Buttress:

Mega Reve – 60m V,5. G. Perroux et al. 4th April, 1994.

Climb a narrow chimney to the left of Jubilee Climb, then snow and a short steep icefall, belay on left. Move up and left leading to the base of the central of three vertical icefalls. Climb this.

North Trident Buttress:

Note: In the description of Fifties Revival (SMCJ 1994, p488), pitch 2 should read: 'Climb the wall 2m left of a bulging crack.'

Carn Dearg Buttress:

The Bewildabeast – 130m VI, 6. M. Garthwaite, A. Wainwright. 21st March, 1995.

A superb route up ice and grooves to the right of Gemini featuring the most 'out there' ice on the Ben on the top pitch. Better and harder than Gemini. Start halfway up Waterfall Gully at the base of a corner just above and to the right of the large detached flake of Gemini.

1. 30m. Climb the ice smear that forms down the left wall of the corner until it runs out at a steep wall. Traverse a thin ledge rightwards to a small ledge in the corner, then climb a short chimney to a larger ledge and belay.

2. 35m. Climb the thin corner, over a small roof, then move right into the base of another corner. Climb this moving over another roof and belay at a small ledge on the right.

3. 20m. Climb the very thin groove in the arete above (to the right of the main corner), then move right slightly to another short corner. Belay on the terrace below the final wall.

4. 45m. Climb the thin tongue of ice above and then move left on to the main icefall and direct to the top.

STOB BAN, Central Buttress:

Rampant – 250m IV, 4. D. Hanna, S. Kennedy. January, 1995.
Takes a line between Bodice Ripper and Skyline Rib on the large triangular face. Climb to the prominent left-slanting ramp and follow this until it fades (Bodice Ripper leaves the ramp at this point). Move up on to another ramp above and follow this to within 20m of the buttress edge. Another narrow ramp leads up steeply rightwards below the crest of the buttress. A steep step leads on to the narrow ramp which is followed for two pitches. A steep leftwards traverse across a small buttress leads to the buttress edge to finish just below the top of the Triad gully. Finish up the ramp of Triad.

South Buttress:

North Ridge Route – 150m IV, 4. S. Kennedy, A. Nelson. 29th January, 1995.
At the lower end of the steep central wall near the foot of South Gully are two corner lines. Climb the left-hand corner for 35m, then move out right to belay just short of the ridge (50m). Continue to the ridge which leads easily to a finish very close to the summit.

AONACH MOR, Coire an Lochain:

President's Buttress – 120m III. S. Richardson, J. Ashbridge (AL). 4th December, 1994.
The slabby buttress left of Hidden Gully. Start roughly in the centre and follow the well-defined depression and groove system to reach easier ground and the top.

Sprint Gully – 120m III. S. Richardson, C. Cartwright (AL). 8th January, 1995.
The wide gully/depression to the left of President's Buttress leads to the plateau in three pitches, with the second one providing a steep crux.

Ribbon on Edge – 120m IV, 6. S. Richardson, C. Cartwright (AL). 8th January, 1995.
The elegant arete to the right of Hidden Gully.
1. 30m. From the foot of Hidden Gully, a break leads right on to a platform on the front face of the buttress. Climb the groove on the right (crux), and continue to a good ledge.

2. 45m. Climb straight up the turfy wall above the belay to gain the crest of the arete. Follow this, turning two towers on the right.
3. 45m. Climb easily up the final arete to reach the summit snow slope.

Maneater – 90m V, 5. S. Richardson, R. Webb (AL). 14th January, 1995.
The prominent wide gully between the buttresses taken by White Shark and Gondola with the Wind. A good direct line.
1. 50m. Climb the gully to where it steepens at an overhung cave. Thin ice on the left wall (crux) leads to a groove and belay.
2. 40m. Climb steep ice directly above the belay to reach the top groove (previously climbed by Tinsel Town) and the plateau.

An Cul Choire:
South Spur – 150m IV, 4. S. Kennedy, S. Thirgood. 21st December, 1994.
The left (south) side of the prominent buttress containing Aonach Seang comprises three distinct buttresses. This route climbs the largest left hand buttress finishing close to the neck just below the plateau.
   Start at the lowest point of the buttress and climb easy ground up leftwards to a narrow ramp which leads to a belay on the buttress edge. Climb up and leftwards into a vague depresion left of the buttress edge. Continue in two pitches over short steps and a steep corner on the left to the easier upper slopes. Finish along the ridge leading to the neck.

Bishop's Rise – 80m IV, 5. P. Moores, A. Nelson. 8th February, 1995.
A small prominent buttress juts out from the back wall of the coire close to the Aonach Mor/Beag col. A two-tiered icefall forms down the buttress with a wide terrace splitting the two pitches.

AONACH BEAG, North Face:
The following two routes may coincide somewhat?
Dragonfly – 200m III. M. Duff. January, 1994.
Start 40m right of Mayfly where a wide gully leads to an iceflow (similar to the start of Mayfly). Climb this and then break left up a small, steep ice pitch. Move up the broken ridge overlooking the upper section of Mayfly and mixed upper face.

Queen's View – 250m III. P. Moores, A. Nelson. 8th February, 1995.
In the centre of the north face, on the area between Mayfly and King's Ransom, is a snow basin. Gain this via a runnel. Exit the basin by a narrow gully which leads directly to the highest point of the face.

BINNEIN SHUAS:
Squeezy – 85m IV, 4. P. Amphlett, M. Sinclair. 25th January, 1995.
Climbs the bottom fault of the summer route Second Prize (below the Terrace). Involves an interesting thrutch under a chockstone.

Fairy Liquid – 85m III. M. Sinclair. February, 1994.
Climbs the bottom fault of Eastern Chimney (below the Terrace).

CREAG MEAGHAIDH, Raeburns Gully Buttress:
Do What Thou Wilt – 200m IV, 4. A. Powell, S. Grayson. 12th March, 1994.
Start on the left side of the buttress behind a small tower. Climb the bay and take the obvious unlikely-looking ramp running across and through the roofs (excellent pitch). Head right, then climb a short wall to easier ground. The groove in the (avoidable) buttress 80m higher up also goes well at V, 6. Traversing right now leads straight to the foot of Smith's Gully.

MONADHLIATH, Carn Dearg, Loch Dubh Crag:
Tunnel Vision - 110m III. B. Findlay, D. Riley, R. Ross, G. Strange. 3rd January, 1995.
Climbs the left edge of Wee Team Gully.
1. 50m. Start immediately left of the gully and climb short walls and vegetation to an obvious rock pillar on the skyline.
2. 40m. Continue up the corner on the left to blocks below the plateau.
3. 20m. Climb either the steep wall on the left or a through-route in the blocks to the right.

BEN ALDER, North face, Maiden Crag:
Tour d' Alder – 300m II A. Nisbet. 22nd April,1995.
Near the right edge of the crag is a big shallow gully which curves left in its top half. This is the route. A steep ice pitch near the start was avoided on the left but in colder conditions would be climbed – probably Grade III.

GLEN COE

BUACHAILLE ETIVE MOR, Creag a' Bhancair,
Curtairean Mairtfheoil – 35m E6 6a. G. Farquhar, C. Carolan. 27th July, 1990.
A serious pitch, climbed on sight, up the wall between Twilight Zone and Meatbeater. Start below the grey groove 5m left of the red groove of Twilight Zone. Climb the groove and rightward-slanting diagonal crack through the bulge to join Carnivore (protection). Step right and climb directly up the steep wall above to a good ledge. Continue up and right to the peg belay.

Conga Reel – 50m E3/4 6a. R. Anderson, C. Anderson. 8th August, 1994.
In the middle of the right-hand section of the crag, there are three parallel cracklines – close together – slanting up the wall. The rightmost, Cayman, is the biggest. The central crack is taken by Walk with Destiny after starting up Cayman. This route takes the leftmost crack. Start at a tree just below and left of the line.
1. 25m 6a. Climb the crack to a grass ledge.
2. 25m 5b. Step up into the groove behind the belay, swing out right and continue to join Cayman and Walk with Destiny at the large grass ledge. Continue up scrappy ground to the tree belay at the foot of the chimney on Cayman. Either continue as for Cayman or 50m abseil.

BIDEAN NAM BIAN, Gearr Aonach, East Face:
Mimsy – 120m IV. P. Moores, A. Paul. 24th January, 1995.
Follow the summer line.

BEINN FHADA, North Face:
Ice Gearr – 250m III. P. Harrop, P. Moores. 13th February, 1992.
Follows the obvious water course immediately right of the nose. Start at about 400m.

AONACH DUBH, East Face:
Basin Chimney – 100m IV. P. Moores, A. Paul. 25th January, 1995.
Follow the summer line.

Diamond Buttress:
Diamond Edge – 130m IV, 5. M. Robson, B. Ottewell. 14th April, 1994.
Start just at the narrows in the left branch of Central Gully, just before the top of Collie's Pinnacle.
1. 50m. Climb ice and turf in a continuous groove for 20m. Step left across a large block and climb ice above trending left to easy snow.
2. 35m. Move up and right to belay below three short, icy grooves.
3. 45m. Move up and climb either groove, then trend right up mixed ground to the top.

Church Door Buttress:
Redemption – 75m VI, 6. R. Anderson, R. Milne. 13th February, 1994.
Climbs the obvious groove just around the buttress crest, some 75m up Central Gully from the start of Crypt Route.
1. 30m. Climb the groove, first on the left, then on the right via a small recess to an easing. Step across left and continue up the groove to pull around a snow crest to a bay.
2. 45m. Step right and climb a stepped groove to a bay and continue up a shallow left trending groove to the top.

West Top of Bidean:
The Fang – 75m V, 6. B. Ottewell, I. Sutton. 26th March, 1994.
The prominent gully separating Bishop's Buttress and the steep buttress of Twilight.
1. 40m. Climb the iced corner exiting right at the icicle (the Fang). Move up over bulges to belay in a large cave. Thin ice on the left wall may have been essential.
2. 35m. Traverse left and climb the steep ice wall moving back right to the gully line. Exit by an icy corner and bulge on the left. The right exit may be slightly easier.

Surely – 60m II/III. I. Sutton, B. Ottewell. 24th March, 1994.
This route lies on the left wall of Hourglass Gully. Start 25m up the gully. Climb ice into a shallow gully leading to a rock wall (40m). Mixed climbing up a corner leads to the top (20m).

BEINN A' BHEITHIR, Sgorr Dhonuill:
Thirty Nine Steps – 100m IV, 6. S. Kennedy, A. Nelson. 18th February, 1995.
This good route lies on the steep granite buttress high up on the left (south) side of the north-most coire (GR 027 563). The buttress is approx. 100m left of the left-most of two wide gullies at the head of the coire. Start up a prominent corner line near the centre just left of a steep wall. Climb the corner for 10m, then traverse out

leftwards along an obvious ledge for 5m to reach a short steep corner. Climb the corner (crux), then move back right above and continue up a chimney to a ledge (45m). Traverse a few metres left to a groove which leads back up rightwards into the main corner line. Follow the corner to easier ground above (55m).

TRILLEACHAN SLABS:
Take Your Chances – 120m E2. C. Stead, D.F. Lang. 14th May, 1994.
This route lies on the left side of the upper slabs, left of Dan. Start at the foot of the leftmost of the three right-facing corners.
1. 45m 5c. Climb the corner (wet, RP runners) to reach holds leading right then left back into the continuing groove which leads to a stance.
2. 40m 5b. Climb the groove to a finger crack, step right and climb the slab to two small overlaps with a heather moustache. Traverse the moustache right and gain a fault line via three tiny finger pockets which leads to a flake belay.
3. 35m 5b. Climb the slab to a large overlap, traverse left and gain a dirty corner, climbed on its right wall to ledges (thread and spike belay). Three abseils to the path.

STOB COIR' AN ALBANNAICH:
Unnamed – 70m II/III. S. Kennedy. 26th March, 1994.
A nice icefall falls directly from the summit down into the north coire. Climb the icefall and vague depression above to the summit. An easy gully 30m to the left provides a convenient descent into the coire.

BEN STARAV, Stob Coire Dheirg:
Desperate Dan – 175m III, 4. I. Dillon, M. Sinclair. 25th January, 1995.
Situated on the right-hand buttress of three, to the right of Shadow Groove, following an obvious gully fault.
1. 25m. Up steep snow to a chockstone barrier. Surmount this at the right-hand side where the chockstone meets the slab. Continue up until a short steep thigh width crack bars access to the gully continuation above.
2. 25m. Thrutch up the crack and pull over into the gully. Continue up and belay to the left of the gully exit slot.
3. 50m. Up right through the slot and over short steep steps to easy ground. Scramble to the ridge (75m).

ARDGOUR, GARBH BHEINN, South Wall of Great Ridge,
The Contender – 50m E3/4 5c. R. Anderson, C. Anderson. 11th August, 1994.
Excellent climbing up the wall between Pincer and White Hope. Start in the centre of the wall beside White Hope, at an embedded pointed boulder. Take plenty draws and wires, particularly in the Rock 1-5 range.
1. 50m. Climb directly to the right end of a short, left-slanting crack at 6m and follow this to gain a jug up on the left. Move up to a large round pocket, step left, climb the thin crackline and continue directly above into a groove, access to which is barred by a boldish hard move over a double bulge. At the top of the groove an awkward move over a bulge gains a rampline beneath the headwall. Follow the ramp a short way, then swing out right and climb the short crack up the left side of the headwall to reach ledges and a wide groove. Climb the niche on the left, swing out left on to the rib and follow the slab to a thin grassy ledge just below the top.

North Buttress:
Too Old to be Bold – 110m V. Diff. E. Fraser, A. Keith. 3rd October, 1993.
The climb is located at the extreme left side of the crag, just right of the 'unnamed gully' p338, Glen Coe Guide. A good line on generally clean, sound rock.
1. 35m. Climb through steep slabs, making an initial traverse right for 5m into a V-groove, then follow this up, trending slightly left, past an awkward move at 20m, to a belay stance.
2. 35m. Climb up and left by slabs and cracks to the exposed edge overlooking the unnamed gully, then follow the edge over easier angled slabs to a niche below a steepening.
3. 40m. Climb steeper rock out of the niche for 15m, then scramble to the top.

SOUTHERN HIGHLANDS

BEINN AN DOTHAIDH, North East Coire:
Valhalla – 150m IV, 5. S. Dicken, H. Pell. 29th January, 1994.
Climbs an icefall starting approx. 10m right of Haar.
1. 50m. Climb the icefall and belay on the right in the narrow gully above.
2. 50m. Trend right and climb steep rock and ice bulges to belay at the foot of the summit snow cone.
3. 50m. Climb the snow cone to the summit.
Note: The route was repeated, unaware of the earlier ascent, by M. Reed and M. Sawyers on 13th February, 1994. They note that the amount of ice varies greatly and some years isn't there. They graded IV, 4, which looks right on the photo provided, but also there was much less ice in January.

THE COBBLER, South Peak:
S-Crack – V, 7. I. Taylor, C. Lyon. 20th March, 1994.
Climb the summer route in two pitches. Well protected.

North Peak:
Right-Angled Chimney – IV, 5. A. Forsyth, B. Goodlad. 25th February, 1994.
By the summer route.

Wild Thing – 40m E5 6b. R. Campbell, P. Thorburn. 20th July, 1994.
'The true finish to Punster's Crack'. Start up Punster's Crack but continue without belaying up the impending crack. The off-width section is the crux (Camalot 4 very useful) but a rest can be contrived in the slot before a spectacular climax is achieved pulling on to the slab. Led on sight (second visit).

Trans-Am Wheel Arch Nostrils – 40m E4 6a. M. Garthwaite. 20th July, 1994.
Start up the first corner of Punster's, then straight up the wide crack to just before the step around on the second pitch of Punster's. Climb the steep groove to the right of the wide crack of Wide Country and pull on to the slab (crux). Easy to the top.

North Peak, South Face, Great Gully Area:
Gimcanna – 105m VI, 7. R. Anderson, R. Milne. 2nd January, 1994.
A good route based on the summer line of Gimcrack. Start as for North Rib Route some 7m right of the entrance to Great Gully, at a steep shallow recess.

1. 35m. Climb the recess and the groove on the right to easy ground leading to a ledge. Move left into Great Gully and go up this a short way to beneath an obvious V-corner.
2. 30m. As for Gimcrack, up the corner to a ledge (possible belay) and ascend the bulging crack to a spacious ledge.
3. 40m. Move up and where Gimcrack traverses the flake away left, continue straight up the left side of a huge block to reach a shallow fault leading to the top.

North Rib Route – 90m V, 7. R. Anderson, C. Anderson, D. McCallum, R. Milne. 4th January, 1993.
Follows the summer line, a first-rate climb with good situations. Start some 7m right of the entrance to Great Gully, at a steep shallow recess.
1. 15m. Climb the recess and groove on the right to easy ground leading to a ledge and a belay on the right.
2. 35m. Move up into the obvious square cut recess, stand on the obvious block on the left and traverse round left, then up to the edge overlooking Great Gully. Climb straight up to slabby ground leading to a belay on the chockstone runner on the third pitch of Gimcanna.
3. 40m. Move back right, climb a short step via a nose, then go right and climb a steep crack up the right side of a huge block to finish up the shallow fault of Gimcanna.

Great Gully Groove – 95m. IV, 6. R. Anderson, R. Milne. 27th December, 1994.
Climbs the obvious groove immediately beside North Rib Route, starting 10m right of that route.
1. 20m. Climb a short step into a shallow bay and continue up and slightly left to belay as for North Rib Route.
2. 35m. Climb the obvious groove up on the left. North Rib Route goes out left on to the rib after the initial block. Near the top of the groove swing out left around a roof with a chockstone and continue up the crack to belay as for North Rib Route.
3. 40m. Continue as for North Rib Route or move left and finish as for Gimcanna.

Lulu – 95m. IV, 6. R. Milne, R. Anderson. 27th December, 1994.
Climbs the groove just to the right of Great Gully Groove sharing its first pitch.
1. 20m. As above.
2. Enter the bay above as for the previous two routes, then pull out right and climb a shallow groove to belay beneath a short corner. Up on the left the short rib of North Rib Route provides an easier finish for those wishing to maintain the standard of the route.
3. 40m. Climb the short corner, and swing out beneath the capping block and gain the ledge. The crack on the left is taken by the other routes hereabouts. Instead climb the blunt arete to gain the top.

CREAG THARSUINN, Sugach Buttress:
Pulpit Grooves – 205m VI, 7. R. Anderson, D. McCallum, R. Milne. 8th January, 1994.
An excellent line approximating the summer route up the prow of the buttress. Start on the terrace beneath a groove, just right of the corner in the lowest rocks.
1. 45m. Climb the groove and pull out left on to the right end of the terrace. Move

up to the central of three possible lines. A small bush beckons from the easy ground ahead, head for this, then continue up the prominent groove over a steepening to belay below another steepening.

2. 30m. Continue up the groove to gain the right side of the Pulpit.

3. 35m. Just left of the edge and above the belay is a short steep groove. Climb it (Original Buttress Route et al are assumed to take the easier groove on the left) and follow easier ground up the blunt crest to the start of the knife-edged arete.

4. 45m. Climb the arete and ensuing easy ground to the top of the buttress.

5. 50m. Cross the neck (don't fall down Maclay's Chimney!) and climb easily to the top.

V Groove, Variation Start – IV, 5. D. MacLardie, G. Szuca. 23rd February, 1994.
Start 5m left of the normal winter start, below an obvious right-slanting corner. Follow the right edge of the slabby wall via a crack until a hard move right on to the arete gains a small niche. Follow the short ramp above until possible to move on to a large ledge. Follow the right edge of the slab above to a large block belay. Traverse rightwards to the original route below the final bulge. This was climbed and the shallow chimney above.

BEINN IME:

Unnamed – 170m V, 6. S. Richardson, C. French, T. Prentice. 21st January, 1995.
The steep buttress to the right of Ben's Fault.

1. 50m. As for Ben's Fault to belay in a cave beneath a steep triangular wall.

2. 30m. Follow Ben's Fault for 15m, then break out on to the slabby buttress on the right and belay in the right-hand of twin turfy grooves.

3. 20m. Climb the groove to a ledge beneath the headwall.

4. 30m. The headwall is cut by two prominent grooves. Move up and left into the left-hand groove and climb this for 15m to where it overhangs. Move 5m right along a turfy break and step into the top of the right-hand groove. Climb this to a good stance.

5. 40m. Continue up short walls and grooves to the crest of the buttress and the top.

Friday the Twelfth – 130m IV, 5. A. Ogilvy, E. Robertson. 12th January, 1995.
A route right of Buttress Route.

1. Start at the lowest rocks on the buttress just left of a small recess. Climb the wall direct to the base of a prominent chimney.

2. Climb the chimney to belay under a groove on the top right of the terrace.

3. Gain the groove strenuously and follow to a second terrace. Move up and left to a thread belay on the left under an undercut corner.

4. Climb the corner and continue on easier ground to the top.

MULL OF KINTYRE:

Graham Little with Kevin Howett, Bob Reid and Bill Skidmore have climbed more than 50 new routes on the schist outcrops of the Mull of Kintyre. Mainly single-pitch climbs ranging from Severe to E4, many of good quality and great character in an attractive setting. Full descriptions in the new edition of the Arran, Arrochar and Southern Highlands Guide due out late 1996.

ARRAN

BEINN TARSUINN, Full Meed Tower:
Baron Samedi – 50m HVS. A. Fraser, K. Douglas. July, 1994.
An Arran off-width, although not the most brutal of its type. Directly underneath the main tower are slabs. At the left end of these slabs is a prominent off-width crack. A gritty and somewhat vegetatious start leads to a traditional struggle up the off-width into a niche (25m 5a). Climb the overhang above to a ledge, then the continuation crack above (25m 5a).

Flat Iron Tower:
Corbie Steps – 30m V. Diff. K. Douglas, A. Fraser. July, 1994.
The 'ancients' recorded routes on the right-hand tower. The middle tower is a fine, narrow pinnacle. Climb this by its frontal face. Enjoyable.

Meadow Face:
Meadow Slabs – IV. P. Hyde, G. Szuca. 15th January, 1994.
Follows the summer line. Climbed during a thaw; should drop a grade in better conditions.
Note: Boggle: G. Szuca and A. Wren did not avoid the through route by choice (SMCJ 1992). It was partially blocked, possibly by rockfall, and future ascenders are recommended to carry an ice axe to attempt clearance.

CIR MHOR, South Face:
Sou'wester Slabs – V, 6. A. Forsyth, B. Goodlad, J. Turner. 10th April, 1994.
Winter ascent by the summer route.

Coire na h-Uaimh, Lower Slabs:
The Key – 115m HVS. G.E. Little. 15th October, 1994.
Start at an elongated pocket to the right of a large, pointed block beneath the slabs (between Hode On and Polhode).
1. 45m 4c. Climb straight up a clean slab to below the overlap. Step right on to a projecting block. On the slab above a thin flake runs out left. Ignore this and climb straight up a slight rib on small pockets and dimples to a wide heather ledge.
2. 30m 5a. Climb a clean slab in two steps (a perched block lies to the left) to a small turf patch left of a small corner. An incipient crack runs out left. Follow it for 3m, then climb boldly up a steep slab, on minimal holds, to gain a keyhole thread belay just above a big crumbly flake.
3. 40m 4a. Ascend the pocketed slab above the belay, then cross an overlap to gain a thin rock crevasse (joining Polhode). Move slightly right, then climb straight up the centre of a narrow slab to finish.

SANNOX BEACH, Conglomerate Crag (SMCJ 1991):
Sci-Fi – E2 5c. G. Szuca. May, 1994.
On the second sandstone buttress on the right past the crag. Start 2m right of the *in situ* peg. Climb to the peg and pull over the roof leftwards. Finish rightwards to a good tree.

Fallen Rocks (NS 006 483):
Howk Howk – VS 4c/5a. G. Szuca. 28th May, 1994.
At the right side of the rocks there is an obvious orange sandstone buttress. The route follows the obvious groove finishing by an interesting move in a good position through the top bulge. Round the corner is a shallow cave with a slabby right wall. Two VS routes were climbed on this wall by G. Szuca.

BEINN NUIS:
Nuis Chimney. J. Irving and F. Bennet note a free winter ascent of this route at IV, 6.

LOWLAND OUTCROPS

GLASGOW SOUTH AND AYRSHIRE, Loudon Hill, West Face:
Planet X – 12m E1 5b. P. Brown, S. McFarlane. December, 1994.
The corner immediately right of Sadist's Groove.

THE GALLOWAY HILLS, Mullwharchar, The Tauchers:
To the right of the Giants Staircase, situated between the two burns in the coire, is a broken area of hillside, identifiable by a pale concave slab at its foot and a tiered headwall at its top.
Concave Slab – 30m HVS 5a. R. McAllister, A. Fraser. 10th May, 1994.
The pale concave slab, the first feature encountered when approaching from Loch Doon. This route takes the shallow corner immediately left of the smoothest part of the slab, reached by the wall directly below the corner.

Tiers for Fears – 40m E1 5b. R. McAllister, A. Fraser. 10th May, 1994.
Good if avoidable climbing up the three tiered steeper side of the headwall. Start 3m left of a boulder perched above the first tier. Climb the thin slab (crux) to gain a finger crack and the top of the first tier. Take the next two tiers directly by steep walls and cracks.

Where Beagles Dare – 15m VS 4c. A. Fraser, R. McAllister. 10th May, 1994.
About 100m down and left of the headwall is a smaller steep wall. This route takes the left-hand crack system.

Craigencallie, Flake Buttress:
At the bottom corner of the buttress is a wide, vegetated crack with two starts (Raven Seek Thy Brother is the left start). Left of this is an undercut slab steepening into a wall, the steepest feature on the buttress.
The Empty Quarter – 50m E2. A. Fraser, S. Mearns. 23rd June, 1994.
A superb route giving unexpected and improbable climbing up the undercut slab and wall. Low in the grade. From the left end of the slab, traverse right into the centre of the slab above the initial overhang, then continue up the centre of the slab and wall, angle and difficulties increasing with height (30m 5b). From the left end of the ledge, traverse 5m left and climb a cleaned crack and slabs to the top (20m 4a).

Corbie Steps – 60m HVS. A. Fraser, K. Douglas. 6th July, 1994.
A fine route taking a direct line up the buttress between the right start of the wide

crack and Cranium Edge. Start 5m right of the wide crack. Climb into a scoop at 5m, traverse right across the top of the scoop, then directly, crossing the diagonal fault of Cranium Edge to gain a steep corner. Up this, exiting left on to the wall, then up to gain a leftward trending grassy crack. Follow this for a couple of moves, then up the wall above to belay on a huge flake (30m 5a). Move left and up the centre of the wall (3m right of the wide crack) to a large grass ledge. Climb the steep wall at the back of the ledge, then slabs above to the top (30m 4b).

Main Wall:
Heinous Venus – 25m E3 5c. R. McAllister, A. Fraser, W. Todd. 14th October, 1994.
The blocky shallow edge 3m right of the crack of Delta of Venus. A steep but civilised lower section leads to a blind and precarious crux.

Odd Mortality – 25m E2 6a. A. Fraser, R. McAllister, W. Todd. 14th October, 1994. Technical and well protected. To the right of the main wall is a huge roof, immediately to the right of which is a smooth corner. Climb this, then the bulge above. Continue up walls rightwards to the top.

Dungeon of Buchan:
Well worth the effort to get there. Do not walk straight across the bog.

Dungeon Buttress:
Take a double rack of Friends and tape up.
Parcel of Rogues, Variation to pitch 1 – 30m E3 6a.** A. Shand, R.D. Everett. 17th July, 1994. An obvious challenge which, when dry, is a little easier than the original way. Climb the original route to the small ledge at the top of the crack. Make hard moves into the hanging niche above, then struggle up the impressive overhanging slot.

Cooran Buttress:
Note: The Direct Finish to Heir Apparent is E3 5c.** Excellent climbing but leave your brain at home. The first pitch of Cyclopath is probably 5b.

Craigencallie:
Note: The Scottish Natural Heritage warden points out that the bird restriction here should run from the beginning of April to mid-July, not as stated in the guide.

THE SOUTH-WEST SEA CLIFFS, Kiln o' the Fuffock:
Note: This crag provides some exciting adventures. Point Break is E2 6a.* Total Immersion is well worth its grade and stars. It is better to pre-clip the protection peg of Burning the Boats by climbing the corner to its right and leaning across to clip it. Then climb back down to the start of the hard climbing. If this is not done, the climbing is not well protected and worth E5.

The Kiln:
The Kiln is the grassy depression or hole inland from the main cliff and separated from the sea by an arch. The following two routes lie in the Kiln on the steep left side of the arch.

The Niche – 6m E2 5c. M. Reed, R. McAllister. 26th June, 1994.
The lefthand crack line.

Suggestive Digestive – 7m E3 6a. M. Reed, R. McAllister. September, 1994.
The right-hand crack.

Money Head, Ecu Wall:
The following two routes may coincide somewhat but Cash Flow Crisis was
received too late to check.
Jug Jive – 20m E1 5b. R.D. Everett, D. Gaffney. 3rd June, 1994.
A good climb which is less fearsome than it appears. About 10m left of Slot
Machine is a hanging yellow prow with a grey overhanging recess to its left. Move
rightwards into the recess, then cross its overhanging right wall on surprising holds
to reach the yellow prow. Traverse across the lip of the roofs to gain and climb the
corner which lies left of the arete of The Root of all Evil.

Cash Flow Crisis – 15m E2 6a. R. McAllister, D. McGimpsey. August, 1994.
Fine athletic climbing over the lowest point of the overhang 6m left of the corner
of Slot Machine. Above the roof finish straight up by easier climbing.
Note: Slot Machine is VS 4c. The parking place identified in the guide has a new
building on it. Since the farmer is extremely aggressive about people parking on his
land, it would be better to park at the cross roads.

Laggantalluch Head, Main Cliff:
The Holy Grail – 35m HVS 5a. R. McAllister, D. McGimpsey, A. Fraser. 6th
October, 1994.
The huge corner at the left edge of the slab gives superb and well protected
laybacking and chimneying.

Lunch Bay:
Truncheon Muncher – 15m E2 5c. R. McAllister, A. Fraser, D. McGimpsey. 6th
October, 1994.
Thin chimneying up the wall right of Sciatic Nerve. Start 2m down and left of the
large boulder jammed in the gully. Climb to the left end of the roofs, move left round
a rib, then climb the wall above.

Island Walls:
PC Plummet – 10m E1 5b. R. McAllister, D. McGimpsey, A. Fraser. 6th October,
1994.
A good although often wet route up the steep, cracked wall at the back of the gully
between the two Island walls.

Crammag Head, Lighthouse Walls:
Firefly – 10m HVS 5a. R.D. Everett, D. Gaffney. 3rd June, 1994.
Start at the right hand end of the ledge. Climb the wall, keeping as close to the right
arete as possible.

Razamatazz – 10m HVS 5a. R. Smith, A. Munro. 24th July, 1994.
A direct line up the middle of Hourglass Slab. Poorly protected.

Gabarunning Zawn:
Note: Matador (25m, E1 5c) was climbed. Details next year.

Viking Zawn:
Ultima Thule – 30m HVS 5a. A. Fraser, R. McAllister. 23rd May, 1994.
A fine continuous route tackling the steep ground at the left end of the face, left of Ragnarok. Climb the initial 6m of the gully of the Four B's until it widens and it is possible to step right on to a slab. Climb this, then up a left-trending corner above. Continue directly to a roof, surmount this, then up the slab to the top roofs. These are split by a leftward fault (just left of Ragnarok), which is climbed to the top.

Kittiwake Zawn:
The steep south-facing wall of the zawn has a wide horizontal ledge at 8m. Down Under starts up the grey corner which springs from the right end of this ledge. To the right of this is another right facing corner, which starts as a wet overhanging chimney low down. Right again is the corner at the back of the zawn. The following route climbs the middle corner, starting at a sloping ledge where the wet chimney closes.
Violently Happy – 20m E3 6a. R. McAllister, S. Mearns. September, 1994.
A magnificent impressive route, steep on large holds. Abseil to the sloping ledge. Climb a short corner to a small ledge, then up to a roof (Friend 1). Climb the left side of this, then move slightly right (wallnut 3) up to an obvious hinged spike, then pull steeply up on large holds to a rest. Finish boldly up the wall above.
Note: Down Under lies some 10m to the right of Stingray and is approached from the foot of that route.

Carrick Walls:
The Krapton Factor – 10m Severe. M. Reed. April, 1994.
The short steep wall right of Yosemite Sam.

Rocky Relations – 25m E1 5b. S. Mearns, R. McAllister. 28th July, 1994.
A very good route. Start just right of the pinnacle of Fragile Edge at a pod. Climb this, then follow cracks up the wall above.

Maiden's Stone – 20m V. Diff. M. Shaw. 17th April, 1994.
This prominent sandstone stack is a geological landmark on the Berwickshire coastline (OS sheet 67, 967604). Walk southwards below the cliffs from Ross, near Burnmouth village. The stack is accessible on foot at lowish tide (west face). A series of three mantelshelves, each one harder and more guano-ridden, takes one on to the north ridge which is followed via another mantelshelf to the top. Best avoided during the nesting season. Wellies recommended.

CENTRAL OUTCROPS, Cambusbarron West Quarry:
The Assassin – 20m HVS 5a. G. Lennox, C. Adam. July, 1994. Climbs the dirty looking slab left of Cha via an overhanging crack on the left-hand side. A second ascent throughout E1 5b.

The Accomplice – 20m E1 5b. G. Lennox, C. Adam. 9th April, 1995.
Climb the corner below and right of the slab taken by The Assassin. Follow the diagonal crack round on to the slab and finish straight up.

Left Crack – E1 5b. P. Brown, K. Archbold. August, 1994.
On the left end buttress, immediately left of Cha. Jamming to a niche. Poor rock above.

Wrong Crack – 20m. E1 5a/b. P. Brown, K. Archbold. August, 1994.
The right crack leading to the same niche. Very loose in places.

Cherry Popping – 20m HVS 5a. C. Adam, G. Lennox. 8th April, 1995. This takes the small corner immediately right of Gobi Roof. Climb past two small trees and finish straight up. Despite the FA claim, it has previously been soloed.

Frustration – 15m E2 6a. G. Lennox, C. Adam. 8th April, 1995.
Takes the arete on the left of the main face. Climb up to a small ledge in a corner and reach round to a crack on the face. Climb straight up, finishing up Easy Contract.

Bo's mantel – E1 5b. C. Adam, G. Lennox. 25th July, 1994.
Start up Easy Contract. Where this traverses left into a corner, move right and mantle on to a small ledge on the face.

Crack Attack – E3 6a. G. Lennox, S. Baker. 8th August, 1994.
Mantel on to a detached block, climb small pockets in cracks to an undercling and join Slot Shot after its rightward traverse.

Decidedly Dodgy – 20m HVS 5a. G. Lennox, C. Adam. 9th April, 1995.
In the back wall of the quarry 20m left of Scaresville is a solid-looking slab. Climb up left of this to a sloping ledge below the slab. Traverse right below the slab and up the right-hand side, finishing up the corner above.

Bo's Girdle – 35m E2 5b. C. Adam, G. Lennox. 7th April, 1995. A diagonal traverse of the main face of the quarry. Start up Easy Contract and aim for the ledge on Not Easy Contract. Climb the layback crack until it is possible to step right. Traverse to the corner of Malky the Alky and round the arete; finish straight up.

EDINBURGH OUTCROPS, Ratho Quarry:
Wounded Knee – 15m F7a. I. Taylor, S. Munro. 19th July, 1994.
Climbs the excellent bolted arete between Wally 2 and Cornered. Start on the right side. At the second bolt, move awkwardly round to the left side, climb up, then swing back on to the arete to finish on large blocks.

THE FAST CASTLE SEA CLIFFS, Fast Castle Head, The Soutar Area:
Something Fishy – 20m VS. A. Matthewson, A. Hume. 12th September, 1993.
An entertaining route up the prow right of the Second Sight descent chimney.
1. 12m 4c. Flounder up a shallow chimney, past a constriction, to belay on a ledge at the base of an obvious wide crack.
2. 8m 4c. Follow the crack steeply and muscle over the final overhang on giant holds.

MISCELLANEOUS NOTES

LETTER TO THE EDITOR

A report from Jon Taylor extolling the virtues of Kiwi climbing.

Gidday! 'A large anticyclone covers the South Island of New Zealand and is expected to bring fine weather for the next few days.' Ah, the words all N.Z. climbers love to hear, but rarely do, or at least if they do they are at work and not out in the mountains enjoying the delights of the majestic Southern Alps.

But I should digress a little to explain the Scottish connection. My climbing career began when I moved to Peterhead and started to explore the sub-Arctic Cairngorms and the sun-soaked Aberdeen sea cliffs with local guides, Wilson Moir, and Peterhead's perennial sunseeker, Niall Ritchie. Knowledge and skills gained in icy gullies and on perfect granite led to the European Alps. A restless need to explore ranges farther afield took me to New Zealand. I came here eight years ago, initially, coming on a whim to climb Mt. Cook, I had heard of nothing else, and then to return. But like so many ex-pats I stayed, enchanted by these uncrowded islands in the South Pacific. As the seasons here are 'back to front', those of you wishing to escape the Scottish winter may like to consider changing your regular holidays from July/August and come over in December/January, our summer. It's perfectly feasible to come here in July and get good weather and climbing, certainly low freezing levels, but, of course, it's winter Alpinism, with short days and storms that can dump huge amounts of snow leaving in their wake a high avalanche danger.

N.Z. Alpinism is quite different from anything you will have experienced in Europe because access is often difficult and arduous. Long walk-ins are the norm, carrying climbing boots and full bivvy gear. There may be a track through the bush and bridges across the rivers but often it's an infrequently visited wilderness. Depending where and what you decide to climb you may be in for some bush-bashing through the tangled growth of temperate rainforest that receives seven metres (25ft) of rain per year that will slow your progress to as little as one mile per hour. But don't let this put you off though, because some of the best mountaineering trips you will ever experience are to be found in these remote ranges.

Perhaps one of the finest I can recall is the S.E. Ridge of Mt. Totoko and at 9042ft it is the highest summit in Fiordland. Three buttresses of perfect granite linked by snow aretes lead to the summit slopes. As you flow up the rock, holds appearing where you want, you can revel in the delight of continuous movement on a fine, exposed route. A true classic.

Moving north of Fiordland National Park brings you into Mount Aspiring National Park. Named after the beautiful pyramidal glacial horn of Mt. Aspiring – the Matterhorn of the Southern Alps. This mountain draws climbers from all over the world and like its Swiss counterpart it seems to have a micro-climate of its own. Hard men can try the South Face, but perhaps the graceful, sweeping curve of the S.W. Ridge is the classical route. Be careful on the descent as the icy ramp on the N.W. Ridge has claimed many lives as jubilant climbers begin to relax after attaining its summit.

But I expect most of you will head straight for Mt. Cook, N.Z.'s premiere Alpine Park. Here you will find extensive glaciers, and their associated moraines, and a

High Peak, Mount Cook, New Zealand. Photo: Jon Taylor.

North Face of Rangrik Rang (6553m) in the Kinnaur Himalaya. Photo: Graham Little.

wealth of routes to suit all grades of climbers. N.Z. rock is notoriously loose, it's greywacke or 'Weetabix' to local climbers which sum up its qualities very well. Despite that, excellent rock does exist and it is usually noted in the guidebook. The red rock of the Malte Brun range provides cragging routes in an Alpine environment. One of N.Z's 30 or 50 10,000-footers – the magic number in N.Z. – Mt. Malte Brun (10,350ft) has many routes on its firm, sunny north face. Descent is usually made via the West Ridge where you'll encounter the famous Cheval. As you straddle this sharp rocky arete one leg dangles down the south face, the other the north.

N.Z.'s guidebooks are deliberately brief. They tell you where the route starts and goes, but little else, so that a spirit of adventure, and a little uncertainty, remains. Unwardened huts are scattered throughout the park, usually without blankets, but otherwise fully equipped with fuel and cooking utensils. A radio schedule in the evening gives the weather forecast and is a means of keeping a watch for overdue parties.

The earliest attempts on Mt. Cook were in the 1880s via the Linda Glacier but progress up this easiest route to the summit was hampered because crampons were not used by N.Z. climbers. The high peak of Cook was first climbed by its North Ridge on Christmas Day 1894 by three Kiwis racing to beat the visiting English climber, Edward Fitzgerald, and his Swiss guide, Matthias Zubriggen. Piqued at missing out on N.Z.'s highest peak they cut steps up the elegant South (Silberhorn) Arete to the summit of Mt. Tasman (11,475ft) the second highest mountain. As you climb up the hard ice look over your shoulder at the steep Balfour Face, which though short (600m) is an ice climber's challenge. Zubriggen eventually climbed Cook via a ridge on the extreme right of the East Face. A popular route much climbed but that has seen fatalities due to rockfall.

The summit of Mt. Cook was dramatically changed in December 1991 when the East Face avalanched sending thousands upon thousands of tons of ice and rock roaring across the Grand Plateau down the Hochetetter Icefall, across N.Z.'s longest glacier (29km) and up the Malte Brun range on the other side. Last year, we climbed the sinuous sharp East Ridge, which merges into the enormous 2000m Caroline Face, to the middle peak of Cook and traversed to its new high peak, a precariously overhung piece of ice through which we could feel the reverberations of the ongoing rockfall down the East Face.

The South Face of Cook is menaced by ice cliffs but the classic White Dreams takes a safe line to the left and leads to the low peak. Top this off with a traverse along N.Z.'s highest mile and you'll be left with a big smile on your face for a while.

I could go on and talk of the South Face of Hicks, if in condition it's another test piece, or its North Face, offering remote rock routes. But I have to stop somewhere. I can think of literally hundreds of trips, climbs, expeditions in the N.Z. Alps, but if I have imbued you with some of my enthusiasm for these mountains then that is enough.

N.Z.'s mountains offer long snow and ice climbs, where you will rarely find another party on your route, though there may be someone else climbing on the same mountain. You probably won't see them, and this enhances the virginal wilderness experience. There is unlikely to be footsteps to follow so reconnaissance and good mountaineering judgment can mean the difference between success and failure. A season spent in N.Z.'s Alps will make you a much more rounded, confident mountaineer ready for the greater ranges.

South East Face of Dansketinde, Staunings Alps, Greenland. Climber – Andy Hume. Photo: Dave Ritchie.

New Zealand Tale

Tom Weir writes:– Looking back on 50 years' membership of the SMC recalls memories of days joyous and sad that so many fine men have passed on; one in particular came to mind when glancing through the 1991 Journal. I read the In Memoriam tribute to Mike Low by Douglas Scott who went round Annapurna with him in 1977. In his potted biography of Mike I discovered that after evacuation from the Dunkirk Beaches, he was posted to Malaysia and Thailand, where he was wounded – escaped to India via Java and Ceylon, but was in action again in North Africa and the Italian campaigns – was awarded the MC after Cassino where he was wounded again and invalided to the UK, later becoming OCTU Chief Instructor with the rank of Major. As Douglas put it: 'It does not take much imagination to appreciate the character and resilience that goes with that sort of history.'

The tale Mike told me, as we descended from Carn Eighe and Mam Sodhail on the 1984 sunny Easter Meet at Cannich, tells that he came from a good stable. It arose when I chanced to remark on the old-fashioned Raeburn-style ice axe he carried. Handing it over to let me feel its weight, he said: 'It's an axe with a claim to fame. It made the third ascent of Mount Cook before either of us was born. It was given to my father by the Rev. H.E. Newton who was with him when they made the summit in 1905. It was while my father was out climbing in New Zealand he met my mother and got engaged. He very nearly didn't make the altar. I'm here because he did.'

The remarkable tale he told me is worth repeating for its survival interest.

First though, a wee bit of background on Bob's father, who was born in Monifeith, in 1875, one of whose earliest recollections was of being roused from his bed on a wild December morning to see the gap in the Tay Railway Bridge following the disaster that cost the lives of 90 passengers. Mike said: 'My great, great grandfather built the first steam locomotive for the Dundee and Newtyle Railway in 1831. My father joined the family business of J.F. Low & Co. which made jute machinery. He trained as an engineer, but went abroad to India, travelled a bit in South Africa and Canada and on to New Zealand to join up with Dr James MacIntosh Bell, a well known geologist engaged on a survey of the South Island. My father married Dr Bell's sister.'

Now we come to the story behind the ice axe. Bob Low was a very experienced climber for those early days, and had decided to separate from his survey companion by crossing a pass at nearly 9000ft known as Graham's Saddle, as the most direct way of getting to the Hermitage Hotel below Mount Cook. Although he didn't consider the crossing to be foolhardy, it was agreed that his companion should accompany him to the first glacier, watch to see he reached the Saddle safely, then he would make his way back to base. Bob said he would send a telegram from the Hermitage to let him know he had got there.

Conditions were good. At 10am Bob was on the Saddle facing a steep descent to the glacier far below. The snow was just right for heeling down, but at a sudden change to icy surface he tried to brake with his axe, was over-balanced by the weight of his rucksack, and careered out of control until slowed down by rocks which halted his slide just above a large crevasse which could have swallowed him up.

He had gashed his knee. His ankle was broken. The only way he could move was by propelling himself with his arms in a sitting position, and this he did until at last he unrolled his sleeping bag for a night on the glacier. Resuming in the morning of February 22 his strategy was to tie his pack to the climbing rope, crawl unencumbered to its full length, then pull the pack after him. That evening he reached a rock, and under its lee found shelter from the snow which fell steadily all next day forcing him to lie up. His food was finished. All he had now was a quarter-pound tin of cocoa.

When he resumed, among stony moraines he had to crawl with the pack on his shoulders, but he reached the place he was making for, the De la Beche bivouac, where searchers would be sure to look for a missing man. It was night when he got there, and for the next six days survived by catching drips of water from the bivouac roof and mixing it with his diminishing supply of cocoa. Expecting to die, as no one came, he scratched some blood from his arm and on his map wrote his will in red.

By this time, however, he was known to be missing and his wife to be had been told there was little hope of finding him alive. But what of the telegram, whose non-arrival should have sparked off a much earlier search party. Because of a breakdown in the telegraph service, and bad weather holding up travelling in the mountains, a full week had elapsed before there was real concern. It was the guides Peter Graham and Jack Clarke, who had been with Bob Low on Mount Cook, who climbed the moraine above the bivouac.

Graham described hearing somebody calling. 'To our relief it was Mr Low. Clarke and I were so excited at finding he was alive we dashed over the rough boulders to the bivouac.' It was 4am. The rescuers had brought a homing pigeon to carry a message over the mountains to the Hermitage, and it flew bringing the good news that nobody expected.

Until Mike Low told me his tale I had not realised how New Zealand and Scottish mountaineering had developed in parallel in the late 19th century when small groups of adventurous professional men began serious climbing for pleasure. In 1882 an Irishman, the Rev. W.S. Green, with a Swiss guide and a fellow Swiss made a bold bid for the top of Mount Cook and narrowly missed. Other parties attempted this heavily-glaciated mountain, but it was to be 12 years before it was climbed on Christmas Day 1894 by an all New Zealand party.

To return to Mike Low, who joined the SMC in 1947. Here is an extract from a letter he sent me on October 31, 1987.

'We had a good day on Ben Ledi on Saturday, the first time I have climbed it since 1931. I have been having quite a bit of trouble with a leg which was badly shot up in the war, with five inches of left femur reduced to chips, but which has all joined up after 43 years. Sadly, the knee joint seems to be packing up a bit now. I had another trip to Nepal last year but failed to get up Mera, chiefly due to a porters' strike and a forced descent of 8500ft down a very rough route to get another starting point for the climb. The leg didn't like it a bit.'

Like his father, it took a lot to stop Mike Low in war or peace. Although living in Oxford he came to New Year and Easter meets, when such events were well attended – when our Club was more of a Club.

THE LETTEREWE ACCORD

By John Mackenzie

The Letterewe Accord was agreed in its present form on the 28th November 1993. It represents a milestone in cooperation between landowners and landusers in that the basic principle of our traditional freedom to roam was incorporated within the Accord. It was the result of two years of closely worked and often fascinating dialogue between the owners and staff of the Letterewe Estate and the principal access groups in Scotland. The net result is as near to the ideal as we can reasonably expect and the result is produced on Page 000.

Readers of the Journal might be interested in some of the historical asides and footnotes of this period, there being many ways to skin the proverbial cat, and I think that together we tried most of them. In the process we also discovered how much we all had in common, regardless of any political differences that may, or may not, have existed within the group. I think if I was asked to sum it up, I would say it was a happy period where a potentially diverse group managed to pull together after a traumatic start. History is full of such stories but it is the first time it has had relevance within the quite narrow world of walking and climbing.

It began, like so many good things, with a bang. 'Estate ban on climbing incurs clan chief's wrath', screamed a fairly inflammatory article by Oliver Gillie in the *Independent* which just happened to be part of 'Forbidden Britain' week. Naturally, other newspapers such as the *Scotsman*, *Glasgow Herald* and the *Press and Journal* were soon publishing articles in that rather uncomfortable October of 1991 and this kick-start which was ultimately to lead to the Accord needed time to simmer down to unruffle all those considerably ruffled feathers. The truth of the situation was that certain notices had upset people and misconstrued intentions on both sides had got stuck like so many repetitively jarring notes. Given the situation, polarised views abounded and, like nations going to war, the 'enemy' was all one colour, while you were, of course, all the other. All this only proved the point that human beings are emotional creatures who are sometimes incapable of seeing beyond the end of their own, often long, noses.

As prime instigator, agent provocateur, or traitor to my own class, depending on your point of view, the first thing to do was to get in touch with Paul van Vlissingen and Caroline Tisdall-Mackenzie, his partner. A long phone call from Caroline smoothed over some of the more contentious issues and she suggested a weekend at Carnmore to discuss the issues more fully. The Accord very nearly came to a wet end when our boat, capably helmed by the inimitable Dougie Russell, threatened to turn itself into a submarine. We returned whence we boarded on the Fionn Loch and walked in like everyone else had to do. The weekend cleared a great deal of misunderstanding and proved to be the real starting point for the dialogue which was to follow.

We arranged to meet at Letterewe Lodge once the various parties had been informed. Obvious contenders on the access side were Dave Morris of the Scottish branch of the Ramblers Association and Bob Reid and Kevin Howett of the MC of S. Affiliated to those two groups were, of course, our own club, the SMC, with John Fowler and Iain Smart as early attenders, the John Muir Trust with Andrew

Thomson, SNH with initially, Dick Balharry, and latterly Tim Clifford, the Scottish Wild Land Group with Anne Macintyre and Highland Regional Council with Alex Sutherland. Adam Watson, an essential member of the group, was at first an independent consultant and latterly affiliated with the John Muir Trust. Not all these groups were initially represented but joined our forum as the talks progressed. On the Estate side were the owner, Paul van Vlissingen; Caroline Tisdall-Mackenzie; administrator, Mrs Barbara Grant; four stalkers, Graeme Grant, Dougie Russell, Norman Kelman, Donald John MacLeod, and river keeper, George Mackenzie.

Our initial meeting, in January 1992, set the tone of what was to follow at six-monthly intervals. We were ferried across Loch Maree either on the launch or on the barge, the latter a miniaturised version of the landing craft as used on D-Day in Normandy. Perhaps in a metaphorical sense we were going 'over the top' in that never before had such meetings taken place with all the pedestrian access groups together in the same place discussing the same issues.

Letterewe Lodge has to be one of the very finest of the classic Highland lodges, a low, elegant building fitting into the hillside, a comfortable retreat against the elements. Inside, we met in the dining room around the table. Being completely cut off from the rest of the world we had little option but to discuss our supposed differences in a civilised manner. Much of the credit for the generally-cosy feel of these meetings has to go to Caroline who invariably produced a succulent venison stew and appropriate puddings, together with good wine. It is simply impossible to get seriously annoyed when well fed and wined.

Obviously, the initial meeting was cautious, generalisations were spoken and a great deal of sounding-out went on on both sides. I was apppointed chairman for the combined groups and Paul corrected some information which had appeared in the Press. The notices were, of course, a contentious issue, and open to misinter-pretation; most of the magazines in the climbing Press carried photographs of them and readers were left to draw their own conclusions. However, the barn at Carnmore had been reinstated at Paul's expense and climbers were welcome to use it, contrary to what had been printed. Wild camping was sensitive and a topic that would be exhaustively discussed and naturally, with such an expert as Adam Watson on board, land management and regeneration were also on the agenda.

From the start we agreed to disagree and to respect each other's positions, and as chairman I had the privilege of listening to both sides of the arguments. Central to the Ramblers' position was the right to roam; not a subject that found immediate favour despite forceful and persuasive argument. The Estate equally argued on the need for proper land management and the appropriate cull without interference or disturbance. The MC of S took the centre ground, which meant that they invariably had the last word, smoothing out the ragged edges that were left. Perhaps the greatest single plus was that Paul always listened to reasoned argument; a fact not lost on the others. Polarised views gradually, in the course of several meetings, got amalgamated into something more workable.

At a meeting at Castle Leod, my home, we were joined by Hamish Leslie-Melville representing the West Ross Red Deer Management Group. Despite some heated moments – perhaps our wine was not quite up to what we were getting used to – I suddenly realised that what separated us was less than what joined us. Since we were by now relaxed in each other's company, a feeling that we were fellow travellers on the same journey became gradually apparent. We began to solve the issue of wild camping and constructively hammered out the points raised over access in the stalking season. Adam Watson, always the last word on things natural, was a voice of authority who greatly clarified sometimes muddy waters.

In between meetings at Letterewe, Bob, Dave and Caroline liaised and the nascent Accord began to take shape. At our final meeting in November 1993 we agreed to the final version, Paul accepting the right to roam in a responsible manner and considerate wild camping, the codes of which were spawned from these meetings. At the moment of agreement, a superb 'royal' appeared on a nearby crest, a symbol we felt that was entirely appropriate.

After our meetings carefully worded Press releases were published in several national and local papers, and to give the Press their due, the final Accord was given quite reasonable coverage in an unemotional and non-partisan way, a fact that made all of us breathe more easily.

Over a year on, how is the Accord working and what has it produced outside Letterewe? The access at Letterewe as per the Accord appears to be working, there is less litter and outdoor folk are respecting a man who took a considerable risk in getting the meetings going. It is worth remembering that there was no legal compulsion for Paul or Caroline to accept our proposals, the whole affair was fuelled by the need for reasoned dialogue between us. Undoubtedly, the timing, the place and the personalities involved had an air of serendipity about them. It was a unique opportunity that was, thankfully, not missed.

Paul also took on the more conservative element of the Scottish Landowners Federation when he addressed them at their annual meeting at Battleby, proving that meaningful discussion requires all the involved parties to sit down and talk to each other, an idea possibly remote in the minds of some of the delegates. The Accord was then welcomed by the Scottish Landowners Federation as a good 'first step' which at least shows that progress was being made.

Government bodies hung well back while all this was going on, then SNH expressed belated satisfaction that such a voluntary solution had been reached and adopted the formula for centralising any similar further discussion under the banner of a 'Concordat', announced by Magnus Magnusson at the Red Deer Management Groups' annual meeting last year in Inverness, where I was also invited to speak on the subject of access.

More recently, I was asked to address the West Ross Red Deer Management Group and it was agreed that the principle of the Letterewe Accord would be adopted by the various individual estates who made up this group. This policy decision will work through the MC of S and a possible further development, an idea of Paul's, is that a centralised 'hill phone' where appropriate information is given by estates could be disseminated via the MC of S.

These are early days as yet, and though the Accord was designed with one particular estate in mind, there is no real reason why its principles cannot be adopted more widely. There may well be more difficulty in its interpretation on some of the heavily deer populated estates on the eastern half of the Highlands and no doubt not all owners will be as co-operative as one would wish. However, to pursue the voluntary principles of access to wild land will require a great deal of effort from all parties and we will have to see whether or not the access issue will ultimately require state legislation in the face of increasing recreational demand.

Letterewe Lodge,
Loch Maree, Wester Ross,
Scotland.

THE LETTEREWE ACCORD

SOME of the finest mountain scenery in Europe is found on the Letterewe Estate in Wester Ross. It is renowned amongst hillwalkers and climbers for its wild land qualities. The Letterewe Accord is a set of principles whose aim is to enhance public awareness of wild land needs and to provide a guide to its use and enjoyment, both on Letterewe and perhaps elsewhere in the Scottish Highlands. The Accord has been drawn up by Letterewe Estate in co-operation with outdoor organisation representatives. It has developed from discussions initiated by the Mountaineering Council of Scotland and the Ramblers' Association with the Estate.

Fundamental to this Accord is the recognition that all who visit, or live and work on the land and water of Letterewe, must cherish and safeguard the area's wildlife and beauty. Such places are increasingly rare in a world where the natural environment is under ever growing pressure. A new approach is needed. Co-operation between individual and community interests in the sound management of wild land is one element. It reaffirms that human needs are inseparable from those of the natural world.

* The prime objective at Letterewe is to maintain, expand and enhance the area's biological diversity and natural qualities. This will ensure that these are central to the experience of all who visit the area and are recognised as an essential element in sustaining the long term economy of Wester Ross.

* Red deer management policy is based on selective culling, aided by scientific research, with the aim of maintaining population levels appropriate to the regeneration of the natural habitat.

* All who visit the area are asked to recognise that red deer stalking is carried out across most of the estate area with the most important period being weekdays from 15 Sept. to 15 Nov.

* Visitors are asked to contact the estate during this period for further advice. Visitors are encouraged to base their visit to Letterewe on the concept of 'the long walk in'. Adequate experience, training and equipment to meet the rigours of travel in this remote area are essential.

* Public use is based on the tradition of freedom of access to all land, subject to any agreed modifications for conservation or management reasons.

* There are footpaths through those areas where there are benefits for land management or for visitor access.

* Car parking, telephone and other facilities are available at Dundonnell, Kinlochewe and Poolewe.

* The estate does not favour the construction of new vehicle tracks or the use of all terrain vehicles. Ponies and boats are used for estate management.

* Mountain bikes should be used only on existing roads or vehicle tracks and not on footpaths or surrounding land.

* Minimum impact techniques should be used when camping overnight using lightweight tents. Pollution and disturbance to wildlife, especially sensitive lochshore birdlife, must be avoided.

* Visitors are encouraged to visit the area in small, rather than large groups.

* Research studies which help to further understanding of the use and protection of wild land are welcome at Letterewe.

LETTEREWE ESTATE WILL BE PLEASED TO ADVISE ON ANY

ASPECT OF ESTATE MANAGEMENT

AND ON WAYS TO MAKE ANY VISIT TO LETTEREWE

AS ENJOYABLE AND REWARDING AS POSSIBLE.

....

THE LETTEREWE ACCORD

produced by Letterewe Estate in association with

John Muir Trust

Mountaineering Council of Scotland

Ramblers' Association Scotland

Scottish Wild land Group

December 1993

(actually agreed at the meeting on 28th November 1993)

The map on the opposite page is reproduced from maps in the Scottish Rights of Way Society office, and shows claimed rights of way in Letterewe and Fisherfield. They are the traditional routes referred to in the Letterewe Accord. Some of these routes are very old, as they were shown in Roy's map of 1755. The route from Kinlochewe to Poolewe is a very old right of way – the route from the south to Poolewe. Part of it was the subject of A.E. Robertson's campaign in the 1930s to establish the right of way from Glen Carron to Kinlochewe over the Coulin Pass.

Donald Bennet.

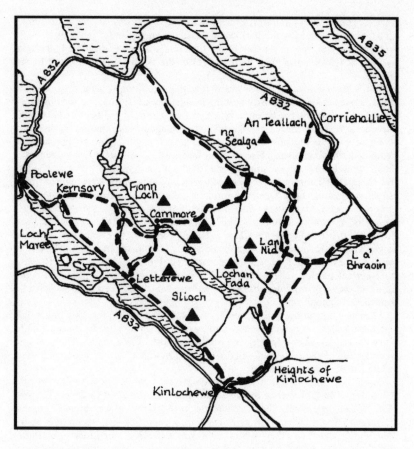

STATES OF ALTERED CONSCIOUSNESS

The following account describes an ascent of Good Friday Route on Ben Nevis, made during the winter of 1984. The route, normally a pleasant Grade III, is not the subject of interest here, but served as a vehicle for an unusual, if not somewhat bizarre happening. The story is true, and I would very much like to hear from anyone who has experienced a similar 'state'. Any correspondence will be treated as confidential, unless otherwise indicated. My two fellow climbers were Bob Richardson and Alastair Walker.

All three of us began soloing the route, front-pointing up the straight-forward initial gully. This led to a barrier, which forced me onto a right traverse on steeper ground. After a few moves on this sense prevailed and the other two tied on and threw me a rope end so that I could continue leading the small bulge. The situation had concentrated my mind, a factor I believe to be the first of three significant factors. I pulled over this bulge, which was the crux of the day, and higher up found, and tied onto, a rocky outcrop. Bob and Alastair came up and climbed on through, belaying up and right at the foot of the final pitch, which was probably the final section of Observatory Wall, farther right of the normal finish to Good Friday Route.

While I was belayed at the rock, with the other two farther on, the mist swept in. I was alone for some time with nothing in sight but my immediate surroundings, the slope below hidden below a bulge, the mist hiding sights elsewhere. This isolation, I feel, was the second significant factor, again concentrating my thoughts.

Finally, the shout came and I untied and set off, leapfrogging my partners and leading up the final pitch. This was snow leading to a well-defined snow runnel of about 40m. It was narrow, straight, and filled with perfect snow-ice. I climbed up for about 10m, chortling all the while about the quality of the snow, pulled over a slight steepening, then began the runnel section, about 25m of a very uniform nature, not hard, but not easy either. The climbing was a delight, crampons and axes going into the snow cleanly first time, with a neat, crispy sound, very secure. I was told later that I suddenly fell silent, though I continued to climb with the same rhythm as before, one axe in, second axe in, one foot up, the second foot up and so on. Near the top of the runnel the slope steepened slightly and the snow became less than perfect, forcing a change of pace. At this point I 'woke up', for want of a better description, gave myself a shake, and realised that I had been in some sort of a trance, or hypnotic state.

I finished the pitch and tied onto the cairn, bringing up the other two. Other than me falling silent, they had noticed nothing out of the ordinary. As for me, I had a very pleasant, peaceful feeling, not tiredness, more of a calmness. There was no recollection of the section climbed while in the 'trance', it had been done in an altered state of consciousness.

Some time later, while a Research Assistant, I came across the report of a Commonweath Conference that had taken place in Jordanhill College, Glasgow. One of the papers rekindled my interest in the event. It was a paper entitled *Hypnosis - Some States of Altered Consciousness and their Application in Sport*. The author was a Dr Peter Weston, who was a medical practitioner working in Edinburgh, and who used hypnosis as a therapeutic tool for athletes. His paper defined hypnosis as 'an altered state of consciousness in which the mind is much more receptive to suggestions.' Or (he continued) it is a state of hyperconcentration in which the power of criticism is either reduced or eliminated. Without the power of criticism the subject allows suggestions to go straight into the unconscious, to be stored there for use afterwards in an automatic way.'

Before providing more definitions, I shall briefly describe an earlier event of a similar 'trance', though one which took place in more mundane circumstances. Several years prior to the event described above, I was watching modern dance on television. I was sitting on the floor, cross-legged, and enjoying two dancers performing to some piece of appropriately modern music. The figures were swirling to the music, and I became focused concentrating on them. After some time, I became aware that I had emerged from some sort of a light trance state. As with the climbing later, I had been in a high state of concentration.

Dr Weston's paper described five stages of altered consciousness. Such states are induced by a subject increasing his concentration, and reducing his global awareness.

The five states are:

1. No Sensory Selection – where there is no sensory selection the subject is not concentrating on anything in particular.

2. Normal Sensory Selection – In this situation the subject is engaged in routine work of a fairly ininteresting nature.

3. Augmented Sensory Selection – This level is present when the subject is concentrating on a very complicated or interesting task.

4. Hyperselection – occurs when the subject's attention is on one regular monotonous stimulus, this may be auditory, visual, tactile or mental and will produce a light or medium state of altered consciousness.

5. Total Sensory Selection – In this state the subject has continued to concentrate on the stimulus, has become completely oblivious of everything except the stimulus and has entered the deepest state of altered consciousness. This is a level of sensory selection which is attainable by only a very small number of people.

As for Sports therapy, Dr Weston has, for example, allowed athletes to perform well by overcoming various fears, phobias, injuries etc. using hypnosis. Autogenic Training also has a place, though this is not the place to go into detail. I wrote to Dr Weston two years after the climbing event, describing my experiences. He very kindly replied, saying that it sounded as if I had '. . . experienced total sensory selection while climbing in a routine monotonous fashion.' As soon as the gradient and texture of the snow altered, he continued, I then '. . . went up into a state of augmented sensory selection.'

Weston's reply continued by pointing out the obvious danger of using the state of total sensory selection while doing something dangerous in that if you are already tired you may go to sleep when you no longer have any control over your functions. He likened this to the experience while motorway driving at the same speed being aware only of the regular white dots passing by. 'It is important,' he continued, 'when taking part in something potentially dangerous to avoid monotony by altering pace or keeping your actions irregular.'

In conclusion, I would like to add that I had been practising yoga for some time before and during these two experiences, that I had definitely not been tired during either, but had certainly been concentrating wonderfully hard. I'm sure that I'm not alone in this experience, and would welcome any similar stories.

Ken Crocket.

John Mackenzie recalls: I note on page 496 of the 1995 Journal some comments on Monolith Grooves. It is gratifying to know that the route now has worthy companions which might entice more to seek out the winter delights on this crag. Readers may be interested on some original comments made about this route before the major rockfall occurred a few years ago.

It was climbed on January 16, 1977 – just pre front pointing, a single cut-down ice axe and an esoteric slater's pick being the chosen weapons. It was in thin conditions and before the rockfall the crux was the chimney below the top corner, a short (15m) but bulging affair that gave considerable angst.

It would be worth V (5) by today's softer standards, but this fine feature has been radically altered to something a grade easier, which is a pity. I do not know if the 'Gallery', a roofed cave, is still in existence. This lay below the final pitch and was an extraordinary feature. The top corner, the highlight of the climb, was fortunately untouched by the rockfall. We started the route from the left, but I note that in better conditions it is possible to climb up the gully adjacent to the Monolith.

Obviously, this direct start decreases the length of the climb, as noted, but the original lengths for the six pitches encountered are accurate (30m, 40m, 9m, 30m, 15m, 30m).

Geologically, the entire crag is very gradually on the move down to the main road; the grassy crevasses at the crest show that 'exfoliation' on a massive scale is the way this crag has formed and the unfortunate rockfall was but an interim process over the eons of time that will gradually eat back into the hillside until a stable slope is formed.

Climbers could provide a useful service by noting any widening of cracks or areas of unsoundness and reporting progress from time to time in the Journal.

The Mad Monk and the Wolf of Dundonnell

Steve Chadwick confesses: Last year I was due to take my winter mountain assessment so decided to carry out some navigation practice and then sleep out for the night. There is an area of high, rough moor behind Dundonnell that does not have too many cliffs on its edge, an obvious essential for practice, else mistakes can be fairly unforgiving. It was about 9pm when I left Ceilidh my Border collie on a high point GR 068858 with orders to *stay*. She looked reproachfully up at me and sat down with a 'grief, where's he going now' sort of flounce.

It was a clear, starry night with the moon about half-full. There was a light breeze blowing through the deer grass and the world felt a lonely place, but I was at peace with it. In order to increase the difficulty of the problems I set myself, I pulled my hood down over my forehead so I could not look up and see location points. With my hands out in front of me holding the compass and my little toggles on the compass cord for counting off the 100m sections I set off.

After reaching the first objective I chanced to look up to check my position against the dark outline of Sgurr Fiona on An Tealach, and there descending the flank of Bidein a' Ghlas Thuill coming towards me were two pin points of light. It was at this moment that Ceilidh began to howl mournfully for her supper. The head torches stopped dead and I could swear that for a second or two they began to go back up the mountain, but the fear of toiling back along the ridge at the end of a long day must have outweighed the dread of a howling hound that lay seemingly on their line of descent. I thought no more of it, and continued setting myself problems across the featureless terrain while the dog continued to howl at the moon.

What transpired 15 minutes later was a misfortune of pure chance. My next objective was the small hillock at GR 069850. It also has to be crossed or contoured on the descent from An Teallach. It was while I was descending this knoll, with my hood low over my face, hands in front holding the compass and counting of steps, 31,32, 33, and so on, that the two nocturnal hill walkers and I met. I came down behind them sounding my liturgy of numbers with only a metre of forward vision, so that they heard me before I saw them. At the sound of my words and slow-measured tread they turned to face me.

I can only assume that the howling 'wolf of Dundonnell' had sufficiently unnerved them to make the sight of me coming down on them out of the dark the final straw. It is true that I must have looked like a mad monk with seemingly a cassock drawn over my face, hands held out as if in supplication and prayer, mouthing a chant and with the toggles on my compass cord looking like rosary beads. Whatever they thought they didn't stay to tell me. Despite having good-sized rucksacks on their backs, they fled down the path and on into the gloom of little Loch Broom.

I sometimes wonder how the conversation went in the bar of the Dundonnell Hotel that night. Or, more likely, they decided to say nothing. Who would believe them? If they read this I hereby apologise for the fright they received. If it's any consolation to them the weather changed and I got very wet before the dawn.

The winter of 1947 – Almost 50 years ago there was a great winter in Scotland. Snow fell in quantity and this was followed by a period of stable weather. There was a six-foot deep cornice on the Cat Nick Gully on the Salisbury Crags and in the anticyclonic haze Arthur's Seat looked Himalayan in stature. The number of people who remember this meteorological event will decrease as the years go by and so John Berkeley has offered to act as the Editor of a 'Winter of '47' archive. Would anyone who would be prepared to write reminiscences or look up the Press reports of the time in the National Library please contact John Berkeley, Drumbeg, Coylum Bridge, Aviemore, Inverness-shire, PH22 1QU.

SHETLAND

For the record, Graham Little notes that he spent six months working in Shetland during 1970 when, with a variety of partners (often coerced), he made a series of first ascents of sea stacks and smaller walls on Unst and the Mainland.

Precise details of these are lost in the mists of memory, although the fin-like stack to the south of Sumburgh lighthouse, well seen when approaching Sumburgh Head from Stromness, gave a sporting little climb by its short side (approach from above down a short, crumbly arete). An attempt with (Stuart Gibson) was made on the great 100m wall that sits below the radar dome on The Compass above Sumburgh Airport (MR 408 094).

The attempt terminated part way up pitch 2 due to technical and psychological difficulties and the threat of a bus-size block that hangs from the wall at half height. A return visit (on business) in 1994 confirmed that the block still defies gravity and that the wall looks as impressive as ever!

THE SCOTTISH MOUNTAINEERING TRUST 1994/95

The Trust has had a busy year which saw the publication of new climbing guides to Ben Nevis, the Lowlands and North East Outcrops with a revised Central Highlands completing the present series of District Guides.

A large number of applications for financial assistance have been processed which have led to a record distribution of funds.

The greater number of applications and their varied natures has, unfortunately, caused Trustees to formally consider the attitude that the Inland Revenue might take towards these awards in relation to maintaining the Trust's charitable status which is essential to sustaining the publishing program at its present level. To that end, legal opinion has been sought from senior counsel on the areas in which it is appropriate for Trustees to make awards and more importantly, the areas in which it is not. The opinion received was interesting and will have a marked effect on the purposes to which Trustees can extend benevolence in future.

Broadly, Trustees will require to see present in any application some element of educational and scientific advancement, these being defined charitable purposes and thus, for example, any expedition seeking assistance will from now on require to demonstrate that in addition to climbing the peak, it has some recognisable and defined scientific or educational goal.

The following grants were awarded during the year of which the most notable was the total exhaustion of the Land Fund towards the purchase of the Strathaird Estate in Skye. Trustees regarded Strathaird as one of the most significant properties to come on the market in recent years (it includes the climbing side of Blaven) and were more than happy to assist the John Muir Trust in the acquisition.

The Trust remains appreciative of those members who give voluntary of their time to manage its affairs either as Trustees or officials. The present Trustees are: D.C. Anderson, R.N. Campbell, J.Y.L. Hay, S. Kennedy, D.F. Lang, R.T. Richardson, R.G. Ross, J.M. Shaw, N.M. Suess and W. Wallace.

J.R.F. Fowler.

General Grant Fund

Grants paid	LSCC – Provision of new sceptic tank at Blackrock	£1500
	JMCS Edinburgh – Re-roofing of Jock's Spot	£3223
	Scottish Rights of Way Society – mapping project	£1000
	Ochils Mountaineering Club – Hut improvements	£5000
	National Trust for Scotland – Field worker	£800
	Head Injuries Trust for Scotland – contribution	£500
	Dundee Mountain Film Festival	£500
Grants committed		£20,125

Footpath Fund

Grants paid	Balmoral Estate – Glas Allt Shiel	£600
Grants committed		£27,950

Snart Bequest

Grants paid	BMC winter skills video	£2000
	SSC navigation courses	£1000

Sang Award

Grants paid	C.I. Watkins – Romania	£400
	1994 Bezingi Wall Expedition	£500
	1994 British Trinity Peak Expedition	£1000
	SMC Staunings Alps Expedition	£875

Lagangarbh Project

Expenditure this year - phase 3	£19,211

Land Purchase Fund

Grants paid	JMT – Strathaird Estate	£50,000

MUNRO MATTERS

By C.M. Huntley (Clerk of the List)

There are 115 new names to be added to the List this year taking the number to 1389. The annual incremental rise has now been constant for the last three years, although there does appear to be an increase in the number of multiple compleations and more compleations of the Tops. The List below gives the Munroists' number, name, year of compleation of Munros, Tops and Furths as appropriate. SMC and LSCC members are identified by * and ** respectively.

No.	Name	Munros	Tops	Furths		No.	Name	Munros	Tops	Furths
1275	David Smith	1994				1319	Robert P Gray	1994		
1276	Alan Findllay	1993				1320	Robert W Gray	1994		
1277	John M.Barrett	1993				1321	Ian Forder	1994		
1278	Allan P. Lees	1994				1322	Ken A Butcher	1994	1994	
1279	Nigel P. Morters	1994				1323	Frankie S Cumming	1994		
1280	Adrian M.Lodge	1994				1324	Ian McVittie	1994		
1281	Carol Lodge	1994				1325	Charles G Elliott	1994		
1282	Lorraine Nicholson	1994				1326	Ben S Cooper	1994		
1283	Harry Blenkinsop	1994				1327	Ian J Brownell	1994		
1284	John D Taylor	1994	1994			1328	Raymond Hay	1994		
1285	Kevin Borma	1994				1329	Gillian M Green	1994	1994	
1286	David William	1994	1994			1330	John E Green	1994	1994	
1287	Robert J Shapperd	1994				1331	John Mackay	1994	1994	
1288	David Fisher	1994				1332	Fraser MacGillivray	1994		
1289	Steve Simpson	1994				1333	Kenneth W C Stewart	1994		
1290	Anne Lochhead	1994				1334	Alex K Kirk	1994		
1291	Keith Work	1994				1335	J P Fish	1994		
1292	Julian P Ridal	1994				1336	F David Smith	1994		
1293	Alistair Maitland	1994				1337	G W Hollins	1994		
1294	J. Sebastian Grose	1994	1994			1338	Christine C Macleod	1994		
1295	William Beattie	1994				1339	Rhoda McKinnon	1994		
1296	Alex D Grant	1994				1340	Andrew Balsillie	1993	1994	
1297	David W Duncan	1994				1341	David Bonham	1994		
1298	Graham T Illing	1994				1342	Irene Crawshaw	1994		
1299	Michael McLaggan	1994				1343	Grahame Crawshaw	1994		
1300	W.Harvey Condliffe	1994				1344	Pat Craven	1994		
1301	Keith Moody	1994				1345	Brian Norman	1994		
1302	Roberta Taylor	1994				1346	Gerry Callaghan	1994		
1303	Charles M. Taylo	1994				1347	George Middleton	1994		
1304	Eiona Conacher	1994				1348	Alistair Patten	1994	1994	
1305	John G. Aird	1994				1349	Carol Harper	1994		
1306	Barbara V. Watson	1994				1350	Keith Harper	1994		
1307	Celia Goodman	1994				1351	Margaret Beattie	1994		
1308	Audrey M Litterick	1994				1352	Carole Strang	1994		
1309	Charles Leggat	1994				1353	Martin Horn	1994		
1310	Fiona Wallace	1994				1354	Murray Smith	1994		
1311	Terry A. Fuller	1994	1994	1994		1355	Carole George	1994		
1312	Paul Krebs	1992				1356	Iain McManus	1994	1994	1994
1313	Michael J Smyth	1994				1357	Iain A B Wallace	1994		
1314	Neil S Dunford	1994				1358	Ken Naismith	1994		
1315	J H Calver	1994				1359	Lyn S Wilson	1994		
1316	N S Hunnisett	1994				1360	Jeremiah J Scott	1994		
1317	Leigh Sayers	1994				1361	Graham Wanless	1994		
1318	Catherine S Gray	1994				1362	Clare Parnell	1994		

1363	Simon Halliwel	1994		1377	John D. Shiel	1994
1364	A. Haveron	1978		1378	John M Griffin	1994
1365	J. Coull	1984		1379	Ruth Hannah**	1994
1366	J. Mitchell	1987		1380	C P Herdman	1994
1367	R. Shafren	1989		1381	Moira Broadhead	1994
1368	J. Smith	1989		1382	Martin J Darling	1993
1369	K. Higgins	1992		1383	A Stuart Duncan	1994
1370	N. Kenworthy	1993		1384	John G Proud	1994
1371	Spencer A. Julian	1994		1385	Allan J Gordon	1994
1372	W. Lofthouse	1994		1386	Colin Scales	1986
1373	M. Lofthouse	1994		1387	Ian H Anderson	1994
1374	J.Weir Brown	1994		1388	Lorna McLaren	1994
1375	Stephen Sharp	1994		1389	John King	1994
1376	Richard Burt	1994				

AMENDMENTS
Multiple rounds only show the year of the most recent Compleation.

148	D Whalley	1991		1989		392	Mervyn Griffin	1994		1989
		x4		x2				x2		
250	Leonard Moss	1994				599	James Taylor	1994		
		x2						x2		
259	Derek A Bearhop	1994				962	Bob Connell	1991	1991	1994
				x3		963	Howard A Sowerby	1991	1991	1994
327	Stewart Logan	1994	1994	1987		1045	Steve Fallon	1994		
		x7	x7	x3				x2		
346	John J S Brown	1994				1160	Peter E. Collins.	1993		
		x4				1192	David Unsworth	1993	1995	
391	Brenda D Griffin	1994	1989							
		x2								

The letters of notification that the Clerk receives cover a multitude of experiences and exhibit almost every facet of hillwalking life in Scotland. I have tried to summarise only a small proportion of the details contained in the letters and apologies to those who haven't had their favourite epic included.

The Families:

The occurance of couples compleating is now relatively common, and this year we have the Greens (1329, 30), the Crawshaws (1342, 43), the Harpers (1349, 50) and the Lofthouses (1372, 73). One break with convention is that Carole Lodge has accepted the second number of 1281, while husband, Adrian, has 1280. I'm afraid that when their letter arrived announcing their compleation together, I misunderstood the wording and thought Carole had only accompanied Adrian for the Last One, not the whole round. I can imagine her consternation, and please accept my apologies again. At least she corrected me so promptly that they still have consecutive numbers.

This year we have a family of three, the Grays (1318-20), which includes son, Robert, aged 15 years, and Terry Fuller (1311) is the third of three brothers to compleat, following on from Richard and Steven (387 and 388). Members of the same family compleating a few years apart is not particularly uncommon and others this year include Moira Broadhead (1381) wife of Dave (690) and Pat Craven

(1344) wife of Pete (827). Where members of the same family compleat some years apart, it is invariably the older member who compleats first. Not so for Ken Butcher (1322) who is following after his son, Chris (1110). One couple who didn't feel the necessity to reach that Last One together are Margaret (1351) and William Beattie (1295). They both kindly sent in the full list of their ascents and I was a little surprised when I received Margaret's to find that when she accompanied William up Ladhar Bheinn on his Last One she only had four to go herself, including Ladhar Bheinn. Obviously, not Ladies first.

Michael Smyth (1313) has been fortunate to find himself absorbed into the wider family of the DMBA (Dutch Munro-Baggers Association). This is a group previously mentioned in SMCJ No. 185, 1993. Michael met them some years ago and they declared they had already attended other Final Munro celebrations and would be only too happy to join his at the 'drop of a clog'. True to their word, four members turned up including the Foreign Correspondent and Michael is now the proud owner of a pair of clogs.

Finally, I obtained news from an even more extended family when the leader of the Kinloss MRT wrote in. D. Whalley (148) has now almost compleated his fifth round and I received notifications from eight of the members (1364-1371). He is also aware of other ex-team members who are compleat and I would be very pleased to hear from any who would like to be added to the List.

Highlights:

Most who have reported have definite highlights to their round, although as we all know there can be a fine line between a long and memorable day out and an epic; with the former often imperceptibly extending into the latter. John Aird (1305) must have had a good many long days out in his round of 43 years, but one in particular was a trip to ascend Mullach na Dheiragain at the head of Loch Mullardoch. By taking advantage of accommodation at the Glen Affric Hotel, a boat was made available to his party, with the warning that the water level was low, and waterway through very narrow. Anyway, they reached the foot of the hill without incident and climbed the hill. The climb took a little longer than intended but worse was to come as the boat, while left unattended, had stuck fast into the mud. Even getting near the boat was difficult on account of the gelatinous mud, and flat stones placed in the mud for footholds simply sunk away. Eventually, by rocking the boat they managed to cast off but by then there was some doubt as to whether they would be able to find a route back through the narrows in the dark. Fortunately, a route was found and there were no uncomfortable questions asked back at the hotel. Water-borne approaches are not all epic and one couple, Gillian and John Green (1329-1330) report that they have managed to gain 35 of their hills starting from a kayak. Epics involving wading can be very unfortunate. Colin Scales (1386) recently elevated to chairman of the MBA decided to improve his credibility among the younger members by declaring belatedly his compleation in 1986. This was on Gairich which was ascended from Kinbreck Bothy and necessitated wading the Kingie to get started. Colin probably made a wise choice to later retreat to the Tomdoun Hotel where he discovered throbbing toes and blackened toe nails. Andrew Balsillie's (1340) worst day (most memorable) was rounding off a winter circuit of Beinns Bhreac, a' Chaorainn and a' Bhuird with wading the Quoich water to retrieve his bike whereupon he found he'd forgotten his cycle lamp.

The Inn Pinn can give a memorable day although Ian Brownell (1327) says it will be a few years before he repeats his somewhat nerve-wracking two hours spent on it. Ken Naismith (1358) left much to chance on his ascent of the Pinnacle, because he simply walked up to the bottom of the climb, alone, early in the morning and waited until another party arrived with the suitable gear and know how. This was really very uneventful for Ken as many years ago he was the unfortunate victim of a big avalanche described in SMCJ No. 168 1977 that hit a ski-mountaineering party. Fortunately, no lasting damage although it was 12 years before he really got back into the hills again. John Taylor (1284) recounts what almost all Munroists know to be a long day when he reached the summit of Lurg Mor at 6p.m. in December and retraced his steps to Gerry's, arriving at 11p.m.

The Final One:

Munroists' choice of final summit varies enormously. Beinn na Lap and Ben More (Mull) are still the most popular venues with Buachaille Etive Mor becoming more in vogue. One of the appeals of Beinn na Lap is obviously the train. Charles Leggat (1309) was so near, and yet so far, when he came to board the train at Rannoch. He found to his dismay that the line was at a standstill due to the North-bound sleeper breaking down between Bridge of Orchy and Rannoch. This delay meant that all other trains were held up and their only hope of ascending the hill and getting back to commitments in Glasgow that evening, was to persuade the sleeper now being pulled by a replacement locomotive to stop and let them on. As luck would have it the train did stop but a very determined guard did not want anyone boarding and did not intend to stop at Corrour. Then actions worked where 'but it's his Last Munro' had failed. Bank notes were glimpsed and claims made that the member of the party with the Australian accent had travelled all the way from Oz just for this day. It worked, and the four climbed aboard well pleased themselves. Neil Dunford (1314) was drawn to Beinn na Lap for his final session as it offered a shortish day for eight under 10-year-olds in the party of 31, and gave the facilities of the Bridge of Orchy Hotel for a celebration meal in the evening.

When Carole George (1355) was only a few hills short she resolved her choice of Last One by checking her Gaelic Guide in the Tables, to find that Sgurr a' Ghreadaidh on Skye fitted her requirements – Peak of Torment/Anxiety.

Your Companions:

There have been a few solo compleations this year including Fiona Wallace (1310) who arrived on Ben More (Mull) alone, perhaps hoping she would find another celebration going on anyway, and Alistair Maitland (1293) decided against waiting months to organise a fitting finale and ascended Carn a' Mhaim accompanied only by his can of coke. Harry Blenkinsop (1283) climbed 90% of his Munros alone but doesn't say whether he made Ben Hope as his final Munro, one of the 10% companioned hills.

Carole Strang (1352) was fortunate enough to call on the experience of Leonard Moss (250) when she began her round in 1988, and they then climbed all the subsequent hills together. Leonard has been reported before in SMCJ No. 173, 1982, as the oldest starter having begun his first round at the age of 61 and compleating at 64. His second round was started aged 72 and was compleated at 78.

Leonard has said that he would be pleased to hear from any other over-70s who started and compleated a round when over 70. I suspect there are very few. Any letters to me and I will pass them on.

The shortest round to be recorded this year goes to Clare Parnell (1362). She compleated on Ben More (Mull) with Simon Halliwell (1363) only three years after starting, and manged to write up her PhD thesis all in the same time period. She obviously felt the two projects were so complimentary that her Munro Log was reproduced in her thesis as an appendix. Simon was only slightly slower speading the pleasure over four years and still working on the thesis.

Assorted Trivia Facts:

1995 was exceptional for the number of Edinburgh-based reports – 18 Munroists.

Number of Compleations on Beinn na Lap this year was five.

Number of Compleations on Ben More (Mull) was three.

Number of Women Munroists is 205 (15%).

Assorted Comments

'Attacked by Man-eating blue bottles on Carn Mor Dearg.'

'Munros tables should be metricated, and a Munro set at 910m.'

'Corbetts are a bit of a disappointment due mainly to their lack of bulk.'

'My first Munro was Ben Nevis, when I wore cotton socks, Start-rite shoes and had some sticky dates in the pocket of my gaberdine mack.'

The Future:

Public awareness of Munros is unlikely to decline. This winter, as in previous years there have been a number of accidents resulting in us finding our activity under closer and closer scrutiny by many who do not understand the interest. I have heard recently that the Press use a walker's Munro tally as a measure of the capability of that person. Unfortunately, everyone expects a quantitative measure or benchmark and unwittingly we are providing it. Having said that, most Munroists know that it is only by being out on the Hills in all weathers and seasons that you really begin to get a feel for how to look after yourself and to make good mountaineering judgments on equipment and our own limitations, and generally the more often you are out on the Hills the better equipped you would be to read a dangerous situation.

Access will continue to be raised as an issue and the SMC would be glad to hear of any problems with access to a route previously used to get to a hill. However, we also hope that a measure of understanding on both sides will ensure that the issues do not become confrontational.

For entry to the list:

Notification of compleation and any amendments to the List should be sent to Dr C.M. Huntley, Old Medwyn, Spittal, Carnwath, Lanarkshire, ML11 8LY enclosing a SAE to ensure a reply. I am always interested in how long you have taken, the first and last hills, age, and plans for the future. In return you will receive your Munroists number and details on the purchase of a tie, or brooch.

SCOTTISH MOUNTAIN ACCIDENTS
REGIONAL DISTRIBUTION

(Geographical Divisions are those used in SMC District Guidebooks)

REGION	CASUALTIES (of which fatalities are bracketed)				INCIDENTS							Non-mountaineering	
					Actual Rescues		Other Callouts						
	Injuries	Exhaustion/Exposure Hypothermia, Hyperthermia	Illness	Total Casualties	Incidents with Casualties	Cragfast	Separated	Lost	Overdue or Benighted	False Alarms	Total Incidents	Animal Rescues	Incidents
All Regions 1993	200 (50)	16 (3)	25 (10)	241 (63)	221	20	16	13	47	7	324	5	15
Northern Highlands	16 (1)	5 –	2 (2)	23 (3)	18	2	4	1	6	3	34	1	1
Western Highlands	12 (1)	– –	2 (2)	14 (3)	11	–	1	1	3	1	17	–	1
Ben Nevis	17 (6)	6 –	2 –	25 (6)	24	7	1	1	1	–	34	–	–
Glen Coe (Inc Buachaille)	27 (5)	2 –	– –	29 (5)	28	7	–	2	4	2	43	–	–
Other Central Highlands	28 (3)	3 (1)	1 –	32 (4)	29	5	1	3	5	2	45	1	1
Cairngorms	34 (5)	4 –	6 (1)	44 (6)	42	1	3	2	8	–	56	–	2+2 not known
Southern Highlands	27 (7)	2 –	6 (2)	35 (9)	34	2	6	–	4	2	48	1	3
Skye	12 (6)	1 –	– –	13 (6)	12	1	1	–	2	–	16	–	–
Islands (other than Skye	5 (1)	1 –	– –	6 (1)	6	–	–	–	1	–	7	–	1
Southern Uplands	4 –	5 –	4 (1)	13 (1)	13	–	2	2	8	–	25	–	1+1 fire
All Regions 1993	182 (35)	29 (1)	23 (8)	234 (44)	217	25	19	12	42	10	325	3	10

TOTAL MOUNTAIN RESCUE CALL-OUTS, EXCLUDING AIRCRAFT, MARITIME AND ROAD ACCIDENTS, AND ANIMAL RESCUES.

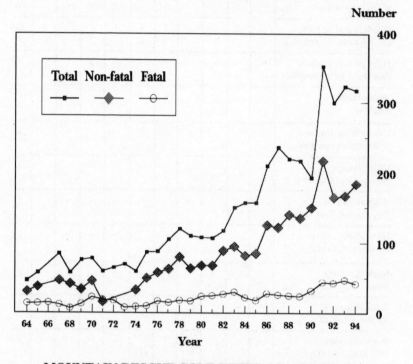

MOUNTAIN RESCUE COMMITTEE OF SCOTLAND
CONTRIBUTORY CAUSES OF SOME INJURIES
(fatalities in brackets)

The mountain injury lists exclude casualties from the following causes, although they are included in the rescue narratives:

Playing in spate burn	1 (1)
Suicide	(1)
Suicide sea cliffs	(1)
Sledged under snow bridge (near piste)	1
Illness on piste	1
Sea cliff injury (not climbing)	1
Collision on piste	1
Swimming	1
Total	8 (3)

Mountain Casualty List Summer 1994 (Fatalities bracketed)	Northern Highlands	Western Highlands	Ben Nevis	Glen Coe (inc. Buachaille)	Other Central Highlands	Cairngorms	Southern Highlands	Skye	Islands) other than Skye	Southern Uplands	Totals
Hillwalking: slip/trip/stumble	4	2 (1)	–	2	6	4	8	3 (3)	3 (1)	1	33 (5)
Hillwalking: Slip etc. known to be descending	2	4	1	6	3	4 (1)	4 (2)	1	–	1	26 (3)
Hillwalking: Rock dislodged by companion	–	–	–	–	–	–	–	3	1	–	4
Hillwalking: Rockfall	–	–	1	–	–	–	–	–	–	–	1
Hillwalking:Injured rescuing companion	–	–	–	–	–	1	–	–	–	–	1
Hillwalking Descending. Blown over	–	–	–	–	–	–	1 (1)	–	–	–	1 (1)
Hillwalking: Descending. Old injury	–	–	1	–	–	–	–	–	–	–	1
Hillwalking: River crossing, slip etc.	–	–	–	1	–	1	–	–	–	–	2
Rock climbing: Roped, slip etc.	2	–	1	1	–	3	–	–	–	–	7
Rock climbing: Roped, rockfall	–	–	–	1	–	–	–	–	–	–	1
Rock climbing: Unroped, slip etc.	–	2	–	2 (1)	1	1 (1)	–	–	–	–	4 (2)
Rock climbing: Unroped, handhold came away	–	–	–	–	–	–	–	2 (1)	–	–	2 (1)
Rock climbing: Seacliffs	–	–	–	–	–	1	–	–	1	–	2
Fell running: Slip etc.	–	–	–	–	–	–	–	–	–	2	2
Fell running: Descending, slip, etc.	–	–	1	–	–	–	–	–	–	–	1
Illness	2 (2)	2 (2)	2	–	1	5 (1)	6 (2)	–	–	4 (2)	22 (9)
Hypothermia	2	–	1	–	1 (1)	–	1	1	1	5	12 (1)

Continued on next page

Mountain Casualty List Summer 1994 (Contd.) (Fatalities bracketed)	Northern Highlands	Western Highlands	Ben Nevis	Glen Coe (inc. Buachaille)	Other Central Highlands	Cairngorms	Southern Highlands	Skye	Islands) other than Skye	Southern Uplands	Totals
Exhaustion	1	–	4	–	–	1	–	–	–	–	6
Scald: Mountain camping	–	–	–	–	1	–	–	–	–	–	1
Canoeing: Mountain river	–	–	–	–	1	–	–	–	–	–	1
Mountain biking	–	–	–	–	–	1	1	–	–	–	2
Paragliding	–	–	–	1	–	2	1	–	–	–	4
Hang gliding	–	–	–	–	–	–	1	–	–	–	1
Sea cliffs, fishing	1	–	–	–	–	–	–	–	–	–	1
Walking: Cause not known	–	–	–	–	–	–	1 (1)	–	–	–	1 (1)
Totals	14 (2)	8 (3)	12	14 (1)	14 (1)	24 (3)	24 (6)	10 (4)	6 (1)	13 (2)	139 (23)

WINTER: (Snow, ice, frozen turf underfoot. Not necessarily winter months)

	Northern Highlands	Western Highlands	Ben Nevis	Glen Coe (inc. Buachaille)	Other Central Highlands	Cairngorms	Southern Highlands	Skye	Islands) other than Skye	Southern Uplands	Totals
Hillwalking: Descending, slip etc.	1	3	9 (4)	3 (1)	3 (1)	4	6 (2)	–	–	–	29 (8)
Hillwalking: Slip, trip, stumble	1	–	–	1	2	3	–	1 (1)	–	–	8 (1)
Hillwalking: Fall through cornice	–	–	–	1	5 (2)	–	–	–	–	–	6 (2)
Hillwalking: Fall through snowbridge	–	–	–	1 (1)	–	–	–	–	–	–	1 (1)
Hillwalking: Fall through hole in snow	–	–	–	–	2	–	–	–	–	–	2
Hillwalking: Slip sitting on icy rock	–	–	–	–	–	–	1	–	–	–	1

Continued on next page

Mountain Casualty List Winter 1994 (Contd.) (Fatalities bracketed)	Northern Highlands	Western Highlands	Ben Nevis	Glen Coe (inc. Buachaille)	Other Central Highlands	Cairngorms	Southern Highlands	Skye	Islands) other than Skye	Southern Uplands	Totals
Hillwalking: Blown over	1	–	–	1	–	1	–	–	–	–	3
Hillwalking: Avalanche	1	–	–	2 (2)	–	1	–	–	–	–	4 (2)
Snow climbing: Roped, avalanche	3 (1)	3	–	–	–	–	–	–	–	–	6 (1)
Snow climbing: Roped, slip etc.	–	–	–	3	–	–	–	–	–	–	3
Snow climbing: Unroped, fall just below cornice	–	–	–	–	–	1	–	–	–	–	1
Snow climbing: Unroped, cornice failure	–	–	–	–	1	–	–	–	–	–	1
Ice climbing: Roped, slip, tools pulled	–	–	2 (2)	–	3	–	–	–	–	–	5 (2)
Ice climbing: Unroped, tools pulled	–	–	–	–	–	1	–	–	–	–	1
Mixed climbing: Roped, slips	–	–	–	1	–	2 (2)	–	–	–	–	3 (2)
Glissading without crampons	–	–	–	–	–	–	–	1	–	–	1
Glissading with crampons!	–	–	1	–	–	–	–	–	–	–	1
Hypothermia	2	–	1	2	2	2	2	–	–	–	11
Total	9 (1)	6	13 (6)	15 (4)	18 (3)	15 (2)	9 (2)	2 (1)	–	–	87 (19)
Summer/Winter totals	23 (3)	14 (3)	25 (6)	29 (5)	32 (4)	39 (5)	33 (8)	12 (5)	6 (1)	13 (2)	226 (42)

SCOTTISH MOUNTAIN ACCIDENTS 1994

Compiled by John Hinde

Rescuers are named in, or just after, the narratives, with the number of rescue person/hours at the end of each incident. Police are not usually mentioned since it is well known that they are always deeply involved – being ultimately responsible for all Scottish rescues. Any incidents mentioned which did not involve rescue services have not been entered in statistics. Some incidents included in the 'Lost' column may be actual rescues, as well as those incidents involving casualties and persons cragfast or weatherbound.

NORTHERN HIGHLANDS

JANUARY 2nd – Party of three were approaching summit Beinn a' Chlaidheimh when a 50m windslab detached and swept two down 80m. Anna Love (22) sustained fractured vertebra. Dundonnell MRT, RAF Sea King17.

JANUARY 8th to 14th – Sgurr Mor, Fannaichs. R. Fields lost his dog and heard it above him next day from the floor of the East Coire. He had fallen 80m and landed in soft snow. Searches and abseils by Dundonnell MRT on 10th and 12th failed to reach the dog, who was found safe in a natural snow kennel on 14th. Team had to climb Easter Gully, traverse to the dog and lower him 250m. HMCG helicopter involved for a training exercise. 80.

JANUARY 16th – A mountain guide soloing, with three students roped together, was climbing Trotters Gully (Grade II, north side Liathach). Snow was falling when a slab avalanche was released causing all four to fall almost the entire length of the gully. Three out of four sustained serious injuries. Woman (28) died from head and internal injuries after rescue. Guide (m40) had head injuries (no helmet), second student (m26) was hospitalised with a broken back. Third student (17) had freed himself and went for help. Torridon MRT, SARDA and RAF Sea King. 246.

JANUARY 23th – A party of three had climbed Wellington's Nose roped. Starting the descent of Fuar Tholl they were blown off a ridge. The guide (m38) dislocated a shoulder colliding with a boulder during a fall of 16m. He was able to get down aided by the others. Scottish Ambulance Service. 7.

FEBRUARY 12th to 13th – Separated from his companion on Seana Braigh, Ian Meek (29) was traced at Loch a'Choire Mhor Bothy by Police and the stalker. 15.

MARCH 19th to 20th – A local man alerted Assynt MRT about 20.00 when he saw the lights of two walkers on Sail Garbh of Quinag. It had been snowing heavily but they descended OK and had not been in trouble. 28.

APRIL 4th to 5th – Vanessa Tonczinska (42) was delayed by an old knee injury returning to the foot of Loch Glass from Ben Wyvis in snowy weather. She and John Done (51) suffered exhaustion hypothermia and were rescued by Dundonnell MRT and RAF Sea King. Three of the party had managed to walk out after midnight, but the two left behind had no maps. No torches or bivvy bags were carried and the party had been equipped with summer gear. 40.

APRIL 4th to 5th – Mark Poulter (29) and Siobhan Poulter (f27) got stuck descending from the summit of Beinn Eighe. Mark had a degree of hypothermia. They had no ice-axes, crampons or navigation gear. They had met the party of three mentioned in the next incident and had been advised to stay put. About 03.00 they were found by four members of Torridon MRT and a SARDA dog. All stayed overnight on the ridge in bivvy shelters and Mark warmed up. Airlift was impossible due to bad conditions. At first light they were roped up and helped down. 80.

APRIL 4th to 5th – In a party of three without crampons or torches, descending fairly steep névé into Coire Mhic Fhearchair of Beinn Eighe, Andrew Ferguson (27) fell 30m and broke an ankle. One went for help. Torridon MRT and SARDA had to spend the night on the hill during the rescue of the other two because of adverse weather. RAF Sea King managed to lift them by 10.30 next day. See incident above. 235.

APRIL 6th – Labour party leader John Smith (56) slipped in snow on Eididh nan Clach Geala injuring an ankle.

April 8th to 9th – Simon Kirkwood (36) did the western group of the Fannichs in mistake for the central group so he descended to Nest of Fannich instead of Fannich Lodge. Found by Dundonnell MRT, after a night search of Meall na Chrasgaig, overdue near the lodge. Dundonnell, Kinloss, SARDA. 182.

APRIL 13th – Without headtorches, John Cartwright (47) and Ben Newton (18) turned up safe at 22.30 overdue from An Teallach. Dundonnell. 14.

MAY 16th to 17th Assynt MRT called out to search for a missing woman in a rural area (Dunnet).

MAY 23rd – Thomas Thomson (70) died of coronary heart disease when he stopped to rest on a path walk between Scoraig and Badralloch. Dundonnell MRT. RAF Sea King. 17.

JUNE 1st – Nick Butterworth (33) was assisted down by other walkers after breaking an ankle on the path down An Teallach. Dundonnell. 7.

JUNE 8th – Janice Brown (60) sprained her ankle on the Shenaval Path. Helped out by Dundonnell MRT and JSMTC Dundonnell. 9.

JUNE 9th – Assynt MRT and HMCG helicopter carried out searches after seven distress flares had been set off in a dump near Lochinver. 40.

JULY 2nd – Without a helmet and unsecured to a belay, Mary Orr (22) was on top of a 10m cliff at Reiff, Coigach. She was bringing up Maxwell Bruce (26) who fell from near the top. He fell 8m and then got 'locked on' but he had dragged Orr down with him. She collided with him, breaking her fall somewhat, but then fell the remaining 2m to the bottom with concussion and cuts. Bruce had a sore back. Kinloss MRT and Inverness Air Ambulance. 10.

JULY 4th – Burn fishing on Meallan Ghobhar, Kinlochewe, Asa Wallen (f22) slipped on grass and broke an ankle. Torridon MRT. 8.

JULY 15th – Separated in mist on Cona Mheall summit, his wife got down first and raised the alarm when David Park (39) was overdue. He walked out as Dundonnell MRT and RAF helicopter were en route. 14.

JULY 20th – Gob a'Gheoda, just north of Loch Ewe. Francis Russell (m48) slipped on wet rocks when fishing below sea cliffs, breaking an ankle. Dundonnell MRT. 30.

JULY 22nd – Well equipped and with five other women at the summit of Sgurr nan Each, Fannichs, Agnes Morrison (50) slipped on rock, breaking tibia and fibula at an ankle. RAF Sea King and Dundonnell MRT. 12.

JULY 26th – Three walkers aborted their ascent of An Teallach due to mist. Descending grass on the lower slopes of Glas Mheall Liath, Hayley Clarke (f26) slipped and injured her knee. Rescue by RAF helicopter. Dundonnell MRT alerted. 11.

AUGUST 10th – Assynt MRT alerted for an old man reported to have broken his leg. In fact, he had broken his glasses and walked out unaided from near Inverkirkaig. 3.

AUGUST 19th to 21st – Searches by Assynt MRT and RAF Sea King for a mixed group of four (aged 15 to 17) who strayed off route on an award hike. They had not identified an indistinct path junction. Kinloss team stood down en route to incident. Loch Choire, Sutherland. 140.

SEPTEMBER 3rd – Twelve cadets and four ATC officers were contouring a wet rock/grass slope on the north-facing aspect of Stuc Loch na Cabhaig (Torridon Beinn Dearg) when Karen Murray (15) slipped and fell 30m cutting her head. She was able to walk with aid till met by Torridon MRT 1.5km from the road. 35.

SEPTEMBER 3rd – Carn nan Conbhairean of Ben More Assynt. Ann MacLeod (37) was exhausted, but managed to walk down aided by six companions (three had gone for help) as Assynt MRT and RAF Sea King arrived. 33.

OCTOBER 3rd – Richard Carlsberg (57) a member of a grouse-shooting party of five died from a heart attack on Bidein Clann Raonaild (466m) a hill 4km west of the head of Loch a'Chroisg, Achnasheen. Recovery by Torridon MRT, SARDA and RAF Sea King. 63.

OCTOBER 10th – Collecting water samples in small hill lochs 3km west of Beinn Eighe summit, Bert Paquin (29) failed to make a rendezvous with a colleague. He did not have a watch and walked back to Coire Dubh in darkness. Torridon MRT, SARDA, RAF Sea King. 66.

OCTOBER 16th – Separated from a companion near the summit of Sgurr Mor (Fannich) Peter Baikie (27) had no navigation gear. He mistook Loch Fannich for Loch Glascarnoch and walked to the road at Lochluicart. Dundonnell MRT and RAF Sea King. 14 .

NOVEMBER 1st to 2nd – Separated in mist on Conival summit (Ben More Assynt) James Herd (48) went down the wrong side despite having a map and compass. He walked out to Kylestrom at low level, rather than climb back up through the mist at night. Found 16km from last known position. Assynt and Kinloss MRTs, SARDA, RAF Sea King. 282.

NOVEMBER 18th to19th – Leaving at 14.30 and going to the top of Slioch from Kinlochewe, William Tate (49) and Geoffrey Telford (40) were benighted. Rescuers were alerted because they failed to make a promised VHF radio contact – their battery was defective. In poor weather they got themselves down by 00.40. Torridon MRT. 20.

NOVEMBER 27th to 28 – Michael Burke (45) and Linda Kimmey (38) suffered hypothermia trying to descend Spidean a'Choire Leith, Liathach. Lost in mist and gale winds they got cragfast above steep cliffs and used bivvy bags. RAF Sea King spotted them on the SW shoulder and winched them off next morning. Torridon, Dundonnell and Kinloss MRTs. 164.

DECEMBER 21st to 22nd – Kinloss team called out to search for a woman missing overnight at Munlochy, Black Isle. found by Police. 45.

DECEMBER 26th to 27th – Stuc a' Choire Dhuibh Bhig, Liathach. Martin Richardson (37) and Andrew Davies (21) got benighted and unable to descend. Found by Torridon MRT. Recovered by RAF Sea King. 50.

WESTERN HIGHLANDS

JANUARY 4th to 5th – Night search by Kintail MRT for three people lost on Carn Loch nan Eun (594m) a rocky peak above Glen Elchaig. Paul Ryder (36), Robert King (34) and Nicola Hibbert (30) had lost their map but carried on. A light on the hill had been spotted and they were found by SARDA dog. Self evacuation. Helicopter involved. 44.

FEBRUARY 16th – Descending Druim Coire a'Bheithe (a shoulder of Sgurr Thuilm, Glenfinnan) Eric Murphy (43) slipped and broke an ankle. Lochaber MRT and RAF Sea King. 34.

FEBRUARY 23rd – Wearing crampons, Steven Cuthill (31) slipped on ice, collided with a rock and fractured a femur. Creag nan Damh (918m), South Cluanie Ridge. Kintail MRT and RAF Sea King. 44.

APRIL 4th to 5th – A party of five were avalanched by a cornice collapse on the NE Face of Sgurr an Lochain (1004m) South Cluanie Ridge. Guide (m40) and one student (m27) had leg injuries. Kenneth Stewart (51) was also injured, but he and two women (both 29) were able to get out themselves. The casualties were night-stretchered by Kintail and Glenelg teams in appalling conditions. Helicopters were unable to operate. 282+.

MAY 17th to 18th – Solo hillwalking, Kevin McCubbin (34) slipped descending snow on NE Ridge, Sgurr na Lapaich, Glen Strathfarrar. Wearing crampons he fell an unknown distance, with head, ankle and knee injuries. Dundonnell and Kinloss MRTs, SARDA, RAF Sea King. 67.

MAY 19th to 20th – Neil MacKinnon (73) was overdue on hills near Fort Augustus. He got confused when following an injured lamb, but found his way to the A82. Kinloss and Dundonnell MRTs, SARDA, RAF Sea King. 191.

MAY 20th – Going ahead of his two companions up Forcan Ridge of the Saddle, John Clayton (69) was seen to lose his balance when scrambling on hands and knees up a rock arete. He was killed after falling 25m down vertical rock, then another 180m down a hard snow gully, striking a large rock near the bottom. Kintail and RAF Sea King. 42.

MAY 29th – The body of solo walker Patrick Raison (60) was found by other walkers on the north shore of Loch Hourn (near Eilean a' Garb-lain opposite Barrisdale). He had died of coronary heart disease. Stretcher recovery to boat by Glenelg MRT. Kintail team alerted. 61.

JUNE 7th – During a solo descent of Sgurr a'Bhealaich Dheirg (Loch Cluanie) D.H. (32) slipped on wet grass and injured an arm. He also suffered breathlessness due to a heart condition. Helped down by other walkers. Kintail MRT. 6.

JUNE 17th to 19th – Party of six schoolgirls (all 15) in the charge of a male leader were overdue in reaching their rendezvous at Dorusduain, Strath Croe (Loch Duich) after walking from Glen Cannich. They were found by rescuers, during spate conditions, near Camban Bothy. The main cause of the call-out was that their route was changed by the leader and no-one knew about it. Dundonnell and Kintail MRTs, SARDA. 147.

JULY 17 – Liz Bondi (39) broke leg in a slip on dry scree in the northern coire of Beinn Tharsuinn, Achnashellach (863m, near Bhearnais Bothy). Evacuated by RAF Sea King. Kintail MRT. 17.

JULY 17th – On The Saddle, man (19) stopped and took off his rucksack. It fell down. Trying to retrieve it he slipped on dry grass and fell 15m. Among other bruises he got head injuries and was unconscious for 20min. He tried to walk out but got dizzy. Stretchered by Kintail MRT from Allt a' Coire Uaine. 33.

AUGUST 1st – Rescuers were called out by a walker who thought he saw a body in the coire west of Mullach Fraoch Coire. He could not get down to it. The team found an abandoned survival bag: owner please contact Kintail MRT. 26.

AUGUST 3rd to 4th – Walking out from Sgurr Mor (Glen Kingie) in wind and rain, Alan Peacock (63) became separated from his companion at 16.00, halfway to Glendessarry (Loch Arkaig). Peacock was reported missing, and made a navigation error, walking out to Tomdoun Hotel (Glen Garry) at 10.30 next day. Lochaber MRT, RAF Sea King. 202.

AUGUST 30th to 31th – Kinloss MRT, SARDA and RAF Sea King searched Glen Moriston for a missing male (30) who had made a despairing telephone call. He was found safe by Police next day on the Tomich to Cougie track. 190.

SEPTEMBER 25th – Set out at 15.30 to climb Beinn Sgritheall, two men got benighted without lights. Both fell over a rock and sustained injuries. Found by Glenelg team leader two miles from their car. 1.

OCTOBER 31st – Stalking near Wester Glenquoich Burn (4km NW of Altbeithe, Loch Quoich) Peter Brown (50) having previously complained of chest pains, died of a heart attack. Evacuated by quad. ATV and trailer. 2.

BEN NEVIS

JANUARY 11th to 12th – Because of severe weather, four male students (18-26) were advised not to leave the summit refuge until Lochaber MRT arrived. There was no search/rescue and they were guided down for their safety. 18+.

JANUARY 11th to 12th – Lost in a blizzard and white-out 300m below the summit which they were attempting by the track, Geoffrey Attwood (41) and Ann Frankum (35) had their map blown away. They descended till dark, then snowholed. Walked into Coire Eoghainn where they were found uninjured by Lochaber MRT and guided down. 63.

JANUARY 14th to 15th – David Little (44) who suffered slight hypothermia and Stephen Jones (31) were benighted at Tower Gap. Airlift RAF Sea King. 24.

JANUARY 22nd to 23rd – Four men glissaded (sitting) Ledge Gully after climbing The Curtain. Wilfred Preston (52) was still wearing crampons, one of which caught in ice which twisted and injured an ankle. Dragged to CIC Hut then stretchered by Lochaber MRT next day to airlift by RAF Sea King. 35.

FEBRUARY 6th – Descending track without crampons or ice-axe, Katrin Bahr (18) tried to stop a slide using her hands, sustaining cut and frostbitten fingers. Helped down by passer-by. Police. 3.

FEBRUARY 12th – Descending to Halfway Lochan from the top of Castle Ridge, Michael Cottam (24), using crampons, slipped and fractured an ankle on rocks. AM Ski Patrol, Lochaber MRT, RN Sea King. 32.

FEBRUARY 16th – Benighted, cold and cragfast at Tower Gap, Sean Turner (25) with mild hypothermia, and John Rothwell (24) were winched before midnight by RAF Sea King. 8.

FEBRUARY 19th to 20th – Nigel Walton (34) and Michael Stork (32) were both killed in a fall from Minus One Gully. Lochaber MRT, RN Sea King. 48.

FEBRUARY 19th to 20th – With a companion, and two that they met, Richard Gordon-Head (33) slipped descending steep snow breaking a leg. They thought they were in Red Burn, but it was Five Finger Gully. Stretcher carry by Lochaber MRT and airlift by RAF. 204.

FEBRUARY 22nd to 23rd – Party of two attempting to descend the track in a whiteout. At 16.00 Kevin Mulroy (29) strayed into Five Finger Gully and was killed by a long fall. His body was recovered on February 23rd by Kinloss and Lochaber MRTs and RAF Sea King. 138.

FEBRUARY 22nd – About 16.00 two walkers attempting to descend the track were sitting lost above Five Finger Gully. About 16.15 visibility improved and one went towards the track. Preparing to follow, Brian Boot (46) slipped and was killed by a fall. Recovery by Lochaber MRT and RAF Sea King. 112.

FEBRUARY 25th to 26th – Late on February 25th, after climbing Orion Direct to the summit refuge, George Gibson (40) attempted to descend the track with a companion. He got above Five Finger Gully and slipped. Fatal. Lochaber MRT, RAF Sea King. 107.

MARCH 3rd to 4th – Poorly equipped with only one torch, light boots, no ice-axes or crampons, three Belgian men (24, 27, 31) tried to go down the track in poor weather from the summit refuge. The 27-year-old was navigating with the one map and compass, but he got separated and was lucky to descend to Steall car park near the Waterslide of Coire Eoghainn. The other two were also lucky to get back to the refuge, whence they were guided down next day by Lochaber MRT. SARDA and RAF Sea King also involved. 255.

MARCH 17th to 19th – Geraldine Westrupp (41) leading William Gorman (38) tried to get him to the Great Tower. However, they had commenced the Eastern Traverse too early. He could not follow so she descended to him and requested rope and jumars by mobile phone. Rescue by RN Sea King was delayed because the wrong couple were contacted who did not need help. Further phoning resulted in rescue by RAF Wessex. Lochaber MRT. 474.

MARCH 19th to 20th – Three men reported overdue on Tower Ridge radioed from CIC Hut at 04.05 on 20th that they were OK.

APRIL ? – A pair were in trouble on the Great Tower, and later, when trying to navigate off the plateau, got guiding instructions by mobile phone from Fort William. Not classed as an incident.

MAY 8th – On slopes of Carn Dearg NW. John Bryde (38) fell 100m descending in crampons, breaking a leg. RAF Sea King. Lochaber MRT. 19.

MAY 16th to 17th – Lawrence Sands (20) separated from his three companions by going ahead on Carn Mor Dearg Arete. They reported him overdue, last seen at Abseil Posts. He was found by a ground party, lost and cold, on the Waterslide of Coire Eoghainn. Lochaber MRT, RN Sea King. 120.

JUNE 12th – Top-roping at Poll Dubh, Alexander MacMillan (23) received arm injuries and general bruising from a fall of 9m. A belay had failed and he landed on grass in a rock cleft and was not badly injured. Stetcher lowered by Lochaber MRT. 17.

JUNE 25th to 26th – A male walker on Ben Nevis got left behind by his group when he got cramp. An early morning message said he got down OK.

JULY 2nd – Without crampons or ice-axe, Robert Hammond (45) was in a group of four descending the track at 760m when he slipped on névé and fell head first for 18m. He sustained a neck strain and a deep leg cut. Stretchered by Lochaber MRT. 46.

JULY 2nd to 3rd – Peter Ward (41) was overdue on track. Solo, he wore inadequate boots (Doc Martens soles). His body was found by Lochaber MRT searching in a gully of Upper Coire Eoghainn below a snowfield. He had no ice-axe, crampons, helmet. spare clothing or navigation gear. Evacuated by RAF helicopter. 110.

JULY 19th – Charles Elias, having taken 10 hours to get up the track was exhausted descending. Escorted from Halfway Lochan by Lochaber MRT.

JULY 29th – At 950m when descending the track, Conni Wilczopolski (f59) slipped and sustained a bad ankle fracture. Lochaber MRT and RAF Sea King. 51.

AUGUST 3rd – At 250m when descending the track, Sandra Prowse (45) took ill. Stretchered to hospital by Lochaber MRT and released after treatment. 34.

AUGUST 4th – A rock rolled on to his foot and fractured his ankle when Colin Hendry (30) was in Observatory Gully. He used a hand-held radio to summon help (Lochaber MRT and RN Sea King) 92.

AUGUST 4th to 5th – Descending the track on a charity walk woman (22) who had a history of knee problems, suffered a dislocation at Halfway Lochan. Night evacuation by Lochaber and RN Sea King. 120.

AUGUST 7th – Lochaber MRT and RAF Sea King were called out to the summit for a hypothermia case. In fact, woman (41) had gastro-enteritis and was detained in Belford Hospital. 52.

SEPTEMBER 3rd – Runner in Nevis Race, Kevin Rogan (37) slipped when descending suffering minor injuries and mild hypothermia. Stretchered from 1220m. to Halfway Lochan, then airlifted by RAF Sea King. Kinloss and Lochaber MRTs. 26.

SEPTEMBER 3rd – Colin Ross (25) suffered exhaustion hypothermia in Nevis Race. Lochaber MRT and RAF Sea King. 22.

SEPTEMBER 17th – Ann Murphy (29) and Alison McLure (28) were climbing Tower Ridge when their rope jammed under a boulder at Tower Gap. They tried to free it for an hour then called for help. Winched off by RAF Sea King. Lochaber MRT. 44.

SEPTEMBER 25th – John Vickers (53) got exhausted at the first aluminium bridge when ascending the track. Aided down by Lochaber team member. 3.

OCTOBER 16th to 17th – Starting at noon on an ascent of Tower Ridge with no ice-axes or crampons, William Kay (33), George Kay (31) and Thomas Ness (30) were delayed by other groups and a heavy fall of snow which quickly froze. They failed to reach the top and descended to Tower Scoop where they stayed overnight. Next morning in Tower Gully two could go down no farther (because of the amount of snow and lack of gear, according to the report) though one got to the CIC Hut for help. Winched out by RAF Sea King. Lochaber MRT. 56.

NOVEMBER 20th – Descending the track with a companion, Gordon Yates (58) got sore ankles and exhaustion at 350m altitude. Escorted down by two Lochaber MRT members. 4.

DECEMBER 27th – Peter Ibberson (30), Richard Moss (26) and John Carmichael (22) left CIC Hut at 09.30 for Tower Ridge. Delayed by unconsolidated windslab they got benighted a pitch below the Eastern Traverse and flashed distress signals. Lifted by RAF Sea King at 20.00 they were released from Belford Hospital after a brief check for hypothermia. Lochaber MRT. 58.

GLEN COE
(Including Buachaille Etive Mor)

JANUARY 1st – On Bidean nam Bian, John Barr (34) walked through a cornice and fell 10m towards the Lost Valley, suffering concussion for three or four minutes. Found by companions who helped him down while one went for help. Met by Glencoe MRT near road. 41.

JANUARY 1st to 2nd – Two women and one man traversing Aonach Eagach east to west got benighted and cragfast due to poor weather and one woman being unfit. Flashed torches alerted Glencoe MRT who roped them off. 10.

JANUARY 2nd – Roped, Katherine Schirrmacher (19) was seconding Crowberry Ridge, Buachaille Etive Mor, by Naismith's Route. She slipped and fell a metre or two on a rock slab, twisting her knee when a crampon caught. She was lowered to easier ground, but then the party of four were subjected to a windslab avalanche (Avalanche Danger 3 Medium Risk). Helped by the rope they managed to hang on. One man was buried but dug out uninjured. Schirrmacher was lowered to the foot of Curved Ridge where Glencoe MRT found them. RAF Sea King. 88.

JANUARY 2nd – False alarm. During the Crowberry Ridge incident a light was seen on North Buttress which did not move for over an hour. Two Glencoe MRT members went up but could not get close because of avalanche danger. Rescue 137 helicopter had to give up a close approach due to mist. Then a man walked into base and said he had dropped his headtorch on North Buttress. 10.

JANUARY 2nd to 3rd – Alison Bull and Matthew Kinsey (both 22) could not find way off Sgurr nam Fiannaidh after traversing Aonach Eagach, so they snow-holed for the night. A search that night by RAF Sea King failed, but another air search next morning found them. Glencoe, Kinloss, Leuchars and Stafford MRTs SARDA. 445.

JANUARY 3rd to 4th – A man and woman bivouacked near the summit of Buachaille Etive Mor after climbing West Route on North Buttress. It was dark and misty when they finished but they spent the night in a good snow cave. Walking off next day, rescuers told them there was an avalanche risk (4) and they would have to be airlifted. The pair were not happy but thought it was a *fait accompli* so they were flown off, reluctantly. Glencoe, Leuchars and Stafford MRTs, RAF Sea King. 232.

JANUARY 23rd to 24th – Separating from a group of eight near the summit of Stob Dubh, Buachaille Etive Beag in very severe winds, Andrea Welz (24), intended to go an easier way and meet the others lower down. Her body, with multiple injuries and without crampons, was found by a SARDA dog about 200m below the summit, on a SE rock and scree slope. She may have slipped or been blown over. Glencoe and Leuchars MRTs, RAF Sea King helicopters. 695.

JANUARY 23rd to 24th – With four companions David McCulloch (39) was descending near the summit of Sgor na h-Ulaidh in severe winds. He was blown down the SE face, fracturing a femur, but his friends thought he was blown down the NW side. Glencoe MRT and SARDA spent more than seven hours that night searching the NW face, but he was not found till next day. Airlift by RAF Sea King. 159.

JANUARY 29th – Near the foot of Curved Ridge, Buachaille Etive Mor, Richard Gleed (21) fell through a snow-bridge down a waterfall, into a gap between snow and rock. Uninjured in the fall, he was in water 3m down. His companion tried his best to haul him out but failed, having to leave him tied off to a dead-man belay plate. When Glencoe MRT reached him he had been swept farther down, and had to be dug and hauled out from under the snow, probably drowned although death from hypothermia was not ruled out. RAF Sea King could not get in due to high winds. 55.

FEBRUARY 3rd – Two men walking to the foot of Crowberry Ridge, Buachaille Etive Mor were hit by a soft windslab avalanche (High Risk 4 that day). One was caught by the edge of the slide and stopped by using his ice-axe. William Murphy (25) was swept down over two rock buttresses by the full force. He was dead from head injuries on the surface of the snow. The slab had started as a channelled avalanche but was open slope when it hit the men. Lower and stretcher carry by Glencoe MRT and SARDA. RAF Sea King returned to base when death was confirmed. 48.

FEBRUARY 10th – Man (26) was traversing Aonach Eagach east to west with a companion, but they descended the south side of Stob Coire Leith. Victim fell 7m and was unconscious from a head injury. He subsequently rolled down another 50m and he is now only slowly recovering. Glencoe MRT, RN Sea King. 59.

FEBRUARY 21st to 22nd – RAF Sea King found Ian Johnstone (33) and Neil Thomson (32) who were reported overdue on Shelf Route, Crowberry Ridge, Buachaille Etive Mor. They had snow-holed for the night and elected to finish the climb. Glencoe MRT. 35.

FEBRUARY 27th – Going down a rough track to a bothy at Allt-na-Reigh in the dark, Tracy Anne Clarke (22) slipped on a snow-covered rock breaking an ankle. Rescue by Glencoe MRT involved a stretcher hoist up a face beside a long ladder in the gorge. 22.

FEBRUARY 27th – Avalanche risk for the day was High Risk 4. Dimitris Andrikopoulos and Zacharias Xypolias (both 24) did a climb on Buachaille Etive Mor and were descending Coire na Tulaich in the dark, roped. At 550m altitude they triggered a windslab avalanche with a crown wall measuring 1m deep and 400m across. They were swept down 150m burying Dimitri head down. Zacharias was buried up to his neck, so that it took him 10 min. to free himself and a further 10 min. to dig out Dimitri who was dead. Glencoe MRT stretcher carry. 44.

MARCH 5th to 6th – David Langrish (29) was abseiling off Pitch 4 of Raven's Gully, Buachaille Etive Mor, in deteriorating conditions when a peg pulled causing the rope to fall down, leaving him cragfast. His companion abseiled from 16m lower down and alerted rescuers who could not recover him that night. He was rescued next day using a rope from top to bottom of Raven's Gully. Glencoe MRT, RN Sea King. 183.

MAY 2nd to 3rd – Traversing Aonach Eagach east to west, Shona Green (32) and her companion slid 12m down the north side of Meall Dearg. Hamilton was uninjured. After eight hours, he went to get help for Shona who was cut and cragfast. He went back over the ridge and got benighted going down the steeper south side. Glencoe MRT and RN Sea King. 90.

MAY 28th – While paragliding, Kenneth MacKenzie (31) crash landed on rock and scree on the Lost Valley slopes of Stob Coire nan Lochan. He walked off the hill with cuts and bruises, but a hillwalker witness thought he had been seriously injured. Glencoe team and RN Sea King alerted. 11.

MAY 28th to 29th – Descending from Sgor nam Fiannaidh after a traverse of Aonach Eagach, Ronald Neil (43) got separated from three companions who went down without him, not realising he was having problems. He slipped on scree causing a slight arm injury, then got cragfast. Guided down by Glencoe MRT. 40.

JUNE 28th – Going down one of the steeper parts of the Lost Valley path, Gertude Spalinger (73) slipped on rock and scree injuring her head. Met by Glencoe MRT and walked down to base. 6.

JULY 17th – Leading The Gut on East Face of Aonach Dubh, man (46) slipped. Some runners pulled out so he fell 25m with severe leg, chest and abdomen injuries. Rescued by Glencoe team setting up a stretcher cableway down the cliff for RN Sea King lift. 52.

JULY 19th – Children (accompanied by adults) shouted in Lost Valley to hear their cries echoed from the rock walls. A couple thought the shouts were distress signals and raised a false alarm. GMRT. 4.

JULY 23rd – Whortleberry Wall on Rannoch Wall of Buachaille Etive More. Mark Litterick (30) had just untied from his belay and was about to lead on when the large ledge he was standing on collapsed. His companion was belayed far to one side, so Mark swung for 16m, sustaining a bad knee injury. His belayer, with other climbers, lowered him down to Glencoe MRT. Airlift by RAF Sea King. 50.

July 24th – Descending solo the East Face of Bidean nam Bian, Thomas Reid (40) slipped on a wet, rocky path, breaking an ankle. Stretchered to below cloud base by GMRT for RAF airlift. 68.

July 27th – Three Dutchmen descended from the summit of Buachaille Etive Mor and went down Curved Ridge, thinking they had seen a path. The route was too difficult for them so that Paul Bertelcamp and Dolf von Voskuilen (both 29) became cragfast (Paul having a slight hand injury). The third went to call out Glencoe MRT. The two cragfast were lowered to the foot of the crag then walked off unaided. 42.

July 31st – Party of three traversing Aonach Eagach east to west descended prematurely. Girl (18) slipped on a steep scree/heather slope with serious spine and pelvic injuries. Glencoe MRT. RAF Sea King. 49.

July 31st to August 2nd – Technical searches of climbing faces of Buachaille Etive Mor in poor visibility resulted in the discovery of the body of solo climber Gordon Sutherland (55) in Crowberry Gully. He was thought to have slipped from North Buttress, or possibly Crowberry Ridge, and fallen about 200m. No route plan had been left so the searches were extensive. Weather had been good till evening on July 31st, but turned to heavy rain and low mist. Glencoe, Kinloss, Leuchars MRTs, SARDA, RAF and RN Sea Kings. 1963.

August 12th to 13th – Steven Blakemore (23) separated from a TA training group of five on Stob na Broige, Buachaille Etive Mor. He was seen running fast down a slope above the Dalness Chasm. Glencoe MRT searched from 21.00 hours but Steven had no torch and was hard to find in the maze of gullies. He was found between the two central forks. He had taken a fall, hitting his head and was unconscious for a time. He was also cragfast. It took the team a few hours to get to him. He was roped and hoisted vertically to a large ledge. It was too dangerous to go on, so everyone waited for an RAF Sea King to winch them out. 92.

August 15th – Descending north from Beinn Fhada two women got separated near a large gully. Cheryl Peppard (27) dropped her rucksack down a 100m crag and tried to climb down to it. She failed and climbed back up to a large ledge where she got cragfast, shouting to her friend to get help. Glencoe MRT lowered her down some vertical cracks, then walked her down the large gully. 60.

August 16th – Descending west from Sgor na h-Ulaidh summit, Michael Burchell (23) had a short slip down a slab. To stop he put out his hand, dislocating a shoulder. Mist prevented RAF Sea King reaching him. Glencoe MRT reduced the dislocation under Entonox, the use of which necessitated a stretcher carry to below the cloudbase for an airlift. 59.

August 21st – River-crossing injury. Crossing Allt Lairig Eilde by jumping between rocks, man (27) slipped wearing training shoes, suffering a serious, but closed, leg fracture. Entonox, splinting and stretcher carry by Glencoe MRT. 25.

August 28th – A 41-year-old man was found in a dazed, hypothermic state on Aonach Eagach by three other walkers. He was poorly clad and thought he was walking from Kingshouse to Clachaig by the West Highland Way. The weather was very cold with gusty winds near gale force and sleet. A very difficult rescue followed for Glencoe MRT. He weighed more than 100kg. He was stretchered east along the ridge, then lowered north to below cloud for winching by RN Sea King. 171.

August 28th to 29th – John Fiddes (48), one of the three walkers who found the dazed man in the above rescue, stayed with the casualty till the rescue, then did not go down with the team. He walked east to Am Bodach, descended too early and got cragfast on the loose south face. Mildly hypothermic, his torch flashes were seen from rescue base. Two team members hoisted him to a large ledge from which they were winched by Rescue 177. (Same helicopter from HMS Gannet). 60.

SEPTEMBER 6th – Glencoe MRT went up Aonach Eagach to rescue Jonathon Miller (24) cragfast on the Pinnacles, but he got down on the north side. 54.

SEPTEMBER 23rd – In a party of four traversing Aonach Eagach east to west, Elizabeth Blake (53) slipped at The Pinnacles, fracturing two ribs. Glencoe MRT prepared her for winching by RAF Sea King. 58.

OCTOBER 9th – Descending the lower slopes of Buachaille Etive Beag into Lairig Eilde, Margaret Anderson (57) slipped on mud. A twisting fall broke her ankle. Companions helped her to walk but it became too painful. Rescued by Glencoe MRT with stretcher and vacuum splint. 24.

OCTOBER 19th to 20th – Lost in mist on Curved Ridge, Buachaille Etive Mor, Douglas Melvin (38) and John Alexander (32) went down near Central Buttress. Abseiling in Waterslide Gully their rope jammed and they got cragfast. Glencoe MRT were alerted by torch flashes and roped them off. 45.

OCTOBER 25th – One of a group of 30 traversing Aonach Eagach east to west, man (30) was seen to slip on wet rock at Stob Coire Leith, falling about 75m on the Glencoe side. Unfortunately, his helmet was strapped on his rucksack so he sustained severe head injuries among others. Glencoe MRT used oxygen, vaccum mat, nasal airway and suction and he was lifted by RAF Sea King to Belford Hospital, then Southern General, Glasgow. He stopped breathing during flight but was revived. 68.

OCTOBER 27th to 28th – Lost in mist and falling snow during a walk from the Lost Valley over Stob Coire nan Lochan to Achnambeithach, George West-Robinson (44) and his two children, Ruth (17) and Owen (14) were found by Glencoe MRT on scree in Upper Coire nam Beith, and guided down at 03.30. They were OK and their headtorches had been seen. 97.

DECEMBER 27th – Paul Barlow (43), Georgina Neville (23) and Nigel Callaghan (22) got cragfast in Crowberry Gully. Snow and ice thinned so that they could not continue. Unable to descend they flashed SOS and were winched off by RAF Sea King. Glencoe MRT. 41.

DECEMBER 27th – At the same time as the above incident a pair of men were stationary on North Buttress of the same mountain. They were also winched off. On reaching base they said they did not want to be rescued and were flashing their torches to say they were OK. The time was 22.00.

DECEMBER 28th – Man (32) slipped climbing the basin below Crowberry Gully. He fell 16m and received back and leg injuries (also head injuries despite wearing a helmet) Winched by RAF Sea King. Glencoe MRT. 64.

DECEMBER 28th – Conveying the above casualty to hospital, Rescue 137 spotted torch flashes in Coire Gabhail and reported them. Robert Staynes (26) had separated from his companion because of burns in spate. When Glencoe team reached him he had crossed but his torch battery had expired. He was escorted down. 6.

DECEMBER 29th – Man (45) was severely injured (head injuries – no helmet) when he fell from the final pitch of NC Gully, Stob Coire nan Lochan. He hit his second, William Canning (27) and dislodged him who also fell and was slightly injured. Rescue by Glencoe MRT and airlift by RAF Sea King in poor weather. 86.

OTHER CENTRAL HIGHLANDS

There have been too many instances this year of people walking through snow cornices, particularly on Beinn a' Chaorainn. Some of the incidents may have ocurred trying to get from the South Top (1050m. GR: NN385845) to the summit named Beinn a' Chaorainn on some 1:50,000 maps, and listed as a separate mountain in some Munro's Tables as Beinn a' Chaoruinn (Centre Top) (1053m. GR: 386851). The curve of the cornice does not look too pronounced in the plan view (map). Have people been trying to go between the tops on a straight line bearing? The danger is obviously insidious judging from the number and experience of people who have fallen through in the last few years. I have used the place a lot for teaching navigation but always rope parties up in white-outs. On the latest Landranger map the Centre Top is given a height of 1049m – but the cartographer has made an error and surrounded the 1049m spot height with a ring contour of 1050m. The Ordnance Survey have assured me that 1049m is the correct height and that the ring contour will be deleted in reprints. The point of all this, in my opinion, is that the Centre Top is no longer the Munro. The South Top is 1m higher, and much easier to find in poor visibility, so perhaps the number of fallers can be reduced. *Mountainmaster* 1:25,000 Map shows Ski Tow D to be 114m north of its actual position. See March 25th and April 5th incidents. Maps are now revised, but old ones are still in use.

JANUARY 1st – Man (27) walked through the summit cornice of Aonach Beag (1236m) in mist fell 300m sustaining serious skull and facial injuries. Lochaber MRT and RAF Sea King were alerted by his two companions. 60.

JANUARY 3rd to 4th – Leuchars and Strathclyde MRTs alerted for an overdue climber who made his own way down. Bridge of Orchy. 10.

JANUARY 8th to 9th – Robert Anderson (36) was found in a snow-hole at 1000m just down the south side of Meall a' Bhuiridh. Piste skiing, he had got lost in mist and wandered about before digging in, wearing ski gear. He was OK but with mild hypothermia. Found by White Corries Ski Patrol. Night searches by Glencoe, Kinloss and Leuchars MRTs, SARDA, RAF Sea King. 795.

JANUARY 22th to AUGUST 27th – Several thousand person-hours were used in searching for the body of Christopher Mitchell (45) who was seen by his son to walk through a cornice on Beinn a' Chaorainn. It was found under névé using a radar device about August 27th. Kinloss, Leuchars, Lochaber, Glencoe MRTs, RAF Sea Kings, SARDA.

FEBRUARY 12th to 13th – Cutting across to avoid cornices and ice bulges on Right Twin and Siamese Buttress (both Grade II) on Aonach Mor, Peter Knox (39) slipped and fell 120m, breaking a tibia and fibula. He also dragged off his second, who fell 60m then went to alert rescuers. Lochaber MRT and RN Sea King. 128.

FEBRUARY 13th – Aonach Mor (SE of summit). Climbing unroped with a companion, Michael Green (27) fell 18m when a cornice he was scaling broke away under him. Ice-axe injuries. Assisted down by Lochaber MRT. 6.

FEBRUARY 13th – With three others, Jonathon Merchant (23) was descending Sgurr a' Mhaim into Coire a' Mhail, Glen Nevis. He tripped on crampons, breaking a tibia and fibula. Carried out by Lochaber MRT. 114.

FEBRUARY 16th to 17th – Bernadette Kerby (29) and Claire Hayes (21) were benighted on the north ridge of Sgorr Dhearg, Ballachulish Horseshoe. They bivouacked and were found by Glencoe MRT next day. Airlifted by RN Sea King. 97.

FEBRUARY 18th to 19th – Staghorn Gully, South Pipe, Creag Meagaidh (Grade IV). Lorraine Parkinson (22) was cragfast and left in a cave belay by her lead climber, who went for help. Lowered overnight by Cairngorm MRT, cold but uninjured. 144.

FEBRUARY 19th – Nicholas Wood (29) leading last pitch of Centre Post, Creag Meagaidh, fell when his tools and crampons did not hold in unconsolidated snow. He pulled Andrew Perkins (38) off his belay and both fell into Easy Gully without serious injuries. Wood was helped down by people in Easy Gully. Perkins was airlifted by RAF Sea King. Cairngorm MRT on standby. 9.

FEBRUARY 19th – Graeme Cornwallis (31) caught his foot in ice in Upper Glen Nevis, fracturing his ankle, 3km. east of Steall Cottage. Lochaber MRT, RAF Sea King. 92.

FEBRUARY 19th – During the above rescue, Lochaber MRT found Ian Currie (48) in Steall Meadow with foot and rib injuries. He was helped to hospital by climbing companions. 5.

FEBRUARY 28th – Harry Windle fell through a cornice when descending from the summit of A' Mharconaich, Drumochter, and was separated from his companion. He ice-axe braked after falling 60m but his friend had initiated rescue alerts. These were cancelled when Windle walked in tired but uninjured.

MARCH 14th to 15th – A compound incident. Andrew Latham (38) and Andrew Dean (27) went down the wrong coire off Am Bodach, Mamores, reaching the top of Steall Waterfall, Glen Nevis. Forced to make an unroped descent over rocks, snow and ice, Latham fell 18m and stopped, breaking a leg. Dean then fell past him, down the waterfall and out of sight, and was killed. Rescue and evacuation by Lochaber MRT. 91.

MARCH 25th – Rupert Hoare (38) fell 45m through a cornice on the East Face of Aonach Mor injuring a knee walking on a bearing from Ski Tow D. See note at the start of this section. Ski Patrol assistance.

MARCH 27th – About 300m SE of the South Top of Stob Coire Sgriodain (960m), Philip Henderson (43) was killed when he walked through a cornice and fell a minimum of 60m towards Lochan Coire an Lochain. He had been walking along the ridge with seven companions. Another member of the party had a similar fall shortly before the fatal fall, escaping uninjured. Recovery by Lochaber MRT, SARDA and RAF Sea King. 63.

APRIL 1st – Woman (52) suffering an illness was found by searching woodlands west of Sherramore Lodge, Upper Strath Spey, Laggan, and taken to hospital. Cairngorm MRT, SARDA, RAF Sea King. 76.

APRIL 2st – Lochaber Team called out to Uisge Labhair, Loch Ossian. RAF helicopter lifted two people to Raigmore – detained overnight. Ann Ramage (40) had fallen into a hole in the snow covered by a thin crust, injuring a leg. Janice MacPhail (37) stayed with her while third woman went for help. 39.

APRIL 2nd to 3rd – Lochaber MRT conveyed male (19) with minor scald injury from a tent at Steall Meadow down Nevis Gorge to hospital. Wind gust blew over a pot of boiling water. 31.

APRIL 3rd – 12.30. Beinn a' Chaorainn, Loch Laggan Hills. At GR: NN 385847 (see note) Nicholas Hinchcliffe (30) was walking alone half-an-hour after midday. In misty, windy conditions he walked through a cornice and was uninjured by a fall of approximately 140m. He dug a snowhole to await improved conditions.

APRIL 3rd – 13.00. Attempting to reach the South Top of Beinn a' Chaorainn (from which they intended to get to the North Top) a party as yet unconnected with

Hinchcliffe of the previous incident: Paul Margison (40) and a companion, Sheridan, missed the South Top. They passed it to the north when walking on a compass bearing. Margison fell through a cornice and landed close to Hinchcliffe, who had fallen half-an-hour before him. Margison was also uninjured. Conferring, they decided to stay put, knowing that Sheridan would seek help.

APRIL 3rd – 13.30. Meanwhile, Sheridan found the correct map reference of his companion's disappearance through the cornice from another pair of walkers. They had lost a Border Collie. It is assumed that the dog also fell through a cornice because it turned up, also uninjured, beside Hinchcliffe and Margison. All three fallers were rescued by Leeming and Lochaber MRTs. 135.

APRIL 3rd – RAF Leeming MRT called out to Black Mount, where Graham Robertson had fallen through a cornice near the top of Stob Gabhar. He managed to climb back up the slope and walk out. 20.

APRIL 5th – A party of three walking on the summit plateau of Aonach Mor had just left the top of the Ski Button Tow. One noticed a change in snow structure and stopped, but Mark Baxter (30) walked past him through a cornice, falling 120m into Coire an Lochain. Rescue by Avalanche Service and Ski Patrol. Hospital treated for shoulder and hip bruises. 18.

APRIL 7th to 8th – After completing four Munros from Culra Bothy, Thomas Gilfillan (31) was exhausted when 2km SW of the bothy. His companion left him in a survival bag and went to the bothy for help, but finding it empty carried on to Ben Alder Lodge. Meanwhile, the casualty recovered some strength and made it to the bothy. Rescue by Police vehicle with Cairngorm MRT on standby. 8.

April ? – Crag near Steall Hut, Upper Glen Nevis. Woman climber cragfast after ankle injury. She climbed down unaided before Lochaber MRT arrived.

MAY 1st – Other walkers alerted rescuers, saying that a couple were cragfast near the waterfall above Steall Hut. The woman (31) had twisted her knee but got down unaided, using a safer route. Lochaber MRT. 23.

MAY 10th – When a couple were walking along Upper Glen Nevis Path near Steall Ruin, the husband, Denis Morl (66) slipped, catching his foot against a stone and injuring it. Lochaber MRT. 45.

MAY 31st to JUNE 1st – Three anglers walked for an hour across Rannoch Moor, then used an inflatable dinghy to get to Heron Island, Loch Ba. The dinghy blew away. Rescue by RN Sea King next morning.

JUNE 12th – Without their leaders knowing, two schoolboys (both 15), went up an easy gully to the top of An Grianan, Beinn Ceitlin, because they could not sleep in their tents. They decided to descend to their camp at Alltchaorunn by climbing down Diedre's Bower on A' Chioch. One got cragfast and the other went for help. When Glencoe MRT arrived the cragfast boy had got himself down. 7.

JULY 4th – 700m East of Staoineag Bothy, Loch Treig, Kathleen Roberts (44) sprained her ankle on a rocky path. RAF Sea King. 13.

JULY 6th – On a path between Kinlochleven and Loch Eilde Mor a very heavy man, Tino Modder (22), wearing trainers, attempted to jump a rock but twisted an ankle. Glencoe MRT and RN Sea King. 22.

JULY 17th – Ian Sommerville (29) got cragfast on steep ground walking to the ridge crest of Sgorr Dhonuill, above Gleann a'Chaolais (Glenachulish). His wife (who had turned back earlier) heard his shouts and called out Glencoe MRT. He was aided down, but had got himself out of trouble. 11.

JULY 22nd – Glencoe MRT called out to search for a 64-year-old man overdue from a walk at Caolasnacon, Loch Leven. He had gone to Fort William and did not know what all the fuss was about. 7.

AUGUST 28th – Norman Hall (61) was in a group of 30 descending from Sgorr Dhonuill/Sgurr Dearg Bealach when he slipped on wet grass, breaking an ankle. Aided part way then stretchered by Glencoe MRT. RN Sea King diverted to Aonach Eagach incident. 30.

AUGUST 29th – In a party of three descending the steep ENE Ridge of Sgurr a' Mhaim towards Coire a' Mhail, boy (13) slipped wearing fell boots on wet grass. He slid 50m gathering speed then hit a rock, sustaining a deep scalp cut and fractured skull. Airlifted by RAF Rescue 137. Released from hospital after overnight detention. Lochaber MRT. 48.

SEPTEMBER 11th – Canoeing River Roy near Brunachan Bothy, Mark Seymour (34) was thrown out of his boat fracturing his leg by striking a rock. Rescued from a 6m gorge by Lochaber MRT using a Tyrolean Traverse. 21.

SEPTEMBER 13th to 14th – A man of 57 returned early from a walk on Binnein Mor/ Sgurr Eilde Mor due to bad weather. He missed a bus and spent the night in a B&B in Kinlochleven without telephoning, causing unneeded searches by Glencoe, Kinloss and Lochaber MRTs, RN Sea King. 344.

SEPTEMBER 17th – Attempting to walk from Ballachulish SSW to Glen Creran. John Drummond (66) went west too soon and got lost in the trees and tracks at the head of Glen Duror. Glencoe MRT spotted his torch and escorted him off. 12.

SEPTEMBER 24th – Having gone up the Meall a' Bhuiridh Ski Lift wearing trainers, Patricia Mellor (42) was hill walking with a companion. At The Canyon (a ski run in winter) she slipped on wet grass breaking a tibia and damaging knee ligaments. Stretchered to Chairlift by Glencoe MRT then chairlift stretchered off. 24.

SEPTEMBER 25th – Solo low-level walking at Corriechoille, Spean Bridge, Scott McNally (17) slipped and fell on rocks gashing a thigh. Treated by a doctor passer-by and transported to hospital by Lochaber MRT, who were alerted by the doctor's mobile phone. 3.

OCTOBER 5th to 6th – Solo walking from Rannoch towards Corrour Station, John Shepherd (83) got lost in mist and darkness. He wandered about part of the night, but eventually he found the railway and waited till dawn. He flagged down a train crew who were aware of the search for him. Tayside, Lochaber and Rannoch School MRTs. 136.

OCTOBER 8th to 9th – Attempting a solo walk of three of the Glen Etive Munros, including Stob Coire an Albannaich, Hugh MacKenzie descended in mist when he ran out of time. His guidebook and compass conflicted and he got benighted without a torch. He was found wandering on low ground by Police near Coileitir. Glencoe MRT. 61.

OCTOBER 12th – Hugh Burden (23) slipped near the summit of An Gearanach, Mamore Forest, when hillwalking with four others. He suffered a broken ankle and was airlifted by RAF Rescue. 137.

NOVEMBER 5th to 6th – A passing hillwalker found the body of John Barden (56) in Allt Rath, about 1.3km WSW of the summit of Stob Ban, Grey Corries, Spean Bridge. Hypothermia. Stretchered by Lochaber MRT. 162.

NOVEMBER 18th – Deborah Quartel (20) slipped wearing Wellington boots on wet vegetation on Beinn Riabhach, above Lower Glen Nevis. She slid and hit a fallen tree, fracturing a humerus and dislocating the opposite elbow. Stretcher carried by Lochaber MRT. 13.

CAIRNGORMS

JANUARY 3rd – Trevor Turner (63) went through ice on the River Spey 2km above Fochabers rescuing a dog. He was rescued by a man (61) and a younger man rescued the dog.

JANUARY 5th – Body of man (59) found under sea cliffs at Dickmont's Den, Arbroath. Not thought to be a climbing accident. Recovery by stretcher hoisted by Land-Rover winch. HM Coastguard. 8.

JANUARY 15th – Beating for hares on hill ground on Phones Estate, Newtonmore, James Dunbar (59) died from a heart attack. Found by his companions sweep-searching and evacuated by RAF Sea King. 11.

JANUARY 16th – 17th – Roderick Ferrier (31) and Judith Leslie (30) left Clova Hotel for a circular walk via Loch Brandy. Because their car was still there about midnight Leuchars and both Tayside MRTs, SARDA and RN Sea King were called out. Roderick staggered in to search control at 04.15 saying that Judith had hypothermia, because of severe weather after a fall. She was airlifted by Rescue 177 from between Corrie of Bonhard and Red Craig at 04.37. She was flown direct to Ninewells Hospital where her core temperature was 22°C. She made a remarkable recovery as that is the lowest temperature from which women in Europe have survived. (Lowest was a male in Finland whose temperature was 17°C.) The party had no map and compass, with poor clothing for the conditions. 120.

JANUARY 21st – Beside the Day Lodge in Coire Cas of Cairngorm, boy (4) was sledging with his father in an area marked as dangerous, when his father let go of the sledge which slid down a burn under a snowbridge. He was located four minutes later with no pulse and no breathing. An off-duty nurse successfully performed cardio-pulmonary resuscitation and boy was later recovering in hospital. Ambulance Service.

JANUARY 23rd to 24th – Planning to walk the six Munros east of the Braemar/Glenshee road, Keith Owens (35) and Frances Robb (f36) experienced strong winds with snow and poor visibility between the first two (Carn an Tuirc – Cairn of Claise). Their map blew away and they stumbled around the plateau for hours eventually descending Allt an Loch and bivouacking. They carried on for another km, then Keith went on alone to Callater Lodge Bothy. He returned to Frances in her bivvy bag, then they both got down to the bothy. Meanwhile, a car check had found their route plan and they were rescued by Grampian Police at 02.40. Frances was hospitalised with fatigue and slight frost trauma. 13.

FEBRUARY 10th – Richard Webb (55) lifted by RAF Sea King from Glenshee Ski Area suffering a heart attack.

FEBRUARY 13th to 15th – Night (2) and day searches in severe weather for Jaqueline Greaves (53) were carried out by Aberdeen, Braemar, Kinloss, and Leuchars MRTs, and RAF Sea King. She was found by SARDA dog handlers walking down Luibeg Burn suffering from frost nip and mild hypothermia. She had become separated from two male companions when they both fell through a cornice. Rescuers had concentrated on the eastern coire of Derry Cairngorm which is where the cornice was reported to have been, but it may well have been somewhere on Ben Macdui. 2000+.

FEBRUARY 15th – After climbing Diagonal Gully in Winter Corrie, Neil Turner (22) was descending steep ground north of Driesh with a companion. There was 16cm of new snow lying over older consolidated snow and ice. There was strong wind with snow falling. Shortly after start of descent they were overtaken by a large, loose, avalanche which carried them down into the Burn of Kilbo at GR: 266745. Neil sustained a small fracture in the spine/pelvic area. He was found staggering by Leuchars and Tayside MRTs alerted by his companion and stretchered off. 210.

FEBRUARY 19th – At 16.00 John Inglis (31) was leading Tough-Brown Traverse on Lochnagar. In the area of Parallel Gully B he fell and pulled off his second, John Buchanan (30) who was killed instantly. He had been belayed to a piton and a snow bollard. Inglis had sustained two open fractures to a femur. His cries for help were heard by other climbers and two reached him at 16.30, but he died at 19.30. Evacuated by stretcher and snow vehicle. Aberdeen and Braemar MRTs, RAF Boulmer Sea King. 246.

FEBRUARY 21st – Aladdin's Mirror Direct, Cairngorm. Paul Lamb (46) broke a leg falling 12m from an ice wall. An axe hold came away and he was unroped. RAF Boulmer Sea King, Cairngorm and Glenmore MRTs. 33.

FEBRUARY 23rd – Two men and two women (31-18) were overdue from climbing Central Buttress of Lochnagar, having been delayed by deep snow. Grampian Police MRT. 6.

FEBRUARY 26th – Alistair Henderson (28) received chest injuries when he slipped on to an ice-axe during an outdoor course on Carn na Cloiche, Cromdale Hills. Rescued by group members.

MARCH 2nd – Cairngorm MRT called out for two climbers cragfast in Red Gully, Coire an-t'Sneachda. They extricated themselves.

MARCH 5th – After completing his first winter climb (Fluted Buttress) Ian Drummond (28) was walking down the Goat Track with three companions. He tripped over a crampon and slid a long way because he did not manage to ice-axe brake. Serious leg injury. Cairngorm and Glenmore MRTs, RAF Sea King. 81.

MARCH 9th – Adam Gray (7) helicoptered to hospital from the Lecht when knocked unconscious from a ski accident. 1.

MARCH 11th to 14th – Searches of River Tay for a missing Dunkeld woman who had been walking her dog near the river.

MARCH 15th – Dawn Hatton (54) was heading towards the foot of The Vent, Coire an Lochan, Cairngorm with her husband. She was blown off balance and fell 75m down a steep snow slope on to rocks, injuring ribs and an ankle. Stretcher lowered by Glenmore and Cairngorm MRTs to airlift by RAF Sea King in very difficult flying weather. 34.

MARCH 28th – Climbing Kiwi Gully, Hell's Lum Crag, unroped, Simon Mea (29) slipped from just below the cornice. He fell to the bottom and suffered a dislocated shoulder and abrasions. RAF Sea King. 9.

APRIL 2nd – Paul Sweeney (27) returning from a climb in the Northern Corries and descending Fiacaill a' Choire Chais with a companion, stumbled in crampons, breaking a lower leg. Stretcher carry by Cairngorm MRT. 72.

APRIL 3rd – Walking in Glen Doll, Nick Morley sprained a knee and ankle and was stretchered out by RAF Stafford MRT. 17.

APRIL 17th – Air ambulance rescued Ruth Blackburn who broke an ankle paragliding on the Bochel (491m) Glenlivet.

APRIL 17th – Air ambulance rescued Philip Marsden (31) with a fractured pelvis from a paragliding crash near the Bochel, Glenlivet.

APRIL 24th – Glen Fender Bridge, Blair Atholl. Virginia Greig (51) slipped on wet grass and fell 12m into the gorge when trying to rescue her dog. She was only slightly injured. Firemen got her out using a ladder, and also rescued the dog.

APRIL 30th – With three friends descending a boulder slope on Beinn a' Chaorainn, Glen Derry, Neil Stewart (47) slipped. In falling he tried to protect a camera in his right hand and he suffered an open fracture of the wrist. Braemar Ambulance from Derry Lodge. 13.

MAY 19th to 22nd – Searches by Aberdeen, Braemar, Grampian Police and Kinloss MRTs, SARDA and RAF Sea King around Ballater for Alfred Clark (69) who did not return home after visiting an eye clinic. Subsequent searches by SARDA and Grampian Police Underwater SU failed to find him. 650.

MAY 22nd – Hamish Reid (13) rescued by RAF Sea King after a fall from the top of a cliff at Newtonhill Harbour, south of Aberdeen. Head wound and severe bruising.

MAY 28th – Two women hillwalkers got separated between Cairngorm summit and the Saddle en route to Linn of Dee. The weather was breezy and snowing. The woman reported missing was traced by Grampian Police at Derry Lodge. SARDA involvement. 33.

JUNE 9th – Sea cliffs at Downie Point, Stonehaven. Teenage boy climber fell with severe injury. Airlift by RAF Sea King.

JUNE 12th – Descending Coire an Lochain Uaine of Derry Cairngorm with her husband, Jane Leveley (56) walked on névé, not realising how slippery it was. Having no ice-axe or crampons, she fell 30m, hitting a rock and sustaining chest and limb injuries. Winched by RN Sea King. 16.

JUNE 18th – Steven Clark (17) became ill in the small hours during an award expedition assessment. His group was camped at the head of Glen Tilt on the old Inverness/Perthshire boundary. He had stomach cramps and was vomiting bile. He had consumed water contaminated by a dead sheep. Braemar MRT walked him out to a track. 17.

JUNE 23rd – In a party of 12 at the top of Fiacaill a' Choire Chais, Cairngorm, Laura Wallace (19) stumbled in a boulder-field and sprained her ankle. Airlifted by RAF Sea King. 10.

JULY 2nd – Walking from Glen Esk to Glen Clova, Ian Redford and Robert Brown (both 33) got separated from 22 others. In low cloud they walked from Ben Tirran and came down at the head of Glen Lethnot. Tayside MRT and SARU. 12.

JULY 8th – Leading Beech Wall at Craigie Barns, Dunkeld, William Snow (23) fell to the ground because his four lower running belays were pulled out. He fell off when inserting his fifth runner, sustaining lower back and shoulder blade fractures. Stretchered by Tayside Police SARU. 3.

JULY 9th – Descending the path south of Mam nan Carn to get to Spittal of Glenshee (11km to SE of them) Helen Reid (55) broke an ankle. She had jumped from a peat hag on to a tussock. Stretchered 3km by Tayside MRT and SARU. 88.

JULY 11th – A party of 12 on an award hike from Loch Lee to Glen Clova Hotel got on to steep ground at the head of the Corrie Burn. The weather was low cloud and rain. They should have been 2km farther east on the path from Green Hill past Loch Brandy. Two went for help while 10 erected tents. Tayside teams and RAF Sea King located them and four were airlifted; a girl with suspected appendicitis was flown to hospital. 62.

JULY 14th – Braedownie Quarry, Glen Clova. Woman (30) was belayed above a 13m climb safeguarding the ascent of Kevin Robb (33). Her harness was incorrectly secured in that the waist strap had not been rethreaded back through the buckle. Robb fell off at 6m, putting tension on the rope, causing woman's belay screwgate karabiner to pull out of her harness. Both fell to the ground. Robb was bruised and woman suffered a compound fracture of her lower spine. Evacuated by Ambulance Service.

JULY 16th – Mick Marquis (45) fell off his mountain bike in deep sand descending the Land-Rover track from Beinn a' Bhuird to Glen Quoich, near the water splash

(Quoich Burn). His companion biked out for help, because Marquis sustained an open kneecap fracture. Due to danger of further injury from vehicle evacuation he was airlifted by RAF Sea King. Grampian Police MRT. 14.

JULY 26th – A 'simple slip' on a path on the east side of the Quoich, 1.6 km north of the Punch Bowl, caused Rose Baird (62) to suffer an ankle fracture. Stretchered to Grampian Police Land-Rover. 3.

AUGUST 1st to 2nd – Without sufficient food, poorly clad, wearing shoes, and with no navigation equipment, a man of 45 left Linn of Dee with no definite plans for his hillwalk. He failed to reach the top of Ben Macdui and descended to Loch Etchachan in mist. Another walker with a map told him how to get back to Linn of Dee, but he went to Glen Avon, over the Saddle and into the Forest of Abernethy. A forester gave him a lift to Nethybridge, then he walked to Tomintoul (07.00) before telephoning his hotel. Meanwhile, Braemar MRT and RAF Sea King had been searching. 50.

AUGUST 11th – Instead of returning to Linn of Dee car park from Ben Macdui, Hans Schlicher (30) went due north over the Lurchers and down to the site of the no-longer Sinclair Hut. Returning over the Lairig Ghru he was stopped by darkness in Glen Luibeg. Grampian Police. 2.

AUGUST 15th – Descending a track when returning from an ascent of Mount Keen, Kathleen Mitchell (67) slipped on loose gravel and broke her wrist.

August 28th – Man suffered from a heart condition when walking with a club at Gannoch Hill (Tarfside to Aboyne by the Fungle). Airlifted to hospital. Braemar MRT. 4.

AUGUST 28th – A woman in her 20s was evacuated from Derry Bothy to Linn of Dee by Aberdeen MRT. She twisted her knee at Fords of Avon and managed to reach the bothy. 10.

AUGUST 28th – Two women (66 and 60) got lost walking from Loch Muick to Glen Doll. They had to ford a river but found their own way down before search teams arrived.

SEPTEMBER 11th to 12th – After walking from Aviemore to Derry Lodge and sleeping in Bob Scott's Bothy, man (27) suffered an irregular heartbeat. RAF Sea King airlifted him to hospital where he was detained 48 hours. Grampian Police MRT. 9.

SEPTEMBER 17th – Saturday walk in area of Lairig Ghru/Glen Lui. Two new female members of a club arrived back late for their bus and probably hitch-hiked home without informing Police. Aberdeen MRT. 8.

OCTOBER 16th – Not knowing the ground James Bayne (31) had been descending the buttress between A and B Gullies of Coire Fee, Mayar with a companion and a dog. The dog refused to descend a small cliff, so Baynes returned and put it on a lead. Bayne was then seen to fall 60m and died from head injuries. Tayside MRTs, RAF Sea King. 30.

OCTOBER 16th – Marlene Adams (56) injured trying to rescue above fatality.

OCTOBER 23rd – Viola Lawlor (47) and Helen Lawlor (12) were watching Peter Lawlor (14) snowboarding at Ciste Mhearad, Cairngorm. About 13.00 the family dog went missing and they all got lost searching for it. When it got dark they sheltered behind an overhanging boulder, where they were found well at 21.40 by Cairngorm MRT and SARDA. 106.

OCTOBER 23rd – Geoffrey Thompson (42) camped for some time on a River Dee island near Mar Lodge, exploring the area on foot. On various occasions over a week, he was warned of the dangers of flooding. On October 23rd after 24-36 hours rain the river rose more than 1m, threatening to engulf the island. The depth and force of water made the river unfordable and the weather showed no sign of clearing. Braemar MRT rescued Thompson plus gear using a Canadian canoe. 8.

NOVEMBER 1st to 2nd – Solo walker, John Hunter (62) tried to cross River Avon in spate at Fords of Avon Refuge. He was blown over by a strong wind gust and tore a calf muscle. Airlift by RAF. 10.

NOVEMBER 5th – The body of Robert James Linton (29) was found by friends at the foot of Eagle Buttress, Lochnagar on November 12th. They had instigated a search by Grampian Police and Braemar MRTs because he had talked about climbing Eagle Ridge and his car had been parked at Spittal of Muick for a week. On November 5th the weather would have been cold and clear and there would have been some wet rock on Eagle Ridge. He had been killed by a fall of up to 200m. His boots and socks had been found in his rucksack, suggesting he had removed them to overcome a slippery pitch. He had been soloing without a helmet and sustained multiple injuries including head injuries. RAF Sea King. 256.

NOVEMBER 13th – Walking on Bynack Mor, Grace Mackenzie (40) collapsed with exhaustion. Airlift by RAF Sea King. Cairngorm MRT. 26.

DECEMBER 24th – James Dunn (46) and Kenneth Stirling (30) were delayed due to lack of snow/ice on their route (Fiacaill Couloir). They got back to Cairngorm car park before midnight. Cairngorm MRT. 12.

DECEMBER 26th – Walking on a level path at the foot of Morrone, Braemar, Samuel Lev (49) slipped on ice and broke his leg.

DECEMBER 26th – Starting from Glen Doll to go up Mayar a pair separated. James Robertson (56) tried to communicate that he was going down but the other wanted to reach the summit. Robertson got lost and followed the Mayar Burn into Glen Prosen. Tayside MRTs. 24.

DECEMBER 30th – Because of poor snow, Kevin Leeson (30) and Guy Farley (24) abseiled from the top pitch of Parallel Gully A, Lochnagar. They got lost on the way down from the foot of the climb and were found by Police near Allt a' Ghlaschoire. Apart from not having a map they were well equipped.

DECEMBER 31st –Three climbers overdue in Coire an-t' Sneachda returned safe before midnight. Cairngorm MRT.

SOUTHERN HIGHLANDS

FEBRUARY 3rd – Cutting short a walk up Ben Cleuc h because of bad weather, Ian Ross (70), with a companion, was descending a path in Alva Glen. He was blown over and killed by a fall. Raised two rope lengths and stretcher-carried by Ochils MRT. RN Sea King turned back. 62.

FEBRUARY 5th to 6th – Male (48) with a history of depression and attempts on his life, left a note and walked up a hill above Brig o' Turk to carry out the threat. Found dead from a drugs overdose by Killin MRT with SARDA sweep searching. Evacuation by RN Sea King. 82.

FEBRUARY 10th – Robert Adam (68) was killed on a solo descent of the steep east side of Dumgoyne, Campsie Fells. Wearing Doc Marten shoes he slipped on wet grass and fell 60m down rock and scree. Lomond MRT and SARDA. Stretcher carry. 96.

FEBRUARY 19th – In a well-equipped party descending Beinn an Lochain towards Rest and be Thankful, Hugh Boyd (56) slipped on ice and fell 120m with broken ribs and bruising. Dumbarton Police and Arrochar MRTs stretcher carry to RN Sea King airlift. 81.

FEBRUARY 26th – Alan Johnstone (17) slipped on snow descending Beinn Narnain causing leg injuries, but those left with him realised he was not too badly hurt after the alarm was raised, so they carried him down. Met by Strathclyde Police and Arrochar MRTs. 18.

FEBRUARY 26th – A party of 12 descending Ben Ledi footpath in mist tried to go down the steep east face. Robert Williams (56) slipped on wet snow and fell 120m (fatal) over a rock buttress. He wore workboots with no tread and had no ice-axe, crampons or navigation gear. Killin MRT. 42.

FEBRUARY 26th to 28th – RAF Leuchars MRT and RN Sea King searched rough ground and agricultural areas around Methil and Leven, Fife for James Selbie (77) who had been out walking. He was found dead.. 300.

MARCH 20th – Walking with a companion in the Kilpatrick Hills, Roy McKeag (40) slipped descending wet grass between snow patches on Auchineden Hill. Ankle injury. Another walker alerted Scottish Ambulance Service using a mobile phone. 4.

MARCH 26th – Because of tiredness, Shelagh Watson (36) stopped on the bealach between Meall Garbh and An Stuc of Ben Lawers. She slipped on steep snow north of Lochan nan Cat and sustained severe chest injuries. Airlift by RAF Sea King. 8.

MARCH 26th – One of a group hang-gliding on Bishops Hill, Fife stalled and injured his back. Companion alerted rescuers using mobile phone. Airlift by RAF Sea King.

MARCH 27th – Ascending a steep slope on Ben Lui with a companion, Colin Hendry (44) stopped for a breather, sat on an icy rock, slipped and fell 90m with back, chest, limb and abdominal injuries. Stretcher carry by Killin MRT. Lomond team on standby. 160.

MARCH 27th – Lomond MRT on standby for woman with epileptic fit on Ben A'an, Trossachs. Recovered by Scottish Ambulance Service.

MARCH 27th – Lomond MRT called out for overdue male walker separated from party on Ben Lomond. Turned up safe.

MARCH 27th – SW Face of Meall Glas, Upper Glen Lochay. In pliable boots, and without crampons or ice-axe, Caroline Small (30) was descending névé with companions when she slipped and fell. She was killed by collision with rocks. RN Sea King, Killin and Lomond MRTs. 68.

MARCH 27th to 28th – James Ovenstone (62) got lost and spent a night near the top of Ben Vorlich (Loch Lomond) sustaining hypothermia and frostbite. He was found just NE of the summit by Strathclyde Police and Arrochar MRTs and stretchered to an airlift by RN Sea King. SARDA involved. 90.

APRIL 23rd – Carrying a heavy sac through deep snow during mountain leadership training, Shirley Stoddart (27) stopped exhausted between the summits of Beinn Ghlas and Ben Lawers. Rescued with hypothermia by both Tayside MRTs and RAF Sea King. 137.

APRIL 25th to 26th – Killin MRT found James Mellis (54) in a bivvy bag near Doune Bothy. He was overdue walking West Highland Way from Rowardennan to Inverarnan. 20.

APRIL 26th – G. I. Lithgow (72) tripped walking a footpath at the Whangie, Kilpatrick Hills, breaking his ankle. Stretchered by Ambulance Service and Central Scotland Police. 5.

MAY 1st – ROSPA rescue boat, two Police forces, SARDA and Police helicopter were all alerted for William Pratt (84) when he got separated from his daughter at Rowardennan. He was spotted by the helicopter between Rowchoish and Inversnaid, then recovered by rescue boat for an airlift. 72.

MAY 1st – In a party of three descending steep ground at Beinglas, Inverarnan, Glen Falloch, man (67) suffered vertigo and got cragfast. Aided down by Killin MRT. 29.

MAY 2nd – Descending east by the tourist route off Schiehallion in mist, Nancy Gordon (40) and Alison Gordon (5) got separated from the main party of walkers. Lost, because the navigation gear was with the others, they did a three-quarter circuit of the mountain to Kinloch Rannoch. Leuchars and both Tayside MRTs, RN Sea King. 75.

MAY 3rd – Night search on steep grass by Police for father and two sons (9 and 6) at 400m near burn at Balquharn, Alva. Ochils MRT not called.

MAY 7th – Hillwalker thought he heard whistled distress signals on Ben Vane. False alarm. Strathclyde Police and Arrochar MRTs, RN Sea King. 70.

MAY 10th – An Ochils MRT member was lowered 16m down a crag on the Nebit, Alva, to rescue a cragfast sheep. A long pole with barbed wire on the end was successfully used to snare the sheep's fleece, then a sling round the horns was used to hoist the sheep uphill. Ungrateful, it ran off with the sling. 5.

MAY 14th – Wearing training shoes on the West Highland Way between Rowardennan and Inversnaid, Teresa MacColl (41) stumbled and suffered a compound ankle fracture. Evacuated by RoSPA boat. Lomond MRT and SARDA. 28.

MAY 23rd – A wife (42) was ascending Beinn Each, Loch Lubnaig, when she became separated from her husband. Party had a map between them but no other hill gear. Overdue, she was found by Police coming off the hill.

JUNE 10th – Tracy Armit (17) rescued and lowered by Police, Ambulance and Fire Brigade when she fell 3m from a path to the bank of the Burn of Sorrow, Castle Campbell, breaking an ankle. Ochils MRT not used. 22.

JUNE 10th – One km up the path from Ben Lawers Visitor Centre, woman (75) suffered a stroke and was rescued by Killin MRT and RN helicopter. 22.

JUNE 18th to 19th – Sheila Lothian (57) had been tourist walking from Roseneath Caravan Park. She was found dead at high-water mark with signs of having been in the water. Strathclyde Police.

JUNE 25th – Phyllis Cochrane (49) injured a leg slipping on grass on Ben Achaladair. Lifted By RN Sea King. Oban Police MRT. 12.

JULY 2nd – Helen Golding (23) carried on when her party turned back in mist on Schiehallion. Tayside teams were called out but she descended safe by a different route.

JULY 3rd – Training for an award, Thomas Nixon (14) fell into a deep gorge near the West Highland Way (30m deep) and sustained kidney bruising. Gorge near Mar Burn, Milton of Buchanan. Stretcher hoisted out by Lomond MRT. 30.

JULY 3rd to 4th – Lost on Ben Ledi with no compass and a photocopy from a guidebook, two women (48 to 25) got down to Glen Finglas after 12 hours despite mist and rain. Killin MRT. 15.

JULY 10th – Upper Gleann nam Meann (above Glen Finglas Reservoir, Trossachs). Mountain biker Stewart Addie (31) fell off when riding down a track in rain and mist, suffering a big scalp cut and torn shoulder muscles. Stretchered out by Killin MRT. 21.

JULY 10th – Accompanied by a relation, man (36) lost his footing on wet rock/grass and fell 90m down a steep rock-strewn slope on the north face of Ben More (Crianlarich). He came to rest against a large rock after colliding with several other rocks, suffering head injuries. Airlift by RN Sea King. Killin MRT. 77.

JULY 17th – When paragliding, Harry Haynes (30) did a tight turn, spilling too much air from his canopy, falling 12m on to Myreton Hill above Menstrie. Lifted by RN Sea King, he sustained a broken arm and severe bruising. Ochils MRT. 23.

JULY 28th – Trying to cycle round Loch Katrine, Julian Leseve (14) got stuck on the lower slopes of Ben Venue. Overdue, he was picked up by a Water Board boat. Lomond MRT standby.

AUGUST 3rd – Tigh Ness Burn, Tyndrum. Playing in the burn in spate, holding on to branches etc., Michael Mathewson (15) was washed away. Found drowned by Killin MRT 1km from Tyndrum. 9.

AUGUST 13th – Red lights were seen and reported on Auchineden Hill (near the Whangie). Lomond MRT and SARDA carried out a vain night search. 53.

AUGUST 27th – John Nicoll (57) and Beatrice Burnside (55) got separated from 12 others on Schiehallion in low cloud. They went down to NW while others went NE to Braes of Foss. Tayside teams were alerted. 12.

SEPTEMBER 1st – Family group of grandfather, son-in-law and two grandsons were descending from Schiehallion summit. David Goodwin (80) was killed by a 60m fall down a rock/scree face. Son-in-law tried to stop the fall, sustaining scalp cuts and a knee fracture. Recoveries by RAF Sea King. 10.

SEPTEMBER 3rd – Walking on the Central Path, Callander Craig (1km north of Callander) Iris Gizeley (61) sipped in dry weather, sustaining cuts and bruises. Stretcher carry by Kilin MRT. 11.

SEPTEMBER 14th to 15th – Comer Farm (2km NE of Ben Lomond summit). Police and SARDA search for missing woman who was found uninjured, but with hypothermia, by SARDA dog. Lomond MRT on standby.

SEPTEMBEr 27rd – Colin McDermid (21) had to be raised 10m by Killin MRT from a pool at the foot of Falls of Falloch, with multiple fractures of a femur. He had slipped on wet rock while swimming. 11.

OCTOBER 11th – Male angina sufferer (40+) got separated and overdue on Ben Lomond. He turned up safe as Lomond MRT assembled at Rowardennan. 9.

OCTOBER 16th – Hanns Fickert (71) took ill with severe abdominal pains, and suffered hypothermia, when deerstalking on Creag Uchdag, Glen Lednock. Killin MRT, RN Sea King. 17.

OCTOBER 23rd – Anne Orr (57) slipped in wet forest at Corrow Farm, Lochgoilhead, injuring her leg. Winched by RN Sea King. Strathclyde Police and Arrochar MRTs. 32.

NOVEMBER 5th – Russell Murray (19) took ill on Ben Vane. He was assisted to walk off. Strathclyde Police and Arrochar MRTS, RN Sea King. 14.

NOVEMBER 6th – Ian Carswell (17) on rescue exercise, slipped crossing a plank bridge over the Menstrie Burn, injuring his leg. Stretcher carry to 4WD by Ochils MRT. 31.

NOVEMBER 13th – Ronald Nield (62) decided to turn back in bad weather when solo climbing Ben More (Crianlarich), but he was seen by other walkers to collapse and die. It was later confirmed he had a heart attack. Evacuation by Killin MRT and RN Sea King winch. 19.

SKYE

FEBRUARY 25th to 26th – Thomas Alves (39) and Sarah Alves (28) got lost in heavy snow descending from Meall Odhar, which is the north spur of Sgurr a' Bhasteir. Next day at 04.45 Police noticed them flashing the mountain distress signal. At 05.55 they zeroed in on the Police car blue flashing light and got themselves down safely. Skye MRT. 14.

MARCH 30th to 31st – The body of John MacFarlane (36), was found and recovered from Greshornish (peninsula), Loch Snizort by HMCG helicopter. Skye MRT, Coastguards and local volunteers. 50.

APRIL 2nd – On Sgurr nan Gillean, Alastair Bell (25) got separated from his companion and fell 180m down a snow slope when trying to find him. With minor injuries only he walked to Sligachan to raise the alarm for his companion, James McAndrew (25). McAndrew walked in just as HMCG helicopter arrived on scene. The reference given for the separation was in Lota Corrie. Skye MRT. 27.

APRIL 12th – Niall Harvey (30) was glissading on wet snow down the Great Stone ˏ Shoot of Sgurr Alasdair when his foot caught in a hole. He sustained a compound ankle fracture, but he continued to the coire floor where a nurse in the party provided first aid. Rescue was by RAF Sea King and Skye MRT. 27.

MAY 21st – Christopher Fry (20) was attempting a climb on Sgurr Alasdair, near the Great Stone Shoot, when a handhold came away causing him to fall 25m, sustaining a dislocated femur, cuts and bruises. Neither he nor his companion were using ropes or helmets. Rescue by Skye MRT and RAF Sea King. 63.

MAY 28th – After his four companions had gone on ahead during an ascent of Bruach na Frithe, Samuel McKee (54) was left alone on the mountain. More than two hours later, other witnesses heard him falling. He was found dead by four more witnesses having fallen between 50-100m. Skye MRT and RAF Sea King. 51.

MAY 29th – Edward Gardner (10) was clambering over loose rocks on Sron Dearg (the ridge west of Sgurr Dearg) about 4-5m behind his father. His father dislodged a rock which slid into Edward's path causing him to lose his footing and fall, sustaining cuts and bruises to the leg. Skye MRT and RAF Sea King. 41.

JUNE 5th to 13th – Body of solo hillwalker John Brittain (66) was found with multiple injuries just north of bealach between Sgurr Thearlaich and Sgurr Mhic Choinnich on 13th. Stretchered out by Kinloss and Skye MRTs down Coire an Lochain slabs and Coruisk to evacuation from Loch Scavaig by local fishing boat. Searches on 12th and 13th by the two MRTs, SARDA, RAF and RN Sea Kings. 977.

JUNE 6th to 7th – Suffering hypothermia when camping at Creag Langall (east of Trotternish Ridge) in a group of six school expeditioners, Andrew Patterson (17) was winched by HMCG helicopter. 15.

JUNE 7th to 8th – Climbing Pinnacle Ridge of Sgurr nan Gillean, two men (36,30) and two women (29/23) had crossed all four pinnacles and descended into the neck before the summit ascent, when they got cragfast by bad weather. Not finding an escape route they were winched out next morning by RAF Sea King. Skye MRT. 50.

JUNE 12th – On Pinnacle Ridge (probably Sgurr nan Gillean) David Holand (58) suffered a broken leg from a rock dislodged by his son. Airlifted to Raigmore Hospital. 14.

AUGUST 4th – Descending the Great Stone Shoot of Sgurr Alasdair, Anne Gaskill (42) got a quarter of the way down when she injured an ankle. It got caught between two rocks. Skye MRT, RAF Sea King. 23.

AUGUST 10th to 11th – Male walker Nevan McGhee was overdue on the Trotternish Ridge. He turned up safe at 05.00.

AUGUST 13th – David Walker (29) was negotiating Collie's Ledge, Sgurr Mhic Coinnich unroped, with one companion ahead of him and Andrew Barcroft (28) behind him. Walker took a grip for a hand hold when a slab of rock approx. 2m x 3m was dislodged carrying him with it. He was killed by a long fall. As a result of further rocks falling Barcroft received leg injuries but managed to stay on the ledge. Skye MRT, RAF Sea King. 54.

SEPTEMBER 6th to 30th – The car of Peter Mace (30) had been parked for some time outside Glenbrittle Youth Hostel, so a search was set up on September 30th by Skye MRT and two RAF Kinloss search dog handlers. Peter's body was found on Sgurr a' Ghreadaidh (GR:443232). He had probably fallen a few hundred metres. Stretcher carry. 126.

OCTOBER 15th to 16th – Separating from fellow club members to go farther on, intending to reach Bruach na Frithe, Alan Mann (43) did not return to Glen Brittle Hut. A search by Skye MRT and RAF Sea King located his body on Bidein Druim nan Ramh. 106.

ISLANDS
(Other than Skye)

JANUARY 2nd to 3rd – Search for Rhona Auchincloss and Paul Davies overdue from a walk to the Carsaig Arches, Isle of Mull.

MAY 29th – In a party of two, Christine Kell (38) was struck by a dislodged rock, sustaining head injuries, at Bealach an Oir (between Glens Dibidil and Harris, Rum). Airlift by RAF Sea King. 12.

MAY 29th – In the NE Corrie below A' Chir Ridge solo hillwalker John Harrison (38) tripped and injured a leg. Lifted by RN Sea King with Arran MRT on standby. 35.

JUNE 3rd – On the very steep NE (facing) slopes of Holy Island, Arran, solo walker John Kennedy (20) got cragfast. He sat and waited five or six hours to alert passing fishing boats and therefore got very cold. Rescued by Arran MRT and RNLI lifeboat. 36.

JULY 2nd to 3rd – Having been seen walking on Canna at 22.30 Saturday, a report was received at 11.00 Sunday that Dr Ian Smith (36) archaeologist, was overdue. A search by Oban Coastguard, Mallaig lifeboat and HMCG helicopter located his body at the east end of the island below a 45m cliff. Evacuated to Mallaig Pier by lifeboat.

JULY 19th to 20th – Alexander Young (74) was believed to have walked into Glen Sannox, Arran to draw sketches, but he went solo hillwalking to near the summit of Cir Mhor where he slipped and fell down the west side sustaining head injuries and abrasions. Arran MRT searched on 19th. On 20th they were joined by SARDA and Police and RAF Leuchars MRTs. RN Sea King from HMS Gannet spotted other walkers waving gaiters so they airlifted the casualty. 431.

JULY 23rd – David Brookes (21) fell from cliffs behind the Island Arts Centre, Ellenabeich, Easdale breaking an ankle. HM Coastguard, Police and Ambulance Service.

SOUTHERN UPLANDS

FEBRUARY 11th – Tweed Valley stretchered out the body of male walker V. G. Lynn (66) who died from natural causes at the edge of woodland in Ettrick and Lauderdale District. 13.

MARCH 4th to 17th – Alastair Hall (54) found dead on Duns Law, Berwickshire. Searches over two days by Borders SRU, SARDA and Tweed Valley MRT. 280.

MARCH 6th – Search of moors and forest at Newcastleton, Liddesdale for two missing walkers, who turned up safe. Tweed Valley MRT. 11.

MAY 3rd – Search of Southern Upland Way for Ellyann Smith (51) who went walking without leaving details. She got lost and very wet and was taken in by a farmer suffering mild exposure. Tweed Valley MRT, SARDA. 36.

MAY 8th – Margaret Glen (54) slipped on a path at Murder Hole, Loch Neldricken (3km SSE of the Merrick) breaking an ankle in two places. Recovery by Galloway MRT and RN Sea King. 69.

MAY 8th – Search of Dingleton Hospital grounds for a youth (16) overdue from a walk. Found by Police. Tweed Valley MRT, SARDA. 48.

MAY 25th – Galloway MRT standby for a man (30) walking on moorland in Glen Dee, Kirkcudbright. Doctor was concerned as he was diabetic.

MAY 28th – Grass fire on fell of Eschoncan, Loch Trool. Police were worried about 30 hillwalkers cut off from their cars. Galloway MRT searched Buchan Burn checking for walkers. Forestry helicopter and workers together with RAF and RN Sea Kings.

JUNE 5th – Tweed Valley MRT and SARDA searched for an elderly woman separated from her walking group in an area she did not know (Lauder). Good weather. Found by Police. 14.

JULY 24th – Tweed Valey MRT standby for a group of walkers on Southern Uplands Way overdue at St Mary's Loch. They turned up safe.

AUGUST 13th – Daniel Danjaune (52) slipped and broke his ankle descending scree on the Eildon Hills, Melrose. Stretchered by Tweed Valley MRT. 29.

AUGUST 28th – Tweed Valley MRT put on standby for person who turned up. 3.

AUGUST 30th – Successful search for missing girl (11) in woods on Abbey Hill, Lammermuir, by Tweed Valley MRT. SARDA alerted. 72.

SEPTEMBER 3rd to 4th – D. Skidmore (50) could not find his way off Corserine (Rhinns of Kells) in darkness, rain and mist so he stayed out till daybreak and got down OK. RN Sea King, Galloway and RAF Stafford MRTs. 68.

SEPTEMBER 6th – Hare Law (GR:380327) Southern Upland Way. Tweed Valley MRT and SARDA found four overdue schoolboys (all 15) on the wrong hill. They then found five overdue girls (all 14) and one teacher (21) in darkness. RAF helicopter used. 124.

SEPTEMBER 6th to 7th – Man (84) wandered off from a home NW of Kelso, became confused and lost in woods. Large scale search by Borders SARU and Tweed Valley MRT. Located by SARDA dog with cold trauma and slight cuts of hands from barbed wire. 153.

SEPTEMBER 12th to 13th – Woman (32) got separated in mist from her husband on Corserine at 14.30. There was some urgency because she was on thrice daily medication for epilepsy, but Police were not informed till 22.00. She was found OK the next afternoon. Galloway and Moffat MRTs, SARDA, RN helicopter. 343.

SEPTEMBER 14th to 15th – Man (68) wandered from Dingleton Hospital, Melrose, became disoriented and fell into a forest ditch. Mild hypothermia. Found by SARDA dog. Tweed Valley MRT, Borders SARU. 75.

OCTOBER 8th – Tweed Valley called out for missing child who turned up OK. 3.

OCTOBER 14th to 15th – Walking beside River Teviot, Hawick, Jessie Murray (88) got hypothermic because she was stuck in dense undergrowth for at least six hours. Found by Tweed Valley MRT and SARDA jammed between trees, well away from paths with no evidence of her route in. 52.

OCTOBER 22nd – Karrimor Marathon fellrunner, Robert Price (30s) tripped and dislocated his ankle on Henderland Hill (531m), St Mary's Loch, Ettrick Forest. Stretcher carry by Tweed Valey MRT. 28.

OCTOBER 23th – Karrimor Marathon fellrunner, man (64) collapsed at Drumelzier Burn (13km SW of Peebles) and was unable to regain his balance. Very cold, he was evacuated by Tweed Valley MRT suffering labyrinthitis (inflammation of inner ear). 12.

OCTOBER 23rd – Karrimor Marathon fellrunner, Martin Oakes (33) slipped on wet heather at Kirkstead, St Mary's Loch, injuring his leg. Tweed Valley MRT. 3.

OCTOBER 26th – Tweed Valley MRT, SARDA and RAF helicopter searched hill area near Hawick for a schoolgirl (13) epileptic and depressed. She was found in a small strip of shelter woodland after missing for six hours. Borders SARU called in. 90.

NOVEMBER 1st to 2nd – Searches by Galloway and Moffat MRTs, SARDA and Coastguards located Karen Panton (33) suffering hypothermia in Munches Forest, near Dalbeattie. 200.

DECEMBER 17th –Three students got lost at the foot of Merrick, trying to reach White Laggan Bothy. They bivvied north of Loch Enoch. RAF helicopter spotted lights and lifted them to the bothy, whence they continued next day. Galloway MRT. 10.

NON-MOUNTAINEERING

FEBRUARY 19th – RAF Sea King rescued a glider pilot from a snow-covered field near Glenbuchat, Strathdon. He had got lost in low clouds and landed the glider without damage, radioing for help.

JUNE 2nd – RAF Chinook helicopter crashed at Mull of Kintyre killing all 29 persons on board. Kinloss, Leuchars, Strathclyde Police MRTs. RAF Boulmer and Lossiemouth and RN Prestwick Sea Kings involved.

JUNE 19th – Labouring in a remote area (Knoydart shore of Loch Hourn below Ladhar Bhein) Lester Standen (27) fell 9m into a deep gully when an eroded banking collapsed. He suffered lacerations to the forehead and was evacuated by RAF Sea King. Glenelg MRT. 26.

JUNE 28th – Assynt MRT, HMCG helicopter and Coastguards and local professional divers were involved in searches for Ewen MacRae, a missing diver. MRT searched foreshore below cliffs inaccessible to others. Search repeated on July 3rd and July 10th. Body not found. 200.

JULY 15th – En route to an MRT exercise, Leuchars team gave first aid to a pedestrian with a dislocated ankle fracture near Tay Bridge. 2.

JULY 27th to August 10th – Protracted and (to date) vain searches for Donald Melville (43). He was last seen at Blackwaterfoot Beach, Isle of Arran on July 27. Extensive searches of coastline and surrounding country as well as air and sea searches were made from July 27th to 29th. Arran, RAF Leuchars, Strathclyde Police MRTs, HM Coastguard, RNLI lifeboat, RN Sea King, SARDA. 2000+.

SEPTEMBER 1st – RAF Tornado (from Marham) crashed at the top of Glen Ogle, Lochearnhead, killing both aircrew. Searches for remains and wreckage by Leuchars, Killin and Kinloss MRTs, RAF and RN Sea Kings. 900.

SEPTEMBER 18th – Returning from exercise, Aberdeen MRT controlled traffic at the scene of a car fire on North Deeside Road.

SEPTEMBER 25th – False alarm. Tweed Valley MRT and RAF helicopter searched Gala Law after a male reported a microlight crash. Police located the aircraft safe 16km away. 44.

DECEMBER 27th – PLM helicopter with animal food slung below in a cage crashed on a hillside not far from Ballachulish, Loch Leven. Both aircrew were killed instantly. Gale winds. Glencoe and RAF MRTs.

ALEXANDRA HOTEL
Fort William

THE PARADE, FORT WILLIAM
SCOTLAND
PH33 6AZ
TELEPHONE: 01397 702241
FAX: 01397 705554

ATTENTION: DR KEN CROCKET
EDITOR - SMCJ

CLIMBED OUR RIDGE REACHING
TOP 15.05 THURSDAY 25/5/95
EXTREMELY DIFFICULT & SENSATIONAL

SHAW, KEITH

P.S. ARRIVING WAVERLEY 22.10 FROM
KINGUSSIE

"Glenisla, Long Row, Menstrie, 27th May, 1995. Keith and Co. will be really over the moon at nabbing this great line. Like Woodentop and his merry men I also eyeballed it from all angles, and was pos it would go. It was cool of Keith to sneak up without telling us, and although I'm obviously hacked off at not being in the team, at least the beezer was grabbed by Team SMC, and not by what the 'droid might call geeks from the deep south. Don't know the pro yet though." ken.crocket@almac.co.uk

IN MEMORIAM

ALISTAIR LORIMER CRAM MC j.1930

IN THE death of Alistair Cram the Club has lost a very remarkable member. We have received so much biographical material about him that we have had to create, in conjunction with Perth JMCS, a 'Cram Archive'.

We start with the following extract from Fraser Darling's *Island Farm* recounting their first meeting in 1939: 'What an extraordinary open and innocent face for a lawyer, I had thought to myself, but soon I saw how his face could be that of the mystic and idealist he is, in one moment, and the sharp, practical man of affairs the next. The dualism was in his character as well as in his face, and the warring of these two sides had brought him here [i.e. to the island of Tanera Mor in the Summer Isles] now the mystic in the ascendant.

He came to stay with us for two or three days, . . . he remained three months and would have gone to [North] Rona with us for the winter had not the war fallen on all our plans.' Prior to the war Cram had been a leading climber in both Scotland and the Alps, a member of the SMC and AC and the pre-war or 'pre-resurrection' EUMC. He had also been in competition with Bill Murray for the first ascent of Clachaig Gully. He next met Murray some six years later when both were prisoners of war.

Murray writes: 'The extraordinary character of the man was not disclosed to me until early 1944, when he turned up at the prison camp of Mahrish Trubau in Czechoslovakia. He had been put in the bag in 1942 at Sidi Rezegh in the Western desert. Like me he had spent 14 months in Italy and gained fame by making 13 escapes, a phenomenal record. He was imbued with the conviction that an officer's duty was to escape. He had complete mastery of the German, French and Italian languages – such was his fluency that he could pose as a French worker speaking Italian with a French accent or vica versa.

Toughly resourceful, he spent more time roaming the Apennines and their coastal strip than he spent in prisons where he paid due penalty in solitary confinement. We had 1500 fellow prisoners in Czechoslovakia, among them Tommie Wedderburn of the JMCS (younger brother of Sandy). We pinned an advert on the camp noticeboard announcing the formation of a mountaineering club, entry qualification: preparedness to deliver a talk on mountains. Soon we had a score of members drawn from Scots, English, Canadian, South African and New Zealand climbers. They gave good-quality performances since no time could be spent on slides but much on preparation. Cram's contribution was outstanding for his Alpine experience (in comparison with other members') was hugely varied.

Our club might well have joined the BMC which had been founded that very year in Britain, had communications been better. But bomber raids were destroying landlinks, not to mention our food supplies. Cram's more usual activities were now frustrated. The Senior British Officer had banned all further escapes. This was not because those who did escape and fell into Gestapo hands were beaten to death, incinerated and their ashes returned to the camp of origin – a rule to which we knew of no exceptions – but over-ridingly because we now had several tunnels excavated under the camp's electrified fence, their use strictly reserved for a possible mass escape at the end. The Czech patriots had warned us that the SS were gunning down prisoners in camps farther east to forestall release by the advancing Russian armies.

Cram's next chance was thus delayed until August when unexpectedly we were packed into cattle trucks and moved westward to near Brunswick. The train was slow and halts so long that prisoners had thrice to be allowed out on the line. Before we had crossed the German frontier, Cram and Wedderburn seized one such chance to escape unseen. The act was of high courage. I never expected to see them again. Three months later I heard one morning that Cram and Wedderburn were back in camp. They had succeeded in reaching Prague where they had tried over many days to contact the Czech patriot forces. They were betrayed to the Gestapo, who catching them in civilian dress believed them spies, and despatched them to Dachau for prolonged and final interrogation.

There Cram fiercely maintained that both were escaped prisoners of war. The Gestapo refused belief, judging that no one of Cram's linguistic abilities would have been wasted on desert fighting. He and Wedderburn too must surely be Secret Service or SOE agents. Ensnared by their disbelief and curiosity, they sent their captive's names, alleged numbers and fingerprints to Berlin with the query: 'Are these escaped British prisoners?'. At Dachau they were interrogated day and night under bright lights, made to watch the torture of Czech women to force disclosure of their menfolks' whereabouts in the patriot bands, then returned to their cells but denied sleep while Jews, screaming in the neighbouring cells, were beaten with rubber truncheons. The truncheon bearers would then visit Cram and Wedderburn and stand around menacingly before bearing them off once more to interrogation rooms. After four weeks of this hell, a written command came from Berlin stating that Cram and Wedderburn were indeed escaped British prisoners ending, 'Return to Oflag 79, Braunschweig'. In the face of that direct order the Gestapo had to comply.

No other of our freedom-bidders had come back from the Gestapo alive. He escaped once more when his place of confinement was hit in an air-raid. This time he made it to the American lines. He and I never met again. I honour his memory. This man was indomitable'.

W. H. Murray

G.J.F. Dutton continues: 'Before and after these cathartic war-time experiences Cram noted his extensive expeditions in the Journal, contributing between 1930 and 1991 over 40 accounts of formidable, new or entertainingly-unusual ascents; a remarkable 61 years' record, further notable in that all but one or two of these contributions appeared in Notes or SMC Abroad. He was our most prolific and distinguished lower-case contributor and – under my Editorship at any rate – firmly ignored requests for 'full-scale articles' while still regularly forwarding his eagerly awaited accounts: rather than risk their indignant (though unlikely) cessation we continued to issue them in Small Print, as perhaps befitted his legal background.

As far as the Journal tells us, he burst on the scene in 1930 fully armed from the JMCS Perth Section, which he had apparently organised into 'recognition' by the previous year, along with Chris Rude (later Rudie) and others, following a suggestion of Donald McKay, SMC.

These early Notes and Meet Reports (some of which Perth still holds on its files) were full of exploratory and technical interest. reflecting a penetratingly-lively mind; in 1932 (SMCJ ix, 392) appeared 'April Climbing in Skye' – snow and ice work on the ridge, unusual then, and part of what would become a typical motorised

ALISTAIR CRAM

ARCHIE MACALPINE. Photo: W.H. Murray.

GEORGE GIBSON. Photo: David Geddes.

expedition (this time in a two-seater Jowett across Scotland) bagging peaks en route with EUMC and CUMC colleagues. More Scottish climbs, Norway and the High Class Alps graced subsequent volumes until the war.

An all-round mountaineer, he had compleated the Munros and Tops by 1938 (with a second round in 1978). August 1939 saw him in the Oberland; and by 1947, having done with the Nuremberg trials, the Alps once more. This latter entry under SMC Abroad (xxiv, 72) introduced the characteristic laconic urbanity, the edged understatement, that enlivened this section of the Journal over the next 43 years ('. . . apart from those engaged in smuggling and counter-smuggling, we had the mountains to ourselves'.)

The 1949 issue carried the first of his African descriptions. He was by then a Senior Magistrate and rose to become Acting Chief Justice in Malawi. He relished the tropics for the spice they added to his remarkable climbs, many of which were solo or first (European) ascents. '. . . A fine ridge walk complicated a little by game . . .'; 'four 7-8000-footers, rocky, and tedious from the need to carry a heavy loaded rifle . . .; '. . . A rhino in every acre . . . sometimes they ran and sometimes we ran . . .'. Rock climbing near Nairobi, he had to compete with baboons, 'as climbers sadly insanitary . . .' or 'dispute with those illiberal occupants of otherwise good stances, the leopards.' Camping was not dull: 'gigantic and tenebrous cliffs . . . the habitations of malicious buffalo and coldly, watchful snakes and the den of lion and leopard . . . In Africa night does not belong to the mountaineer . . .' One can only hint at these colourful activities. Home on leave from Africa – June in the Cuillin, July to October in the Alps (Mediterranean to Adriatic), the Apennines, Alban Hills, Dolomites (all major peaks), Chamonix rock-climbing school, Jura, gritstone at Fontainebleau. And of course Scotland – such as the one about this time, off north from Perth in the back of a butcher's van with Ian Robertson of the JMCS.

From the early '50s his wife accompanied him, a partnership providing further delightful asides, and motoring to the hills and back proved as attractive as ever. For example, on their very successful private expedition to the Himalaya: 'We drove from Bombay to Manali. Twelve crates and bales of equipment and food went by train and lorry (mostly to outfit porters). Our own modest equipment . . . fitted into our Silver Dawn Mk V . . .' At the end: 'Drove back to London via Lahore, Karachi, Baghdad, Beirut, Damascus and through the Iron Gates Pass to . . . Istanbul . . . the Rolls clocking 60 road miles every hour through the night in the Arabian desert . . .' and, of course, bagging peaks on the way. (On home leaves the hapless Rolls was harnessed to a caravan and driven north.)

Latterly, in '82 and '84 (53 and 55 years after his first first-ascents in Glen Clova) they drove walked and climbed along the whole S-N traverse of the Great Dividing Range of Australia, on off-days visiting places like sapphire mines from which 'after a near tearful abduction' of his wife they forced 'the raging floods of Cyclone Grace across a (laterally) unfinished viaduct' where the car '. . . did a sidewinder, affording stunning scenic views first on one side and then on the other. I observed my wife was not to be separated from her sapphire under any eventuality . . .' Regarding that disastrous Cyclone Grace: 'Anyone who has camped at the head of Loch Etive on a January night will have had a similar experience.' The Mediterranean hills and Near East featured more often as they grew older; on Mount Sinai they appreciated the difficulties of Moses, and the Red Sea cliffs afforded treacherous rock and difficult route finding: '. . . at times like these my wife, like Lot's, took care to look back'.

Crete, Cyprus, Corfu and neighbourhood were the last visits, in the late '80s and early '90s, yielding, at age 79, a solo bivouac on a 8350ft peak reminiscent of Scottish experiences and where after a good climb, 'One may also walk to the Cave of the Nymphs (be prepared for disappointment) . . . A mule relieved the load on the shoulders if not on the mind: 'Our muleteer bounding along the narrow Skye-like ridge' and warmed by 5-star brandy 'passed me riding a bank of gravel. This cast him headfirst down a slab, lubricated by small stones, into a cleft where he was imprisoned by the clamping of spiny spinifex bushes round the middle . . . as he emitted a dismal hiss, my wife, in whom minor male lesions evoke a sensible response, aptly equated the sound to a punctured tyre.'

Motoring back from a rock mountain in Cyprus in typical Scottish conditions of rain and mist: 'Where the road ran along the rims of gorges I was reduced to looking for the road surface on my hands and knees and to scattering handfuls of gravel – walking on to place a quartz block on the road . . . driving on . . . and repeating the tedious exercise. My wife attributed the total absence of local drivers to their good sense.' A fitting close is the final contribution. It describes a return to the island of Kephalonia, 'climbing the familiar tops of 'Enos Eros' (5075ft) and Gioupari' and discovering below, the presence of two Royal Navy warships – flags, dazzling white uniforms and full-dress gold braid – 'to remind the populace that the navy had been first on the scene . . . after the great earthquake of 1953. As a climax to the memorial service taking place at the foot of the mountain, without warning a great deluge broke over Argostoli, lachrymae rerum, as it were. Yet it remained dry on the sunlit hillside, a curious inversion of experience.'

I have tried to quote the flavour of these extraordinary contributions, quite ignoring the high quality of the climbing and the wealth of helpful detail they provide. Perhaps a full article or – as Perth JMCS are considering – a reprint, may be devoted to the mountaineering adventures, described in such imperturbably-zestful terms, of one of our most accomplished, courageous and civilised members, whose memory is indeed to be honoured.

Below is a list of Cram's notes or mentions in the Journal; compiled during an eye disability, I cannot guarantee its completeness. Roman letters refer to volume and arabic numbers to page. Pre-war: xix 71, 139, 142, 157, 158, 217, 222, 293, 424, 430, 437; xx 67, 372, 459, 462; xxi 137, 293, 435; xxii 86, 153. Post-war: xxiv 72 (Austria 1947), 256, (Central Africa 1949); xxv 88 (Africa 1950-51, Alps 1951, Skye), 276 (Africa 1953); xxvi 297 (Africa 1955-57), 298 (Alps 1956); xxvii 103 (Africa 1959) ; xxix 170 (Himalayas 1960, 1963), 175 (Brazil 1966), 177 (Africa 1961, 1966), 180 (Pyrenees 1968); xxxi 219 (Spain 1976), 220 (Sinai 1976). 317 (Spain 1977); xxxii 302 (Australia 1981); xxxiii 108 (Australia 1983), 231, (Australia, ecology), 546 (Crete 1986); xxxiv 172 (Crete 1987), 350 (Corfu 1958, Crete 1988), 555 (Cyprus 1989), 730 (Kephalonia 1990).

I thank Ian Robertson of Perth JMCS for helpful reminiscences.'

G.J.F. Dutton.

We end our tribute by quoting this final sentence from his wife Isobel, his companion in adventure: '. . . and then at 84 years of age . . . he fought the greatest battle of his life, never giving in to weakness, his brain sharp and clear to the end. He died in his own bed beside me in his sleep as quietly and efficiently as he had lived.'

ARCHIE MACALPINE j.1945

I MET Archie MacAlpine when I was a boy of 14, and he an undergraduate at Dental College in Glasgow. His interest, therefore was not at all in me, but in my elder sister, Margaret, whom in following years he wooed and won. Ben Humble had been one of his fellow students, but Archie, no more a mountaineer than I, was instead a university oarsman – shelves loaded with the silver cups he'd won. At that first meeting in Kintyre, where my sister and I were on holiday, he had rowed to Skipness from the Clyde around Ardlamont Point – a distance of nearly 60 miles – hands not even blistered. I was impressed.

After he had set up practice at Ibrox and married my sister, he became concerned for her brother's sanity. I had found mountains. This to him was a puzzlement. What on earth could be the point in sweating up hills? My sister, reversing the safety-first trend of the times, encouraged him to try. I persuaded him to think of Glen Coe, to which I had not yet found my way. I owned no car, but he did. I had so newly joined the JMCS that I knew no members. The trumpet-call of the Buachaille Etive Mor was sounding in my ears. On a sunny September morning of 1935, we rounded that last bend of the Rannoch road and for the first time saw that huge rock-cone lift high out of the moor. Our breath was taken from us. We stopped the car. Every detail of the cliffs showed clear and sharp, to our eyes unclimbable.

We found our way up by the easy route from Glen Etive. Archie not yet fit, dubbed the trudge laborious, but his attitude changed on reaching the summit screes, where we could walk in delight to the cairn. He needed just one look over that wild, far scene – and was hooked, just as I had been five months earlier on the Cobbler. Spurred by curiosity we climbed down to the top of the North Buttress, and saw a party of three rock-climbers starting up the Crowberry Tower. They were SMC, and made our 'impossible cliff' look feasible even for us. Now doubly hooked, Archie promptly joined the JMCS.

Entirely to him I now owed my chance to climb with Bill Mackenzie and Kenneth Dunn, who were two of the club's leading rock-men. The club held a May meet at Glen Coe, from which I was absent (fighting a Cairngorm blizzard). In these days the only club hut in Scotland was the CIC, so Archie pitched his big tent, called 'the canvas palace', at Coupal Bridge. It proved so popular in heavy rain that his camp-bed broke under the weight of parked bodies, two of them Dunn and Mackenzie. Mackenzie said brusquely to Archie: 'We'll have a climb in the glen the week after next,' to which he replied: 'Sorry, but I always climb with Bill Murray.' Mackenzie blurted: 'Bring him along.' And that was how I came to join what became the strongest team with whom I have ever had the good fortune to climb, especially on winter rock and ice.

All could give a firm lead when wanted; none, whatever the foulness of weather, ever looked like coming off on a climb, and that bred the mutual confidence that counts for so much on mountains. We each had our different gifts. Archie was quite outstanding as a mirth-provoker. His keen sense of humour was backed by two other gifts: a good mimic's ear (enabling him to catch to perfection Macphee's drawl or Bell's Fife accent); and what he called 'a flypaper memory', which allowed him to retain without effort a near-inexhaustible fund of good stories. These were real talents. One sometimes hears of a story-teller having his listeners 'rolling in the aisles', but only once in my life have I seen this literally happen –

when Archie spoke at a JMCS dinner in the old Constitutional Club of Glasgow. He gave a simple recitation of Longfellow's *Wreck of the Hesperus,* delivered as if by an upper crust English gentleman, just slightly sozzled. The result was so hilarious that members could hardly keep upright in their seats, and some did, in fact, have to throw themselves on to the floor. I have never seen the like again – for Archie would never give a repeat performance despite all urgings.

On mountains, the worse conditions became, whether on hard climbs, or in wet tents or bleak bothies, he never failed to lighten the fix we were in, and to lift drooping spirits. This rare talent being his to high degree, it made him a most valued member of any rope. Although a top-class performer on rock and ice, he would rarely consent to lead, yet would climb without trouble or hesitation any rock or ice on which Mackenzie or I were able, even with much trouble, to find a way up or down. Since we could rely on him to the limit, his presence helped us to get up routes like those high-angle slabs of Rubicon Wall, on which Mackenzie's variation involved very long run-outs with no protection, or the second ascent of Agag's, made within minutes of the first, or down Garrick's Shelf in a blizzard, or the first ascent of Clachaig Gully, and many another good route.

The JMCS used to hold fortnightly winter lectures at Archie's house in Ibrox, where his wife was hostess. On the outbreak of war in 1939, he joined the Army Dental Corps and was posted to the South of England. He took training in advanced dental surgery at the hospital of East Grinstead, where McIndoe, the great plastic surgeon, repaired the terrible facial injuries to Britain's airmen. He became one of McIndoe's famous team, whose skills were giving new hope to broken-up men. When the war ended, he returned to Scotland and joined the SMC, only to find that his Ibrox practice had evaporated into thin air. With a wife, two sons, and a daughter to support, he moved back to England and opened practice anew at Tunbridge Wells. He was, of course, at once appointed consultant in dental surgery at East Grinstead.

Archie continued to visit the Scottish hills over the next 20 years. His first son, Roderick, with whom he and I often climbed, became a rock climber of high skill in Norway, where he had gone to live, but was killed in the Jotunheimen by a fall of rock in 1969, aged 30. Archie died in a nursing home last November, aged 88. He had introduced me to a tough winter-climbing school, and to many of the best mountain days of our lives.

W.H. Murray.

RICHARD NAPIER RUTHERFURD j.1922

WHEN the Secretary invited me to write an obituary for Dr Dick Rutherfurd on the grounds that I was the only member he could think of who had met him, I realised that I might well be faced with a formidable task. This was not to prove the case. I took a chance and telephoned the only Rutherfurd in Kirkcudbright and found that I was speaking to his son, Harry, now senior partner in his parent's medical practice, who generously sent me his father's climbing log for 1920-24.

This proved a fascinating insight into the climbing scene of long ago. Expeditions were largely confined to the New Year, Easter and the Glasgow Fair. Travel was by bicycle, train and on foot. The weather was as fickle as it is today and the only complaint made in the log concerns a home-made tent and a groundsheet both of which leaked regularly. It records that on Sunday 30 December 1923 at the Blair Atholl meet a number of members attended the evening church service. Changed days!

Dick started climbing before leaving school and joined the Club in 1922. He first appears in the Journal at the New Year Meet in 1922 at Brodick and he was a regular attender for the next 30 years besides making a number of visits to the Alps. His last meet was at New Year 1951 at Dalmally, the one at which Percy Unna died.

His lasting mountaineering memorial lies in the fact that in 1925 he founded the Junior Mountaineering Club of Scotland along with Arthur Rusk and Archie Hutchison. This was planned during an expedition to the Bernese Oberland in July 1924 and the idea was that it should be a training organisation which would be a feeder club to the SMC. The fact that few JMCS members nowadays come into the SMC and that there are now six large and prosperous separate JMCS groups could not have been foreseen by the founders. Several accounts of the founding of the JMCS and their hilarious initial meet at the Cobbler appear in the 1975 Journal and are well worth reading.

Born in Glasgow in 1902, Dick Rutherfurd had an exceptionally full and varied life. Educated at Glasgow Academy and Sedbergh, he obtained a degree in engineering at Glasgow University and served an apprenticeship with Sir William Arrol in Bridgeton. Engineering was at a low ebb in the 1920s and Dick went to the Argentine for a three-year contract to supervise the building of a breakwater and a golf course. On his return in 1931 he worked for a while with Sir Robert McAlpine and Partners until an aunt offered to finance a medical degree. He graduated MB, ChB in 1938. During the Second World War he served in the Royal Army Medical Corps and served in the Middle-East.

In 1946, he took over a practice in Kirkcudbright with his wife, Elinor, who was also a general practitioner. Besides becoming a much loved GP his contribution to the life of the town was very considerable. He was a member, and later president, of the Choral Society, and a founder member, and later Commodore, of the Sailing Club and was a member of the RNLI for 30 years and received the RNLI gold badge for his outstanding service.

His tremendous enthusiasm and interest in the welfare of others is illustrated in the many offices he held. He was a founder member of the Royal College of General Practitioners, and elder of St Cuthbert's Parish Church, a Justice of the Peace, an Honorary Sheriff, the president of the local Rotary Club. He was a member of the Town Council and became the Dean of Guild and Senior Baillie before being elected Provost of Kirkcudbright in 1973.

Bill Myles.

JOHN BUCHANAN (Edinburgh JMCS), (1963-1994)

WHEN John tragically died on Lochnagar on the February 19, 1994 with his climbing companion and friend, John Inglis, while attempting an ascent of the Tough-Brown traverse, the section was shocked by this double loss.

I came to know John when he moved to the Stockbridge area of Edinburgh and approached the Edinburgh Section of the JMCS during Autumn 1992. Quickly, he was marking himself out as a keen prospective member, joining the Club during December 1992, becoming our first and only parapenter.

It was on the Dinner meet during late November 1992 when six of us decided to make a Club ascent of Twisting Gully in Glen Coe, that the rest of us discovered just how strong and powerful John was. From the car park to the base of the route he snow ploughed the way for the rest of us to the first belay stance. Long legs put to use from early days walking with the Youth Group attached to the family's local church in Cambuslang, and later days at Strathclyde University saw John, a gentle giant, walk, climb and explore many parts of Scotland. Later trips to Alaska with Operation Raleigh and an ascent of Mt. Kilimanjaro while working in Africa occurred.

It is fair to say that Club social events brought out John's character. Memorable moments at the 1992 and 1993 Annual Dinners, notably the toothbrush incident with John Inglis at Jock's Spot. The list of members with whom he climbed during his short time spent in Edinburgh was extensive and bears witness to his popularity. Ascents during this time included Crowberry Gully, Comb Gully Buttress, Comb Gully and numerous ascents of An Teallach. In spite of his popularity he never managed more than solo descents by his parapente. One of the best of these during his time in the club was his descent from Creag Meaghaidh, down over Loch Laggan, coming in to land on the foreshore following a most spectacular stack over the water.

During the late autumn of 1993, John was transferred to Aberdeen with his job as an electrical engineer, choosing to live in Stonehaven. From there he continued to attend the winter meets during early 1994 and from where he and John Inglis planned to explore Lochnagar. Sadly, we never were able to put in to fruition the planned sea-cliffs meet based in John's front room. The only solace we can take from this far-too-short friendship and association with the JMCS is that John will be at rest with his faith.

C. Stupart.

JOHN INGLIS (Edinburgh JMCS).

EARLY in February 1994, John and I drove up to the FRCC hut at Kinlochleven in the evening gloom, with vague plans of climbing North Buttress on the Buachaille on the Sunday. We had a disturbed night in the Civil Defence building, with various parties leaving in wreaths of pipe smoke at hourly intervals for the Ben. Uncertain of the conditions, we changed our plans and headed for Stob Coire nan Lochan. Fortunately for me, by the time we arrived there were already parties queuing up for the harder routes. I was able to divert John onto something more within my capabilities and much below his (not without some discussion). A few days later, walking down from Creag Meaghaidh with another JMCS party, my main thought was that I should contact John to tell him how good the conditions were. Sadly, I heard that evening of John's death at the age of 31 in a fall from near the top of the Tough-Brown traverse on Lochnagar. That had occurred on the previous day, February 19, and John's companion, John Buchanan, also died in the fall.

John first started climbing with the Edinburgh JMCS in 1989, and despite other pressures on his time, he soon became one of the club's most active members. I got to know him well about a year later, and we discovered a common interest in science. It turned out he was a rising star in the field of molecular genetics at the MRC Human Genetics unit in Edinburgh, though as a mere physicist I only learned of the full importance of his work after his death. (Fuller details are given in the *Scotsman* obituary of February 21, 1994.) We soon became friends and frequent climbing partners, with John's rising abilities on rock overlapping for a time with my declining ones. John had come to climbing late, and had little time to devote to the frequent outings and training sessions that make modern climbers rise quickly into the higher E grades. In any case his climbing heroes were from an earlier age when a few pints in a pub was a much more inviting prospect than a night in the gym. In particular, he had read widely the mountaineering literature of the Fifties and Sixties and was in the midst of preparing an article on Robin Smith when he died.

What John lacked in finger strength and experience he made up with a driving determination to make his mark in the climbing world, as in any activity he engaged in. He first came to notice with a series of bold and poorly-protected new routes on a local Edinburgh crag, Dalmahoy. This had been climbed on in the Sixties and rediscovered in the Seventies, but the central steep part of the crag, with a series of smooth grooves and overlaps, had always remained inviolate. John cleaned up the buttress (in more ways than one) with four new ascents after much activity with a wire brush. Unfortunately, recent quarrying activities nearby have accelerated the growth of a powdery lichen that will make further re-ascents problematical. John went on to climb another new route in Ratho Quarry, and an attempt on a second route here resulted in a prized photograph of him with John Buchanan that now adorns the JMCS hut at Laggan. Further exploration on the Buachaille led to a new pitch on Cuneiform Buttress, described in the 1994 SMC Journal, and John was planning to return to do a continuation pitch in the spring. One of his last summer routes was a fine lead of Kipling Groove, another of his ambitions being to 'tick off' all the routes in *Hard Rock*.

I have the consolation of a host of outstanding memories of days out with John on the crags and mountains. His zest for life was infectious. I recall one day climbing Savage Slit in heavy rain when the sun suddenly broke through the clouds. The possibility of a piece of dry rock somewhere in the vicinity revitalised John and he dragged me down the sunnier side of the mountain to the bottom of Hell's Lum Crag. Needless to say his optimism about the conditions was somewhat misplaced, but I had the pleasure of seeing him leading up through the mist on the big corner of Clean Sweep in grand style.

I have another memory of a late autumn meet in Wasdale. We had had a good day on Pillar, but John was still feeling rather smug after his conquest of KG, so I brought him down to earth by introducing him to Engineers Slabs on Gable Crag. I had done it many years before so I knew what to expect. A climb that is 'only' two 30m 4c pitches, but when you find that every move on the whole exposed route is at this level, the measured length and book grade become purely abstract concepts. John reached the top in a state of total adrenaline-enhanced exhilaration 'floating on high o'er vales and hills'. For John, that was what climbing was all about.

John leaves a wife, Dr Julia Dorin, herself a leading molecular geneticist, and two young daughters, Jenny and Joanna. He will be missed by all who knew him.

Chris Eilbeck.

WILFRED LENNOX COATS j.1934

Here in Scotland and – alone or with his son Alasdair – in the Canadian Rockies, Wilfred Coats was out on the hills, enthusiasm undimmed, well and truly into his eighties. Sadly, illness took over for a number of years and last October, at the age of 97, he had to admit defeat.

His membership of the Club spanned exactly 60 years. Prior to joining he had at least two good spells in Skye and these clearly played a big part in dictating how he chose every opportunity to return there, both for meets and otherwise.

However, it wasn't only the Ridge which claimed his attention. In those old tricouni days there was plenty to attract elsewhere too; notably, the still unclimbed Rannoch Wall was a prize much discussed and sought after. Eventually, Route 1 went in June 1934. Wilfred followed up with a lead of the second ascent in May of the following year.

Up until the war there were good opportunities to enjoy the home hills. Graduating B.Sc. (Eng) at Glasgow University, Wilfred worked for Shell-Mex and BP, first as assistant then as branch manager for the West of Scotland. Thereafter, however, he was based farther afield as resident engineer for the company – in Orkney and South Uist, Norfolk, Hampshire and finally at head office in London. More conveniently back North again, he lectured in engineering drawing at Glasgow University from 1957 to 1962, finally retiring aged 65.

From the three meets which he attended in the pre-war years Wilfred obviously extracted excellent value – for example, on Speyside a formidable step-cutting tussle on Braeriach, out from Ullapool a memorable four-Munro marathon. But it was really only after he had retired that he majored on meet attendances. As Meets Secretary he notched up a list of more than a score with almost no blank years, the last at the Glen Brittle Hut when, aged 81, he traversed Ghreadaidh, Thormaid, Banachdich and Sgurr nan Gobhar! Mostly he managed to land the chore of official chronicler, a fact which speaks quite a few volumes for his enthusiasm.

Outdoors otherwise in Scotland he was a member of the Scottish Ski Club and the St Kilda Club. Abroad he had four seasons, the first at Arolla in 1947, the others in the Fifties – two at Saas Fe and Zermatt, one at Zinal.

Personal memories of Wilfred are mostly of far-off Glen Brittle days – on and off the rocks – with friends who are merely names today and that to only a few. But they were great days and no mistake, often enough ending at the hospitable fireside of Mrs Chisholm's Post Office. Wilfred as an engineer – and a particularly high-powered one at that – was never short of inventive ideas, often, I remember, having to do with theory of rope management and belaying, or the breaking strain of ropes. The laughs were many as we egged him on to wilder and wilder theories till finally he diagnosed the leg-pulls and laughed at himself as heartily as the rest of us. Good days indeed – long past maybe, but very far from forgotten.

Wilfred was a keen Christian, an elder of the Kirk for many years, above all a real family man. To his wife, Agnes, his son and daughter and the grandchildren sincere sympathy – and thanks for the memories.

Campbell R. Steven.

ANDREW ROBB MacCORQUODALE j.1961

OUR paths first crossed on the hills during the mid-Fifties, when he ran with the Falkirk MC and again in the city, where he was in the thick of his studies and so we gradually came to appreciate one anothers' opinions and interests.

Korky as he came to be known, was a virtual life-long friend, the kind you may not see very often but when the occasion arose, it was always stimulating, for he was forthright, highly entertaining, well read and possessed of a devastating ability to deflate cant and pomposity wherever it appeared.

He was an all-round sportsman with particular skills in climbing, cricket and rugby, but when the great surge in explorative climbing and emergence of the dynamic young stars occurred, he decided it was time to set aside other sporting interests, concentrate on climbing and threw his lot in with us.

We made a few good new routes together, but sadly, it was not to last as one night in 1958, when motorbiking home from a dance he made to overtake a lorry and was involved in a smash, sustaining injuries which rendered him paraplegic.

Whilst on the mountains, I had recognised his physical and emotional strengths, but I and many others were astonished when, after being virtually written off by the specialists, he fought back from the brink of death, with surprising humour and the heart to offer sympathy and encouragement to his fellow unfortunates of Killearn. He joined the Club, post-accident in 1961.

Accepting his chairbound mobility with resolution, he then set about rebuilding his life with customary vigour and enthusiasm to establish a sound marriage with Helen and their two children Lynn and David, eventually to achieve notable success in his profession and make considerable contribution to the organisational side of young Scottish rugby.

When an athlete is dealt such a blow, one would expect bitterness and remorse to influence the new life but this was never so with Korky.

Even in our occasional debauches there wasn't a hint of such, though he did complain it was unfair that he must start off 'legless'; however, it was brother Ronnie and I who drew the long straw, in that we had to humph him up umpteen flights to my top-floor flat, with stances on the landings to ease our Sherpa muscles, debate topical affairs and tank up for the severe stretches above.

On retirement, he entered Stirling University in order to expand his knowledge.

As climbers, we are familiar with courage, often performed in dramatic settings which seem at times heroic, yet Korky's resolution of his Kismet was to me a greater display of courage, more so as it was accomplished unstated and with a selfless compassion and concern for others right to the very end.

He inspired and influenced many and diverse associates and left us all the legacy of his unquenchable spirit and irreverent humour as typified by the bogus titles adopted in our exchanged letters which seems appropriate to cite on this occasion to illustrate the nature of the man Korky. e.g.

A.R. MacCorquodale,

FRICS, FRVA.

(Ex-sergeant 1st Larbert Boys Brigade).

J.R. Marshall.

PROCEEDINGS OF THE CLUB

New Members

The following 14 new members were admitted and welcomed to the Club in the year 1994-95.

Rick Allen (40), Petroleum Engineer, Aberdeen.

Keith J. Anderson (32), Composer, Edinburgh.

Jim Beaton (40), Telecommunications Engineer, Erskine.

Andrew J. Forsyth (27), Veterinary Surgeon, Malton, N. Yorks.

Andrew A. Fraser (34), Solicitor, Ayr.

Andrew R. Hume (27), Energy Engineer, Edinburgh.

Adam Kassyk (38), Corporate Management Officer, Edinburgh.

Alan McDonald Kerr (30), Sales & Marketing Executive, Hamilton.

David J. Myatt (37), Consultant, Lumphanan.

Robert A. Smith (46), Schoolteacher, Dunbar.

Ian P. Stevens (31), Chartered Physiotherapist, Glasgow.

Colin P. Stewart (22), Electronic Engineer, Glasgow.

Gavin N. Williams (38), Outdoor Education Instructor, Perth.

Iain McKenzie Young (35), Geologist, Killearn.

EASTER MEET – ELPHIN

The meet was attended by nine members and gravitated back to the Strangs' superb facilities and hospitality in Sutherland. Betty's meals seemed bigger and better than even our fondest memories, and alcohol appeared to have been placed on drip-feed. These home comforts were entirely necessary as the weather was abysmal – where oh. Where has the Greenhouse Effect gone?

Very little was done. Some presidential quality people felt they needed to demonstrate superiority by venturing up Cul Mor and returned glowing with apathy. The verdict was 'cool mor'. Assorted secretaries, treasurers, trusties and other such plebs couldn't have mustered a Munro with their combined footage, but sea-levels were closely scrutinised at multifarious locations, proprietorial inspection was made of Sandwood Bay, and waterfalls (land-based rather than those coming out of the sky) were given a real hammering. Scott Johnstone temporarily abandoned geology for anthropology when he announced the discovery of a chambered cairn within the Strang estate. However, this was later thought to have

been a gathering of the afore-mentioned presidential elite in the sauna. The meet concluded with significant depths of frozen snow on the roads and most of the Sutherland traffic through the hedges.
PRESENT: Doug Lang (President), Bryan Fleming, Mike Fleming, John Fowler, Scott Johnstone, Malcolm Slesser, Iain Smart, Colin Stead and Oliver Turnbull.
Mike Fleming.

CIC MEETS

Once again seven weekend meets were organised on the hallowed mountain. Unfortunately, the thaw and freeze cycle was not evident and when the snow finally did arrive it was overwhelming. As a result very little ice was present and there was virtually no névé.

The meet attendances were below par with an average of 10 per meet. By February, the golf club finally closed access to their car park for climbers. This may have dissuaded some members and by the lack of numbers on the mountain it appeared to have repelled the multitudes. Having said that the weather did play a part; in the fortnight between the February meets not a single climb was recorded in the log.

Last year's gloomy hut decor has been restored to civility with the added bonus of an independently supplied central light being greatly appreciated. Well done to Kev Wilson for his plumbing work.

Hopefully, the car-parking problem will be resolved with a new car park for climbers to the east of the golf club house.

I request members to get off their backsides and make an effort to attend these enjoyable meets.

After 15 years As CIC Commandant the Richardson dynasty is soon to terminate. During this time Bob has ruled and maintained the roost in a most professional manner. We are indebted to Bob for his magnificent call to duty. We wish him well and good climbing in his retirement.

D.F. Lang.

The One-Hundredth-and-Sixth AGM and Dinner

The 1994 function was a repeat of 1993 based in the Alexandra where they seemed pleased to see us return.

The AGM again took place in the local school hall where at least the debates were lively and not influenced by the dreary surroundings. The customary business was uneventful with only the implications of the Criminal Justice Act initially exciting the 130 or so members present.

Last year's executive error in permitting discussion and indeed a vote on abolition of the Loyal Toast required a re-match between the chief protagonists Messrs Cousins and Ross. Unable to agree on a composite, independent motions were discussed with the President calling time after a full 15 rounds and exercising his casting vote in favour of the *status quo*.

The Club then turned to much more relevant issues by embracing the established principle of Freedom to Roam in the Constitution through Bob Reid's motion that Rule 4 be amended to read: 'While enjoying the freedom to roam in Scotland, Members of the Club shall act responsibly at all times.' The meeting grappled uneasily with a really topical issue – the crampon marking of classic summer climbs and wisely perhaps, no positive decision was reached as prevention is surely impossible and anyway according to Milne, the good guys don't do damage.

The Committee proposal for the disposal of the Ayscough bequest roused the meeting one more time – a new hut in the North-west! But who is going to find it? Another prolonged Speyside affair asked Richardson? Possibly, said the Committee. Hope not, said the Club! Probably!

And on to Dinner. Isn't it always the case that the second cup of tea is never as good as the first. The 1993 Dinner was a classic Club affair to which perhaps this event could never aspire. President Lang, however, dealt neatly with the smouldering dissatisfaction of the Loyal Toast debate by borrowing Godfrey Solly's toast from the 1909 Dinner to the Old Brigade and Stan Pearson was kinder to the guests, who included for the first time the Irish Mountaineering Club, than had previous speakers. The reply was given by Bob Allen who it seems pays subscriptions to all of England's senior clubs but who riskily strayed into lines of humour never appreciated by members even pre-1990.

And so with Campbell wielding Raeburn's axe for the next two years, the 1994 function came to a close. It seems that we may be on the move again next year as now the Alexandra is too small and Arrochar is being considered. As we continue to outgrow the Highlands, perhaps a return to the central belt will have to be contemplated for 1996?

J.R.R. Fowler.

JMCS REPORTS

Glasgow Section:– During 1994 the Section has continued to meet approximately fortnightly in the hills and monthly for a pub meet. A total of 23 meets occurred, and Niel Craig's achievement in attending 20 was notable.

Within Scotland, meets were held to the usual popular haunts of Glencoe and the Cairngorms, however, a number of trips were made farther afield, including Skye, Torridon and Jura.

Throughout the year members have been Munro and Corbett bagging, ski-mountaineering, downhill skiing, rock and ice climbing, mountain biking, sailing and fishing. This, of course, leaves lots of other activities not attempted including caving, paragliding and canoeing – perhaps next year.

The good winter conditions of 1994 started early and enabled an extended New Year meet to be held at the Raeburn Hut. (Two members stayed at the hut for 10 consecutive nights, a record for the hut). Highlights of the stay were ski mountaineering days from the road and a mass ascent of 'Oui Oui' at Newtonmore. Later in the season many good ice routes were climbed with members active in all of the main ice-climbing centres. A joint meet in February with the London and Edinburgh Sections left Jock's Spot seriously overcrowded.

Early summer saw increased activity on the rock, although usually confined to the lower crags due to the snow on the higher cliffs. The May meets were met with lots of snow on the hills and there was still snow on the Skye ridge at the Coruisk work meet at the end of the month.

Although no formal meet was held abroad this year, a number of members travelled overseas, including the secretary, who tried climbing near Washington D.C. in late June – a mistake. Elsewhere others ventured to the Alps including John Park and Stuart Fish who climbed the Chèré Couloir and a number of rock climbs around Chamonix.

Later in the year a group, including Niel Craig, Neil Marshall and David Ritchie visited Wadi Rum, Jordon and came back with tales of impressive sandstone climbing and deserts full of abandoned shoes.

September proved to be a month for long weekends. A memorable trip was had to the North-west (the return journey included visits to Elgin, Ben Rinnes, the Lecht, Braemar and Perth). Later in the month the Club visited Jura, where an enjoyable walk was undertaken from the Gulf of Corryvreckan at the north end of the island down its western shore to the bothy at Glengarrisdale.

Overall, an enjoyable year of mountain and outdoor activity for those who attended the meets, unfortunate, therefore, that the average attendance at meets was only six out of a section membership which now stands at 87, including 20 life members.

Expanded newsletters, including meet reports on all Section meets, have been produced this year, a development that seems to have met with approval from the membership. Also this year the Glasgow Section went 'on line' and information on the JMCS can now be found at URL "http://www.mech.gla.ac.uk/JMCS/" on the Internet. The secretary can also be reached by Email.

At the AGM in November the following officials were elected: *Hon. Member,* W.H. Murray; *Hon. President,* Iain Cumming; *Hon. Vice-President,* Benny Swan; *President,* Sandy Donald; *Vice-President,* Peter Cairns; *Secretary,* Donald Ballance, 1/R 11 Airlie Street, Hyndland, Glasgow, G12 8QQ, (Tel: 0141 357 3073, Email; d.ballance@mech.gla.ac.uk); *Treasurer,* Andrew Sommerville; *Coruisk Hut Custodian,* Sandy Donald, 15 Smeaton Avenue, Torrance, Stirlingshire, G64 4BG, (Tel:01360 622541); *Committee :* Niel Craig, David MacDonald, Neil Marshall, John Park and Ian Thomson.

Donald Ballance.

Edinburgh Section:- Membership of the section remained steady at around 70 members, six new members were admitted during the year.

Meets were held throughout the year with 27 official weekend meets. These were held throughout Scotland with several meets held south of the Border. As ever the weather resulted in varying attendance. Despite this ever-present factor in Scottish life, half the section's members were active and achieved a high level of mountaineering activity. The last winter meet of the year to the Ben during April saw several of the classic ridges being climbed as well as an enjoyable evening with fellow climbers in the CIC. On rock, the meets during May to the Lake District and Skye saw a successful traverse of the ridge by two members, plus several ascents; including the Great Prow on Blaven and Amphitheatre Arete in Sron na Ciche. Mid week rock climbing meets were well attended, a total of 22 were organised.

In common with most years a large part of the activity happened on unofficial meets. However, on one of these to Lochnager on February 19, the low point of the section's year occurred when John Buchanan and John Inglis died as a result of an accident while climbing Tough-Brown Traverse. Both were very active and extremely popular characters. The section was stunned by the loss of two friends.

Activity abroad was down on previous years, although the following areas were visited: Separate parties were ski-touring in the Bernese Oberland and Austria; later in the year one group visited Arolla in the Swiss Alps while others visited various locations throughout France for some sun rock. Two members visited Colorado in July where many superb ascents were made.

Once again both huts were in demand throughout the year. Jock's received a major renovation to the roof resulting in vastly-improved fire exits being put in place. This work was jointly funded by the section and a generous grant from the Scottish Mountaineering Trust, to whom the members are gratefully thankful.

As ever there were several social events during the year. November saw nearly 40 members and guests congregate at the Gaskmore Hotel, Laggan to hold the AGM and then the Annual Dinner. For the first time in several years a guest speaker was arranged. David Whalley (Heavy) from the RAF Kinloss Mountain Rescue Team presented a thoroughly entertaining and well illustrated talk on the 50 years of the RAF Mountain Rescue Service. Earlier during the day a large number of members had gathered on Meall Chuaich to celebrate a member's last Munro, the section's first new Munroist for several years. During the year Mike Fleming stood down as Honorary Vice-President after many years as a committee member. In recognition of his services to the section he was awarded a life Honorary membership.

Office Bearers: *President*, David Buchanan; *Hon. President*, John Fowler; *Vice-President*, Kate Holden; *Hon. Vice-President*, Nigel Suess; *Treasurer*, Brian Finlayson; *Secretary*, Charles Stupart 4 Comely Bank Place, Edinburgh, EH4 1DU; *Smiddy Custodian*, Fraser Fotheringham, Tigh na Sith, Braes, Ullapool; *Jock's Spot Custodian*, Alistair Borthwick, 2 Aytoun Grove, Dunfermline. *Committee:* Nicholas Cruden, Brian Donaldson, Beryl Leatherland, Robin Sinclair, Frederike Van Wijck.

Charles Stupart.

Perth Mountaineering Club (JMCS Perth Section):–During the past year, Perth MC has been active with organised day/weekend meets from Giggleswick to Durness and Lochnagar to Skye using feet, ski, fingers, axes and bikes.

Away from the organised meets, members reported trips to South America, Asia and Europe as well as plenty around Scotland, the Lakes and Wales.

The Club held several evening meets throughout the year, whether to climb outdoors, indoors or just to imbibe (with or without slides).

Our Honorary Vice-President, Robin Campbell, and President, Ray Lee both gave excellent presentations on the history of climbing. Robin showed us the tweed and clinometers of the early Scottish scene, while Ray showed the denim and perms of his early years.

This year saw the resurrection of the Club's photographic competition. So close were the entries that it was difficult to tell them apart. Many thanks to Grahame and Mel for their work in getting it going again.

Now an advert: The Club organises regular day/weekend meets throughout the country and evening climbing meets around Perth or to a wall in Dunfermline or Edinburgh. If you want to get involved call me on 01738 828058.

The Club dinner was held in the Royal George Hotel in Perth where we were addressed by Geoff Dutton – mainly to celebrate the life of Alastair Cram and to chastise us for not having female members in the JMCS.

The Club was invited to all the major dinners in the country – many thanks to our hosts for their kind words and hospitality.

At the AGM in December the following officials were elected: Hon. President, Donald McIntyre; Hon. Vice-President, Robin Campbell; Hon. Members, David Wares, Chris Rudie, Bob Milne, Walter Perthers and Iain Robertson; President, Ray Lee; Vice-President, Chris Bond; Secretary, Antony Lole; Treasurer, Tom Rix; Auditor, John Rogers; Meets Secretary, Alex Runciman; Newsletter Editor, Melanie Crother. Committee: Iain Robertson, Alasdair Dutton, Pet Thomas, Grahame Nicoll.

Antony Lole.

Lochaber Section:– Membership currently stands around 55, with most of the members living in the Lochaber area and the rest being ex-Lochaber residents now spread throughout the country.

The section held several meets throughout the year with old favourites like Ling Hut and Dundonnel and a very successful camping trip to Arran on a sunny May weekend. As well as organised weekends, most members are active during the year doing their own thing, whether it be walking, climbing, bothying or whatever takes their fancy.

Members meet in the Nevis Bank Hotel on Thursday evenings, usually just an informal social night but sometimes incorporating a slide show or lecture.

Steall Cottage in Glen Nevis is the Section's main source of income and bookings have been very steady over the last year. As well as the normal maintenance a porch has been built onto the hut which when finished will serve as a drying room. The wind generator installed last year is now working well, supplying lighting to some of the rooms.

In November the Glen Clova Hotel was the venue for the Section's annual dinner which was the best attended to date with 47 members, friends and guests sitting down for the meal on the Saturday evening.

Officials elected were: *Hon. President,* D. Watt; *Hon. Members,* B. Bissell, D. Scott; *President,* W. Anderson; *Vice-President,* I. Walker; *Secretary,* K. Foggo, 19 Abrach Road, Inverlochy, Fort William. Tel: 706299. *Hut Custodian,* J. Mathieson, 43 Drumfada Terrace, Corpach, Fort William. Tel:772599

K. Foggo.

SMC AND JMCS ABROAD

Several of the reports which follow may indicate some of the mental stresses that can follow trips abroad. Either that or some funny travel medicine was taken along.

Europe

THE 1994 YACHTING MEET

By Drew Sommerville

Or How Mistress Malin treated her cohorts (A tuneless opera in many acts – some dafter than others)

The Cast

The Ancient Mariner (Skipper) – Tam for short, a bold and courageous man.
The 1st Mate, Ewa – the only person to have any control over Tam, and then only sometimes.
The 2nd Mate, name of Chalmers, Robin for short – eat your heart out Vatman – valiant mast-man.
Bosun Bennet – nuff said.
(Reasonably) Able Seaman Sommerville, Rasds for short – he has the answer to the question: 'Where's yo dust bin?' – please ask him.
Halina – a gorgeous Swedish stowaway of Polish extraction.
Bjorn and Odd – two Norwegian part-time joiners.
Christina – a gorgeous Swedish single hander with meteorological tendencies.
The Turtagro Family.
Ship's Parrot – an enigmatic bird that kept a low profile.
And many more forbye.

(Tam was in his cabin baking some more bread. Some of the Crew were down with flu. The Parrot it was dead.)

Act The One.

Scene – Newcastle Docks; Time – the immediate past (June 1994).
THE Bosun and Rasds report to the good ship Venus, would you believe? A poor replica of the real thing – nae figurehead and they didn't think much of the mast either.
Bosun: 'Take me to my Stateroom vassal!' and the two bold lads were immediately escorted to the Admiral's superbly appointed cabin (relatively) high in the stern of the good ship Venus, well a few surly non-European seamen grudgingly pointed the way vaguely backwards.
The action leaps forward to Egersund, no relation of Elsinore – nae mermaids and Hamlet's not in the cast anyway. It's a dreich night, there's no sign of the Mistress Malin and the rain is getting ever heavier; the original plan of kipping under/on top of the picnic tables at the Gjestehavn appears increasingly less desirable, it is decision time – what will the poor mariners do? Fortunately, they are repelled from the best place in town, the Eiger Sentrum Hotell (is this an omen?). B & B at the more economical outpost of the Eiger Motell, a mere half-day's camel journey

away, is the happy alternative, and if you are a discreet mover your packed lunch is included at no extra cost. On the completion of the second portage back to the Gjesthavn lo and behold the Mistress Malin and her gallant passage crew. She's a fine looking craft, as many a Norwegian and fellow yachtsman will agree before the epic voyage is complete.

The voyage continues northwards into ever colder waters and glorious views of (still) snow-covered mountains, Hardangervidda in particular, in fairly busy sea lanes. Bergen is skirted on a quiet Saturday morning and a new sport is discovered – fjord orienteering. There is a myriad of sheltered passages between Bergen and the Sogne Fjord and the navigators were hard at it deciding whether it was right hand down a little or left hand. Ironically, a very favourable wind also brought rain, but this was a blessing in disguise as the whole expedition would have run out of film had the sun been shining, the scenery was so glorious. The cosy little harbour of Eivindvik was reached and the crew settled down for a typical wet Scottish weekend, not that there was much rest to be had as our workaholic skipper talked himself into some major surgery on his Mistress – floorboards up and we'll just do a wee bit of significant rewiring. It has to be said that when the Norwegian mist eased some of the crew went for a long walk – it was a short pier.

Monday dawned bright(er) if not clear – they could actually see some of the way up the surrounding hills. Sognefjord was just round the corner so off they set and by the time they reached the main fjord the day was becoming better and better, suffice to say they had a glorious sail to Ballestrand, dinner being served in the cockpit with Tam overhauling his winches between courses.

They now had to think about climbing – a major psychological shock. How to get to the Jotunheim – the wee lassie at the Informasjon had hardly heard of the Jotunheim, far less Turtagro, but she soon learned. It was bus/ferry/bus/taxi – nae bother. A good deal was struck at Turtagro – bed in the annexe, breakfast in the main hotel which meant a packed lunch at no extra cost, of course; this only left the problem of dinner, solved by setting up the camp kitchen under the verandah – the management were aware of this, but fortunately, had a well-developed sense of humour.

There was fresh snow at Turtagro, and this mid-June, but Wednesday morning was promising so the bold quartet set off up the gently-sloping Ringsbotn to the more steeply-sloping glacier below the Ringstindane. Bosun Bennet gave them a sparkling lead on superb snow with a glorious front-pointing finish to the shapely top of Store Ringstinde (2127m). Due to the unaccustomed land-type exercise Tam began to suffer leg cramps, it was fortunate that his foredeck gorilla-type activity of recent years allowed him to reverse the top 100m by an interesting arm technique – let this be a lesson to all youse chaps wot do too much marinading. The rebellious crew were somewhat impatient with all this delay but were even more displeased later in the day when the anthropoidal one took a more favourable course farther down the glen (and he didn't even have the chart, sorry map), found his second wind and was back at Turtagro and into the showers first. What was even worse, he hadn't put the Primus on for the whisky toddies. He had to go, which he did the next morning, giving the poor excuse that he wanted to play with his Mistress.

And then there were three. It had snowed again, but Store Dyrhaugstindane called so off they went on a good compass bearing and the 2nd Mate's altimeter at hand; there had been talk of liberating the GPS from the Mistress but Rasds became uncooperative when he discovered who was to carry the 12-volt battery. Into the murk they went and after one-and-a-half interesting pitches found themselves on the top. The 2nd Mate had the most patience and was rewarded by a brief clearance to record yesterday's peak on his Nikon.

The joiners were still working away on the annexe on the trio's return and expressed knowledgable interest in their achievements; over dinner that night reasoned opinion came down from on high that they were doubtless part-time guides who possibly did a bit of langlauf tuition in the winter – this was proved to be just a little inaccurate when Rasds discovered that the bigger of the two was actually Odd Eliasson, the first Norwegian to reach the top of Everest and a 'big' expedition man to boot, while his pal Bjorn (just an ordinary guy in his own estimation), must have been pretty high too as there is a glorious colour print in the hotel dining-room of Odd holding the Norwegian flag on the top taken by that 'ordinary guy' Bjorn.

Like all good Norwegian part-time joiners they keep their weather eyes and ears well tuned and so were able to tell the bold, and tiring, trio that good if not excellent weather was forecast for the morrow and they had the very peak for their delectation – Austanbotn tindane. At least one of the trio was hoping for a rest but, alas, Friday dawned absolutely gloriously and Bjorn's kind offer of a lift six miles up the road could not be refused. Straight off the road and on to the snow, crampons on as they get into the shade of the Vestle-Austanbotnen ridge but off again when they swing south and back into the sun. Great views all round as they plod up the main ridge with just a trace of cloud on Austan's south peak – a bad omen, by the time they reach the main gap the visibility is so reduced that the bealach is hardly visible. The bold trio are not put off (yet) and despatch the Bosun on the end of the rope which runs out before the bealach is reached. Decision time and, discretion being the better part of idiocy, the Bosun is retrieved as momentary clearances show a formidable summit ridge leading from the yet unreached bealach. Their mentors had indicated that there would be absolutely no problem in hitching a lift back to Turtagro – alas it was only in the last mile that the first bus of the season stopped to pick up the weary climbers.

This is definitely the trio's last night – the Mistress awaits and time is running out on the 'three-week passes' for two of the crew. There is one last task to be done however, to check that Bill Mackenzie's new route on Storen in the summer of '36 has been suitably recorded by the Norwegians; a little bit of backroom work by the hotel hierarchy and the Norwegian equivalent of the Journal shows that it has – how's that for service?

Warning about Saturday travel in Norway – it's not easy, especially when the bus to Hella is marked Voss. The crew are pleased to note that the Skipper has not only been playing with his Mistress he's been playing the fish as well – lots of lovely herring plus an abandoned mini-shark – all delicious.

Back to the sea-faring life – water that boat, pull that rope and if the Mistress puts her elegant backside on the sand, haul her off sharpish. Tam was beginning to get just a touch annoyed with Rasds at four in the morning after a nice easterly wind had got up and there was a funny rasping noise as the wheel rubbed against the (newly-installed) self-steering – it was only when (in desperation to prove that absolutely nothing was wrong) Tam switched on the echo-sounder he accepted that the depth was zero. It's quite amazing what 'all hands on deck', (very) taut anchor chain, full revs on the engine and a rising tide, not to mention sheer desperation, will do to shift a boat in an embarrassing situation. The result of all this was that Rasds got his wish of a good blow westwards down the Sognefjord, only to spoil it when he gave the command: 'Lee ho,' and promptly jibed! It didn't impress the Skipper.

They almost became tourists – Vik church; walkies along fjords, chatting up fellow-yachtpersons – especially delectable Swedish ones who can take down weather forecasts in three languages and then give a synopsis in English. This actually happened at Fedje, their nearest point of departure for Lerwick.

Fedje to Lerwick in 36 hours, nae bother when you view it through the mists of time.

Rasds takes full and total irresponsibility for the foregoing – all lawyers' letters will be returned postage unpaid – you have been warned.

ALEC KEITH reports:- Derek Bearhop and I enjoyed a compressed Alpine season this year, fitting a trip into the confines of a normal weekend in July. Leaving from Edinburgh Airport after work on Friday afternoon, we flew via Heathrow to Geneva, where we hired a car. After exhibiting our inexperience with left-hand drive vehicles, we reached Lauterbrunnen some time after 2a.m. Saturday dawned overcast, and we spent most of it flogging up 6000ft from Stechelberg, past the Rottal Hut, and into clouds on the lower reaches of the Inner Rottal Ridge on the Jungfrau (AD and apparently a 'splendid long climb', and 'the only satisfactory route on the West flank of the mountain', which means the other lines must be pretty shocking.) We evacuated a bivvy-trough in steep shale beneath the initial difficulties and slept uneasily.

Overnight the weather perked up; we set off at 4a.m., soloing up slabs in the dark, excitement quickly mounting as we lost first the route, then each other. Reunited, we scrambled up 3000ft of worrying choss interspersed with rock, snow, verglas and fixed ropes. A 1000ft of easy snow took us to the summit (4158m) at 8a.m. We descended by the same line, then plunged at knee-wrecking speed to Stechelberg. Three hours of fraught driving later and we were in Geneva at 5.30p.m., with a few minutes to spare before the flight home. Heathrow gremlins, however, ensured we were without luggage by the time we returned to Edinburgh. And so back to work on Monday morning.

IAN ANGELL writes:– The 1994 Scottish Mountaineering Club Staunings Alps Expedition members – Ian Angell, Tim Pettifer, John Morrison, David Ritchie, Ian Blackwood, Andy Hume, Stephen Deykin and Colin Wornham – flew on May 9 with Flugfelag Nordurlands hf (Sigurdur Adelsteinsson) from Akureyri in Iceland to Constable Point in Greenland where equipment freighted in earlier was picked up. From there we went north to land on the Berserkerbrae glacier at about 1170m, latitude 72° 06', Longitude 24° 44' 44" west by the pilot's GPS. The magnetic variation was later calculated to be -30° west.

During the next 16 days various climbs and excursions were made.

Danaketinde 2930m, climbed from the north and by a new route on the South-east face – Alpine D. The record on the top showed this to be the third ascent of the mountain.

Hjornespids 2860m, was climbed from the north via the Dansketinde col. Iced rock – D+.

C. F. Knox Tinde 2750m, climbed by the North Spur – D.

Tintagel c.1800m was climbed by a new route up the South-west ridge – A.D.

Harlech 2040m, by the south flank and the South-east ridge. The record left by
the SMC in 1992 was added to.

A hard mixed route with IV/V ice pitches was made to the ridge between False
Col and Hjornespids.

The following mountains had no record of previous ascents and so names have
been suggested to the Greenlandic Place-Name Committee:

'Crossmyloof' 2000m, situated on the ridge on north side of the Berserkerbrae
connecting the Berserkerspire and Tintagel. This peak was next to the Berserkerspire
and was climbed by the south flank. P.D.

'Pardshaw Peak' 1840m, the peak on the ridge to the west of Tintagel and next
to Crossmyloof. Climbed by the south flank. P.D.

'Shirley's Peak' 2400m. Immediately to the south of the Col Major (Majorpasset)
and climbed from the Col. F. Attempts were made on the Berserketinde by the
North face and Royal Peak.

At the end of the trip all members skied out to the coast, two by crossing from
the Dunottar glacier to the Skjoldungbrae, (probably the first crossing) and the
others by descending to the mouth of the Skel. One night was spent at Mestersvig
before the flight back on May 26.

All food and fuel were wrapped in combustible material and remains were
burned thoroughly to ash before being buried. The rifle and EPIRB were not
needed. The weather remained fine for the duration. A break towards the end gave
a few inches of snow and cloud but was not serious. Snow conditions settled during
the three weeks from being very powdery on arrival to a stable condition later.
Above 2000m it remained cold and on steep slopes hard ice was found beneath the
snow. Towards the coast melting of the river ice was occurring in the afternoon and
this was the only place where any significant thaw was evident.

Travel was on skis with small sledges to distribute loads. Tracks of a fox were
seen near the camp but no food was taken. Low down the Skel the remains of a
recently dead musk ox and a new born calf were found. On an outcrop near the Skel
mouth two musk ox were grazing.

This was the third SMC party to visit the area in the spring months which is
proving a good time for travel and weather. It is a small part of a small area of
Greenland and the opportunities are still immense.

Greenland

BOB DUNCAN writes: *What follows is almost directly transcribed from the diary I
kept on an expedition to the Little Switzerland area of East Greenland in 1980. I
do not expect many to believe the unusual story it tells, especially as it is so long
since the events in question took place, yet they have received no mention until now.
I ask you to read with an open mind and judge for yourself. Obvious questions, in
particular why it has taken so long to come out, will perhaps, with a little reflection,
be seen to have equally obvious answers.*

THE SCENE: A cluster of tents high on the Knud Rasmussen glacier, surrounded by
a mess of sleds, skis, pots, mugs and torn and empty cardboard boxes. Behind them
a steep, black-streaked gneiss wall disappears upwards into the sleety smirr.
Nothing stirs.

Inside the tents, lying in damp and mildewed sleeping-bags, five mountaineers pass the time dozing, reading, reciting nonsense rhymes, occasionally making a brew, or dreaming of something to eat other than porridge and butter. Somewhere down the glacier, they hope, being dragged towards them by the other three expedition members, is the big sledge, heavily laden with the remaining glacier rations. The hazards still in the way of a decent meal, however, are many. The combination of wet snow and hidden crevasses, for example, could claim a victim at any moment. Of more immediate concern to the waiting group, though, as they consider their dwindling culinary resources, is the gender mix of the relief party. One male, two females, with a complex, evolving and still (at that point) incompletely understood web of inter-relationships. Might they, even at this moment, be tent-bound and in deep discussion, oblivious to the plight of their fellows at Advanced Base?

Now read on . . .

I was awakened from my dozing (conserving energy) by the thunder of hooves and the crackle of small-arms fire. On sticking my head out of the tent I was very surprised to see a smallish band of ageing American Red Indians, on scrawny and scabrous ponies, charging our feeble encampment. After a couple of half-hearted and obviously ill-practised circlings of the tents they came to an indecisive halt, and stood among themselves, muttering hoarsely.

An ancient and enfeebled character in what looked like a North American Cavalry jacket and hat gestured our way (for we were all by this time stood outside, somewhat mystified), bared his toothless gums in an evil grin, and loosed off a couple of rounds into the air from an antiquated Winchester. This galvanised the rest of his party into some sort of action, and they turned and charged towards us, firing their rifles and giving awful, bloodcurdling whoops.

The effect was ruined, however, by the ancient's pony, which was in the lead, losing its footing on the wet snow and slithering on to its belly, the remainder of the group falling over it and its groaning rider. The tangled mass slid to a gentle halt in front of Willy, who was watching the proceedings idly, munching an oatcake.

The ancient, obviously the leader, extricated himself from a confusion of legs, hooves, bows and arrows, removed a billy which had been firmly rammed on to his head, and brandished his now useless rifle in Willy's face.

'Now Custer, you pay dearly for what you done' . . .

'Did,' corrected another of the Indians, consulting a battered and torn Sioux/English phrase book, while straightening the feather in his head-band.

'Did,' the ancient spat out, casting a jaundiced eye over his corrector. 'One day, Splitting Hair, I will cut out your tongue.' After an exchange of glares the ancient returned his gaze to Willy, who was by now quietly chewing an Opal Fruit. He removed his tomahawk and made to brain Willy with a mighty sweep.

'Now Custer, you die!'

Noel stepped across, raised his hand, and intercepted the tomahawk, a concerned look in his eyes. 'I say, old chap, you've got it all wrong. This isn't Custer.'

The ancient looked slyly out of the side of his eyes at his fellows, who were watching with some interest. 'No, and I'm not Running Bullock.'

He laughed hugely, thinking he had cracked the joke of all time.

Dick, meanwhile, looked up from mending his stove (for we were needing a brew, fuel shortage and unexpected visitors or not), grabbed the ancient's tomahawk, and started pounding furiously. Pieces of MSR stove began to fly around the camp site. Each vicious blow was accompanied by a heated curse, uttered in an eerie and disturbing whine. As Dick worked himself up into a blind fury his blood pressure rocketed, the scar on his forehead bulged alarmingly and a twisted grin distorted his normally homely features into a terrifying manic mask. The Indians drew back, obviously impressed and not a little intimidated. The ancient scuttled back to join them.

'You no' Custer?', he demanded of Willy, who stood impassively, crumbs on busy jaws. The answer was mumbled through a mouthful of Digestive.

'Nuh.'

The raiding party muttered loudly, then quietened.

'This no' Little Big Horn, then?', said Running Bullock, whose stock was obviously falling rapidly among his peers.

'Well no, actually, this is the Knud Rasmussen Gletscher, East Greenland,' said Noel helpfully, pointing at a photocopied map.

'Shag a wild man,' said Ian ungraciously, shaking his head.

I sniggered to myself and turned away, nearly tripping over Willy, who was rifling through empty food boxes.

The war party held a hurried pow-wow, while we painstakingly rebuilt Dick's stove. The ancient, now totally disregarded by his fellows, crept towards us, casting anxious glances over his shoulder.

'Looky here, you sure this no' Little Big Horn?'

Noel looked sympathetic, but repeated our location: 'I think you've rather missed the party,' he added, by way of conversation.

The ancient ignored him and dug in his jacket, pulling out a battered Silva compass, which had 400° on it.

'What magnetic variation you use?'

'30° West, I'm afraid,' said Noel.

'Oh bugger!' exclaimed Running Bullock, flinging his compass into a nearby crevasse and leaping on to his pony in one arthritic movement.

Within seconds pandemonium broke loose, and the whole group charged off on to the 16th September Glacier in hot pursuit of the ancient, who had built up a considerable lead.

A few minutes passed. Soon the only sound was the gentle patter of rain on the tents, the rumbling of Willy's stomach, and a couple of anonymous farts.

IAIN SMART writes:- *Madeira wine improves in flavour when carried around the world in the hold of a ship. So is the memory of a good expedition if allowed to rock around for a few years in the bottom of your mind. The original experiences grow or diminish in relative importance and achieve a balance unsuspected at the time when they were being harvested from the ambient universe. The immediate account of an expedition is the new wine drunk fresh from the bottle, sparkling and youthful. The Beaujolais Nouveau for the 1985 summer expedition to Petermann Peak in North East Greenland has already been provided by Malcolm Slesser (SMCJ, 1986, xxxiii, 177, 283-287). As expeditions go it was a good vintage and what follows is a flagon drawn from the same cask 10 years later. It seems to contain endless glasses unequally filled and obviously poured from the bottle of the mind by a shaking hand. Since few readers reach this remote corner of the Journal – maybe one every half century – now that you are here, why not relax by this little campfire in the wilderness of time and savour a glass or two of vintage '85 while I enjoy your company.*

Moveo ergo sum:– The weather in August 1985 was perfect for travel, the sun shone day after day and there was no wind. The big fjord leading north, however, was filled with heavy pack-ice. After a day or two of pushing floes apart, we made it as far as a little island in the sun that lay a few miles offshore, the top of a drowned escarpment of red columnar basalt an acre or two in area. We landed in a minute bay on a few yards of dark sand. From a nook at the top of its northern cliff we watched the surrounding ice for signs of movement. The hours passed and merged into days. The sun circled the horizon. The pack drifted to and fro with the tide but didn't loosen. The island meanwhile, started to make itself felt. It was a colourful, intricate place. Little terraces led off from a central basin of red gravel patched with grey, black and bright orange lichens, white and yellow flowers, light green willow and dark cassiope. It was like living on the palette of an artist confident with primary colours and bold forms. From the centre of the magic island the outside world was invisible except for the bright, blue sky. The patterned terraces led the few yards to the sea and the sight of the surrounding hills: the jagged Staunings, the distant profile of Ella Island and the long horizon of Traill Island, 15 miles to the east. A peace began to descend on the mind. The magic of this island was unused, very different from the more experienced magic of a Hebridean island. Ideas started to stir. A month spent here would be an interesting educational experience. This led to questions. Was all this desire for movement merely an excuse to avoid thinking? Were we missing the point? We had maps of everything ahead of us, aerial photographs too; others had been this way before. Were we passing the time playing a hands-on computer game in real time in a sort of actual reality instead of trying to do something original? This island suggested there were unexplored territories on offer to a mind not preoccupied with movement. Intellectual vistas on the other side of the backdrop of the apparent scenery kept opening up for attention. This would never do; people were fidgeting and pacing about restlessly. We were getting nowhere fast. We must set off and at least try to accomplish something; otherwise we would have no story to tell, no slides to give a show with, no achievement to show our worth, no sense of fulfilment, no story to sell. As we loaded the boat I had a wild urge to throw out a few food boxes and say: 'Pick me up on your way back.' If I had, I might have done some original journeys into wild and wonderful new territory. It was very tempting to snatch such an opportunity for original exploration but, alas, I had not the strength of character to bring off so bold an action. I got into the boat reluctantly, the last to do so. I had to go. I was supposed to be the leader.

Quinquireme of Nineveh:– The south side of Ella Island presents a wall of near vertical rock rising straight from the sea for 4000ft. A waterfall at its centre bounces once or twice on the way down. The rock looks good, a prize ascent for some lucky climber of the future. We sailed below it in a matronly fashion in an underpowered inflatable boat towing another smaller one behind and making about four knots. We were also grossly overloaded with ration boxes crammed with food from half the world: pineapple from Hawaii, spices from the Indies, royal game soup from Fochabers; we had high-tech tents, sleeping bags of the finest feather and clothing of such oversophistication it was almost chic; we had jerry cans of refined fossil fuel and the complex engineering to transform it into movement; we also had a state-of-the-art radio with which to talk to the world and a rifle to neutralise the local wildlife should it become too uppity. We chatted urbanely about the hundred and

one exotic places we had visited at one time or another. We read sophisticated
novels, some of us indulged in the affectation of playing liar dice to while away the
time. From time to time we looked at the view through the portholes of our minds.
And so we crawled along the foot of this beetling cliff like a caddis fly grub, our
soft parts armoured against the world by a carapace of material and psychological
comforts or, more vaingloriously, (and why not) we sailed like a quinquireme of
Nineveh, our five banks of oarsmen rowing rhythmically within our engine like
genies in a bottle bearing us along with our cargo of apes and peacocks, cedarwood,
sandalwood and sweet white wine.

Respect for the professionals:– As you travel the empty coasts of North East
Greenland you come across good campsites and find that someone has been there
before you. The most humbling of these are low walls of stone and turf with a
lintelled doorway, the winter houses of an Inuit population that survived here for
a few hundred years, dying out last centuries just as Europeans reached this area.
Scoresby described their empty settlements. A small band was seen once in the
middle of last century and then no more: maybe they were the last of a population
that once numbered a few score, the maximum this bare land could support. These
were the professionals and one ought to tread deferentially in their empty home-
land. Their minimal technology was of such a high standard that they were able to
survive entirely on the thin resources of this indifferent land. The only import they
had was driftwood from the Siberian rivers delivered by the sea currents. All other
materials were of local origin: bone, skin, sinew and a stone or two. Even in what
might pass as good times, North East Greenland is borderline survival country even
for an Inuit band. It is a chastening and therefore beneficial exercise for the summer
visitor to pause for a moment and in his mind switch off the daylight and imagine
the vulnerability of life here in the winter dark at the absolute zero of human ability
to survive. An oil lamp under a low roof with a squalor of meat and blubber
represented security for the foreseeable future. In this minimal condition they
created some sort of psychological home to protect their souls from the stark
pressures of an uncertain, ungenerous land; they told stories, made jokes, sang
songs, made poems, carved toys for their children. Sooner or later a hunter did not
come back from the ice and his dependants died, for in hard times the remaining
hunters, if there were any in the area, could not take on the demands of someone
else's widows and orphans. It was of no great moment anyway because death was
only the process you had to go through before rejoining your ancestors in a generous
hunting ground in the sky where there was no cold and hunger; such a place
certainly existed because those who had gone before held parties up there that were
so wild they could be seen in this world as the northern lights. Or then again the dead
might wander about in the cold moonlight, malicious and restless and envious of
the living. More prosaically premature death by accident or hunger depleted a
dangerously small gene pool, some diminishing the ability of those remaining to
cope with a borderline existence.

Nansen survived one winter in an underground house with a skin roof but he shot
enough animals in the autumn to leave a pile of meat and blubber outside the door
sufficient to last till spring. Steffansson speaks of the 'friendly Arctic'; he lived off
the land for three years but in a much more prosperous part of the Arctic than this.
Both Nansen and Steffansson had guns, steel knives, matches and other locally
irreplaceable artefacts. Also they had companions as resourceful as themselves
who didn't get killed or incapacitated to leave the survivor frighteningly alone or

worse still lethally burdened with an invalid. Most importantly they didn't have families of vulnerable children to maintain; without these, individual survival is of no biological value. Mighty men though they were, they were essentially visitors from another planet living on imported psychological and material reserves. Our expedition by these standards was a summer holiday or at best an educational tour for aging yuppies long past their Arctic shelf life.

Playboys of the western world:– We entered the shadows of Kaiser Franz Joseph's Fjord towards midnight. It is a lonely, forbidding place at this shadowy time, a narrow slit, steep-sided and filled with unstable icebergs calved from the glaciers at its head. The event I remember so clearly is the occasion Slesser and I had our turn in the small boat. Unloaded and powered by the spare outboard it could get up on the plane and scoot around at 10 or 12 knots. We did this occasionally as a relief from the sedate progress of the stately quinquireme. We skimmed away into the shadows and slalomed among the icebergs which rocked decorously and dangerously in the wake. We paused a couple of miles away on the smooth black water out of sight and sound of our material support. The bergs caught what little light remained and glowed spookily in the gloom, dimly teetering around their centres of buoyancy as the universe worked out the mathematics of whether they were going to topple into the here and now or remain ghostly metaphors of uncertainty. As we all know there is a wild delight in voluntarily playing under the paw of the great cat, putting a toe over the line and imagining what it would be like to cross it without the possibility of coming back. We, of course, were playboys and kept well on the safe side of the line. After frightening ourselves for a little we returned to the mother ship and rejoined our lumbering capsule of protective artifacts.

A sense of place:– We emerged from the narrow part of the fjord into the broad waters at its head just as the light was improving. This is a magic time in the Arctic and it coincided with reaching the inner sanctum of this mountain fastness. Awe is an unfashionable word and it has lost most of its emotional charge from overuse. However, the feeling it used to describe is still to be experienced in places like this if you are that way inclined. Here there was space and silence, a wide sea filled with icebergs and reflections of icebergs and all around were mountains of light and shadow and great valleys leading into a mysterious interior. Emotionally, it was a bit like crawling out of a window in your mind and finding yourself exposed on a high smooth face without a hold in sight while the mind rummaged around for a metaphor to chock into some crack to provide the semblance of security. I think the trouble was that we had passed a psychological barrier and had entered territory not yet appropriated into our scheme of things. This was not a place you could walk back from either on foot or in your mind. Maybe I was alone in this feeling but I think the rest of the party was also a bit subdued.

Holiday camp:– Half a day after our arrival we had tramped down a platform in the emptiness and were well secured with psychological belays. Our tents were pitched on a sandy platform a 100ft above the icebergs. The sun shone; there was no wind; it was very hot; we sunbathed in our underpants. It was a moment of detente before back-packing into the interior. Slesser to show how at home he was in the Arctic lay around starkers reading a racy novel. Pat set up the radio aerial and after unfankling a wandering musk ox from its coils chatted urbanely to the Danes in Mestersvig; he also recorded the sweet twitterings of Horneman's redpoll. Phil tootled endlessly on his penny whistle, cogitating on his future. Roland remained quiet; he was lean fit and self-sufficient; he had no need to do anything else. I continued to investigate who was in charge of this remote area. Thus each of us was making a statement, some more amusingly than others.

The room at the top:– One day we did get to the topmost rocks of Petermann Peak by two routes of modest difficulty. It was a magic day of light and cloud shadows. We were on the highest point for 600 miles; it was all there below us: mountains and glaciers, receding eastward into the mysterious inland ice. This was the fourth ascent but we were so bemused by all the ambience that we quite forgot to scrubble in the cairn for any record left by previous visitors. In order to achieve this remote position we had exercised a fair amount of organising ability, physical effort, determination in the face of adversity and frank mountaineering competence. These virtues are already the stuff of a thousand climbing narratives and their further consideration here would be boring. The uniqueness of our situation was that we had a special freedom denied to most other expeditions in the sense that we were self-financed. We had no need to do science; we had no need of success or disaster to enhance the sale of a book, no obligations to have something interesting happen to entertain future audiences with slide shows. There was untrammelled room at the top of this particular mountain and the freedom to be conscious in the present without past or future strings.

The scale of it all:– We had travelled the 125 miles from Mestersvig to the head of KFJ Fjord at an average speed of four to five knots. This is equivalent to putt-putting from Oban to the head of Loch Torridon by the Sounds of Mull, Sleat and Raasay at a time when Scotland was emerging from the ice age. No human artefact would be lying around in this proto-Scotland except for, maybe, the ruined camps of some dead nomadic hunters who had arrived before the country was really open for business. The St.unings, like the Cuillins, rise straight from the sea but are well over twice the height and cover several times the area. The fjords were anything from two to 20 miles across; some were narrow passages with steep walls, others were bordered by musk ox pastures. From the head of the Arctic Loch Torridon we relayed our food and equipment for 35 miles inland, say from Inveralligan to Beinn Mor Fannich elevated to three times its height. I am not telling you all this to solicit your admiration. This type of journey after all, if you watch your step, is a lot safer than driving from Blairgowrie to Glasgow. I think I'm trying to make myself realise what a high privilege it was to travel in this vast unpopulated wilderness.

The hunting band:– The experience of being a member of a small free-travelling band of competent equals exploring new territory is satisfyingly atavistic. It was what the much-maligned male version of the human mind is good at. There are, alas, no longer any unknown oceans to navigate or Bering land bridges to be crossed into unpopulated worlds. Failing the real thing we are driven to do something unusual requiring skill and nerve. It is apparently something to do with mate selection. To do something bold and original with a bit of violence thrown in shows you have plenty of biological reserves at your disposal and so demonstrates that you are the possessor of a genome with spare capacity for the competitive game of life. Some biolgically-aware female may therefore select you for matrimony after which your biological competence is utilised for supplying the resources for raising a family of dynamic offspring. Thereafter the demonstration of exploratory prowess for its own sake becomes socially taboo. The various substitutes on offer, such as beating a commercial opponent into the ground or its somewhat more respectable analogue, namely, ram-raiding a shopping mall with a borrowed Range

Rover are both said to be pretty good, but they can't possibly be as satisfying as the real thing. The present journey through the wilderness of East Greenland with self-reliant companions was a homeopathically-diluted version of fulfilling of our basic design and gave a vestigial feel of what the Real Thing must be like.

The chocolate mountain:– On our return journey we made a side trip along a sound running to the north into a curiously different landscape. Its western shore was dominated by ruined mountains shaped like ziggurats, the highest about 4000ft, they presented a striking horizon when silhouetted against the setting sun. The other shore, the one we followed was steep too and made up of loose contorted strata of browns, yellows and whites. Some of the strata were wavy and as thin as biscuit; others were monstrous layers of flaky pastry. We reached a small bay which marked a transition to a stepped hillside cradling little lochans in its treads. Above this stepped pedestal there was a mountain of chocolate coloured rock, steep but disintegrating. One of its hanging glaciers had pushed a steep frontal moraine of chocolate rock onto a grassy meadow; you could see the bright greensward disappearing under the rich brown jumbled blocks as if they had toppled on to the fresh, green grass the day before. I showed a photograph to a world famous glaciologist who also found its origin mysterious. Whoever constructed this area had unconventional ideas about mountains. Being here broadened the mind. This area was actually brilliantly original, a virtuoso performance in the art of orogeny, free of repetition and without a single orographic cliche.

The iceberg in the distance:– We camped that night at the little bay on the east side of Ymir's Island looking west across to the ruined ziggurats of the opposite shore. The sound was three miles across here. Maybe a score of icebergs were scattered around. If a big berg coups the wave it creates can be substantial and in a narrow fjord its front is throttled by the walls and a tsunami can flood 30ft vertical up the shore. We were safe here in calm wide open water so we moored the big boat to the shore by its bow keeping its stern out with an anchor. Nevertheless, from force of habit we pulled the small boat 12ft above high water. After supper as we sat communing with the work of the Great Artist one of the distant icebergs slowly keeled over and its new summit spire metronomed against the dark opposite shore. Thank goodness it was such a small one and so far away. So we could relax. Then there was a roar. Sound travels slower than light of course. Then there was this wall of water coming at us. Help! Get the boat farther up. We had moved it a few feet when the wave hit carrying the boat still farther up the shore. The bigger boat lifted its stern anchor off the sea floor and give a mighty twanging tug at its bow rope and then almost crashed against the bottom of the bay as the wave receded. That was the worst over; the subsequent tsunamis scaled themselves down progressively. It was only a small iceberg as icebergs go – about the size, say, of Edinburgh Castle, well at least the size of Stirling Castle, certainly as big as St Gile's Cathedral and we were at, say, the bottom of Calton Hill or the Abbey Craig. A bit bigger and we might have been bereft of everything, facing the winter without even skin, bone or sinew, well not as bad as that, but we would have been very humbled by our carelessness, particularly if the magic, all-singing, all-dancing radio had been silenced. This was not a place you could walk back from.

Personal Glimpses:– Phil was wont to tootle endlessly on his penny whistle as he worked out in his mind the next decisions in his life. The tootlings were semi-competent renderings of folk tunes. One day Roland picked up the whistle and played exquisitely a fragment of Mozart with all the twiddly bits. He then put the flute down and made no further comment. Phil seemed to miss the point and continued his tootlings unabashed.

Leading an expedition with Slesser in it is a complicated business. Things have to be stratified into several levels with minimal intermixing. Occasionally, leaks occur. At one time I heard him remark with some irritation: 'There are decisions being taken in this expedition that I don't know about.' Pat was a man of many talents: internationally-acclaimed birdsong recordist, technically competent in many fields from tram-driving to hawking, aficionado of Haydn quartets and possessor of vast stores of arcane lore; on the downside, alas, he had lost the original lenses in both eyes due to cataract; nevertheless, he drove sports cars and motor-cycles and had retained his pilot's licence and was proficient in aerobatics. Roland was wiry, superbly fit and utterly competent, a widely-experienced mountaineer. Without him and Phil we geriatrics would never have made it. He flew aeroplanes, too, from microlights to his own upmarket monoplane. In the former, specially adapted to carry a variety of sensors, he surveyed territory in Third World countries and in the latter went week-ending from his home in North Italy to Crete and Malta.

An intended member, a friend of Malcolm's, who couldn't make it at the last moment was the former Italian ambassador to Argentina during the Falkland's War. His presence would have enhanced the texture of the group by another magnitude. So we had to make do with what we had.

Sunset Song:– North of Ella Island five sounds meet and at the centre of their wide confluence is a flat-looking island with a rounded hill on it. The map indicated its height was 530m. As we emerged into the confluence from Antarctic Sound on our way home it looked like a good place to camp with a view point for an after-dinner stroll. We approached over a calm sea amid lengthening shadows. The form of the island became more complex; the level base was a barren expanse of dark jumbled rock, the hump a fin of steep unstable slabs. The coast presented a line of low fractured cliffs with a few black sandy beaches. We landed on one and tried to break in to the interior. There was no level ground for a tent, only jumbled rocks. There was also an atmosphere of hostility. The place had an aura. This was one of these islands that didn't like to be visited, at least in its present mood. We coasted the southern shore to the far end where we found that the edge of the fin came down to the sea. We landed again in the shadows of a narrow strip of cold gloomy beach. I sensed that we were not welcome. Fortunately, we had people with us who were able to handle situations like this and we began to climb the revolting unstable rocks. The beginning was a series of steep loose gullies. Perseverance lead on to a ridge of stable rock which took us by pleasant scrambling to the top. We made it in under an hour; we were fit by now. The summit of this shadowy citadel was paradoxically a bright friendly place like the top of an iceberg emerging into sunshine from gloomy submarine depths. We were above the horrors in a still evening of soft colours with the sun just about to descend below the northern horizon. It would take too long to describe the total experience: the colours, the silence, the feel of air so clear the furrows made by a family of eider ducks were clearly visible on the smooth sea far below, the mysterious Vega and Sofia Sounds leading easterly to the bear-prowled outer coast, the sunny unexplored northlands and the dark, sunless south whither we were bound.

We reached Ella Island later that night and rounded its eastern cape deep in the gloaming, feeling our way along the dim shoreline, hitting a fearful rock that was lurking beneath the surface but nothing worse. We camped at the head of a bay. A driftwood fire made a little globe of yellow light on the edge of the immense darkness to come. Thank God we didn't have to face a winter here using skin, bone and sinew to win sustenance from a bare land so far beyond everything that the northern lights flicker in the southern sky.

A few days later we were back in Scotland, one of the better-off residential estates of the world, living among intellectually well-to-do friends who weren't stuck for the odd sirloin steak and bottle of good claret. By and large, balancing this against that, taking one thing with another and when all is said and done it is really not all that bad being a playboy; there are worse belays on the Eigerwand of life.

Thank you for joining me. I'm sorry I've rambled on so long; you may be the only person ever to reach this remote corner of the Journal so I have had to make the most of it.

Asia

JOHN STEELE reports:– John Steele and Barbara Gibbons spent five weeks during October and November 1992, trekking and climbing in the Rowlwaling and Khumbu regions of Nepal. Ascents were made of Parchemo (6200m) from the high pass of Trashi Labtsa followed by a descent into the Everest foothills and a view from Gokyo Ri (5300m).

GRAHAM LITTLE reports:– In 1994 I was a member of an Indian British expedition to the Tirung Gad valley in the beautiful Kinnaur region of the Indian Himalaya. Climbing with Jim Fowler, I took part in the first ascent of the hitherto highest unclimbed peak in the area. It was named Rangrik Rang (6553m) and was climbed by its long North-east Ridge from the head of the Racho Khad glacier. The climbing, although never technically harder than Scottish II/III, proved fairly serious due to a deep layer of unstable snow overlayering ice. The weather was superb and the summit provided stunning views over Garhwal, Gangotri, Kulu, Spiti and Tibet. Two fine unclimbed 6450m peaks lie to the south west of Rangrik Rang and the very shapely Phawarang (6349m) lies to the north west providing excellent future expedition objectives if political restrictions can be overcome.

South East Asia

WITH a base in the Far East since 1993, John Steele and Barbara Gibbons have been exploring that which stands above the tropical jungle. So far ascents have been made of Mt. Kina Balu (4100m) in North Borneo and two volcanos in Java, Gunung Gedi (2900m) and Merapi (2900m), the latter now somewhat lower having erupted violently several weeks after the climb. Exploration continues.

Australasia

JOHN Steele and Barbara Gibbons spent several weeks in South Island New Zealand in December 1994. The first week was spent in Mt. Aspiring National Park where ascents were made of Mt. French (2300m) from the Mt. French hut and Mt. Aspiring (3000m) from the Colin Todd hut. During the second week in Mt. Cook National Park ascents were made of Horschetter Dome (2800m) and Mt. Aylmer (2600m) from Tasman Saddle hut. A two-day exit was made down the Tasman glacier (20k) including a ceremonial crossing of Aoraki's debris which acts as a permanent reminder of Mt. Cook's partial collapse three years ago. The final sojourn coincided with the centennial celebrations of Cook's first ascent on Christmas Day 1894.

JORGE Y LOS ALTARES

The obituary notice of George Gibson appeared in last year's Journal; Raymond Simpson has sent in the following account of his experiences in South America with this overlarge character.

Ayacucho, August 1977 – Only dust whipped up by the scouring winds of the altiplano ever obscured the sun at this time of year. The clarity of the atmosphere was remarkable, throwing into relief the details of the architecture and the mountains, and casting long evening shadows which quickly chilled the thin air. From our room we could watch the Quechua women, heads bowed as they scurried to and from the market place, their produce sold mainly by Mestiso shopkeepers, the proud bourgeoisie of the highland capital. One girl, an olive seller, had me enthralled by her handsome, dark looks and large eyes which glistened like the delicious olives which she proffered to us so seductively: 'Olivos Gringo, quire olivos Gringita.' At that time Ayacucho was innocent of the passion and horror of the Sendero Luminoso and Gringos followed naively in the footsteps of the original Inca imperialists along the length of the Peruvian Andes.

It was in the marketplace that we met with other travellers and gleaned crucial information about the state of the roads over the mountains, where and when the trucks/buses left, on which days were the borders open, who needed bribes, where you could find toilet paper.

'You're mountain climbers,' drawled the Yank. 'No kidding, we met a guy up in Quito, he was looking for climbing partners, Scots guy like yourselves, red beard, something to do with forestry in the Oriente, what the hell was he called now? George, but the locals called him Horhe,' the girl added with a look which suggested that this Scots guy was not without a certain charm.

That was about as much as they could tell us, but we were intrigued enough to risk a few soles on a card addressed to Snr. Jorge, Red-haired Scottish forester c/o Embajada Britanica, Quito.

Several mountains and countries later we were picking up films and mail at a Poste Restante address in Lima when we came across a rather cryptic card from one George Gibson which suggested we meet him on the last Wednesday of any month in El Pub (ask anyone where it is, it's the only Pub in Ecuador).

Quito, October 1977 – The Hotel Grand Casino, or as it was more commonly known in Quito, The Grand Gringo, had an air of decaying opulence. A tall narrow building, formed around a courtyard containing a dried-up fountain and peopled by dope heads and travel-weary gringos of all nationalities. It resembled something between the Tower of Babel and Gormenghast. As in the prison we visited (briefly) in La Paz, you locked yourself in, pulled down the shutters and explored other realities in your own way. Some got stoned, some read, wrote, made love, became quietly alienated or noisily paranoid. What did we chose to do? We made mince and tatties on a Primus stove.

The crowded, jolting bus ride took us to the other side of the tracks, the Hilton, Sheraton and squeaky clean diplomatic enclaves and there it was, nestling in the noonday equatorial glare between the Embajada Britanica and the U.S. embassy El Pub. My eyes took some time to adjust to the smokey gloom, my nose trembled with the all-too-unfamiliar reek of strong ale and whisky; like Alice I had passed through a door into another world. George was at the bar, he was unmistakable, a gap-toothed smile with a fag hanging from the corner framed by an outrageous beard and lank red hair. 'What'll ye hae?' From that moment our fortunes changed, George was up from the Oriente on leave and had no time to waste, we partied for days with the great and the good (and the bad) of Quito. We discoed, danced eightsome reels, dined and wined with the local Baron and his dame.

At the weekend we went off in the 'Queens Land Rover' to attempt a new route on Illiniza Snr. George and I failed in the mist and the dark at 2a.m. We jogged round the mountain to catch the others who had joined forces with some Irishmen on the north face. About 2000ft of brittle 50° ice and a couple of hairy 'schrunds and seracs later we were strolling along the summit ridge. George had soloed the route in better condition earlier in the year. From the summit he pointed out the main Ecuadorian summits, mainly volcanoes, and regaled us with his exploits and ambitions, chief of which was the then unrepeated ascent of Altar. This peak was George's *Bete Noir*, technically the hardest, most remote peak in Ecuador. Buried in the mists of the rain forests it had defeated him on several occasions. By the time he left to drive back to the Oriente we had planned a Christmas assault on the peak.

While he was away we ticked off Cotopaxi, Chimborazu, and Tungerawa. Linda and I visited the coast for a week of sun, sand and seafood, Annie and Stuart were lucky and caught a Logistical flight to the Galapagos.

Los Altares, Christmas 1977 – We rendezvoused just before Christmas at the home of a Marxist architect from Edinburgh called Charles Hooper who was living on a self-help housing project in Riobamba. We had met Charles on Chimborazu, where we had also picked up a pair of wacky carpenters Bart and Ed, from the Green Mountains of Vermont. This was the team. Reinforced by a bottle of Scotch and a take-away roast guinea pig each we crammed into the Queens Land Rover and headed out towards Altar.

George described Los Altares as the Black Cuillin with glaciers and seracs, a vast exploded caldera alive with the noise of crashing rock and ice and bellowing of the torros (a herd of fighting bulls pastured on the grassy floor of the caldera). For only a few days each year these mythical peaks revealed themselves above the cloud sea which billowed up from the Amazon jungle.

We established a base camp in the caldera, the burros and their arrieros left to return to their villages for Christmas, and we prepared for a feast. Our spirits undampened by the equatorial drizzle we sat in our ponchos around the fire, sharing roast guinea pigs, roast potatoes and a crash helmet full of trifle. The torros roared and the peaks drifted in and out of sight as we drifted in and out of consciousness. The whisky bottles were passed round for innumerable toasts, George entertained us with readings from his holy trinity Humble, Murray and Burns. Bart and Ed revealed a vast folk, rock, country repertoire and Stuart told hilarious and improbable tales of an apprentice plumber.

Not surprisingly, we surfaced late on Christmas Day to sort out the loads for the carry to the 'Italian campsite' on the other side of the mountain where the ice crashed less. After an arduous haul up the vegetated side of the caldera we saw our proposed route for the first time and realised that we would have to climb most of it at night and climb it quickly. Two consecutive 2000ft couloirs, both threatened by serac fall and guarded by gaping icicle-fringed 'schrunds led to a steep black tower on the summit ridge. As we were all acclimatised and had slept late from our excesses of the night before we decided to leave at midnight after six hours of darkness had frozen the mountain. Ed opted out, Linda and Annie volunteered to guard the base camp from the torros which left George, Bart, Stuart and myself to make a dash for the summit.

George quoted W. H. Murray as I grappled in the pitch black of midnight with the ice wall overhanging the first 'schrund. As we tiptoed up the rotten ice of the couloir the moon came out and the neighbouring volcanic peak of Sangay erupted billowing sparks and phosphorescence into the night sky. Streams of lava poured down its flanks, this display continued all night illuminating our progress in a dramatic yet eerie manner.

George tried the fringe of icicles leading into the next couloir but the pillars of ice just tinkled into the 'schrund as he sought placements. He stepped up and around the lip and launched himself onto a verglas-coated black wall mumbling something about Bill's 'soaring like a bird' somewhere in Clachaig Gully. Once into the upper couloir we found it narrower, steeper and the hard ice seamed with highly-polished chutes, an evil place. We climbed as fast as our bursting lungs would allow, front points barely penetrating the ice. At the top the rock pitch again fell to George, steep, loose and volcanic, but George was in his element. He said later that it reminded him of the Furgen Ridge of the Matterhorn which was the sort of obscure characterful route from a bygone era which fascinated him.

We gathered on top of the black tower for the final section of the ridge just as the sun was bursting over the Amazon cloud sea. The Glenfiddich was drained on the summit and planted, with Linda's tartan ribbon round its neck, deep in the cornice which overhung the caldera.

I have a photo on my wall of George, wearing 'the breetches faither once courted mother in' (with the arse looking sadly distressed) standing nonchalantly far too near the edge of that cornice.

Knowing we were sitting on a time bomb we hastily abseiled the length of the upper couloir and having used all our gear, precariously down-climbed the lower one. We leapt the bottom 'schrund just ahead of the first volley of ice.

George was elated with the speed of our ascent of Altar which he had coveted since his arrival in Ecuador. We celebrated by moving the party from Quito to his jungle residence in Lago Agrio for Hogmanay.

Lago Agrio, New Year 1978 – Going from the altiplano to Lago Agrio was like the descent into hell. Cliff-hugging mountain roads spiralled down 10,000ft past roadside shrines and tiny upturned buses in inaccessible gorges into the cloud filled Amazon basin. In those days it was a 10-hour journey protracted by mud slides, quagmires and on this occasion a head-on collision with a timber truck. We abandoned the mangled jeep and hitched the rest of the way on a variety of overcrowded vehicles.

The Oriente was George's domain, the steamy jungle where the humid night air was punctuated by loud and violent noises; the screeching of birds and monkeys and the droning of insects, gun shots, women screaming, and men roaring drunk – for Lago Agrio was a mining town with bars and bordellos lining its street.

George lived in a shack on stilts on a half-acre section demarcated by a moat forming a sewage ditch like a medieval Scottish burgh. On our arrival he produced the assortment of kilts which he had begged, borrowed or stolen for the occasion, in order that we would have at least one properly-dressed set for an eightsome reel.

He had also procured – as if from nowhere – a contingent of Australian lassies to provide partners, George was good at that sort of thing.

We were already merry when the bells rang for the Scottish New Year at 6p.m. local time. Six hours later the brass bands and rockets went off to bring in the Ecuadorian one and we were still dancing when the sun came up, birling even faster and more furiously on the brink of the sewage ditch. George regaled us with quotes from Rabbie Burns and Billy Connolly. Ed chased, caught, and rang the necks of George's scraggy chickens for the N'er day broth and there was mony the sair heid swinging in a hammock in the shade of the noonday sun of the first of January 1978.

Last year George died on Ben Nevis. Many who will miss him gathered with his family, to share their grief and our stories of his zest for life. This is only one of these stories, there are and will be many more.

Ireland

Dave Broadhead writes:– LAST year Des Rubens and I had a vague summer plan for a week away rock climbing which eventually crystallised into a trip to the North of Ireland. Researching the cost of ferries almost changed our destination to somewhere closer to home, but a '6-Day Return' on 'SeaCat Scotland' seemed a good deal. It saw us trying to snatch a few hours' sleep huddled in the car, parked in a wet lay-by outside Stranraer, ready to catch the first sailing at 6a.m. Cruising along at 37 knots is more like travel by train than ferry boat, and 90 minutes later we were driving out of Belfast as the morning rush was just starting to stream in. We had a contact in Annalong, County Down, in the person of Phil Holmes, one of the small group of enthusiastic and much-travelled Irish climbers, and after a second breakfast with him we were walking up the Annalong Valley into the Mournes.

Lamagan Slabs, Lower Cove, Upper Cove, Slieve Beg, Annalong Buttress and Hares Castle were all crags in easy reach of our campsite beside the burn. Apart from a group of three climbers from the Sports Council Centre and four schoolgirls with the grim looks of Duke of Edinburgh's Award determination we did not speak to another soul in two days – remarkably quiet for the first week in August, the hills gleaming a vivid purple with heather. On Lower Cove; Agags Wall (HS); Pillar Variant (S); First Corner (HS), and Dots Delight (HVS) are all excellent routes on rough compact granite. No wonder Phil Gribbon always has a smile on his face. After dinner, hungry midges discouraged sitting around, so we climbed Slieve Donard (850m) highest point in Ulster and a fine viewpoint across to the neighbouring Slieves dotted with warty tors and traversed by the amazing granite wall built by the Belfast Water Co. to enclose the catchment of its reservoirs. Despite some drizzle, next morning we sampled the mountain atmosphere of Slieve Beg, diverted from Devils Rib (VD) in a half-hearted attempt to rescue a cragfast sheep, just time for Poetic Justice (VS) before our dinner engagement in Annalong and a few welcome Guinesses in the Harbour Bar.

Another early start saw us on the road west, crossing the Province and into County Donegal. Entry into the Republic was marked by a sudden deterioration in the quality of the road surface and under the additional burden of two canoes on the roof, extra careful driving was required to minimise the alarming scraping of my new exhaust on frequent humps and bumps, so it was a great relief to arrive at last at Malinbeg on the Rossaun peninsula. Des was disappointed by the demise of the donkey cart and thatched cottage since his first visit to Eire, but despite the comforts of their cosy new kit bungalows there were plenty of folk out working in the long strips of fields stretching down to the sea and it still seemed to be in order for climbers to park and camp at the top of the cliff. Not that there were any other climbers, just the ubiquitous German campervan.

Malinbeg's steep walls and slabs of clean quartzite offer a great selection of single-pitch routes with a friendly atmosphere unless the tide is high, but much more spectacular, around the headland to the south, the cliffs of Slieve League (595m) are rated among the highest in Europe, plunging from summit to sea. Too broken to offer much in the way of climbing they are spectacular enough to merit closer inspection from the sea, especially having taken two canoes as a wet weather contingency. Paddling the seven miles or so along the foot of the cliffs from Teelin back to Malinbeg took us past the impressive concave sweep of Sail Rock which attracted Doug Scott's attention in the Sixties. Exploring a series of rocky archways, caves and tiny gravelly beaches, huge amphitheatres with waterfalls spraying into the sea, it turned out to be a fantastic trip. Even the walk back to collect the car, following the top of the cliffs and over the summit in the quiet of the evening seemed like an added bonus. A local farmer, scanning unlikely pastures for errant sheep was the only person I met. He explained that it was the weather which caused the problems ... 'when it's good they stay up, but when it's bad they try to go down.' A lesson there for us all I suppose.

Another day, another delight, heading inland to experience one of Donegal's mountain crags at Lough Belshade, an hour or so from the road end above Lough Eske. The first part of the approach follows the Donegal Way, a long-distance footpath. Despite the spell of dry weather we were enjoying, the path confirmed the worst about the nature of much of Ireland's wilderness. Fortunately, the bog trotting was well worthwhile for behind Lough Belshade an astonishing amount of granite lies scattered across the hillside in the form of broken slabs, boulders and outcrops bristling among the heather, along with the inevitable shepherd gathering up a few sheep. For all this rock there is only one crag of any size, Belshade Buttress, but Lest We Forget (HVS) and Land of Hearts Desire (HVS) were both excellent routes. Boots were carried up the latter so we could carry on upwards and see some more of these unique Blue Stacks, despite the haze and our lack of a map.

Our final day started with a long drive up past Londonderry into County Antrim, to Fair Head. The high quality and number of climbs on these magnificent cliffs has attracted a regular band of SMC enthusiasts including Des, on his third visit. Although at the easy end of things Girona (VS) and Roaring Meg (VS) confirmed the quality of the vertical dolerite. No sheep to be seen, just the smelly remains of a cow which had taken a fatal tumble and a party of American tourists. Certainly no other climbers. Des was able to recover some gear still sitting at the foot of the crag where it had landed when he dropped it a month or so before. With so many excellent climbs on literally miles of cliff we could only look forward to a return visit, as we tucked into a fish tea in Ballycastle before hurrying back to Belfast to catch the evening SeaCat home.

For anyone planning a trip, there are excellent rock climbing guides available for the Mournes, Donegal and Fair Head. As in Scotland, new-route activity renders these out of date as soon as they are published but even the recently-out-of-print Constable Guide *Rock Climbing in Ireland* edited by Calvin Torrans and Dawson Stelfox has enough three-star classics, particularly in the easier grades, for an exploratory visit. *Walking Ireland's Mountains* by David Herman (Appletree Press) and *Ireland: The Rough Guide* by Margaret Greenwood and Hildi Hawkins have up to date background information, bibliographies and useful addresses. Please don't all rush at once.

REVIEWS

Review of *The First Munroist,* by Robin Campbell (SMCJ, 1994, pp. 555-557).
*The review section of the Journal is, I hope, one of perennial interest to readers,
and one which serves a double purpose of being both readable and informative.
None of us like the bland, always polite type of review, which fills space but little
else. A reviewer should be able to say what he or she thinks, within limits, otherwise
we are doing a disservice to reader and publisher alike. It is possible, on the other
hand, that a reviewer's passion for the subject under scrutiny can lead to an
energetic and perhaps overheated exchange, where both sides may get their gaiters
muddied. In response to the review, the authors have sent in the following detailed
and spirited defence of their book, published here in full. This is followed by a letter
from Robin Campbell. With the publication of these two responses, we regard the
matter as closed. (Ed.)*

This is a response to a review of *The First Munroist* in SMCJ, 1994, in which Robin
Campbell makes the two assertions: 'Drummond and Mitchell are worthless as
historians,' (p555) and, 'Almost any fact which the reader takes the trouble to check
will turn out to be false or misrepresented in some way.' (p555). We believe that
these statements are totally untrue, are malicious, and indeed libellous. We further
assert that he has made more errors in his review than he claims to have found in
our book: and that the errors he claims to have found are quite peripheral to the
book, being largely from photo captions or side issues.

Let us look at his points in the order they appear in the review.

1. AER's rock-climbing.

* The book's phrase '. . . he took up rock-climbing after his Munro completion'
was (p3) – in the context of the introductory chapter painting a broad picture first
– intended to emphasise the shift in AER's concentration, from Munro-bagging up
until 1901 (compleation year), to rock-climbing for the next few years. It is made
quite clear in the book that he did some rock climbing in the 19th century – see the
1898 ascent of Pinnacle Ridge detailed in the *Big Walks* chapter (p21) – this indeed
being the only rock climb he appears to have done before 1901. And in the chapter
on his mountaineering exploits we say... 'Much – though not all – of his use of four
limbs rather than two on the mountains was concentrated in the period between
finishing his Munros in 1901 and . . . 1907' (p40).

* To say as Campbell does that '. . . but (AER) was an enthusiastic climber from
the moment that he joined the club' as if in criticism of the p3 sentence quoted is
disingenuous, because the SMC Meets were at New Year and Easter and, naturally,
snow and ice work – not rock work – predominated. We make his 'enthusiasm'
abundantly clear (e.g. – p13, Dalmally Meet '. . . every hour of which I enjoyed').

2. The Goatfell Murder. Three errors are claimed about a half-sentence reference
in the book (p7) to the murder of Edwin Rose. We will leave aside the very
tangential nature of this reference to the main story of AER, it being in relation to
a stranger he and his pals met as a teenager.

* Campbell has got one of these points correct in that Lawrie should be Laurie.
* But the spot where his body was located was just off the ridge leading down
from North Goatfell to the Saddle (a col, joining it with Cir Mhor) and is therefore
clearly part of the Goatfell massif into which the coire headwall bites (see attached

map): one account of the search party relates '... others descended the ridge which runs from Goatfell to the Saddle. About halfway to the Saddle a Corrie fisherman named Francis Logan suddenly hallooed wildly. The search was over.' (J. House, *Murder not Proven* p31). SMC guides (e.g. – 1952 edition *Islands of Scotland* p10) refer to the incident and spot of death under the heading of Goatfell for the very good reason that it is part of that mountain's mass to anyone but the most pedantic!

* Although the post-mortem conclusion was that the injuries to Rose's head had been caused by repeated blows from some heavy instrument, it was widely believed and reported at the time (which the young AER would have heard) that this was an attempt to finish him off (if indeed he was not already dead) AFTER being pushed over the cliffs dropping from the ridge. Not only is there no conclusive proof that a boulder was the 'heavy instrument', our book's phrase 'murder-by-pushing' reflects not only what may have been the principal cause of death – widely contemporaneously so believed – but also the initiation of the incident.

* Campbell himself appears to make an error when he refers to 'Coire na Fhuaran', when the map (and correct Gaelic) shows it is Coire nam Fuaran: we could point out that this is twice as many spelling mistakes as Lawrie contained!

3. Ben Nevis.

* Ben Nevis had a hotel facility on the summit in 1890, and refreshments were also served in the Observatory. Travellers such as AER could take a cup of tea there. When is a cafe not a cafe? Is a little humour and hyperbole really beyond the pale?

4. Percy Unna and the NTS.

Campbell says he finds these errors 'particularly reprehensible'. (Perhaps partly because they have very little to do with the book's main subject!)

* Our sentence on p67 is worth quoting in full without Campbell's excisions. It says: 'Unna, *one of the Trust's main benefactors, whose* grants enabled the Trust to buy – inter alia – Glencoe.' Campbell has omitted the part in italics, thus twisting the meaning of our sentence, which clearly says that he was a substantial contributor, (which he was) while only one of several, the 'whose' referring to benefactors, plural. Again, we make the point on p119 of the book that Glencoe was acquired by the NTS 'due MAINLY to the legacy of Percy Unna'.

* Percy Unna was a modest man, and whatever his 1937 letter stated, it is known now that he made huge anonymous donations to the fund. Let us quote from a recent (1991) book *The Nature of Scotland*, where a box within a chapter by outdoor writer Roger Smith states: '(In 1937) Unna took the initiative and organised an appeal among all the mountaineering clubs in Britain . . . He gave most of the money anonymously himself.'

5. Munro names.

Much of Campbell's outrage seems to be directed at the captions to photos. Here he claims that The Saddle is not the only English name, but there are many others, three being listed by him.

* The three he lists are not English, except in appearance, and it is surprising that a Scottish mountaineer like Campbell does not see that. The Cairnwell is an anglicisation of Carn Bhalg, pronounced locally carnwall, close to its original Gaelic sound approximately carn valluk (Adam Watson et al. *Placenames of Upper Deeside* p34). Mount Keen is likewise an anglicisation, from the Gaelic monadh caoin or chaoin, via the Scots mounth (op cit., p119): and Broad Cairn is not even the Scots that it seems, for it is not a broad hill and the broad may well derive from braghad (as in Breadalbane – see H. Alexander, SMC *Cairngorms Guide* 1928, p78).

*We accept his point about the date when Garbh Chioch Mhor was revised into the tables. There IS one other Munro with an apparently English name, one Campbell didn't name, The Devil's Point (a Victorian polite translation of the original Gaelic Bod an Deamhain, penis of the demon): unlike The Saddle which was not apparently a translation, the Devil's Point's English name is a temporary 20th century aberration from the true Gaelic: indeed, Harvey's current 1:40000 walkers' map of the Cairngorms calls it by its proper Gaelic name, and hopefully, the OS and the SMT guidebooks will follow suit.

6. Pinnacle Ridge.

Another picture caption complaint. Here Campbell really is struggling to nitpick.

* He accuses us of 'inferences' – the inferences are entirely his own. We do NOT infer that AER and Clark made the first ascent of the ridge, nor do we infer that it had only recently been done. We state that Pinnacle Ridge was 'completed' by the trio (not 'conquered' or 'first climbed'), and we refer to two quite other climbs (King's Chimney, Basteir Tooth) which had recently been done.

7. SMC membership.

Campbell claims that we distort the picture of the SMC by highlighting landowners. We feel that the distortion is on his part.

* The fact that landowners happens to be the first of a series of eight professional occupations, that are clearly alliteratively-linked, does not constitute a highlight, since landowners are not picked up and reinforced.

* Not only does Campbell's phrase for clerks, etc., i.e. a 'modicum' (dictionary = a small quantity), square with Drummond's '... but little else': Drummond's next sentence in the book is: 'This was naturally a circumstance born of necessity in the social and economic state of the times' – hardly an effusion of an author 'giving his prejudiced views'! And later on p59 we go on to say that '... a majority of the early climbing club activists were members of the urban bourgeoisie and the professional classes, not landowners.'

*8. The tent.

Another complaint about a caption to a photo, which he THINKS might show something or someone else.

* His wild speculation about who is there is rather spoiled by the absence of any artist's materials around (and where is Philip – in the tent?) and by the clear evidence of a rope on the left. There is also a striking similarity between the hat and nape of the lady on the right and that of his wife, Kate, in another photo (compare p93 and p103 – same year, same early summer, and we know that Kate did come with him and McKenzie to the Cuillin (e.g. – book text)). We cannot be absolutely sure, so we – unlike Campbell – will not speculate to that degree.

9. Faces from the past.

And another photo caption! He claims that two of the people on two of the photos are mistaken, and that lots of (presumably important SMC) people are not identified in another.

*We were naturally largely dependent on AER's own labelling of his slides – which is where such information came from – we did not indulge in speculation. And in slides over half-a-century old it is neither possible, necessary, nor desirable to identify every Tom, Dick or Harry. Finally, there are some points which are not 'facts' but matters germane to his assertion regarding our worth as historians.

10. He says '... the sourcing of their 'facts' is capricious, unsystematic and... not secured by adequate footnotes'. On the contrary, we believe that it is perfectly

clear where most of the information comes from, and in particular there are 83 direct quotations (mainly from his [AER's – Ed.] logs, from SRWS files or from the SMCJ) in the book, all clearly identified by being indented in the text: 72 of these are labelled as to source after the last word in the quote, and a further 10 are clearly located by the preceding or subsequent text. Only one – a newspaper cutting of the late 1930s which we found (as a physical cutting) but were unable to locate the publication source – is unidentified or 'secured by adequate footnotes'. Indeed, can our critic be the same Robin Campbell who wrote in SMCJ volume 34 (1989), page 221, in an article on Munro himself: 'However some unofficial histories tell a different story (about Munro's climbs). It would be invidious to identify those responsible, but we read in various quarters stories that imply . . .' Where are the 'securing footnotes' or systematic securing of facts here?

11. Robertson's rock-climbing.

Campbell complains we undervalue AER's achievements in this field, and lists some climbs on Nevis we did not include.

* We say on p40: '(AER was) able to cope with rock climbing up to Very Difficult in standard – though not leading . . .' None of the climbs cited by Campbell alter this verdict, in our opinion. The standard work on Ben Nevis is Crocket's, and he mentions only one of those on Campbell's list, Recess Route on Tower Ridge, which made the climb easier (page 69). That book devotes as much space to AER's work for the CIC Hut, as chaplain and table-maker, and we think Crocket got the balance right for his contribution. The 18-Minute Route is only a Moderate and was not a first ascent. AER himself describes the descent of Observatory Ridge as 'tedious' and 'really a thing to ascend not to descend' (SMCJ 8, p221). The variation on Staircase, on which AER seconded Raeburn, is described in part by MacPhee (1954 Nevis Guide, SMC, p23) as 'much inferior to the direct ascent of the pinnacle'. And Pinnacle Arete of the Trident (now known as South Trident Buttress) is a Difficult, and not a first ascent (Crocket, op cit p72). Given all this, we neither alter our assessment of AER nor do we accept Campbell's description of them as 'most interesting climbs'.

In conclusion, we can say that precisely two of Campbell's list of our 'errors' are substantiated: Laurie spelt with a u not a w, and the date of Garbh Chioch Mhor's ascension. The remainder of his assertions about errors of fact, we believe we have disproved: and we have pointed out that he has made several errors himself, about spelling, about mountain names, about Unna, and that many of his other points are, frankly, distortions of what we said.

We do not for one minute believe that he quotes the 'errors' that he does to 'give a flavour only', since many of them have nothing to do with the central thrust of our story and its main character. (Only points 1, 6, and 11 above relate to AER directly, and yet he is the central figure on almost every page in the book!)

Every non-fiction book contains some errors, and most fair reviewers note those they spot as part of a balanced critique. He has failed to point out any major flaws in fact, or interpretation. Instead he has scraped around looking for crumbs from photo captions and textual cul-de-sacs (e.g. – the Goatfell murder), in an attempt to malign the whole of the book, suggesting that any errors are merely the tip of the iceberg. Campbell's assertions about our 'worthlessness' as historians falls, his review goes beyond fair comment, and in our opinion is libellous. We regard ourselves as fair men, and would not stoop to calling into question Campbell's 'worth as a reviewer', nor to suggest that 'almost every error he claims turns out on investigation to be unfounded'. Nor shall we conclude our response with vitriolic calls for printed matter to be stuffed into orifices, as he did! We simply ask for fair comment, and for an apology for the unjustified slur on our work and worth.

R.N. Campbell writes: 'I agree that I may have used Drummond and Mitchell rather harshly in last year's review. In particular, I regret the description of them as 'worthless as historians', which went beyond the boundaries of ordinary civilised discourse. Moreover, I wish to make clear that this outburst, and any other overstatements, were occasioned not by any malice towards the authors. Although I do not accept that the foregoing response to my review disposes of my criticisms, I am content to leave interested readers to study the book and form their own opinions about the various points at issue between us.'

Environmental Protection of the Himalaya – A Mountaineer's View:—Edited by Aamir Ali (Indus Publishing Co., New Delhi, 112pp., ISBN 81-7387-012-8).

Regular readers of this Journal have already heard of the benefits of membership of the Himalayan Club (SMCJ, 181, 1990) whose worthy Journal now sports a full-colour cover. Celebrating and accompanying the 50th issue of the Himalayan Journal came this slender booklet, whose 112 pages pack a powerful punch. Suddenly, the problems in the hills at our own back doors of access, footpath erosion, funicular railways, crampon scratches, bolts, the CIC toilet etc. pale into insignificance. Sadly, I have never read such a depressing book about mountains but a 'Symposium on the Environmental Protection of the Himalaya' was an excellent way to commemorate a significant anniversary. Aamir Ali, an Indian with a wide knowledge and interest in the Himalaya who has lived most of his working life in Switzerland has a unique perspective as General Editor and the contributors, 10 familiar names from the West and 11 less familiar (to me) but no less authoritative from the East put their points of view succinctly. Problems there are in plenty, going far beyond the familiar garbage and human waste of the 'toilet paper treks'. Deforestation, over-population, over-grazing and poverty are the main ones, spelled out in some detail, along with suggestions for solutions and examples of good practice already in operation.

While the problems look harder to overcome than the mountains, those of us who have not visited the Himalaya for some years can reflect on our good fortune at having experienced a relatively-unspoiled environment (but how much did we contribute to the damage?) Anyone looking forward to heading off on a climbing or trekking trip should be wondering what they can do to help the problem (yes, every little helps). Users of Ling Hut will be familiar with the 'Kathmandu Declaration' which has adorned the wall for many years now. There is an 'Alpine Club Policy Statement on Climbing in the Alps and Greater Ranges' and this book finishes with 'The Himalayan Code of Conduct', but rules, as we all know, are made to be broken. Way ahead in environmental awareness as usual, an American, Robert McConnell hits the nail right on the head for me.

'Awareness is not enough. Awareness must be translated into action. We must each adopt a personal commitment to leave as little trace as possible of our passing through the mountains. That personal commitment should be part of our planning for every trip . . . part of your thought process every day.'

Which brings us right back to the problems in our own back yard.

'Doing it right means doing it in such a way as to leave no trace of your passing.'

Dave Broadhead.

Altitude Illness, Prevention & Treatment:- Stephen Bezruchka (Cordee, 1994, 96pp., ISBN 1-871890-57-8).

Unpredictable and a killer, altitude sickness can affect anyone from the most experienced climber to the recreational skier. Anyone travelling above 7,000ft is at risk, and this slim, diary-sized book contains essential information for climbers, skiers, hikers and trekkers undertaking trips to altitude.

The book is designed to travel with you, and is written in an easy-to-use format which describes the following topics in a systematic way: preparing for altitude, acclimatisation, recognition and assessment of the signs and symptoms of altitude sickness, and how to make a decision on treatment.

Current medical education provides negligible training in the recognition and prevention of altitude illness, and this book should provide – doctors interested in sports medicine; those who run travel clinics; expedition doctors – with the knowledge and information to impart appropriate advice and treatment for anyone going to altitude. For the lay person, its great advantage is that it does not assume any medical knowledge, nor is it written at too basic a level.

If planning to go on a guided trip, it provides the necessary information to inquire whether the organisers are adequately prepared in the recognition and treatment of altitude illness, and whether they carry the appropriate equipment.

For those with pre-existing health conditions, including diabetes and high blood pressure, it gives sensible and practical information on the increased hazards or otherwise of going to altitude.

Drug treatments used for the prevention and treatment of altitude illness are concisely described, and advice is given as to what you should include in the high altitude medical kit. As a practical point, all the drugs mentioned are available, only on prescription in the UK (Private, rather than NHS prescription – if for use when travelling abroad.) Most medical practitioners should be willing to prescribe the altitude traveller with the necessary drugs, providing their indications and effects were explained as set out in the book.

All in all, an up-to-date, well-researched book, not to be left at home or base camp when travelling high.

Graeme Abel.

Spirits of the Air:– K. Diemberger (Hodder & Stoughton ISBN 0-340-59367-9, £17.99).

This book is a compilation of stories, covering expeditions and trips not covered in his previous books. ie. *Summits and Secrets, The Endless Knot, K2, Mountain of Dreams and Destiny.*

Now, I have not read these other books but I would have to say that if the content is similar to *Spirits of the Air,* then I will not be reading them.

I found the accounts very disappointing and really struggled to finish the book. I am not sure what style of writing Diemberger is trying to emulate but he comes nowhere near the writing and story-telling of his great companion, Herman Buhl, with whom he climbed on his first 8000m peaks; he does, however, continually tell you how great they were.

His other great adversary was and is Reinhold Messner, and the book goes on and on about how great they both are, the question is, however, who really is the foremost mountaineer – is it me or Reinhold.

The content of stories I found pretty boring except for some of the Himalayan expeditions to Makalu, Lhotse and Everest. In these expeditions he does capture the feeling and excitement that you would expect on the big peaks.

Many of the other stories seem to have been thrown in to fill up the book. I was not impressed by a *Night on Stromboli, How to Catch a Millionaire, Milestone in California, The Grand Canyon etc.* Even the ending of the book with notes and heights, a chronology of his main climbs and expeditions was just filling up space.

His trip to K2 in which he lost Julie Tullis was, of course, quite devastating for him, however I found it out of place to keep mentioning it in this book, as it was well covered in *Summits and Secrets.*

As mentioned earlier, throughout the book he continually knocks Messner and keeps going on about their race to complete the most 8000m peaks, and climbing Alpine Style in the Himalayas or West Alpine Style in the Himalaya, which was started by Herman Buhl on Broad Peak with his then climbing partner, who was none other than Kurt Deimberger himself.

So there we have it; if you have a spare £18 to invest in his book I am sure the royalties will come in very handy to sponsor the Kurt Diemberger fan club.

Gordon Ross.

The Central Highlands Fifth revised edition:– Peter Hodgkiss. (Scottish Mountaineering Club, 210pp., illus., maps. £17.95. ISBN 0-907521-44-4.)

To describe this as the 'Fifth Edition' may be technically correct, but it rather reminds me of my old 'Icelandic' sleeping bag, which, in its 40 years' of hard service was relined and recovered many times, yet the core of eiderdown remained the same. This edition of the guide is completely rewritten, re-illustrated (superbly), and the maps redrawn. Only the hills it describes remain unchanged.

It covers in text and illustration the area bounded by the Great Glen, Drumochter Pass, Rannoch Moor, and the Western seaboard. The maps, by Jim Renny and Noel Williams, are lucid and uncluttered, so that the relationships between the various tops are clearly and easily grasped. The workmanlike text is not only easily read for information, but also for sheer pleasure and, although on the whole strictly factual, the author occasionally lets his love of the hills he is describing slip through . . .

This means that, apart from being a thorough and accurate guide to the active climber and hillwalker, it has great appeal to those who through age or infirmity, can no longer go on the hills . . .

The illustrations, mainly in colour, not only give a vivid depiction of the area they represent, but are as good as many so-called 'coffee table' collections of photographs, and a great deal better than many recent publications.

This volume completes the Publications Sub-Committee's remit to republish the entire series of the Club's District Guides, and they must be congratulated on their work. The Club is exceedingly fortunate to have among its members those writers, photographers and, not least, cartographers of the standard shown in this series, and also the production skills of Donald Bennet and the marketing talents of the late Graham Tiso . . .

Any reviewer has to try to find at least one fault. The only one that I can list is the pricing at £X.95. Could this not be rounded up or down to a simple figure? At least, however, it isn't £X.99!

Ross Higgins.

The Wilderness Experience:– John McLachlan (1994, 81pp., photographs, ISBN 0-95116911-1-2).

The author, who also published this book, is a walker who has found spiritual upliftment in the wilder, and more mountainous areas of the world. Accordingly, he has decided to set down some thoughts (meditations?) on paper. I have no idea whether it is self-published through choice or because a publisher could not be found to accept what would probably be a loss-maker. Perhaps it really doesn't matter. The so-called 'Vanity Press' arena is one to be approached with caution. In either case the good Dr McLachlan has obviously travelled the world a bit and has certainly done some reading.

Wilderness is defined in the book by a quotation from John Muir, as being '. . . an area where the earth and its community of life are untrammelled by man, where man himself is a visitor who does not remain . . .'

The text is in places heavy going, being liberally dosed with quotations which are interspersed with the author's words. There are, to be fair, longer sections dealing with some of the author's trips, and, of course, his meditations, but in the main some editing might have helped. There are one or two quotes which come as a surprise. Ex-President Jimmy Carter is there, along with our Hamish Brown. The Lakes poets have pre-eminence.

There is an Index, but no Bibliography, sources being given in the text. More details and presumably copies of the book may be obtained from the author, Dr John McLachlan, 112 Brincliffe Edge Road, Sheffield, S11 9BX.

Ken Crocket.

The Last Hundred – Munros, Beards and a Dog:– Hamish Brown. (Mainstream, £14.99, ISBN 1-85158-607-5).

For someone like me, involved in a long-standing love affair with the Scottish hills, Hamish Brown's latest offering, *The Last Hundred,* will provide a few hours of pure nostalgia and pleasure.

It's all there; the soakings, the midges, the steaming bothies, the wildly flapping tents through the long dark nights, coupled with the pure joy and contrast of a summit attained, resting in calm airs by the cairn so that you feel god-like, atop the world and surveying it in all the glow of sunwarmth and achievement.

For those who have not yet been smitten with such a body-and-soul-destroying affliction, you had better read this book with a certain in-built mental resistance or you, too, will succumb to the dreaded disease, abandoning wife, family or lover every weekend, every holiday, every snatched hour that you can find, in order to achieve the fulfilment of this desperate desire. Beware!

Hamish Brown is not just a human being who writes books, he is one who allows us to feel that we have come to know him well from his writings. He gives himself his own character -in his words: 'sometimes loquacious, sometimes Spartan, whiles cheery, whiles dour.' That, joined to his evident ability to keep many reliable hillgoing friends and his obvious care and affection for his dogs, and we have indications of a strong and rather complex character. Without such strength, he would never have become the first multi-Munroist; he would never have survived his pioneering induction of numerous ebullient and characterful schoolchildren into the harsh realities of hill-walking, camping, bothying and sharing with them the sheer physical hell of the worst that Scottish Hills can sometimes produce. Nor do I imagine him continuing to walk the same hills in repetitive rounds unless he got considerably more pleasure and satisfaction from this task than is gained from merely completing yet another round of the Munros.

He refers to his new book as a 'rag-bag'. Well, yes, I share this view. However, there are rag-bags and rag-bags. Some contain scraps of ermine and purple velvet. Others are full of pieces of blue serge and strips of denim. There are many pieces from the first category and maybe just one or two from the more mundane collection. But, taken broadly, it's all here: short articles, long articles; some old, some new. Some poems, some pictures, and a longer appreciation of Storm, a dog with a huge personality who accompanied his master on a full round of the Munros. Yes, even the 'In Pin'! (Since I've never met a dog capable of controlling an abseil, I presume he had to be lowered down. But, who am I to quibble; it may happen to me one day.)

To become completely serious, I really found this book to be an excellent distillation of all that is best in Hamish Brown's writings. It gave me great pleasure, not only helping me to relive my own visits to the hills, but enabling me to recall with considerable pleasure and nostalgia, many of my own frightening moments, moments of joy, calm pleasure and sometimes great satisfaction or even euphoria. For anyone who has walked the Scottish hills, it MUST do something similar for them. For those who are just starting out into the mountains it not only lets them know just where they are bound, but also gives them some extremely sound advice on how to walk and climb in the Scottish hills, how to understand them and how to come to love and respect them as Hamish Brown has so patently learned to do.

David H. Jones.

Alps 4000 – 75 peaks in 52 days:– Martin Moran. (David & Charles, 1994, 288pp, illus., £17.99, ISBN. 0-7153-0268X).

This book chronicles the efforts of Martin Moran and Simon Jenkins in making the first continuous self-propelled traverse of the Alpine 4000m peaks in summer 1993 on foot, ski and bicycle. More than one list of such peaks exist, and for the purposes of this outing any protuberance above the Plimsoll line with more than 35m of reascent was deemed to be fair game, a prosaic but practical definition. Starting on Piz Bernina the climbers covered 620 miles and 229,000ft of ascent on the way to Barre des Ecrins in a season of poor conditions that would have had Patey's apocryphal Alpine guide climbing down gracefully to the valley before the modern linkers of faces-nord could say 'media circus'.

A typical British Alpinist will take three days to ascend a route or peak: a day to walk in, a day to climb and walk out, and a day to recover. That Moran and Jenkins continued over the peaks for day after day testifies to both their endurance and their enthusiasm. Take, for instance, the 33-hour non-stop traverse of Mont Blanc de Tacul by the Diable Ridge, Mont Maudit, Aiguille de Bionnassay, Mont Blanc and Mont Bronillard; the pair then had a five-hour rest before a quick blast up the Aiguille Blanche de Peuterey.

Motivation came partly through carrying out the exploit for a charity, Blytheswood Care. To his credit, Moran comments on the inherent ambiguity of such backing, as success would benefit his and Jenkins's guiding careers as much as the charity's bank balance. Will McLewin is quoted as suggesting 'in typically blunt fashion', that charitable involvement 'was just a big ego-trip'. An interesting topic, unsurprisingly avoided by most mountaineering authors, and worthy of greater analysis.

As the routes used by Moran and Jenkins frequently coincide with those of the early pioneers, the book gives some interesting historical perspectives. Particularly noteworthy are the efforts of Karl Blodig, the first ascensionist of all the 4000m peaks, who, when the Alps later underwent a sort of Brown-Donaldson revision-ism, duly returned to climb six new tops at the age of 73, one solo by a line then only recently climbed, and today graded at TD-. Potential effigy-bearers can rest easy. No doubt Blodig would also have succeeded on Beinn Teallach.

The book itself is illustrated with some very good photos and helpful maps. As a piece of writing, the book is held together by the content of the story rather than how that story is told, the prose tending at times towards the wooden and the purple. The author's emotions are well documented, but at the end the reader is little wiser about Simon Jenkins other than knowing he benefits from 'inner strength', to me suggesting an individual mixing the characteristics of Popeye and David Koresh. The book lacks the idiosyncracies and anecdotes of its obvious competitor, McLewin's In *Monte Viso's Horizon,* a comparison which is also to be made between the author's *Munros in Winter* and *Hamish's Mountain Walk.* But Moran is not a grizzled soothsayer, so he shouldn't be expected to write like one. His book, however, comes alive only in those sections where the reader has some familiarity with the peaks and routes being climbed.

Alps 4000 is nonetheless a worthwhile read for anyone interested in Alpine peak-bagging, and recognition is due both to the climbers and to their admirable support teams.

Alec Keith.

The Social Climbers:– Chris Darwin and John Amy (Mainstream, Edinburgh, 1991, 156pp., nominally £9.99, now remaindered. ISBN 1-85158-463-3).

I bought this book at a sale, much against my better judgment. The cover shows a crowd of nyaffs in formal attire purporting to be having an equally formal dinner party on top of a high mountain. I bought it cheap in order to look down my nose disdainfully at this example of the way mountaineering is being degraded by upper-class twits.

However, once I started to read I became fascinated by the counterpoint between the absurdity of the concept and the sustained determination that kept this unlikely show on the road to success.

The object was to perpetrate a surrealistic visual joke by having a formal dinner party on top of Huascaran, Peru's highest mountain. The nearest parallel is Apsley Cherry-Garrard's account of the similarly pointless journey to Cape Crozier for an equally useless penguin's egg.

It is written in a rueful style with excellently underwritten humour. The organisation was complex, sustained and difficult. The dining party (three of each sex) had strong characters but no mountaineering experience and was looked after by a team of professional mountaineers.

The expedition was mounted from Australia and made up of natives and ex-pats.

You can imagine the tensions within such a disparate collection of perversely motivated, individualistic oddballs.

The adventures of this psychologically diverse group in the social and seismic instability of Peru (their base seems to have been the town that was swept away when a large part of Huascaran fell off in an earthquake and is now a headquarters for the Shining Path) are quite hair-raising. However, their eccentricity seems to have been such that both the local tectonics and Shining Path seemed to have acknowledged that they were beyond the remit of either.

A delightfully discordant note is introduced by the temporary intrusion of a German TV producer who thought that the point of the expedition was to make the fairly heavy statement that standards must be retained in the face of adversity, whereas the participants maintained that all that heavy stuff, while true, was secondary to perpetrating the visual joke as immaculately as possible.

As I read, my respect for the zany determination of the group and its leader (who maintained a Cherry-Garrard like diffidence in his descriptions) increased.

On their initial practice peak having erected the furniture, set up the meal and taken the photographs, they were overtaken by a storm and forced to evacuate the summit forthwith.

Back at base they realised they had not eaten anything at the table so the achievement was technically invalid. They repeated the exercise properly the next day. In the end they had their dinner party on the top of Huascaran at 6200m in a storm – an evocative picture of the event shows a guest holding a vase with the contents bent at right-angles by the wind.

I recommend this book highly. It is a delightful relief from the immaculate but conventional pot-boilers of the great Bonington. There is even an unexpectedly poignant ending.

I.H.M. Smart.

The Voice Of The Hills: The Story of Ben Humble MBE:– Roy M. Humble (The Pentland Press, 1995, 233pp, £17.50, ISBN 1-85821-249-9).

Ben Humble died 18 years ago at the age of 74. Most people who came into contact with him will have at least one vivid memory because he was in all respects a character. I doubt, however, if many from a later generation will have heard of him. His books are out of print, including a fairly recent re-issue of *The Cuillin of Skye* and ill health curtailed his activities well before his death.

Ben had an interesting life, although perhaps not a happy one. He came late to the hills, beginning with a walking holiday in Skye in 1929. After the war he devoted much of his life to the Scottish mountains through writing, work at Glenmore Lodge and his great interest in mountain safety and rescue.

It is easy to see why the publisher thought there would be a market for this book. Ben's involvement in the development of mountain training for young people and in the progress of mountain rescue from the *ad hoc* state of 40 years ago make his life an ideal framework for the scrutiny of these aspects of post-war Scottish mountaineering. There is also the bonus of Ben's acquaintanceship with people like Bill Murray and the almost proprietary oversight he exercised in Arrochar at a time when it was at the leading edge of rock climbing development.

If that was the ambition then this book falls well short of it. Roy Humble provides an episodic account of his uncle's life but does not seem to have been adequately intimate with Ben's personality or to possess the necessary background detail about the activities that obsessed him. Can these bones live? Not in this account.

It isn't prurience to seek more information than this book provides about Ben's personal life. There are tantalising flashes of revelation that are never pursued. It is understandable that Ben's own outline of his life, which is used as the core of the book, is reticent over personal matters, but a biographer should not be so inhibited. One can construct an image of an insecure and unhappy person from what is revealed and late, sad diary entries emphasise depression and loneliness. This may be an inaccurate view of the whole life. There is very little about his relationships with others and almost nothing on relationships with women. We are given no information about his opinions on politics or social affairs. A reference to his father as a socialist comes across as an expression of scorn, but is that a correct interpretation?

If Ben was an unhappy man then it doesn't seem that deafness was the primary cause. Most contributors emphasise Ben's success in overcoming the handicap. The first time I met him, about 33 years ago, I barely knew who he was and didn't know he was deaf. I remember the conversation as a bit odd – off key – but thought that he was slightly drunk. I learn from this book that others made the same mistake. My ignorance lasted through three or four casual encounters in a dozen years and an exchange of correspondence about some long-forgotten query concerning Arrochar. I only discovered that he was profoundly deaf on the last occasion I heard him speak. This was at the AGM in 1974 when he opposed Bill Skidmore's motion to admit women to the SMC. His characteristic 'aaaaah!' sounded like a warcry and I have no doubt that he was fully aware of the effect.

There is scant reference to the SMC in this book. The most explicit is over Ben's hurt feelings about the Arrochar Rock Guide of 1971. I can remember hearing Jimmy Houston's side of the story and seeing some of the correspondence. This didn't enhance Ben's reputation, but he was elderly and completely out of touch with contemporary events at Arrochar. Ben and Houston were an impossible mix who should never have been brought together.

Probably his most significant contribution was to mountain safety and rescue. Again this book provides an inadequate record with too much reliance on familiar published sources. Here also Ben was a centre of controversy who defended his ideas vigorously. I recall a meeting I attended, reluctantly, as a member of the Greenock Mountaineering Club in place of someone else. It was enlivened by a loud slanging match in which Ben had the better of two or three people who opposed his views. His contribution of the accident list to the Journal also provoked criticism from members who felt that it was a source of entertainment rather than information to support mountain safety. I confess that I treated it as the former. There was a mischievous side to Ben which came across in the occasional item – always with a happy ending – where he pointed up the ludicrous aspects of some incident. Ben would be deeply disappointed by how little effect his other efforts have had as the death toll rises year by year in Scottish hills.

I'm sorry that I cannot be more enthusiastic about this book but it is a wasted opportunity. If you can think of nothing better to do with £17.50 then buy it as an inadequate memorial to a decent man who deserves to be remembered for the work he did on behalf of all hill users. Better still, spend it on a second hand copy of *The Cuillin of Skye*.

Jim Crawford.

At The Rising of The Moon: A collection of short stories:- Dermot Somers. (1994, Baton Wicks and The Collins Press. £8.99. ISBN 1-89573-05-0.)

The content of the stories is extremely varied, and although the author is an experienced mountaineer, this is definitely not a collection of climbing adventures. Instead, he concentrates on the emotions and relationships of his characters, who often emerge as figures to be pitied rather than heroes.

This is certainly not easy reading – meant for the last 10 minutes before you fall asleep – but demands concentration if the stories are to be understood, as Dermot Somers adopts some strange tricks in his storytelling. In *A Tale of Spendthrift Innocence,* he keeps you on your toes by jumping from the climbers, high on a lightning-whipped Dru, to the musings of the author, debating what to do with his characters, in addition to leaping to and fro in time. Sounds confusuing? It can be!

Although this book lacks the mountaineering interest of Dermot Somers's earlier collection, *Mountains and Other Ghosts,* these strange tales are worth a read.

Hamish Irvine.

Fear and fascination – The 100 Best Rock Climbs in England and Wales:– Geoffrey Odds. (1995, Crowood Press, £18.95. ISBN 1-85223-607-8).

Nothing in this book is as good as the front cover. If the photographs were of the same quality, even ignoring the text, then I would say: 'Buy it, at last we have a true artist who has crossed the divide between the factual and the abstract.'

Unfortunately, such images revert to the normal as soon as the book is opened and are not helped by the combination of fuzzy black and whites interspersed by some quality colour action shoots. It is a mistake to mix coloured with black and white, a photographic apartheid that should be kept. Even if the black and white shots were less fuzzy and full page it would have helped as undoubtedly there is a market for pin-sharp black and white in the John Cleare style.

As for the text, there are many bones to pick and gnaw over. The author has chosen to ignore accepted 'classics' for the reason that they do not necessarily give the best climbing. As he has cited the chosen 100 as 'the best', then he sets himself on a dangerous pedestal. If so, then I, and many others are confused as to why the classic routes became classics in the first place; not just because of their history but also, surely, because of their quality.

The *Pocket Oxford Dictionary* definition of 'classic' states: 'Of allowed excellence, cited as a model, often referred to, standard . . .' The choice of exactly 100 routes is suspect; excellence is not restrained by numbers and it would be better to describe more fully 50, or even expand to 200 in a bigger volume. As it is, the routes are crammed into short, subjective, paragraphs that say more about the author than the route. The basic flaw, one suspects, is that many routes have been chosen more for their athletic flair than other qualities. The greatest crime is that only one route, The Axe, comes from that greatest of cliffs, Clogwyn Du'r Arddu; your average Welsh climber will be speechless about that.

The reviewer's knowledge and experience of Yorkshire helps increase the ire somewhat and is used to illustrate examples. On the short climbs, the choice of three southern sandstone routes at the expense of only one – Great Western – from Almscliff in Yorkshire, says much, particularly when Almscliff is described as 'uninspiring'. Uninspiring! That home of the acknowledged classic wherein lie routes such as Wall of Horrors, Big Greeny, Falklands Green Crack and Overhanging

Groove, not to mention the North-west Girdle, all as good as Great Western and all at least up to the quality of any southern sandstone top-rope route.

The right wing at Malham is ignored for the inclusion of two bolt-protected climbs up the admittedly magnificent central wall. As good would be Carnage, particularly Left Hand, Wombat, Slender Loris, Doubting Thomas, Midnight Cowboy, Sundance Wall and, best of all, the Right Wing Girdle.

Likewise, Gordale and Kilnsey only get the 'sports' treatment, and the most telling remark in the book perhaps explains why sports climbs figure so highly on the limestone: 'The classic cave routes not yet bolted. If, or rather when, they are, their popularity will be assured. . .' Retrobolting championed! Popularity does not alone indicate quality, it only indicates popularity, perhaps due to regular protection. So, with the dismissal of the two Cave Routes, what about Face Route, Light or Rebel, just to mention three brilliant climbs or back at Kilnsey, The Diedre or the splendid Directissima and Central Wall? And so it goes on, all rather depressing given the omissions.

A glossary at the end has a fair amount of humour as well as a few revealing statements: 'Bumbly. The sort of person who does not like bolts. A derogatory term used in connection with people who are not very good at climbing.'

'Camping. An activity only carried out by bumblies and punters. Real climbers doss.'

'Doss. Sleeping somewhere where you do not have to pay and can be quite untidy and smelly, such as a friend's house, a football stadium, park bench, cave and so on.'

Just as well Scottish routes have been thankfully ignored; I mean what with the lack of park benches and football stadia at places like Carnmore or Creag an Dubh Loch, dossing could be considerably harder than the routes, particularly since they are only classics devoid of bolts.

John Mackenzie.

Review of Camp 4 – Recollections of a Yosemite Rock Climber:– Steve Roper. (1994, Baton Wicks, £17.99, ISBN 1-898573-10-7).

As I clipped the last bolts of the Nose Route on El Capitan, I recalled the stories I had heard about Warren Harding drilling all night in order to complete the first ascent of El Capitan. This gave a sense of history and added another dimension of excitement about the pitch. An even greater excitement than the thousands of feet of exposure below me. I can still remember that I wish I knew more about the history of the famous route. Who thought of making stoveleg pitons? Why is there a Dolt hole? How long did the first ascent really take? In fact, I have always been intrigued with the significant steps and advances that helps climbing to move forward. If you have a similar curiosity, then this book is for you. If you don't have this curiosity, you should read the book anyway. For those that fail to understand the past are doomed to repeat it.

Steve Roper is uniquely placed to write Camp 4, and he has risen well to this fate. Although I knew he wrote the first guidebook, I never realised that he was one of the first full-time Camp 4 climbers. He superbly presents the growth and evolution of Yosemite climbing. I had expected a chronicle of the major first ascents and landmark climb. I was not disappointed either. But the book also contained two bonuses. The first was a better understanding of the heroes of my youth and the second a clear perspective on the evolution of equipment, technique and ethics.

As a young climber in Colorado, I could never figure out whether Warren Harding was a hero (for the first ascent of the Nose) or a goat (for placing too many bolts on the Dawn Wall). The majority opinion of the early Seventies was for the latter. Camp 4 provides the real answer. Harding was clearly a hero of his time. It was his vision, drive and determination that persevered over two years to make the first ascent of the Nose. Surprising to me, at the time, they climbed as best they could and then placed bolts when it got too hard. As this ethic changed, Harding was driven by a vision of pure 'lines'. Following the old ethic, his epic first ascents placing bolts was quite reasonable. The parallel to modern bolt discussions is fascinating to consider.

Roper provides a sincere view of how the bolting philosophy changed as their experience and confidence grew. Bolts were acceptable in the days of great exploration, when no one knew if they could climb the big walls. But as they learned they could survive the big climbs, the use of bolts faded out. Salathé is another famous name in Yosemite. Because of the Steck-Salathé Route on the Sentinel, I always assumed that Salathé was a superb climber. I was shocked to learn that he was a relatively old man, not much of a free climber, but one of the most important people in the early days of big wall climbing. It seems that in most fields, innovation takes place when someone with skills in one area brings them to a new area. Salathé was not much of a climber, but he was a great blacksmith. He was introduced to climbing just when something better than soft iron pitons was needed. He made the first hard metal pitons, starting with parts of Model A Ford axles and opened up a new world of technical climbing. His legendary almost first ascent of Lost Arrow spire was almost more for the purpose of testing his new pitons than a first ascent. This model of new skills leading to great innovation has happened many times, and I am sure it will happen many more times. Something to remember when climbing gets stuck.

Chouinard and Frost continued the innovations in gear development. When I started ice climbing, I knew of Frost's name only in connection with ice tools. Roper details how important Frost was in working with Chouinard to create new equipment to allow new levels of difficult climbs to be achieved. Now, I will always regret that I didn't know what a great contribution he made when I was using his equipment. I am also glad that I now understand that Chouinard's contribution to climbing was more as a pioneer of new routes than a manufacturer of pitons and an ice climber.

One of my greatest rock climbing heroes as a child was Royal Robbins. I learned to climb from his books and my first climbing shoes were the blue Robbins shoes. But again, I never realised how great he was. For a decade he drove the Camp 4 climbing scene. When El Cap had seven routes, he had done them all. A feat that is more amazing when I realised that they really did prussik up ropes before jumars were available! He set records for fastest ascents such as the Steck-Salathé in 3 hours, 15 minutes. This last event was motivated by the 'young climbers' setting the record at eight hours. Most indicative of his motivation was during a rainy spell in Yosemite. While the other climbers chased the waitresses and moped about, Robbins disappeared for a few days. Only when he finished did they discover that he was making the first solo ascent of the major overhanging face of the Leaning Tower. This was also the first solo ascent of a big wall, and makes one wonder whether he has Scottish blood in him. It is characters like this that help to move climbing forward.

Camp 4 is full of insights of this nature. It details the problems, the mood at the time and how someone always discovered a way forward. It also illustrated how many characteristics of the sport of climbing started, often by chance. The anarchy of the climbers, how the elitist attitude to outsiders grew, the roots of the climbers derelict lifestyle, the role of bouldering, the drive for first free ascents. The book is essential reading for all climbers. Not just for clarifying history and the past heroes, but for providing an insightful chronicle of how climbing itself has, and will continue to, evolve. However, the sentence that triggered the most thought was this comment by Pratt after a British visit in 1967: 'The climbing techniques required in Yosemite presented no problem to the British, whose talent and versatility place them at the pinnacle of the sport'!

Rob Milne.

Weir's World:– Tom Weir. (Canongate Books ISBN 0-86241-480-6.)

Subtitled An *Autobiography of Sorts,* this is the book all of us fans of Tom's writing have been waiting for. As one who cannot pass by a copy of the *Scots Magazine* be it on a news stand or in a waiting room without flicking through to find *My Month* – I have been hooked for years.

Camps and Climbs in Arctic Norway was one of the first mountaineering books I read, in the austere surroundings of the school library, making a lasting impression. His dozen or so other books are all worth a read and *The Ultimate Mountains,* my favourite book on Garhwal is a collectors's item.

Aye, Tom tells a good tale and never a more interesting and entertaining one than this, forsaking a job for life in the Co-op to become 'world traveller, climber, photographer, writer and naturalist'. With so much to cover he deliberately avoids the predictability of strict chronology and skilfully blends in his mixture of interests, home and abroad, business and pleasure, family and friends.

So what is there of particular interest to readers of this journal? There is no appendix or life list of climbs that one sometimes finds in this sort of book, but there is a comprehensive index and our former president's climbing career is well documented, ranging far and wide in time and place. The enthusiasm of the grocer's boy heading for the hills on a Saturday afternoon has never faltered.

It is probably easier now for most of us to visit the Alps or even the Himalaya than it was for Tom and his pals to visit the North West Highlands in those early days, but they made the effort, eventually ranging farther afield as travel became easier. These were no tigers seeking fame and notoriety on hard routes, just a group of like-minded friends eager to grasp the opportunity to climb in exciting new places, though the Scottish Himalayan Expedition of 1950 remains a milestone in the history of the Indian Himalaya. Norway's Lofoten Islands, the Julian Alps of former Yugoslavia, the High Atlas of Morocco, Greenland's Staunings Alps and the mountains of Corsica and Turkish Kurdistan all felt the tramp of Tom's boots and are vividly recalled with the perspective of time adding to the accounts. The publisher has done a good job too. The book is well produced and the photos, colour and black and white are all sharp and bright.

Tom writes warmly of his association with the Club, particularly since many of his climbs were and continue to be with fellow Club members and the pages are packed with fascinating detail. I was particularly interested, for example, to learn that the familiar photo of the elderly Willie Ling and George Glover which hangs above the fireplace in the Ling Hut was taken by Tom.

The book is full of characters, not just pillars of the establishment, but ordinary folk too and he recalls the people as vividly as the places. It is not all looking back through rose-tinted glacier glasses since Tom gives plenty of space to air his views on politics and conservation.

Does this autobiography tell us what makes Tom Weir 'one of Scotland's best-known and best-loved figures'? Tom modestly puts it down to Pelmanism, but I think it confirms his gift for communication, with the people he meets, with his readers and with his viewers (though I have to admit to never having watched *Weir's Way.*)

While the streets of Glasgow have long been crowded with communicators, this one stood out, with his shrewd sense of purpose and direction and a lot of determination.

Well Tom, you are up there now on my bookshelf, alongside Tom Longstaff, Frank Smythe and Seton Gordon and I look forward to dipping into *Weir's World* over and over again.

Dave Broadhead.

The Edge – One Hundred Years of Scottish Mountaineering:– Cameron McNeish and Richard Else. (BBC Books, 128 pp. IBSN 0-563-37084-X. £16.99.

This slim, large-format book purports to deal with some aspects of the themes raised in the six-part documentary series screened on Channel 4 following the superb winter climbing conditions of 1994, when a galaxy of stars were assembled, professional guides recruited as safety men, and under Richard Else – one of the most experienced producer/directors, with Cameron McNeish, Editor of The Great Outdoors, formerly of Climber and Hillwalker, as presenter.

Alas, whatever the merits of the television programme, the book has all the hallmarks of a rushed job, and could have done with the keen eye of a good editor who would have surely rescued it from many of its inaccuracies.

The title of the book is even a misnomer. It is more to do with how the television series was made, than a century of Scottish mountaineering. As for the 13 colour photographs and 30 monochromes I picked only three which could be called outstanding, Nisbet and Crocket on Smith's Route on Gardyloo Buttress, walking off the summit of Ben Nevis at sunset – both double-page spreads – and Dave Cuthbertson on Mega-route X, Central Trident. Too many of the black and whites are muddy.

The sunset red on Ben Nevis summit was appropriate for the words spoken over it, as written by Bill Murray: 'While we walked slowly off the plateau it became clear to me that only the true self, which transcends the personal, lays claim to immortality.' What is missing elsewhere in this book, as in the TV series is the poetry of the mountains. We had the gymnastics without the beauty of the mountains. Action was more important than the mountains, and too much of the dialogue was banal, to say the least.

The re-running of the ascent of Tower Ridge by actors Moss, Cain and Diggins, was to me the most satisfying of the six programmes because it got to the bottom of what climbing is all about, war and peace if you like. How strange that the text credits our Bill Murray with the first winter ascent of the Upper Couloir on Stob Ghabhar when, in fact, it was climbed 16 years before he was born by A.E. Maylard.

Bill Murray has described Douglas Scott as the neatest climber who ever tied to his climbing rope, but it is another Doug Scott, a contemporary of Chris Bonington who features in the index. Douglas Scott of the SMC who holds the post of Hon. Vice-President, is mentioned only in passing as a member of the first Scottish Himalayan Expedition, but he it was who adapted a slater's hammer for use on hard ice pitches, and it can be seen in the museum of Scottish Mountaineering in Glen Coe.

As for Tom Mackinnon, he does not even rate a mention, yet he was chosen for the successful attempt on Kanchenjunga, and for his important part was awarded the Mungo Park Medal. Read Scottish Mountains by W.H. Murray, revised by him in 1993 if you want the true story of 100 years of Scottish climbing.

Tom Weir.

Journals of Kindred Clubs

BERG '94.
The Alpenverein's year book maintains its very high standard of photography, of interesting sidelights on the mountain scene, and above all of variety. This year's special focus is on the Brenner area, that 'gateway to the South' between the Otztal and the Zillertal Alps, much described throughout the centuries, from medieval monks to adventurous modern climbers. Many aspects are covered from early history to geology to mining (including a medieval silver mine). But hard modern routes are not neglected, with descriptions, for example, of climbs in the Tribulaun group on the Italian Border.

Grading of climbs is touched by Robert Jasper, a young freelance guide from the Black Forest, already known for his many first ascents and referred to once as 'the Shooting Star of the German climbing scene'. Describing climbs on Mont Blanc and on the Jungfrau, he classifies parts of the routes as 'schottish', interpreted as 'combined climbing in partly ice-encrusted rock'.

History of mountaineering plays a role this year, with an article on early first ascents, and on the astonishing number of clergy who took part in these in the 18th and early 19th centuries. Notable among them was Pater Placidus a Specsha from Disentis in Switzerland who, between 1782 and 1806, made numerous spectacular first ascents. (It might be added that at one stage he had his pay cut by the village whose pastoral care he held, because he spent too much time in the mountains and too little in the church).

Another article describes the relationships of famous writers to the mountains, including Goethe's descriptiopn of Mont Blanc in 1779, and Ernest Hemingway's ski-touring in the Silvretta in 1925-6. The article on mountains and surrealism is less directly connected with climbing, but Max Ernst and Rene Magritte do have spectacular views of mountains, the latter with one in the shape of an eagle. The seaside cliffs in Salvador Dali's 'Soft Watches' painting are perhaps less convincing as a mountain motif.

Other topics covered include international expeditions from the Pamirs to

Patagonia, environmental issues, including the pros and cons of mountain bikes (mostly pros), and Alpine ways of life which are now gone or fast disappearing. This is only a very small taste of a book/journal which so successfuly celebrates the glories of the mountains, and at the same time puts them into context in the non-mountaineering world.

Iseabail Macleod.

The Polar Record. 1944, Vol 30, Nos 192 –195.
The Polar Record, the Journal of the Scott Polar Research Institute, is received each year and languishes unread in our under-utilised library. I find it a treasure-house of interesting polar lore.

It contains a wealth of information about contemporary literary, biological, historical, political, geological and archaeological goings-on at both polar regions of the planet in the form of articles, notes and book reviews. In the 1994 numbers there are articles on wolves in East Greenland, the first Antarctic voyage of Edgar Allan Poe, non-governmental flights to Antarctica, spying on the Russsians in Siberia during the Crimean War, Antarctic Tourism, unsolved mysteries of missing ships and, as they say, much, much more.

There is a review of a new book on John Rae, the Orcadian who broke the rules of Arctic travel last century. Rae, you remember, went native; he travelled in the Eskimo style and emerged after years of travel in the Canadian north without losing his health. As no gentleman would ever go native (part of the test of true heroism was to die rather than 'lower' your standards) he was never accepted into the British pantheon of great explorers.

He also found the first evidence of the fate of the lost Franklin Expedition but spoiled it all by repeating Eskimo reports that there had been cannabalism among some of the survivors, a story only a cad would repeat. Rae is only now receiving the attention he deserves. The Polar Record makes absorbing reading. Go to our library and spend a fascinating afternoon among its pages.

Robin Chalmers.

Yorkshire Mountaineering Club 50th Year Journal 1941-1991.
At this year's annual dinner of the John Buchan Society, Bill Todd of the Yorkshire Mountaineering Club was kind enough to present me a copy of his club's 50th anniversary journal. This is a slim, nicely-produced volume of 88 pages, containing 34 articles reflecting the activities of the club from its foundation in 1941.

Article titles such as *Club Cottage, New year in Rhum, Snow at the Equator, the North Face of the Taschorn and YMC Characters* give some idea of the contents. The quality of the writing, and the enthusiasm of the contributors makes it a pleasure to read.

The front and back cover photographs – the Bonatti route on the Chandelle and Green Crack on Franklands – are a fair indication of the spirit of the club and the black and white photographs in the text have been well chosen.

This journal is a credit to its editor, Ken Tilford, and it now reposes in our Club library for your enjoyment.

Bryan Fleming.

The Fell and Rock Journal, Vol. XXV, Nos. 72,73 and 74.

There is a lot of very interesting reading in these three issues. Not surprisingly, the expeditions furth of the club's home territory of the Lake District provide many of the stories.

Crossing the Border northwards, Stephen Reid describes a succession of sorties on a mountain bike to the wilds of Galloway to clean up the climbs on Dungeon Hill of Buchan, while research of the property market in Argyll led to the club's acquisition of the old police Station in Kinlochleven as its Scottish hut.

Climbing and expeditions in more distant places gives some interesting reading. There is ski-mountaineering in the Ural mountains and ordinary mountaineering in the Pamirs; rock climbing in South Korea that looks rather like the Etive Slabs and the Mediterranean sunshine on Corsica and Mallorca. On Mont Blanc the Via della Pera contrasts with the via ferrata of the Brenta Dolomites.

The In Memoriam section also makes interesting reading. One has to admire the longevity of many past Fell and Rock members whose careers embraced much of the history of English climbing, as well as mountaineering in the Alps and elsewhere.

The Fell and Rock Journals are produced to a uniformly high standard, enhanced by the quality of their colour illustrations.

Donald Bennet.

Also received:
The Munro Phenonenon, by Andrew Dempster (Mainstream Publishing).
100 Walks in the French Alps, by Terry Marsh (Hodder & Stoughton).
One Hundred Walks Around Manchester, by David Frith (Mainstream Publishing).
The Boardman Tasker Omnibus – including *Savage Arena, The Shining Mountain, Sacred Summits, Everest the Cruel Way,* all for £14.99 (Hodder & Stoughton).
The MAM Journal, 1993-4.
Consolidated Index to the *The Himalayan Journal.* Volumes 1-50.

OFFICE BEARERS 1994-95

Honorary President: W.H. Murray, O.B.E.

Honorary Vice-President: James C. Donaldson, M.B.E.

President: Robin N. Campbell

Vice-Presidents: James A. Crawford, Geoff Cohen

Honorary Secretary: John R.R. Fowler, 4 Doune Terrace, Edinburgh, EH3 6DY. **Honorary Treasurer:** T.B. Fleming, West Lynn, Dairy, Ayrshire, KA24 4LJ. **Honorary Editor:** K.V. Crocket, Glenisla, Long Row, Menstrie, Clackmannanshire, FK11 7EA. **Assistant Editor:** I.H.M. Smart, Auchenleish, Bridge of Cally, by Blairgowrie, Perthshire. **Convener of the Publications Sub-Committee:** D.C. Anderson, 17 Hugh Miller Place, Edinburgh, EH3 5JG. **Honorary Librarian:** R.D.M. Chalmers, 14 Gamoch Drive, Glasgow, G20 8RS. **Honorary Archivist:** D.B. McIntyre, Luachmhor, Church Road, Kinfauns, Perth, PH2 7LD. **Honorary Custodian of Slides:** D.G. Pyper, 3 Keir Circle, Westhill, Skene, Aberdeenshire, AB32 6RE. **Convener of the Huts Sub-Committee:** G.S. Peet, 6 Roman Way, Dunblane, Perthshire. **Custodian of the CIC Hut:** Robin Clothier, 35 Broompark Drive, Newton Mearns, Glasgow G77 5DZ. **Custodian of Lagangarbh Hut:** R.G. Ross, 16 Milton Court, Dunbartonshire G82 22UD. **Custodian of the Ling Hut:** D.J. Broadhead, Cul Beag, Blackwood, Urray, by Muir of Ord, IV6 7UL (01463 871274). **Custodian of the Raeburn Hut:** W.H. Duncan, Kirktoun, East End, Lochwinnoch, Renfrewshire, PA12 4ER. Committee: P.V. Brian; R.D. Carchrie; A. Tibbs; D.A. Bearhop; A. Jane Naismith; R.G. Ross; Phil Gribbon; Niall Ritchie: Roger Webb.

Journal Information

Editor: K.V. Crocket, Glenisla, Long Row, Menstrie, Clacks. FK11 7EA (email: ken.crocket@almac.co.uk)
New Routes Editor: A.D. Nisbet, 20 Craigie Ave., Boat of Garten, Inverness-shire PH24 3BL.
Advertisements: Tim Pettifer, 35 Irvine Road, Largs KA30 8LS.
Distribution: D.F. Lang, Hillfoot Hey, 580 Perth Road, Dundee DD2 IPZ.
Editor of Photographs: Niall Ritchie, 37 Lawsondale Terrace, Westhill, Skene, Aberdeen AB32 6SE.

INSTRUCTIONS TO CONTRIBUTORS

Articles for the Journal should be submitted before the end of January for publication in the following issue. Lengthy contributions are preferably typed, double-spaced, on one side only, and with ample margins (minimum 30mm). Articles may be accepted on floppy disk, IBM compatible (contact Editor beforehand). The Editor welcomes material from both members and non-members, with priority being given to articles of Scottish mountaineering content. Photographs are also welcome, and should be good quality colour slides. All textual material should be sent to the Editor – address and email as above. Photographic material should be sent direct to the Editor of Photographs – address as above.

Copyright. Textual matter appearing in the Miscellaneous section of the Journal, including New Climbs, is copyright of the publishers. Copyright of articles in the main section of the Journal is retained by individual authors.

FREEZE DRIED
1 2   y e a r   m a l t

The
GLEN
AGED **12** YEARS
Pure Single Malt
Scotch Whisky

"DRIED SINCE 1824"

Before even the inaugural meeting of the Scottish Mountaineering Club, the smooth mellow taste of Glen was the toast of the Glens. Now available in freeze dried crystals Glen can be the toast of the Bens.

Open the 100 gram sachet, add sparkling burn water to the dark amber crystals to enjoy the distinctive taste of a full 70 cl, 40% proof, 12 year old malt anywhere you choose.

Imagine the pleasure of a good "swally" before leading off from a collapsing stance and a nervous second. Just add snow (which rapidly melts because of the lower freezing point of the crystals), a chunk or two of ice (available in a good winter) and you can enjoy a smooth malt, in a blizzard, with an English refinement.

It's been estimated the CIC loft can take 4 cwt of the crystals exclusively for Members, available individually in four pounds bags, strictly through the advertising manager of the journal, on a first come first served basis.

SCOTTISH MOUNTAINEERING CLUB
SCOTTISH MOUNTAINEERING TRUST

DISTRICT GUIDES

Southern Uplands	£16.95
Southern Highlands	£16.95
Central Highlands	£17.95
The Cairngorms	£17.95
Islands of Scotland (including Skye)	£19.95
North-west Highlands	£17.95

SCRAMBLERS GUIDE

Black Cuillin Ridge	£4.95

CLIMBERS GUIDES (Rock and Ice Guides)

Ben Nevis	£14.95
Northern Highlands Vol. 1	£13.95
Northern Highlands Vol. 2	£14.95
Glen Coe (including Glen Etive and Ardgour)	£13.95
The Cairngorms (Out of print, new ed. 1995)	
Skye and the Hebrides (Out of print, new ed. 1995)	
Arran, Arrochar and Southern Highlands	£9.95

Outcrop Guides

Northeast Outcrops	£13.95
Lowland Outcrops	£14.95

OTHER PUBLICATIONS

The Munros	£14.95
Munro's Tables	£9.95
The Corbetts and Other Scottish Hills	£14.95
A Chance in a Million – Scottish Avalanches	£4.95
A Century of Scottish Mountaineering	£15.95
Ski Mountaineering in Scotland	£12.95
Ben Nevis – Britain's Highest Mountain	£14.95
Scotland's Mountains	£17.95
The Cairngorms Scene – And Unseen	£6.95
Heading for the Scottish Hills (1993 Edition)	£5.95
Scottish Hill and Mountain Names	£9.95

MAPS

Black Cuillin of Skye (double-sided)	£3.95
Glen Coe	£2.95

Distributed by:

Cordee, 3a De Montfort Street, Leicester LE1 7HD
Telephone: Leicester 543579

These books and maps are available from many bookshops and mountain equipment suppliers